D1282449

POTTER'S NEW CYCLOPAEDIA
OF
BOTANICAL DRUGS AND PREPARATIONS

Fragment of the frontispiece to the Herball written by John Parkinson, King's Herbalist and printed in 1640

POTTER'S NEW CYCLOPAEDIA OF BOTANICAL DRUGS AND PREPARATIONS

By

R. C. WREN, F.L.S.

RE-EDITED AND ENLARGED BY

R. W. WREN, M.P.S., F.L.S., F.C.S.

FOREWORD BY

T. E. WALLIS, D.Sc. (Lond.), F.R.I.C., F.P.S., M.I.Biol.
Emeritus Curator of The Pharmaceutical Society of Great Britain and sometime Reader in Pharmacognosy, University of London

HEALTH SCIENCE PRESS
Rustington, Sussex, England

First published 1907
Second edition 1915
Third edition 1923
Fourth edition 1932
Fifth edition 1939
Sixth edition 1950
Seventh edition 1956
Reprinted 1968
Reprinted March 1970

ISBN 0 85032 009 7

MADE AND PRINTED IN GREAT BRITAIN BY
COMPTON PRINTING LIMITED, LONDON AND AYLESBURY

FOREWORD

MANY plants and parts of plants, usually in a dried condition, are still largely used in Britain as household remedies or as ingredients of orthodox medicine. It is important that reliable information should be available to enable dealers in these remedies to judge of their origin and quality. Some of them are defined and regulated by the descriptions in the *British Pharmacopoeia* and in the *British Pharmaceutical Codex*. There is, however, a very large number of materials, derived from the vegetable kingdom, which lie outside the scope of the two volumes named above. It is desirable, therefore, that some book or cyclopaedia should be compiled with the object of providing particulars by which the botanical drugs can be correctly authenticated. This kind of information is frequently needed by physicians, pharmacists and analysts, who receive inquiries relating to the identity and uses of numerous household remedies as well as those included in the pharmacopoeia and codex.

Potter's *New Cyclopaedia of Botanical Drugs and Preparations* brings together much valuable information which is scattered throughout botanical and medical literature and thus supplies a reference book which meets a need felt by both professional people and the lay public. This book has been carefully prepared and not only provides an account of characters for identification, but also gives a brief summary of the action and uses of the herbs described, together with a note of the preparations made from them. The descriptions are often illustrated by sketches of the plants from which the herbs are derived; these drawings are taken from the well-known *Illustrations of the British Flora* by W. H. Fitch and W. G. Smith, a book which is a companion to the standard Flora of Bentham and Hooker, and since they are constantly in use by professional botanists they can be relied upon to supply the essential details for identifying the plants illustrated.*

Another direction in which difficulties frequently arise is in relation to nomenclature and this is helpfully treated in the Cyclopaedia. In addition to the accepted or scientific names, the popular names and other vernacular synonyms are included in the heading to each description and the full scientific name of the plant of origin is also given. All these names are carefully indexed and this index adds much to the value of the book and frequently enables the inquirer to ascertain the source of some obscure remedy and also to find an account of its reputed uses. The book is unique in the English language and is a valuable source of reference for all who are interested in the origin and uses of botanical drugs.

T. E. WALLIS

* The Publishers regret that it is impossible to include the illustrations in this edition.

PREFACE

THE first edition of Potter's Cyclopaedia was published in 1907 and the reason for its appearance was made plain in the Preface in these words: "For many years there has been a demand for a work which would, in a concise and matter of fact manner, be a guide to all who use Botanic Drugs." My father, Richard Cranfield Wren, F.L.S., after working on it for some years, produced a book of reference on medical plants which was at that time more complete and up to date than anything previously published. It proved an immediate success and of supreme interest not alone to those who practised the art of curing ailments by means of the use of herbs, roots, barks and seeds and preparations made from them, but to many others who were students of the art and still others who believed in collecting the herbs of the countryside for their own personal use in treating minor ailments. Briefly the volume contained the common and botanical names of each plant and its synonyms. There were paragraphs dealing with its action on the human system and any well-known preparations were named. Some three hundred monographs appeared in alphabetical order.

The second edition appeared in 1915. E. M. Holmes, F.L.S., so well remembered in his day as curator of the Pharmaceutical Society's museum, and a firm friend of all students there, was brought into collaboration with R. C. Wren. At that time, E. M. Holmes was no doubt the best-known authority in England on the subject of medicinal plants. He was mainly responsible in that edition for drawing up accurate descriptions of the distinctive characteristics of each drug so that it could be identified with ease. He likewise revised the botanical terms and list of authorities.

In 1923 it was found necessary to produce another edition, and to this were added 200 line illustrations from Bentham's *Handbook of the British Flora* from drawings of W. H. Fitch, F.L.S., and W. G. Smith, F.L.S. The great accuracy of these drawings proved a valuable asset to those who wished to recognize medicinal plants growing in the country and the permission of the publishers so readily given was greatly appreciated.

The original author of Potter's Cyclopaedia died on 24th July, 1930. During a very full life, R. C. Wren had travelled to all parts of the world and wherever he went he learned something of the growing, collection and preparation of medicinal plants. He was at the time of his death a Fellow of the Linnean Society, Fellow of the National Association of Medical Herbalists, a Justice of the Peace and one of the greatest authorities of his time on the subject of medicinal plants. The work he had so ably started had to go on. In 1932 it became necessary to publish the fourth edition and in collaboration with H. A. Potter, Ph.C., I produced a publication which was little different from the former edition, except that, through the courtesy of Cassell & Co., Ltd., several coloured plates of well-known medicinal plants were included.

The fifth and sixth editions which I produced were more or less on the same lines, although a fair amount of revision was carried out to bring things up to date. References to preparations in the *British Pharmacopoeia, British Pharmaceutical Codex* and the *United States Pharmacopoeia* were included as additional items where they applied.

Every edition of the book has proved an outstanding success and copies have gone to many parts of the world.

When the sixth edition showed signs of rapid exhaustion, my thoughts turned to the subject of producing something perhaps on a more grandiose scale and a volume which would contain an even greater amount of interest for all who turn its pages. This book is the result. It will be seen that the background of the last edition has been used and that what has been added has been built round this. The main additions may be summarized as follows: (1) an indication of where the plant grows; (2) the plant's flowering time and sometimes its seeding time; (3) extracts from ancient Herbals where they are of interest (this is dealt with more fully later on); (4) Biblical references where they apply; and (5) four colour plates. These have been specially painted from living plants for inclusion in this edition. Great attention has also been paid to the style of printing and size of page and it is hoped that a volume has been produced which will have an interest for a wide range of readers.

Concerning the extracts from old Herbals, a special word must be said. They have been added because of their historical interest, and the language of the Elizabethan herbalists is so beautiful, amounting to poetic prose, that extracts from these books form delightful reading, even if the subject-matter deals with mundane complaints. Herbalists like Parkinson, Gerard and Culpeper frequently quote the ancient Greek and Roman herbalists, translating the Greek and Latin into quaint Elizabethan English. Notes concerning the individual herbalists who are from time to time quoted should be of interest and I will give them now, dealing first with well-known English writers.

John Gerard, of London, was born at Nantwich in Cheshire in 1545, but came to London, settling eventually in Holborn. The introduction to his book is "From my house in Holborn within the suburbs of London." Gerard became a "Master of Chirurgerie." His best known work is *The Herball or General Historie of Plants*, first published in 1597. A second edition of this work was published in 1636, twenty-five years after his death in 1611, and it is described on the title-page as "very much enlarged and amended by Thomas Johnson, a Citizen and Apothecarye of London."

This edition runs into 1,630 large pages. The original author's name is spelt variously as Gerard, Gerarde and Gerrard.

John Parkinson, a contemporary of Gerard, was born in 1567 and died in 1629. He became an Apothecary of London and King's Herbalist, also a director of the Royal Gardens at Hampton Court. He wrote two well-known works, the first *Paradisus Terrestris,* published in 1629 and the second *Theatrum Botanicum, or an Herbal of large extent . . .* which was printed in 1640.

Nicholas Culpeper was the man of whom Dr. Johnson wrote "Culpeper, the man that first ranged the woods and climbed the mountains in search of medicinal and salutary herbs, has undoubtedly merited the gratitude of posterity." He was the son of a clergyman and grandson of Sir Thomas Culpeper, Bart. After studying at Cambridge he became apprenticed to an Apothecary. In his leisure hours he studied Physics and Astrology and eventually set up his practice as an Astrological Doctor "in Spitalfields, next to the Red Lion." The district is interesting, as up to two years ago one of the few firms still dealing in herbal products had its warehouses near this spot. Culpeper's herb gardens are commemorated by the names of streets, such as Wormwood Street, Camomile Street, in the City. He died in 1654 and his best-known work is entitled *The Complete Herbal and English Physician.*

Joseph Miller was the author of *Botanicum Officinale, or a Compendious Herbal,* published in 1722.

John Hill, M.D., wrote *A general Natural History, or new and accurate descriptions of the Animals, Vegetables and Minerals of the different parts of the World,* printed in 1751, and *British Herbal, an History of Plants and Trees Native to Britain, cultivated for use or raised for Beauty,* in 1756.

William Salmon, M.D., wrote *The English Herbal or History of Plants* in 1710.

Benjamin H. Barton, F.L.S., and Thomas Castle, M.D., F.L.S., collaborated in the production of two volumes entitled *The Medicinal Plants of Great Britain,* published in 1845.

Of the more ancient herbalists, there were many, starting with Solomon and continuing through the ages. Of these, I can mention only a few.

Theophrastos Eresios, of Eresos in the island of Lesbos, lived from about 370 B.C. to 285 B.C. He succeeded Aristotle in the government of the School at Athens about 322 B.C. He is the earliest known European botanical author and wrote his works about 314 B.C. He is said to have shown a great amount of excellent observation and it is likely that some of his works originated from Aristotle. These were printed as early as 1483 and have been translated into several languages.

Pliny—Caius Plinius Secundus—lived from A.D. 23 to A.D. 79 and is the well-known author of *Naturalis Historia libri XXXVII*, subsequently translated into French. He met with an untimely end by reason of an eruption of Vesuvius. As Thomas Johnson put it "He was suffocated by the sulphurious vapours that came from Mount Vesuvius falling at that time on fire: he through overmuch curiositie to see and finde out the cause thereof approaching too nigh."

Dioscorides, whose main writings were accomplished about A.D. 77 or A.D. 78, lived at Anazarba in Cilicia, Asia Minor. His work on *Materia Medica* is considered to be the most valuable source of information on the botany of the ancient herbalists.

Galen (Galenos) lived from A.D. 131 to A.D. 200 and whilst he was Imperial Physician in Rome wrote many distinguished medical books which were held in high reputation right down to the Middle Ages. The term "galenical," used to describe many medicinal preparations, is derived from his name.

Hilarius, Matthiolus, the Italian Physician, Clausius, best known for his translations of Spanish herbal writings, Sammonicus and the Swiss Physician, Paracelsus, are among many others that contributed their quota to the knowledge of herbs which has been passed down to us through the ages.

Perhaps Paracelsus should be mentioned apart from the others as he introduced many unsavoury things into medicine, some of which had been used by the Egyptians, such as various forms of excreta. His writings went so far as to influence the London Pharmacopoeia of 1617 to introduce some of these. He also did much to make popular the Doctrine of Signatures in which many believed at that time. This was a belief that the colour or shape of a plant, or part of a plant, indicated its use in the cure of ailments where the colour or shape had some relationship to the complaint. It was thought that this stamp or signature was laid on the plant by a guardian angel. Thus, because the leaves of the Lungwort were spotted, it was thought to be useful for pulmonary complaints. Plants with yellow flowers or roots with yellow sap would be suitable for jaundice. Red-coloured roots were used for bleeding. The root of the Bryony, because it is shaped like a swollen foot, was thought to be good for dropsy. Poplar leaves, which, because they shake in the breeze in a peculiar way are known as Quaking Aspen leaves, were, of course, the right thing for shaking palsy. One could instance many other examples of the same kind of thing. It was a doctrine subscribed to by a great number of eminent herbalists, and led to the belief that heavenly bodies, the planets, the stars, the sun and the moon, had an influence on plants. This was developed by Culpeper, who made a great study of

Astrology, and in *The Complete Herbal* he sets out his method of astrological diagnosis and treatment as follows—

1. Consider what planet causeth the disease; that thou mayest find it in my aforesaid Judgment of Diseases.
2. Consider what part of the body is affected by the disease and whether it lies in the flesh or blood or bones or ventricles.
3. Consider by what planet the afflicted part of the body is governed; that my Judgment of Diseases will inform you also.
4. You may oppose diseases by herbs of the planet opposite to the planet that causes them; as diseases of the Luminaries by the herbs of Saturn and the contrary; diseases of Mars by the herbs of Venus and the contrary.
5. There is a way to cure diseases sometimes by Sympathy and so every planet cures its own diseases; as the Sun and Moon by their herbs cure the eyes, Saturn the spleen, Jupiter the liver, Mars the gall and diseases of the choler, and by Venus diseases in the Instruments of Generation.

Culpeper in his *Judgment of Diseases* sets out this theory in much greater detail.

The vegetable life of the world has become surrounded by fables, legends and superstitions. The reason for this is probably contained in a paragraph of Charles M. Skinner's *Myths and Legends of Flowers, Trees, Fruits and Plants* where he writes: "To primitive people who thus symbolized natural phenomena, vegetable life was, in a manner, glorified, because it sustained all other life. The tree supplied lumber, fuel, house, thatch, cordage, weapons, boats, shields and tools, as well as fruit and medicine." Many of these myths and legends form interesting reading, but there is not much opportunity of dealing with them exhaustively in a book of this description. The subject forms an absorbing study on its own and only a few instances have been referred to here.

The period of modern pharmacognosy is young, dating from the early nineteenth century, and some of the best work in modern times has been carried out by the late Dr. Henry Greenish. His *Text Book of Pharmacognosy*, first published in 1899, has run into many editions since. The study of herbs, roots, barks, fruits and seeds has now become a fine art. Theories like the Doctrine of Signatures and the Doctrine of Planets, although remaining interesting historically, have been laid aside and have given place to scientific investigation. Much good and useful work has been, and still is being, done by the chemist to discover and extract the active principles of those plants which appear to have an action on the human system. There is, of course, yet much to be done in this direction. Whereas it is known that a great number of plants used by the herbalist today have a beneficial effect upon a human being in the case of the ailments for which they are prescribed, yet in many cases the reason for the effect is not known. Because of this, some people are inclined to scorn the use of herbs. Many of us believe, however, that as the chemistry of plants advances it will be discovered that there is a very good reason for their use and that some may prove superior to many of the synthetic chemical drugs used today.

A fitting conclusion to this Preface is the following extract from Thomas Johnson's "Letter to the Reader" in the 1636 edition of Gerard—

> God of his infinite goodnesse and bounty hath by the medium of Plants, bestowed almost all food, clothing and medicine upon man.

CONTENTS

ABBREVIATIONS FOR WEIGHTS AND MEASURES

THE following abbreviations are used in this work for the more common weights and measures—

cc	cubic centimetre(s)
dr	drachm(s)
fl dr	fluid drachm(s)
fl oz	fluid ounce(s)
ft	foot (feet)
g	gramme(s)
gr	grain(s)
in.	inch(es)
min	minim(s)
oz	ounce(s)
pt	pint

CYCLOPAEDIA

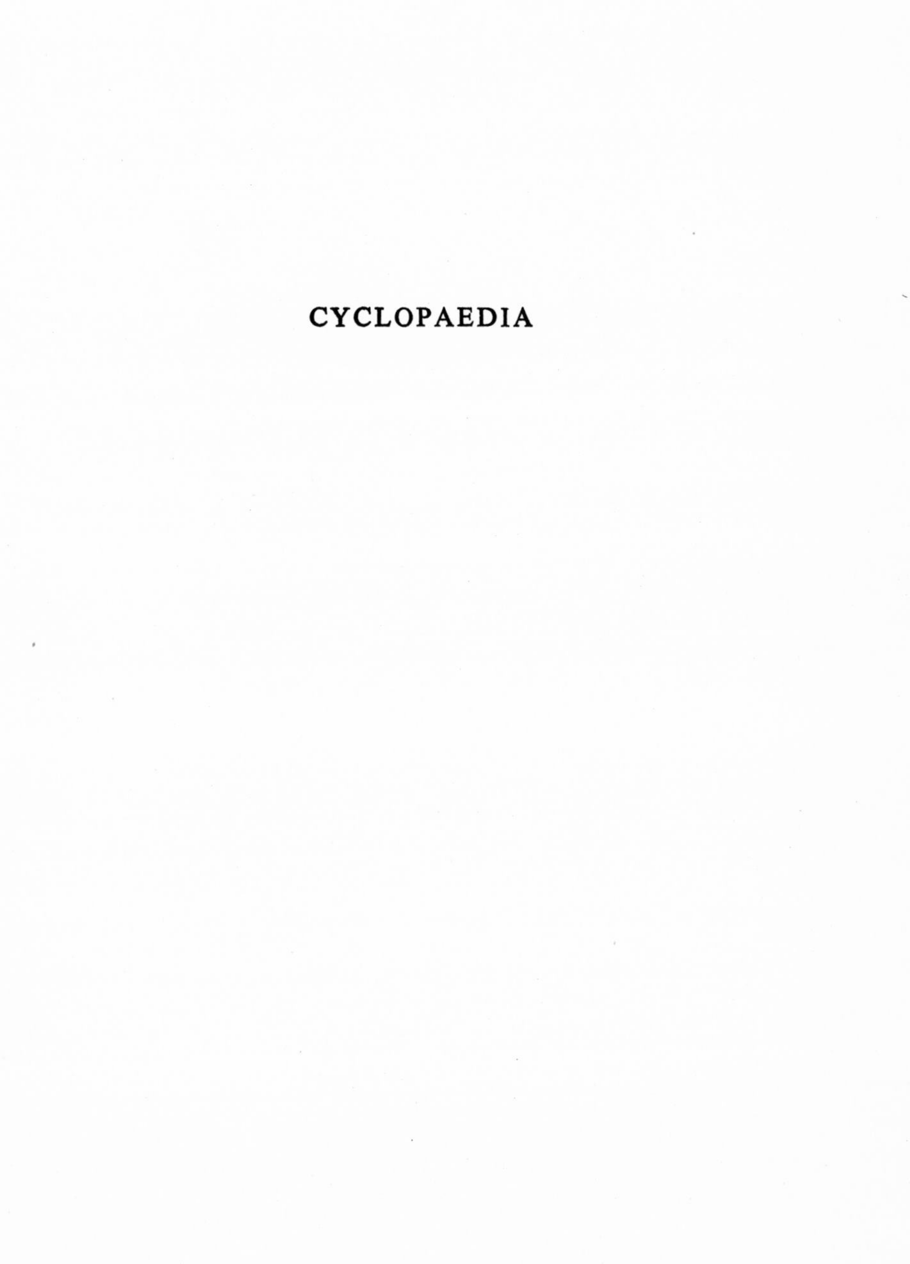

A

ABSCESS ROOT *Polemonium reptans*, Linn.
Fam. Polemoniaceae

Synonyms: American Greek Valerian, False Jacob's Ladder, Sweatroot.
Habitat: Native of Denmark and Sweden and other Northern countries.
Description: Root rhizomatous, slender, 1–2 in. long, and $\frac{1}{8}$ in. in diameter, with the bases of numerous stems on the upper surface, and tufts of slender, smooth, wiry, pale, brittle roots below. Taste, slightly bitter and acrid.
Part Used: Rhizome.
Medicinal Use: Diaphoretic, astringent, alterative, expectorant. This drug has been recommended in febrile and inflammatory diseases, pleurisy, etc. It is useful in coughs, colds, and bronchial or lung complaints. The warm infusion of 1 oz in a pint of boiling water, taken in wineglassful doses, produces a copious perspiration.

ACACIA BARK *Acacia arabica*, Willd.
Acacia decurrens, Willd.
Fam. Leguminosae

Synonym: Babul Bark.
Habitat: North Africa, from Abyssinia to Senegal.
Description: The bark appears in commerce as hard, rusty-brown pieces 3 to 10 mm thick, readily dividing into layers, much fissured; inner surface striated and fibrous. *Acacia decurrens* smoother than *arabica*.
Medicinal Use: This bark is not often used in medicine. Owing to the tannic acid content it has been used as an astringent and Joseph Miller states: "It helps ulcers in the mouth and gums and fastens loose teeth."
Commercial Use: It is used in the tanning industry.
Biblical References: Exodus xxv, 10, 23, xxvi, 26, 32, 37, xxvii, 1, xxviii, 1, xxx, 1, 5, xxxv, 24, xxxvi, 20, xxxvii, 1, 4, 10, 15, 25, 38, xxxviii, 1, 6; Numbers xxxiii, 49; Deuteronomy x, 3; Isaiah, xli, 19; Micah, vi,5.

The references are to Shittim Wood, a variety of Acacia thought to be Acacia arabica. It was probably chosen for the construction of the ark of the covenant because of its hardness and the fact that it would take an excellent polish.

ACACIA GUM

Acacia senegal, Willd.
(and other varieties)
Fam. Leguminosae

Synonyms: Gum Acacia, Gum Arabic.

Habitat: North Africa, from Abyssinia to Senegal.

Description: The gum exudes from the tree naturally, but larger yields are obtained by making incisions. It appears in rounded or angular pieces, which are cracked externally, transparent internally. With hot water it gives an adhesive mucilage which is not ropy or glairy. The mucilage keeps better if made with boiling, than with cold, water. The gum appears on the market in many varieties. The finest is known as Kordofan gum.

Medicinal Use: Demulcent, mucilaginous. Often used as an ingredient in medicinal compounds for the treatment of diarrhoea, dysentery, catarrh, cough, hoarseness, fevers, etc., when a demulcent is required.

Preparations: Mucil. Acac. B.P. (40 per cent in Chloroform water); Mucil. Acac. U.S.P. (35 per cent in Distilled water): Dose, 15 cc; Pulv. Acac. et Trag. B.P.C. 1949; Pulv. Trag. Co. B.P.: Dose 10–60 gr.

Domestic Use: As an adhesive.

ACONITE

Aconitum napellus, Linn.
Fam. Ranunculaceae

Synonyms: Wolfsbane, Monkshood, Friar's Cap, Blue Rocket. There is a tradition that wolves tear up the roots of some plants in winter for their food, and sometimes mistaking this plant, perish by its poison; hence the name Wolfsbane.

Habitat: According to Pliny, the name Aconite is derived from the ancient Black Sea port, Aconis. The many varieties of Aconite are widely spread over the world and were used medicinally by the ancient Chinese. *Aconitum napellus* is indigenous to the Alps and Pyrenees and has since been cultivated in both England and America.

Flowering Time: July.

Description: The root is blackish, conical above, tapering below. The fracture shows a five- to seven-angled star in the centre; otherwise it is white and starchy. The taste is tingling and numbing in less than two minutes. The stalk is robust, erect, round, and smooth. The leaves are alternate, large and deep green in colour, the lower leaves having longer peticles than the upper. The flowers are violet-blue, carried on the top of the stem upon a spike-like raceme. The flowers are followed by capsules filled with angular, wrinkled seeds.

Other Varieties: *Aconitum uncinatum*, Linn.: var. *japonicum Regel*, Japanese Aconite Root, smaller and less wrinkled, paler than English root. Another variety of Japanese Aconite Root is obtained from *Aconitum fisheri*. *Aconitum deinorhizum*, Stapf., Indian Aconite Root. Yellowish brown, coarsely wrinkled, horny fracture, larger than English root.

Parts Used: Root, leaves.

Medicinal Use: Sedative, anodyne, febrifuge. This plant is poisonous and should not be used except under medicinal advice. It is useful in all febrile and inflammatory diseases, scarlatina, gastritis and facial neuralgia, also in acute catarrh, tonsilitis, and croup. In palpitation of the heart spasm, it has been used with success. Overdoses should be carefully avoided as no certain antidote is known. In cases of poisoning, sal-volatile and brandy may be given as first aid.

Preparations: Aconite and preparations containing it have now been omitted from the *British Pharmacopoeia*, 1953. The B.P.C. preparations containing Aconite are the following: Lin. Aconit.; Lin. Aconit. Bellad. et Chlorof.; Syr. Bromof. Co. B.P.C. 1949: Dose, 60–240 min; Syr. Codein et Creosot. B.P.C. 1949: Dose 30–120 min; Tinct. Aconit. B.P.C. 1949: Dose 2–5 min; Tinct. Aconit. Fort. B.P.C. 1949.

JOHN HILL, M.D., in the "British Herbal" (1741), mentions that five persons who ate this root [Aconite] by mistake in their food at Antwerp all died.

ACORNS

Quercus robur, Linn.
Fam. Cupuliferae

Description: The well-known fruit of the Oak.

Medicinal Use: Astringent. An old remedy for diarrhoea. The Acorns are grated or powdered and washed down with water. Roasted and ground acorns have been used as a coffee substitute.

ADDER'S TONGUE, AMERICAN

Erythronium americanum, Ker-Gawl.
Fam. Liliaceae

Synonyms: Serpent's Tongue, Dog's Tooth Violet, Yellow Snowdrop.

Habitat: U.S.A.

Distinctive Character: Leaves, two only, lanceolate, 2½ in. long by 1 in. wide, minutely wrinkled, veins longitudinal, parallel, leafstalk 2–3 in. long. Flower yellow, star-shaped, 1 in. wide, with six stamens. Corms slender, spindleshaped, $\frac{1}{3}$–1 in. long. Taste, sweetish. The drug should be kept in a dry place.

Medicinal Use: Emetic, emollient, antiscrofulous. The fresh leaves are used as a poultice in scrofulous ulcers and tumours, together with an infusion taken internally in wineglassful doses. Is reputed of use in dropsy, hiccough, and vomiting.

ADDER'S TONGUE, ENGLISH

Ophioglossum vulgatum, Linn.
Fam. Filices

Synonyms: Serpent's Tongue.

Habitat: It grows in moist meadows in Great Britain.

Flowering Time: April or May. The plant quickly perishes with the advent of warm weather.

Description: The plant has a solitary leaf, lanceolate with forked veins, and bearing a stalked, linear spike of spore-cases in a double row. The spike is green at first, afterwards becoming brown. The name is obviously chosen because of the likeness of the spikes to an adder's tongue, although as Culpeper says "only this is as useful as they are formidable." The root is fibrous.

Part Used: Herb.

Medicinal Use: Emetic, emollient, antiscrofulous. The fresh leaves are used as a poultice in scrofulous ulcers and tumours, together with an infusion taken internally in wineglassful doses. It is reputed to be of use in dropsy, hiccough, and vomiting. It is said that the plant boiled in oil or fat is a panacea for wounds and to reduce inflammation. According to Culpeper this herb is under the dominion of the Moon and Cancer and therefore "if the weakness of the retentive faculty be caused by an evil influence of Saturn in any part of the body governed by the Moon or under the dominion of Cancer, this herb cures it by sympathy."

ADRUE

Cyperus articulatus, Linn.
Fam. Cyperaceae

Synonym: Guinea Rush.

Habitat: Turkey.

Description: Blackish, somewhat top-shaped tubers, with bristly remains of former leaves $\frac{3}{4}$–1 in. long and $\frac{1}{2}$–$\frac{3}{4}$ in. in diameter, sometimes in a series of two or three connected by means of an underground stem $\frac{1}{8}$ in. in diameter and 1–2 in. long. Transverse section pale, showing a central column with darker points indicating vascular bundles. Taste, bitterish, aromatic, recalling that of lavender.

Part Used: Root.

Medicinal Use: Anti-emetic. It possesses aromatic properties, diffusing a feeling of warmth throughout the system and acts as a sedative in dyspeptic disorders. Is particularly useful in vomiting of pregnancy, etc.

Preparation: Fluid extract: Dose, 10–30 drops.

AGAR-AGAR

Gelidium amansii, Kütz.
(and other species)
Fam. Rhodophyceae

Synonym: Japanese Isinglass.

Habitat: The various seaweeds from which Agar is prepared are indigenous to Japan. Agar is the dried mucilaginous matter extracted with boiling water and dried after being made into strips by forcing through wire netting.

Description: In slender, shrivelled, translucent strips about ¼ in. wide and 9 or 10 in. or more long, or in quadrangular sticks about 1 in. in diameter; colourless and tasteless. Capable of taking up 200 times its volume of water to form a jelly.

Acetic, hydrochloric, and oxalic acids prevent its gelatinization.

Medicinal Use: Nutritive. The commercial varieties are used in bacteriological investigations, and for technical purposes in sizing silks and fabrics. 1 oz – 20 oz of boiling water makes a suitable jelly for invalids, etc. This may be flavoured with lemon or as desired. The powdered Agar in doses of 1 dr given with stewed fruits is recommended for constipation. It is also frequently used in the form of an ingredient in an emulsion of liquid paraffin for this purpose.

Preparations: Emuls. Paraff. Liq. c. Agar B.P.C. 1949: Dose, ¼–1 fl oz; Emuls. Paraff. Liq. et Mag. Hydrox. B.P.C. 60–240 min; Emuls. Paraff. Liq. et Phenolphthal. B.P.C.: Dose, 60–240 min.

Agar is described in the B.P. App. 1.

AGARICUS

Fomes officinalis, Faull.
Fam. Polyporaceae

Synonyms: *Boletus laricis*, White Agaric, Larch Agaric, Purging Agaric.

Habitat: It is a fungus growing on trees in the Larch forests of Russia.

Description: In white, spongy, friable masses, sometimes with the lower portion attached. The surface is usually brownish and the internal structure whiter and porous. The odour is meal-like and the taste sweetish, then bitter and acrid. The powder shows typical threads and minute calcareous concretions.

Medicinal Use: Astringent, purgative. Used in small doses to check night sweats, diarrhoea, and milk secretion after weaning. In large doses it acts as a purgative and may cause vomiting. Dose: 3–30 gr.

AGRIMONY *Agrimonia eupatoria*, Linn.
Fam. Rosaceae

Synonyms: Cocklebur, Stickwort.

Habitat: According to Parkinson's *Theater of Plants* (1640) there are seven varieties of Agrimony. The first and most important is the common Agrimony growing in the borders of fields, by ditches and in hedges throughout the land. The second is Sweet Smelling Agrimony, a plant found in Italy but sometimes cultivated in English gardens. The third is Bastard Agrimony also found in Italy. Although resembling Agrimony it is not a variety of this plant. The fourth is known as Hemp Agrimony, *Eupatorium cannabinum*, and grows in damp places such as ditches and water courses in England (for description see under Hemp Agrimony). The fifth, sixth, and seventh come from America; the fifth and sixth being varieties of Hemp Agrimony and the seventh known as Water Agrimony. This last named is known also as Burr Marigold (*Bidens tripartita*, Linn.). It is said to be a plant originating in North America. John Parkinson says: "it groweth huge and great in our garden grounds coming first unto us out of New England, among the earth that John Newton, a Chirurgeon of Colliton in Somersetshire brought me . . ." (for description see Burr Marigold).

Flowering Time: July and August. The seed ripens quickly afterwards.

Description: The leaves, green above and greyish underneath, are hairy, 5 in. or more long, having 3–5 pairs of lanceolate, toothed leaflets, with intermediate small ones, and half-cordate stipules, toothed. The flowers are small and composed of five small petals, yellow in colour, placed on long, slender spikes. The fruit is small, obconical, ribbed, with hooked bristles at the apex. Each fruit contains two seeds. Taste, astringent, slightly bitter.

Part Used: Herb.

Medicinal Use: Mild astringent, tonic, diuretic, deobstruent. Useful in coughs, simple diarrhoea and relaxed bowels, 1 oz of the dried herb being infused in 1 pt of boiling water, sweetened with honey or sugar and taken in frequent doses of half a cupful.

Nicholas Culpeper in *The Complete Herbal* (1653) states that this plant is under Jupiter and the sign of Cancer ". . . and strengthens those parts under the planet and sign and removes diseases in them by sympathy, and those under Saturn, Mars, and Mercury by antipathy if they happen in any part of the body governed by Jupiter, or under the signs Cancer, Sagitarius, or Pisces and must needs therefore be good for the gout. . . ."

John Hill, M.D., in the *British Herbal* (1751) states that Agrimony was greatly recommended by the ancients but is "very much neglected in the present practice." He recommends it for opening obstructions to the viscera and for jaundice.

John Parkinson in the *Theater of Plants* (1640) recommends that a decoction of the plant "made with wine and drunke, is good against the sting and biting of Serpents." Outwardly applied, a decoction in wine ". . . doth draw forth the thornes and splinters of wood, nayles, or any other such thing that is gotten into the flesh. . . ."

Preparation: Liquid extract: Dose, ½–1 fl dr.

WILLIAM SALMON, M.D., in the "English Herbal" (1710) recommends a formula to stop bleeding composed of the following: Powdered Agrimony 1 ounce mixed with Catechu, Powder of Toads, Man's Blood dried and powdered half an ounce of each. He states that this mixture is incomparable to stop bleeding internally or externally and continued ". . . it dries up Catarrhs and is good against Dropsy. Dose from half a dram to a dram at night."

ALDER, BLACK, AMERICAN

Prinos verticillatus, Linn.
Fam. Aquifoliaceae

Synonyms: Winterberry, Feverbush.

Habitat: United States and Canada.

Description: Bark brownish grey, in quilled, thin pieces about $\frac{1}{20}$ in. thick, with whitish patches having black margins and dark, circular spots, or, in older pieces, short, oblong, transverse marks. The outer layer easily separates. Inner surface greenish or yellowish white. Taste, bitter and astringent.

The berries resemble those of the common Holly in size, colour, and shape, and contain six cells and six seeds. The taste is bitter and somewhat acid.

Parts Used: Bark, berries.

Medicinal Use: Cathartic. Used for constipation generally. Very similar in action to Cascara, to which it is preferred by some practitioners.

Preparation: Liquid extract: Dose, ½–1 dr.

ALDER, ENGLISH

Alnus glutinosa, Gaertn.
Fam. Betulaceae

Habitat: It grows commonly in England, chiefly in moist woods and watery places.

Flowering Time: April and May. The seeds ripen in September.

Description: The alder tree is well known. The bark which is frequently used appears in curved or quilled pieces $\frac{1}{20}$ in. thick, brownish grey externally, and brownish orange on the inner surface. The fracture is short and uneven. Taste, astringent. The so-called "berries" are the woody, nearly globular, female catkins, after the seeds have fallen, about $\frac{3}{8}$ in. long and $\frac{1}{2}$ in. in diameter. The scales of the catkins are ovate and undivided.

Parts Used: Bark and leaves.

Medicinal Use: Tonic. The bark, being astringent, is used in a decoction as a gargle for sore throats. The leaves are glutinous and were used to cure inflammations.

CULPEPER states: "the [Alder] leaves put under the bare feet galled with travelling are a great freshing to them. The said leaves gathered while the morning dew is on them, and brought into a chamber troubled with fleas, will gather them there unto, which being suitably cast out, will rid the chamber of these troublesome fellows."

ALKANET

Alkanna tinctoria, Tausch
Fam. Boraginaceae

Synonyms: Dyer's Bugloss, Spanish Bugloss, Anchusa, Orchanet.

Habitat: Alkanet is a common garden plant in England but is not often found growing wild. In the days of Parkinson and Culpeper it was said to grow wild in Kent at Rochester and in many places in the West Country, both in Devonshire and Cornwall.

Flowering Time: July or the beginning of August. The seed ripens soon afterwards and the root is said to be in its prime at harvest time.

Description: The root is 2–4 in. long, rather thick. The rootbark is purplish and easily separated from the woody centre, which is porous and yellow. The leaves are long and narrow, hairy, and green, somewhat like the Bugloss. The larger leaves cluster round the crown of the root. The plant produces numerous stalks and grows to a height of 1 ft. The leaves are placed alternately. The flowers are beautiful and quite well known. Although there are many varieties of Alkanet producing different-coloured flowers the one generally known produces a beautiful deep-blue blossom. The sap from the root colours paper purple and fats, oils, and spirits red. It will not, however, colour water.

Part Used: Root.

Medicinal Use: At the present time the root is rarely used for medicinal purposes which are stated to be emollient. It is mostly used as a colouring agent for oils and ointments, pomades, etc.

Culpeper placed the plant under the dominion of Venus and states that it helps to cure old ulcers, inflammations, burns. Dioscorides said that it helps those bitten by venomous beasts whether it is taken inwardly or applied to the wound. He goes so far as to say that to chew the root and spit into the mouth of the serpent will instantly kill the reptile.

WILLIAM SALMON, M.D. (1710), in "English Herbs" describes a formula [using Alkanet] invented by John Ardern said to be of use for ". . . deep wounds and punctures of the nerves made with thrusts, stabs or pricking with any pointed weapon, etc., it eases pain and prevents convulsions." The recipe is as follows: "Olive Oil 2 lbs., Alkanet Root 3 or 4 ounces, Earthworms cleaned and purged number 40. Boil them well together, then strain out whilst hot and keep it close for use."

ALLSPICE

Pimenta officinalis, Lindl.
Fam. Myrtaceae

Synonyms: Pimento, Jamaican Pepper, Clove Pepper.

Habitat: Native of West Indies and cultivated in Central America. Mainly imported from Jamaica.

Flowering Time: June, July, and August. The berries appear soon after.

Description: It is an evergreen tree growing from 25–40 ft in height, bearing small, white flowers. The fruits are brown, globular, about $\frac{3}{10}$ in. in diameter, with a rough surface and a ring formed of the remains of calyx teeth at the apex. Seeds two, kidney-shaped. Shell of fruit aromatic, with a mixed clove taste. Gathered unripe, and dried in the sun. They yield from 1 to 4 per cent of volatile oil on distillation.

Medicinal Use: Aromatic, stomachic, carminative. A good addition to other medicines in the treatment of flatulence, dyspepsia, and diarrhoea.

Domestic Use: As a condiment and in mixed spices.

Preparations: Powdered fruit: Dose, 10–30 gr; Liquid extract: Dose, $\frac{1}{2}$–1 fl dr; Ol. Piment. B.P.C. 1949 (distilled from the unripe berries): Dose, 1–3 min.

The oil distilled from Pimento leaves is sometimes used as a substitute, but it is inferior in quality.

ALMONDS, BITTER

Prunus communis, Arcang.
var. *amara*, Schneid.
Fam. Rosaceae

ALMONDS, SWEET

Prunus communis, Arcang.
var. *dulcis*, Schneid.

Synonyms: Sweet Almonds, Jordan Almonds, Bitter Almonds.

Habitat: Although the almond tree grows in England it is not a native of this country, but probably of Asia Minor and Persia.

Flowering Time: Early spring.

Description: The almond is so well known that it does not require description.

Medicinal Use: Apart from their culinary use, the principal use of almonds is for the extraction of Almond Oil. Both bitter and sweet varieties contain a fixed oil which is largely used in the preparation of toilet creams. Its action is emollient. It is also administered internally as a nutrient, demulcent, and slight laxative. Bitter almonds, in addition to the fixed oil, also yield on distillation an essential oil containing from 4 to 7 per cent of prussic acid. This oil is more usually supplied with the prussic acid removed. Essential Oil of Bitter Almonds from which the poisonous ingredient has been removed is largely used for flavouring essences, the flavour of almonds being supplied by the Benzaldehyde which is present in the oil. Peach Kernel Oil (q.v.) is sometimes used to adulterate Almond Oil, but is easily detected by shaking with equal parts of sulphuric acid, nitric acid, and water. Peach Kernel Oil gives a reddish brown coloration, whereas pure Almond Oil remains colourless.

Preparations: Ol. Amygdal. B.P. (expressed oil): Dose, $\frac{1}{2}$–1 fl oz; Ol. Amygdal. Vol. Purif. B.P. (Bitter Essential Oil from which the prussic acid has been removed): Dose, $\frac{1}{4}$–1 min.

From Sweet Almonds: Lot. Ros.; Mist. Amygdal.: Dose, $\frac{1}{2}$–1 fl oz; Pulv. Amygdal. Co.; Lot. Ol. Amygdal. Ammon.

Ground Sweet Almonds contain all the oil. Almond flour is the powdered cake left after pressing, and contains only a small amount of oil. Owing to the absence of starch and high protein content, Almond Flour has been used as a food for diabetics.

Biblical References: Genesis XLIII, 11; Exodus XXV, 33, 34, XXXVII 19, 20; Numbers XVII, 8; Ecclesiastes XII, 5; Jeremiah I, 11.

ALOES

(i) *Aloe vera*, Var. *officinalis*. Linn.
(ii) *Aloe perryi*, Baker
(and other species)
(iii) *Aloe ferox*, Mill.
Fam. Liliaceae
The above form the official varieties.

Synonyms: (i) Curaçao Aloes, Barbadoes Aloes.
(ii) Socotrine Aloes. Zanzibar Aloes is regarded as a variety of the same plant.
(iii) Cape Aloes.

Habitat: (i) West Indies; (ii) East Africa; (iii) South Africa.

Description: Aloes is described officially as "the Liquid evaporated to dryness which drains from the leaves" of the above plants. Socotrine is the mildest in action and the most expensive, but varies much in quality. The powder touched with nitric acid does not give a crimson colour. Barbadoes or Curaçao Aloes has a disagreeable odour and is livery or opaque. Two grains of it are equal to three of Socotrine in purgative action. Cape Aloes is translucent and has a red-currant odour, a greenish tinge, and breaks with glassy fracture. Good Aloes should yield 40 per cent of soluble matter to cold water. Both Barbadoes and Cape Aloes in powder give a crimson colour with nitric acid.

Medicinal Use: Emmenagogue, purgative, anthelmintic. Used in constipation, dyspepsia, menstrual suppressions, and piles. Generally given in pill form combined with anodynes and carminatives; also in liquid forms. Given to nursing mothers it causes purging in the suckling infant. Acts particularly on the lower bowel.

Preparations: Aloin B.P. and U.S.P. (the active principle of Aloes): Dose, ¼–1 gr.

Preparations made with Aloes: Dec. Aloes Co. B.P.C. 1949: Dose, ½–2 fl oz; Dec. Aloes Co. Conc. B.P.C. 1949: Dose, 60–240 min; Ext. Aloes B.P.C. 1949: Dose, 1–4 gr; Ext. Colocynth. Co. B.P.C.; Dose, 2–8 gr; Pil. Aloes B.P.C. 1949: Dose, 4–8 gr; Pil. Colocynth. et Hyocy. B.P.C.: Dose, 1 or 2 pills Pil. Rhei Co. B.P.C.: Dose, 1 or 2 pills; Pil. Aloes et Asafoet. B.P.C. 1949: Dose, 1 or 2 pills; Pil. Aloes et Ferr. B.P.C. 1949; Dose, 1 or 2 pills; Pil. Aloes et Myrrh B.P.C. 1949: Dose, 1 or 2 pills; Pil. Aloes et Nuc. Vom. B.P.C.: Dose, 1 pill; Pil. Colocynth. Co. P.B.C.: Dose, 1 or 2 pills; Tab. Aloes et Nuc. Vom. B.P.C.: Dose, 1 or 2 tablets; Tab. Rhei Co. B.P.C.: Dose, 1 or 2 tablets; Tinct. Aloes B.P.C. 1949: Dose, 30–120 min.

Preparations made with Aloin (active principle): Pil. Aloin Co. B.P.C. 1949: Dose, 1 pill; Pil. Aloin et Podoph. Co. B.P.C. 1949: Dose, 1–4 pills; Pil. Aloin et Strych. Co. B.P.C. 1949: Dose, 1 or 2 pills; Pil. Ferri.

Carb. Co. B.P.C. 1949: Dose, 1–3 pills; Pil. Phenolphthal. Co. B.P.C.: Dose, 1 or 2 pills; Tab. Aloin Co. B.P.C.: Dose, 1 or 2 tablets; Tab. Phenolphthal. Co. B.P.C.: Dose, 1 or 2 tablets.

Biblical References: Psalms XLV, 8; Song of Solomon IV, 14; Proverbs VII, 17; John XIX, 39.

ALSTONIA BARK

Alstonia constricta, F. Muell.
Alstonia scholaris, Brown
Fam. Apocynaceae

Synonyms: *Constricta*—Fever Bark, Australian Quinine, Australian Febrifuge.

Scholaris—Echites scholaris, Linn., Dita Bark, Devil Tree.

Habitat: *Constricta*—Native of Australia; *Scholaris*—India and the Philippine Islands.

The name Alstonia Bark is applied to both the above in the *British Pharmaceutical Codex*, 1949, Appendix XII.

Description: *Constricta*—Bark in large quilled pieces, 1¼–2 in. wide and ½ in. thick, brown and corky externally, fissured deeply lengthwise and transversely, the inner surface yellowish brown and coarsely striated. In transverse section, a corky layer showing alternate lighter and darker bands, and an inner fibrous yellow layer in which shining particles can be seen with a lens. Taste, bitter. The yellow infusion has a blue fluorescence.

Scholaris—In irregular fragments ⅛–⅓ in. thick, fracture short and granular, externally rough, brownish grey, often with darker spots. Internally bright buff colour, showing numerous small medullary rays in the transverse fracture. Taste, bitter.

Part Used: Bark.

Medicinal Use: Anti-periodic, febrifuge, tonic. An efficacious remedy for certain forms of rheumatism. The *constricta* variety is used in Australia as a remedy for all kinds of fevers.

Preparations: Powdered bark: Dose, 2–8 gr; Liquid Extract: Dose, 4–40 drops; Infusion (1 oz to 1 pt water): Dose, ½–1 fl oz; Tincture (1 in 8): Dose, ½–1 fl dr.

AMADOU

Polyporus fomentarius, Fries
Fam. Polyporaceae

Synonyms: Surgeon's Agaric, German Tinder, Oak Agaric.

Habitat: A fungus growth upon oak and beech trees in Europe and the British Isles.

Description: A hoof-shaped, obliquely triangular, sessile fungus. The inner part is composed of short tubular fibres arranged in layers. It is prepared for use by being cut into slices, beaten, soaked in a solution of nitre, and dried.

Medicinal Use: Amadou has for long been used for arresting local haemorrhages, being applied with pressure to the affected part. When inserted between the nail and the flesh, it is one of the best-known substances for treating ingrown toe-nails.

AMARANTH

Amaranthus hypochondriacus, Linn.
Fam. Amaranthaceae

Synonyms: *Amaranthus melancholicus*, Linn., Red Cockscomb, Love-Lies-Bleeding, and in Culpeper's time Flower Gentle, Flower Velure, Floramor, and Velvet Flower.

Habitat: A common garden plant.

Flowering Time: From August until the first frosts.

Description: Flattened stems bearing rounded tufts of minute flowers, hidden by crowded, linear, tapering, chaffy, crimson bracts. Seeds lens-shaped, black, about $\frac{1}{20}$ in. in diameter.

Part Used: The flowering herb.

Medicinal Use: Astringent. Highly recommended in menorrhagia, diarrhoea, dysentery, and haemorrhages from the bowels. The decoction is taken in wineglassful doses. Externally this is used as an application in ulcerated conditions of throat and mouth, as an injection in leucorrhoea, and a wash for ulcers, sores, etc.

Culpeper, relying on the doctrine of signatures, recommends the red flowers for stopping all kinds of bleeding, but this idea is not shared by Gerard, who quotes Galen as saying: ". . . there can be no certainty gathered from the colours, touching the vertues of simple and compound medicines: wherefore they are ill persuaded that thinke the floure Gentle to stunch bleeding because of the colour only, if they had no other reason to induce them thereto."

Preparation: Fluid extract: Dose, $\frac{1}{2}$–1 dr.

AMMONIACUM

Dorema ammoniacum, G. Don.
Fam. Umbelliferae

Synonym: Gum Ammoniacum.

Habitat: In the region from Persia to Southern Siberia, but exported from Persia.

Description: The gum resin occurs in rounded nodules, or rarely compacted into massed, opaque, whitish, becoming brownish with age, fracture glossy. It forms an emulsion with water. Taste, acrid, slightly bitter; flavour, characteristic. The solution in warm water is turned orange red by chlorinated lime.

Medicinal Use: Stimulant, antispasmodic, expectorant. Has been found especially useful in chronic affections of the respiratory organs, also in cough, asthma, bronchitis, catarrh, etc.

Preparations: Powdered gum-resin: Dose, 5–15 gr; Pil. Scill. Co. B.P.C. 1949: Dose, 1 or 2 pills.

ANGELICA, EUROPEAN

Angelica archangelica, Linn.
Fam. Umbelliferae

Synonym: Garden Angelica.

Culpeper has some caustic things to say about synonyms in general and in particular concerning one that was used in connexion with this plant. After mentioning several synonyms for other plants which he considers blasphemous, he continues: ". . . our physicians must imitate like apes (though they cannot come off half so cleverly) for they call Phansies or Heartsease, an herb of Trinity because it is of three colours . . . and therefore some called this an herb of the Holy Ghost; others more moderate called it Angelica, because of its Angelical virtues."

Parkinson mentions other synonyms, but concludes by saying that "all Christian nations . . . follow the Latin name as their dialect will permit. Only in Sussex they call the wild kind Kex and the weavers winde their yarn on the dead stakes."

Habitat: Angelica is a common garden plant in England. It also grows wild in many southern counties and in European countries. America produces a similar plant known as *Angelica atropurpurea*.

Description: The root of the European Angelica is 2–4 in. long and 1–2 in. thick with many fibres. The transverse section shows a brown bark and white inside showing numerous oil cells in the bark. The fresh root when cut yields a thick, yellowish juice. The taste is warm and aromatic and somewhat bitter and the smell fragrant and agreeable. The plant grows to a height of about 6 ft. The first leaves are large, standing upon large, fleshy footstalks. They are broad, pointed with serrated edges. The upper leaves are similar but smaller. The stalk is round and hollow, and green in colour. The fruits are whitish, plano-convex, oblong, and rounded at the ends, $\frac{1}{4}$ in. long and $\frac{1}{8}$ in. broad, winged at the margins, having three longitudinal ridges on the convex and two on the flat side. *Angelica atropurpurea* is less branched than the European *Angelica* and is paler in colour and less aromatic. The flowers are also different, resembling Lovage, whereas those of the European Angelica are small and of a greenish-white colour.

Parts Used: Root, seeds, herb.

Medicinal Use: Angelica is known as an aromatic, stimulant, carminative, diuretic, and diaphoretic. The root, fruits, and herb are all used, but more frequently the herb by making an infusion of 1 oz of the dried herb to 1 pt of boiling water and taking wineglassful doses frequently. The fruits were used as an ingredient in Warburg's Tincture which was included in the 1934 *British Pharmaceutical Codex*, but omitted from the next edition. It was prescribed as an antispasmodic.

Culpeper describes this plant as a herb of the Sun in Leo. He recommends it for all epidemic diseases caused by Saturn and continues: "It resists poison by defending and comforting the heart blood and spirits; it doth the like against the plague and all epidemic diseases." Also: "The root in powder, made up in a plaister with a little pitch and laid on the biting of mad dogs or any other venomous creature doth wonderfully help."

Preparations: Powdered root: Dose, 10–30 gr; Liquid Extract root: Dose, ½–1 dr; Liquid Extract herb: Dose, ½–1 dr; Infusion root, 1 in 20: Dose, wineglassful.

The fruits were an ingredient in Tinct. Antiperiodica B.P.C. 1934, but this preparation is now omitted from the B.P.C.

Culinary Use: The dried leaf stalks preserved with sugar form the confection generally known as Angelica which is used in sweetmeats and to decorate cakes.

ANGOSTURA

Galipea officinalis, Han.
Fam. Rutaceae

Synonyms: Cusparia Bark, *Cusparia febrifuga*, D.C., *Bonplandia trifoliata*, W., *Galipea cusparia*, St. Hil.

Habitat: Indigenous to Venezuela. First used in England about 1788.

Description: A small tree 12–15 ft high from which the bark is stripped, appearing in commerce in slightly curved or quilled pieces ⅛ in. thick, with thin laminae on inner surface, yellowish grey externally, outer layer sometimes soft and spongy. Transverse section, dark brown. Taste, bitter; odour, musty.

Part Used: Bark.

Medicinal Use: Aromatic, bitter, tonic, stimulant. In large doses, cathartic. Recommended in diarrhoea, dysentery, intermittent fevers, and dropsy, in doses varying from 5–15 gr of the powdered bark. Large doses of ⅓–1 dr cause emesis and purging.

Preparations: Powdered bark: Dose, 5–15 gr; Liquid extract: Dose, 5–30 drops; Inf. Cuspariae Conc.: Dose, ½–1 fl dr.

Domestic Use: It is used to make a "bitter" for adding to gin.

ANISEED

Pimpinella anisum, Linn.
Fam. Umbelliferae

Synonym: Anise.

Habitat: It is supposed to have come from Egypt and Asia Minor but is grown commercially in the warmer parts of Europe and North Africa. It is also cultivated in India and South America.

Description: Fruits (or so-called seeds) greyish or brownish grey, ovate, hairy, about $\frac{2}{10}$ in. long, with 10 crenate ribs, often having the stalk attached. Taste, sweet; odour, characteristic. They should be free from earthy matter.

See also Star-Anise, p. 290.

Part Used: Fruit.

Medicinal Use: Carminative and pectoral. Used in cough medicines and lozenges. The powdered seed is largely employed in condition and other condiments for horses. Aniseed was known to the ancients in many parts of the world and was valued as a carminative.

Biblical Reference: Matthew XXIII, 23.

ANNATTO

Bixa orellana, Linn.
Fam. Bixaceae

Synonyms: Annotta, Arnotta, Orellana, Orleana.

Habitat: Venezuela and Brazil.

Description: In small, circular cakes about 1½ in. in diameter and ½ in. thick, or in sausage-shaped rolls.

Part Used: Pulp of seeds (described above).

Use: "Annatto," the colouring matter of the pulp covering the seeds, is mostly used as a dye for fabrics, etc., and in pharmacy to colour plasters, ointments, and oils. It is also employed in various butter and cheese colours.

ARACHIS

Arachis hypogaea, Linn.
Fam. Leguminosae

Synonyms: Ground Nuts, Monkey Nuts, Pea Nuts, Earth Nuts.

Habitat: Tropical Africa.

Description: The lower flowers develop nuts which bury themselves in the earth and ripen. The seeds are reddish brown, containing about 45 per cent of nut oil.

Part Used: The oil expressed from the nuts.

Medicinal Use: The oil is largely used as a substitute for Olive Oil, but it is liable to go rancid.

Domestic Use: Soap-making. The cake, after the oil is expressed, forms a popular cattle food.
Preparations: Ol. Arach. B.P. and U.S.P.

ARBUTUS, TRAILING

Epigaea repens, Linn.
Fam. Ericaceae

Synonyms: Gravel Plant, Ground Laurel, Mountain Pink, Winter Pink, Mayflowers.
Habitat: America.
Description: Leaves stalked, broadly ovate, 1–1½ in. long and about 1 in. broad, leathery, reticulated with a cordate base and a short point at the apex. Lateral veins spreading, wavy, with short hairs on the under surface. Taste, astringent and bitter; odour, none.
Part Used: Herb.
Medicinal Use: Diuretic, astringent. This American plant is reputed to be superior to Buchu and Uva-ursi in all diseases of the urinary organs attended with irritation. It is of value in gravel, debilitated or relaxed bladder, and in urine containing blood or pus. The infusion of 1 oz of leaves in 1 pt of boiling water may be drunk freely.

ARCHANGEL

Lamium album, Linn.
Fam. Labiatae

Synonym: White Deadnettle.
Habitat: A common wild plant in England.
Flowering Time: Early spring and summer.
Description: Stem quadrangular, leaves opposite, reticulate veined, with spreading hairs, chiefly on the prominent veins below and on the stem, margin with large serrate teeth. Flowers, large, white, two-lipped with two long and two short stamens. Taste, slightly bitter; odour, none, when dried.
Part Used: Herb.
Medicinal Use: Similar to Nettle (q.v.).

ARECA NUT

Areca catechu, Linn.
Fam. Palmaceae

Synonym: Betel Nut.
Habitat: Throughout India and the islands of the Eastern Archipelago.
Description: Seed conical or nearly spherical, 1 in. or more in diameter,

hard and horny, marbled with brown lines internally. Taste, astringent and slightly acrid. The larger and more conical seeds are more active than the globular variety.

Part Used: Seed.

Medicinal Use: Astringent, taenicide. It is chiefly used to expel tapeworms. The powdered nut is administered in doses from 2–4 dr. The smaller dose is generally given in syrup, followed by a purgative.

Areca is mainly used in the veterinary practice. The fresh nut is also largely chewed by natives of eastern countries to counteract the relaxation of the bowels caused by climatic heat.

Preparations: Liquid extract: Dose 1–4 dr; Pulv. Arec. B.P.C.: Dose, 15–60 gr.

ARENARIA RUBRA

Lepigonum rubrum, Fries
Fam. Caryophyllaceae

Synonyms: *Spergularia rubra*, Pers., Sabline rouge (Fr.), *Tissa rubra*, Adans., *Buda rubra*, Dum., Sandwort.

Habitat: Malta and S. France.

Description: Herb with jointed stems and flat, linear leaves, about $\frac{1}{16}$ in. wide and nearly $\frac{1}{2}$ in. long, with ovate, pointed stipules, flowers small, pink, in spreading, loose panicles, seeds not winged. Taste, saline and slightly aromatic.

Part Used: Herb.

Medicinal Use: Diuretic. A popular remedy in Malta for diseases of the bladder. Recommended in cystitis, stone, etc.

Dose of infusion, 1 oz to 1 pt, a wineglassful frequently; Fluid extract, 1 dr.

ARNICA

Arnica montana, Linn.
Fam. Compositae

Habitat: It grows in the Northern hemisphere but not in England.

Description: Rhizome $\frac{1}{6}$–$\frac{1}{4}$ in. in diameter, 1–2 in. long with rather distant wing, unbranched rootlets below. Transverse fracture showing greyish pith and oil cells in the bark. Taste, acrid and bitter; odour, like that of apples. The flowers have yellow florets, and brownish fruits, with a single row of whitish, barbed hairs, and a hairy receptacle. Usually collected entire.

Parts Used: Rhizome, flowers.

Medicinal Use: Stimulant, vulnerary. Largely used as a local application to bruises, swellings, etc. As it is an active irritant, care should be exercised in internal employment. Severe and fatal cases of poisoning are on record.
Preparations: Tinct. Arnic. Flor. B.P.C. 1949: Dose, 30–60 min; Tinct. Arnic. Rad.; Lin. Arnic.

ARRACH

Chenopodium olidum, S. Wats.
Fam. Chenopodiaceae

Synonyms: Stinking Arrach, Goosefoot, Dog's Arrach, Goat's Arrach.
Habitat: A British and European wild plant growing mostly in waste places or on dunghills.
Flowering Time: June and July.
Description: Herb with oval, stalked leaves, about ½ in. long, entire at the margins; having a strong, fishy odour and powdery surface.
Part Used: Herb.
Medicinal Use: Nervine, emmenagogue. Useful in hysteria of females and as a remedy for menstrual obstructions. The infusion of 1 oz in 1 pt of boiling water is taken three or four times daily in wineglassful doses.

CULPEPER says of Arrach "... therefore if you love children, if you love health, if you love ease, keep a syrup always by you, made of the juice of this herb and sugar, and let such as be rich keep it for their poor neighbours. ..."

Preparation: Fluid extract: Dose, ½–1 dr.

ARROWROOT

Maranta arundinacea, Linn.
Fam. Marantaceae

Synonyms: Bermuda Arrowroot, Maranta.
Habitat: Tropical America and West Indies.
Description: The plant itself, which is not seen in this country, is herbaceous and grows to 4–6 ft in height. Arrowroot of commerce is prepared from the rhizomes to form a white powder containing small masses consisting of the starch. Under the microscope seen to consist of irregularly oval grains, having the hilum at the larger end or near the middle. Average diameter, 30–40 μ.
Medicinal Use: Demulcent, non-irritating, nutritive. Well suited for infants and convalescents. Two or three teaspoonfuls may be boiled in a pint of

water or milk and seasoned to taste, with sugar, lemon juice, fruit jellies, essences, or aromatics. Other kinds are the Natal and St. Vincent Arrowroot.

THE name Arrowroot was given to this plant because the natives used the mushed root to apply to wounds caused by poisoned arrows.

ASAFETIDA

Ferula foetida, Reg.
Ferula rubicaulis Boiss.
and other species.
Fam. Umbelliferae

Synonyms: Asafoetida, Gum Asafetida, Devil's Dung.

Habitat: Persia. Western Afghanistan.

Joseph Miller in the *Botanicum Officinale* (1722) writes that the plant grows in the mountains of Heraat, in the province of Chorafan in Persia.

Description: The plant itself is never seen in this country and modern descriptions are not available. Doctor Kempfer in his *Amoenitates exoticae* states that the oleo-gum-resin is drawn from the roots and stems of a plant called by the Persians "Hingisch." This has large, thick roots with but few fibres, of a blackish colour outside and very white within. The root is full of a white foetid juice. He states that the leaves are large and winged, the stalk more than a finger thick, much branched and full of a fungous matter; it bears large umbels of pale whitish flowers.

The gum-resin is distinguished by its powerfully alliaceous odour. Occurs in more or less sticky lumps of variable size, sometimes with a pinkish tint. When it is immersed in water, and ammonia is added, a bluish fluorescence appears; touched with nitric acid it gives a green colour.

Part Used: Oleo-gum-resin.

Medicinal Use: Stimulant, antispasmodic, expectorant. Useful in infantile convulsions, croup, and flatulent colic. It allays gastric irritation, hysteria, and spasmodic nervous diseases. Owing to its nauseous taste, it is mostly given in pill form.

Domestic Use: It has been used for generations in the East to give flavour to sauces and is said to be an ingredient in a well-known sauce of the present day in England.

Preparations: Powdered gum-resin: Dose, 5–15 gr; Pil. Aloes et Asafoet. B.P.C. 1949: Dose, 1 or 2 pills; Pil. Asafoet. B.P.C. 1949: Dose, 1 or 2 pills; Tinct. Asafoet B P.C. 1949: Dose, 30–60 min.

ASARABACCA *Asarum europaeum*, Linn.
Fam. Aristolochiaceae

Synonyms: Hazelwort, Wild Nard.

Habitat: It grows in woods and shady places in Europe, Siberia and the Caucasus. It is also an English and American garden plant.

Flowering Time: June, the seeds ripening in August.

Description: A herbaceous perennial plant. Leaves kidney-shaped, smooth, leathery, stalked, remaining green all the winter. Flowers solitary, bell-shaped, with three segments, purplish within. Rhizome slender, 2–4 in. long and $\frac{1}{8}$ in. thick, quadrangular tortuous, thickened at intervals where rootlets are given off, with stem scars on the upper surface.

Parts Used: Root, herb.

Medicinal Use: Emetic, purgative, sternutatory. Is stimulant in doses of 10–12 gr; emetic in doses of 1–2 dr. In France it is said that drunkards use it to produce vomiting. Useful as an errhine in headache. For this purpose 1–2 gr of the powder is sniffed up the nostrils, producing intense irritation and a copious flow of mucus. This is also said to relieve apumatic pains in the mouth or throat.

Culpeper writes; "The common use therof is to take the juice of five or seven leaves in a little drink to cause vomiting; the roots have also the virtue though they do not operate so forcibly . . . the leaves and roots being boiled in lye and the head often washed therewith while it is warm, comforts the head and brain that is ill affected by taking cold, and helps the memory."

ASH *Fraxinus excelsior*, Linn.
Fam. Oleaceae

Synonyms: Common Ash, European Ash, Weeping Ash.

Habitat: Great Britain and Europe, America.

Flowering Time: Early spring.

Description: The ash tree is well known and derives its name from the fact that its leaves are ash coloured and from the grey nature of the bark. The bark (which is the principal part used) is thin, greenish, or greyish-brown in curved pieces about $\frac{1}{8}$ in. thick and about $1\frac{1}{2}$ in. broad, with distant longitudinal furrows, inner surface pale brown, laminated, transverse section showing many thin layers, outer surface rough and scaly in older bark. Taste, faintly bitter; odour, none. American white ash bark has numerous small circular depressions externally, and slightly less laminate fracture.

Parts Used: Bark, leaves.

Medicinal Use: Antiperiodic, laxative, purgative. At one time the bark was extensively used in intermittent fevers, ague, etc. The leaves are used with success in gouty, arthritic, and rheumatic complaints.

The ash had a considerable reputation as a cure for the bites of snakes and other creatures and according to Parkinson, Pliny "writeth that those serpents will not abide the shadow that the Ash maketh in the morning and the evening which then are longest, nor will come neere it, and further saith of his own experience, that if a fire and a serpent be encompassed within a circle of the boughes of the Ash Tree, it will sooner flye into the fire than into them. . . ."

Biblical Reference: Isaiah XLIV, 14.

ASPARAGUS

Asparagus officinalis, Linn.
Fam. Liliaceae

Synonym: Sparrowgrass.

Description: Root about 2 in. long and $\frac{1}{2}$–$\frac{3}{4}$ in. thick with loose, laminate texture internally, giving off long, compressed, tough rootlets several inches long, and $\frac{1}{8}$–$\frac{1}{4}$ in. in diameter, nearly hollow, with a central woody cord. Taste, insipid; odour, none.

Part Used: Root.

Medicinal Use: Diuretic, laxative, cardiac, sedative. It is said that this plant produces a copious diuresis, and it has been recommended in dropsy, enlargement of heart, etc. The fresh expressed juice is taken in tablespoonful doses. It can be made more palatable in the form of a syrup and is used as such in doses of 1–2 tablespoonfuls.

Domestic Use: The young shoots are used as a well known food.

AVENS

Geum urbanum, Linn.
Fam. Rosaceae

Synonyms: Colewort, Herb Bennet, *Radix caryophyllata*, Geum.

Habitat: A hedgerow plant growing wild in shadowy places in Great Britain and Europe.

Flowering Time: May or June.

Description: Root 1–2 in. long, obconical, abrupt below, hard and rough, with light-brown rootlets. Transverse section light purplish-brown with thin bark, a narrow, woody ring and large pith. Taste, astringent, slightly bitter, with a clove flavour. Plant is more conspicuous for its seed than flower. When the petals have withered a round, brown ball of awned seeds succeeds them. The seeds are covered with hairs or bristles which fix themselves on any passing object; stem slender about 1–2 in. Leaves on stem, two leaflets and one margin-toothed terminal lobe. Flowers yellow. Taste, astringent; odour, none.

Water Avens is a distinct species with purple flowers.

Parts Used: Herb, root.

Medicinal Use: Astringent, styptic, tonic, febrifuge, stomachic. Its constant use is said to have a highly restorative power in weakness, debility, etc. Also useful in diarrhoea, sore throat, and leucorrhoea. The infusion is made of 1 oz of powdered herb or root to 1 pt of boiling water and taken in wineglassful doses three or four times a day.

Preparations: Liquid extract herb: Dose, 1 dr; Liquid extract root: Dose, $\frac{1}{2}$–1 dr.

AZEDARACHA

Melia azedirachta, Linn.
Fam. Meliaceae

Synonyms: Nim, Margosa, Neem, Indian Lilac Tree.

Habitat: Native of the Levant and Northern India but cultivated in the Southern United States.

Description: A large, deciduous tree. The bark is described as follows: greyish brown, rough, and cracked externally; inner surface bright buff, in pieces about 2–3 in. wide and $\frac{1}{5}$ in. thick. Transverse fracture fibrous, the inner portion showing distinct layers. Taste, astringent and bitter; odour, none.

Part Used: Bark.

Medicinal Use: Anthelmintic; it is also said to be cathartic and emetic. Used in Southern States of America for worms in children, and generally given in form of a decoction made of 4 oz of bark to 1 qt of water and boiled down to 1 pt. Dose, a tablespoonful every three hours or a dose evening and morning followed by castor oil or some other active cathartic.

Preparations: Infusion, $\frac{1}{2}$–1 oz; Tincture, $\frac{1}{2}$–1 dr.

B

BAEL *Aegle marmelos*, Correa
Fam. Rutaceae

Synonyms: Bel, Indian Bael, Bengal Quince.
Habitat: India.
Description: The tree attains a height of from 30–40 ft. The fruit, which is the part used, appears globular or sometimes oval, with a hard shell divided internally like an orange, flesh reddish, hard when dry, seeds numerous, covered with a gummy layer. Taste, mucilaginous, slightly acid.
Part Used: The unripe dried fruit.
Medicinal Use: Astringent. An Indian remedy and almost a specific for diarrhoea, dysentery, etc. It does not constipate.
Preparation: Liquid extract: Dose, 60–120 min.

IN India the Bael tree is regarded as sacred by the Hindus. It is supposed to increase fertility. It was introduced into this country about 1850 and found a place in the "British Pharmacopoeia" from which it is now omitted. It is not frequently used here.

BALM *Melissa officinalis*, Linn.
Fam. Labiatae

Synonyms: Sweet Balm, Lemon Balm, Honey Plant, Cure-all. The old herbalists knew it as Bawm.
Habitat: A common garden plant.
Flowering Time: Spring.
Description: Leaves opposite, stalked, about 1½ in. long, thin, broadly ovate, with a rounded base (wedge-shaped in the upper leaves), coarsely serrate and wrinkled. Taste and odour like lemon.
Part Used: Herb.
Medicinal Use: Carminative, diaphoretic, febrifuge. Induces mild perspiration and makes a pleasant and cooling tea for feverish patients. To make the tea, pour 1 pt of boiling water upon 1 oz of herb, let it stand for a quarter of an hour, allow to cool, then strain and drink freely. A very useful herb, either alone or in combination with others.

Culpeper quoting Serapio writes "... it causeth the mind and heart to become merry, and reviveth the heart fainting into swoonings, especially of such as are overtaken in their sleep, and driveth away all troublesome cares and thoughts out of the mind arising from melancholy, or black choler. . . ." He also reports that Pliny when writing on bawm "informeth us, that, if it be tied to a sword which gave the wound it instantly stoppeth the blood."

Preparation: Liquid extract: Dose, ¼–1 dr.

BALM is a favourite plant for bees. Pliny stated that it is profitable planted in gardens where bees are kept because they are delighted with this herb above all others, and that when they stray away they find their way home again because of it; also that the hives of bees rubbed with the leaves cause the bees to keep together and others to join them.

BALM OF GILEAD

Populus candicans, Ait.
Fam. Salicaceae

Synonym: Mecca Balsam.

Habitat: About Mecca in Arabia.

Description: A small tree or shrub bearing green, pinnate leaves. It bears small, six-petal, whitish flowers followed by roundish, rugged fruit. It is the buds which are used in medicine and they are about 1 in. long and ¼ in. broad; scales brownish, narrow, ovate, closely overlapping, polished, inner scales sticky and resinous. Odour, balsamic; taste slightly bitter.

Part Used: Buds.

Medicinal Use: Stimulant, tonic, diuretic. It is of great benefit in all affections of the chest, lungs, stomach, and kidneys. As an ointment it is good for colds and pains in the chest, cutaneous diseases, rheumatic and gouty pains. In addition Joseph Miller states: "Outwardly it is of greater excellence than any Turpentine for wounds and ulcers."

Preparations: Solid extract: Dose, 5–10 gr; Tincture: Dose, 1–4 dr; Liquid extract: Dose, 1–2 dr.

Biblical References: Genesis XXXVII, 25, XLIII, 11; Jeremiah VIII, 22, XLVI, 11, LI, 8; Ezekiel XXVII, 17.

BALMONY

Chelone glabra, Linn.
Fam. Scrophulariaceae

Synonyms: Bitter Herb, Snake Head, Turtle Head, Turtle Bloom.

Description: Leaves opposite, oblong lanceolate, shortly stalked, fruits crowded in a short spike, ovate, ½ in. long, two-celled with nearly circular, winged seeds, having a dark centre. Taste, very bitter; odour, slightly tea-like.

Part Used: Leaves.

Medicinal Use: Antibilious, anthelmintic, tonic, detergent. Used largely in constipation, dyspepsia, debility, and jaundice. In all diseases of the liver it will be found very valuable, and is a certain remedy for worms in children. An infusion of 1 oz to 1 pt of boiling water may be taken frequently in doses of a wineglassful.

Preparations: Powdered herb: Dose, 5–10 gr; Liquid extract: Dose, ½–1 dr; Chelonin: Dose, 1–2 gr.

BARBERRY *Berberis vulgaris*, Linn.
Fam. Berberidaceae

Synonyms: Barbery, Berberidis, Pipperidge-Bush, *Berberis dumetorum*, Gouan.

Habitat: A common garden bush, growing wild in some parts of Europe and the British Isles.

Flowering Time: April and May. Berries ripen in September.

Description: The bush with long, brittle branches bearing sharp thorns is well known. It bears yellow flowers among the leaves. The stem bark is thin, externally yellowish grey, orange yellow on the inner surface, separating in layers. Root-bark dark brown externally, fracture short. Taste, very bitter.

Parts Used: Root, root-bark, berries.

Medicinal Use: Tonic, purgative, and antiseptic. Used in all cases of jaundice, liver complaints, general debility, and biliousness. It regulates the digestive powers, being a mild purgative, and removes constipation. Its action is due to the presence of a bitter alkaloid, Berberine, which has been isolated. The berries make a pleasant acid drink of great utility in diarrhoea, fevers, etc.

Culpeper writes: "Mars owns the shrub and presents it to the use of my countrymen to purge their bodies of choler. The inner rind of the Barberry Tree boiled in white wine, and a quarter of a pint drank each morning, is an excellent remedy to cleanse the body. . . ."

Preparations: Powdered bark: Dose, ½ teaspoonful three to four times daily; Liquid extract: Dose, ½–1 dr; Solid extract: Dose, 5–10 gr; Berberine: Dose 1–5 gr.

BARLEY

Hordeum distichon, Linn.
and *Hordeum vulgare*, Linn.
Fam. Graminaceae

Synonyms: Pearl Barley, Perlatum.

Description: Two forms of decorticated barley are sold, known respectively as Scotch hulled or Pot Barley, which is not entirely deprived of the husk, and Pearl Barley. Pearl Barley should always be washed before being boiled, as it is apt to accumulate dust.

Part Used: Decorticated seeds.

Medicinal Use: Nutritive, demulcent. As an article of diet for the sick and convalescent it is largely used. Barley-water is a demulcent food beverage for children suffering from diarrhoea, catarrhal inflammation of bowels, etc. The decoction made from the washed barleycorns—2 oz to 1 pt of water—is an unirritating food in chronic exhausting diseases.

Preparations: Extract of Malt, and its various combinations, is made from Malted Barley.

Domestic Use: Malted Barley is used in the manufacture of beer and whisky.

BASIL

Ocimum basilicum, Linn.
Fam. Labiatae

Synonyms: Sweet Basil, Garden Basil.

Habitat: It grows in gardens throughout the British Isles.

Flowering Time: Midsummer.

Description: The plant, growing to about 8 in. in height, usually has one upright stem diversely branched and obtusely quadrangular. The leaves are opposite, stalked, broadly oval, and pointed. They are of a pale-green colour and dotted with dark oil cells. The calyx has the upper lobe rounded and spreading. The root is long and fibrous. The flowers, which are small and white with a faint dash of purple, are in long, loose spikes. The seeds are brown and obtuse. The plant is easily distinguished by its taste which is aromatic and recalls the flavour of Tarragon. This plant must not be confused with Wild Basil (*Calamintha clinopodium*) which has little clusters of red flowers and produces very small, black seeds.

Part Used: Herb.

Medicinal Use: Ancient writers appear to differ in their assessment of the usefulness of this plant in medicine. Culpeper says: "This is the herb which all authors are together by the ears about and rail at one another (like lawyers)."

It is today considered to be an aromatic with carminative and cooling properties and it is said to have been used with success in mild nervous disorders. In South America the juice is used as a vermifuge.

Culpeper calls it a herb of Mars and under the Scorpion. As with so many other herbs it is recommended to draw out the poison from those bitten by venomous beasts, because as he says: "Every like draws his like."

Domestic Use: Basil is a well-known culinary herb used in cooking as a flavouring agent.

GALEN and Dioscorides hold Basil not fit to be taken internally and Chrysippus rails at it with downright Billingsgate rhetoric; Pliny and the Arabian physicians defend it.

Hilarius, an ancient French physician claims that from his own knowledge an acquaintance of his, by merely smelling the herb, caused a scorpion to be born in his brain.

BAYBERRY

Myrica cerifera, Linn.
Fam. Myricaceae

Synonyms: Candleberry, Waxberry, Wax Myrtle.

Habitat: A widely distributed plant in Europe, America, and the British Isles.

Description: Bark in short, quilled pieces about $\frac{1}{16}$ in. thick, with a white, peeling epidermis, covering a red-brown, hard layer beneath, fracture granular, slightly fibrous on the inner surface. Taste, astringent, bitter, and pungent; odour, slightly aromatic.

Part Used: Bark.

Medicinal Use: A powerful stimulant, astringent, and tonic. If not absolutely the most useful article in botanic practice, it is certainly nearly so. It enters largely into many of the compound powders and forms the basis of the celebrated composition powder. In cases of coldness of the extremities, chills, clamminess, etc., it will, combined with Cayenne, cause that action in the system which generates heat and induces perspiration. For canker of the stomach and bowels it is invaluable, being an effectual deobstruent and cleanser. The powdered bark is generally used in an infusion of 1 oz to 1 pt of boiling water. To promote heat it should be drunk warm. The powder may also be added to poultices, as it has a very healing and cleansing action on all scrofulous ulcers, sores, etc.

Preparations: Powdered bark: Dose, 10–60 gr; Liquid extract: Dose, $\frac{1}{2}$–1 dr; Myricin: Dose, 1–3 gr.

Domestic Use: The wax covering the berries has been used in the manufacture of soap.

The oil distilled from the berries forms an ingredient in Bay Rum for a hair dressing.

BEARSFOOT, AMERICAN

Polymnia uvedalia, Linn.
Fam. Compositae

Synonyms: Uvedalia, Leaf Cup, Yellow Leaf Cup.

Habitat: N. America.

Description: Root greyish brown, finely furrowed longitudinally, from $\frac{1}{4}$–$\frac{1}{2}$ in. in diameter with a tough, coarsely fibrous fracture, the woody column splitting off into laminae, the bark thin, brittle, easily scaling off. Taste, saline, faintly bitter; odour, none.

This is a N. American plant and must not be confused with English Bearsfoot (*Helleborus foetidus*).

Part Used: Root.

Medicinal Use: Stimulant, laxative, anodyne. Has been used with good effect in congestive states of liver and spleen; also in inflamed glands and dyspepsia from these causes. Used externally as a hair tonic or in the form of an ointment.

Preparation: Liquid extract: Dose, 15–60 drops.

BEEBEERU BARK

Nectandra rodioei, Hook.
Fam. Lauraceae

Synonyms: Greenheart Bark, Bibiru Bark, Bebeeru Bark.

Habitat: British Guiana.

Description: Flat, heavy, hard pieces 10–15 mm long, 5–10 mm thick, grey brown in colour with shallow depressions on the other portions. Inner portion coarsely striated. Granular fracture. Imported from British Guiana.

Part Used: Bark.

Medicinal Use: Stomachic, tonic, and febrifuge. It is not very often used.

Preparation: Powdered bark: Dose, $\frac{1}{4}$–$\frac{1}{2}$ dr.

BELLADONNA

Atropa belladonna, Linn.
Fam. Solanaceae

Synonyms: Deadly Nightshade, Dwale.

Habitat: Native to central and southern Europe, but growing quite commonly in England particularly in the southern counties. It is also cultivated in England for medicinal use. Joseph Miller writes: "It is to be found in a Ditch at the end of Goswell Street, in the road to Islington. . . ."

Description: Root pale brown, $\frac{3}{8}$–$\frac{3}{4}$ in. in diameter, 6 or more inches long, with short, transverse scars, easily abraded by the finger nail, showing white, starchy tissue beneath. Transverse section whitish, with a thickish bark, and woody bundles scattered through the central column, but more crowded near the bark. Leaves ovate, not toothed, thin and brittle when dry, showing under a lens numerous minute, pale, prominent points on the surface, corresponding to cells filled with sandy crystals of calcium oxalate.

The plant should be collected when in flower. The larger stalks should be rejected, as they are weak in alkaloids.

Parts Used: Root, leaves.

Medicinal Use: Narcotic, diuretic, sedative, mydriatic. Used as an anodyne in febrile conditions, night-sweats, coughs, whooping cough, etc.; also in spermatorrhoea. Suppresses glandular secretions. Used externally in gouty and rheumatic inflammations.

Preparations: From leaves: Bellad. Praep. B.P.: Dose, $\frac{1}{2}$–3 gr; Ext. Bellad. Virid. B.P.C.: Dose, $\frac{1}{4}$–1 gr; Ext. Bellad. U.S.P.: Dose, $\frac{1}{4}$ gr; Glycer. Bellad. B.P.C.; Mist. Bellad. et Ephed. pro Infant. B.P.C.: Dose, 60–120 min; Mist. Bellad. et Ipecac. pro Infant. B.P.C.: Dose, 60–120 min; Mist. Bellad. pro Infant. B.P.C.: Dose, 60–120 min; Mist. Casc. et Bellad. B.P.C.: Dose, $\frac{1}{2}$ fl oz; Mist. Casc. et Bellad. pro Infant. B.P.C.: Dose, 60–120 min; Mist. Pot. Brom. et Bellad. pro Infant, B.P.C.: Dose, 60–120 min; Mist. Pot. Cit. et Bellad. pro Infant. B.P.C.: Dose, 60–120 min; Pil. Aloes et Nuc. Vom. B.P.C.: Dose, 1 pill; Pil. Aloin. et Strych. Co. B.P.C.: Dose, 1 or 2 pills; Pil, Casc. Bellad. et Nuc. Vom. B.P.C. 1949: Dose, 1–3 pills; Pil. Phenolphthal. Co. B.P.C.: Dose, 1 or 2 pills; Pil. Zinc. Oxid. et Bellad. B.P.C. 1949: Dose, 1 pill; Tab. Aloes et Nuc. Vom. B.P.C.: Dose, 1 or 2 tablets; Tab. Phenolphthal. Co. B.P.C.: Dose, 1 or 2 tablets; Tinct. Bellad. B.P.: Dose, 10–30 min; Tinct. Bellad. U.S.P.: Dose, 10 min; Ung. Bellad. U.S.P.

From root: Emp. Bellad. B.P.C.; Emp. Bellad. et Capsic. B.P.C.; Emp. Bellad. in Mass. B.P.C.; Ext. Bellad. Liq. B.P.; Lin. Aconit. Bellad. et Chlorof. B.P.C.; Lin. Bellad. B.P.C.; Lin. Bellad. cum Chlorof. B.P.C. 1949; Supp. Bellad. B.P.C. 1949; Ung. Bellad. B.P.C. 1949.

BELLADONNA is an extremely poisonous plant and should never be used except under medical supervision. Commenting on its poisonous nature, Culpeper writes: "There is a remarkable instance of the direful effects of this plant recorded in Buchanan's History of Scotland; wherein he gives an account of the destruction of the army of Sweno when he invaded Scotland, by mixing a quantity of these berries in the drink which the Scots, by the truce, were to supply them with; this so intoxicated the Danes that the Scots fell upon them in their sleep and killed the greatest part of them; so that there were scarcely men enough left to carry off their king."

BENNE

Sesamum indicum, Linn.
Fam. Pedaliaceae

Synonyms: Sesame, Sesam, Gingelly.

Habitat: Indigenous to India but cultivated in other warm climates.

Description: Leaves alternate, ovate, or lanceolate, the lower ones three-lobed, often prominently veined beneath. Taste, mucilaginous. Seeds $\frac{2}{10}$ in. long, $\frac{1}{20}$ in. broad, flat, obovate, usually white or black but there are yellowish and reddish varieties. Taste, mucilaginous, oily.

Parts Used: Leaves, seeds.

Medicinal Use: Demulcent, laxative. The fresh leaves are very useful in catarrhal affections, diarrhoea, dysentery, affections of kidney and bladder. The Indian natives steep a leaf or two in water and drink the resulting mucilage freely. Externally they also apply this in ophthalmic and cutaneous complaints.

From the ripe dried seeds is extracted an oil known in commerce as Oil of Sesame. This is used in a similar manner to Olive Oil. It has a mild laxative action.

BENZOIN

Styrax benzoin, Dry.
Styrax paralleloneurum, Perkins
Fam. Styraceae

Synonyms: Gum Benzoin, Gum Benjamin, Sumatra Benzoin, Palembang Benzoin.

Habitat: Sumatra and Java.

Description: Sumatra Benzoin, from *Styrax benzoin* and *S. Paralleloneurum*, are the only official varieties. It is obtained by making triangular wounds in the tree, from which the sap exudes. The first flow forms the almonds of Benzoin followed by greyish-brown, resinous lumps; these are mixed in various proportions and pressed into a solid mass. Benzoin should not contain more than 20 per cent of substances insoluble in 90 per cent alcohol and not more than 2 per cent ash.

Other varieties: Siam benzoin, *Styrax tonkinense*, Craib. Generally occurs in separate tears coated with a reddish-brown resin and has an agreeable odour of vanilla. It is used principally in perfumery and fumigating pastilles. Palembang Benzoin is derived from *Styrax benzoin*, but is an inferior and cheaper quality. It consists principally of the greyish-brown resin.

Part Used: Gum.

Medicinal Use: Stimulating, expectorant. Used as part of Friar's Balsam in coughs, bronchitis, and externally applied to wounds, sores, etc. Contains Benzoic Acid, and thus enters into the preparation of Paregoric.

Parkinson gives a description of Benzoin but states: ". . . it is not used inwardly in Physicke, neither by the Indians, nor by us that mistake it not, but is wholely spent in perfumes either water or oyle, pouther, Pomanders, burning perfumes and the like, and is of an excellent sent where or howsoever it is used."

Preparations: Adeps Benzoin. B.P.C.; Pig. Iodof. Co. B.P.C.; Sev. Benzoin. B.P.C. 1949; Tinct. Benzoin. B.P.C.: Dose, 30–60 min; Tinct. Benzoin. U.S.P.; Tinct. Benzoin. Co. B.P.; Tinct. Benzoin. Co. U.S.P.; Ung. Zinc. Oxid. and Benzoin. B.P.C. 1949; Vap. Benzoin. B.P.C.; Vap. Menthol et Benzoin. B.P.C.

Domestic Use: It is sometimes used in incense.

BERBERIS

Berberis aristata, D.C.
Fam. Berberidaceae

Habitat: India.

Description: Greyish-brown strips of the dried stem, greenish-yellow internally—generally covered with moss or lichens. Conspicuous yellow medullary rays.

Part Used: Stem.

Medicinal Use: Used in India as a bitter tonic in intermittent fevers. Similar in action to Golden Seal.

Preparations: Powder: Dose, 10–60 gr; Tinct. Berber.: Dose, $\frac{1}{2}$–1 fl dr.

BETEL

Piper betle, Linn.
Fam. Piperaceae

Synonyms: *Chavica betle*, Miq.

Habitat: India and Malaya. Cultivated in Madagascar and West Indies.

Description: Leaves cordate below, called female, oval, tapering above, with 5–7 radiating ribs, $2\frac{1}{2}$–$3\frac{1}{2}$ in. long, and about 2 in. broad, dark green above, paler below, called male, with numerous transparent, minute, reddish points due to oil cells. When chewed the leaves produce a flow of saliva. Taste, feebly aromatic.

The lower, or female, leaves are generally used and exported.

Part Used: Leaves.

Medicinal Use: Astringent. Largely used by Indian natives, who chew the leaves with Areca Nuts mixed with Lime and Tobacco as a stimulant and as a preventive of worms.

BETH ROOT

Trillium pendulum, Willd.
and *Trillium erectum*, Linn.
Fam. Liliaceae

Synonyms: Birthroot, Lamb's Quarter.

Habitat: North America.

Description: Rhizome dull brown, subconical, more or less compressed, 1½–2 in. long, and ¾–1 in. in diameter, transversely ringed with numerous oblique lines, and with numerous slender, transversely-wrinkled rootlets on the lower surface. Transverse fracture, whitish, horny, and starchy. Taste, sweet, recalling that of podophyllum.

Part Used: Rhizome.

Medicinal Use: Astringent, pectoral, alterative, and tonic. Will be found of use in all cases of internal bleeding, profuse menstruation, and pulmonary complaints. In female disorders it is especially valuable both as a medicine and as an enemata. It acts as a general astringent to the uterine organs and should be used in fluor albus, menorrhagia, etc. The infusion, made by pouring 1 pt of boiling water on a tablespoonful of powder, should be drunk freely in most cases when it is required as an astringent, in doses of a wineglassful or more. In coughs, etc., 10–20 gr of powdered root may be taken in a little water three times a day. A good antiseptic poultice may be made of equal parts of powdered Beth Root and Slippery Elm with a small quantity of powdered Lobelia Seed.

The American Indians used to use this drug as an aid to parturition; hence the synonym Birthroot.

Preparations: Powdered root: Dose, 10–20 gr; Liquid extract: Dose, 1–2 dr; Trillium: Dose, 2–4 gr.

BILBERRY

Vaccinium myrtillus, Linn.
Fam. Vacciniaceae

Synonyms: Huckleberry, Whortleberry, Hurtleberry.

Habitat: It grows in the United Kingdom chiefly in boggy soil.

Flowering Time: May. The fruit ripens in July.

Description: Berries blue-black, globular, with the calyx ring at the apex. Contains numerous small oval seeds. Taste, sweet acidulous; odour, slightly valerianic.

Part Used: Ripe fruits.

Medicinal Use: Diuretic, refrigerant, astringent. The fruit may be eaten by itself or with milk and sugar as a cooling nutriment. The dried berries are used in medicine and have proved of much benefit in dropsy and gravel. A decoction of 1 oz in 1 pt of boiling water is used in tablespoonful to wineglassful doses in diarrhoea, dysentery, and derangements of the bowels. It has been found particularly useful during typhoid epidemics in the following form: 1 lb Bilberries, ¼ lb Cream of Tartar, 1 gal water; boil for twenty minutes, strain and make up to 1 gal with water. Drink a teacupful several times a day. Externally the decoction is used as a gargle, as a wash for sores, wounds, and ulcers, and as an injection in leucorrhoea.

Bilberries were at one time used against the scurvy in Norway and other Northern countries.

Preparation: Liquid extract: Dose, ½–2 dr.

BIRCH, EUROPEAN

Betula alba, Linn.
Fam. Betulaceae

Synonym: White Birch.

Habitat: It is found commonly in Europe and Great Britain, especially in woods.

Description: It is a fairly large tree with stalked leaves, rhomboidal, ovate, pointed, shiny, biserrate at the margin, about 1–1¼ in. long, and ¾–1 in. broad. Young bark having externally white, papery layers marked with linear brown lenticels; inner dark brown, glanular, with numerous hard, white points, the old bark rough, blackish-brown outside, with white lines showing in the brown, transverse section. Fracture short. The branches produce catkins containing male and female flowers. Taste, astringent and bitter.

Parts Used: Bark and leaves.

Medicinal Use: Bitter, astringent. The bark, by destructive distillation yields Birch Tar Oil (Oleum Rusci B.P.C. 1949) which is used in the preparation of Russian leather, and also in ointments for skin diseases. Mixed with other oils it is used as an insect repellent. Most of the old herbalists say that the juice of the leaves while they are young or water distilled from them, or water that comes from the tree after it has been bored with an auger, being taken for some days together breaks the stone in the kidneys and bladder and is good to wash sore mouths. Joseph Miller adds that the wood makes good fire-wood, and next to Juniper is preferred to burn in times of pestilence and contagious distempers.

Preparations: Ung. Resorcin. Co. B.P.C. 1949; Ung. Resorcin. et Bism. Co. B.P.C. 1949; Ung. Rusc. Co. B.P.C. 1949; Ol. Rusc. B.P.C. 1949.

Domestic Use: Before the invention of paper the young bark was used to write upon. The slender branches are also bound together to make garden brooms.

BIRTHWORT

Aristolochia longa, Linn.
Fam. Aristolochiaceae

Synonym: Long Birthwort.
Habitat: Europe and Great Britain.
Flowering Time: May.
Description: Root somewhat cylindrical, 1 in. or more in diameter, externally pale brown, smooth, striated, or warty. Transverse fracture whitish, with brown dots due to vascular bundles containing oleo-resin. Taste, sweetish, then acrid and disagreeable.

The plant is about 2 ft high producing alternate leaves of a yellowish-green colour and shaped somewhat like those of ivy. From the junction of the leaf stalk and stem arise the flowers, one to each leaf, each flower consisting of a long, hollow tube with a flap at the end, of a brownish-yellow colour.
Part Used: Root.
Medicinal Use: Aromatic, stimulant. Used in rheumatism and gout.

Joseph Miller writes that the root "Cleanses the stomach and lungs of tough phlegm . . . outwardly it is useful in cleansing sordid ulcers."
Preparation: Powdered root: Dose, $\frac{1}{2}$–1 dr.

DIOSCORIDES states of Birthwort that the powder being drunk in wine "brings away both birth and afterbirth and whatsoever a careless midwife hath left behind."

BISTORT

Polygonum bistorta, Linn.
Fam. Polygonaceae

Synonyms: Snakeweed, Adderwort, English Serpentary, Dragonwort, Osterick, Passions.
Habitat: It grows in shaded places in woods in the North of England. It is also a garden plant.
Flowering Time: End of May. The seeds ripen in July.
Description: The root, which is the part used, may be described as about 2 in. long and $\frac{3}{8}$ in. broad, twice bent as in the letter S, red-brown, depressed or channelled on the upper surface and transversely striated, convex, and with depressed root scars below, fracture short, light reddish-brown, bark thick, ring of woody wedges small, enclosing a pith equal in thickness to the bark. Taste, astringent; odour, none.
Part Used: Root.

Medicinal Use: Astringent. Used chiefly in haemorrhages and mucous discharges as a medicine, injection or a gargle.

Culpeper states: "The root with Pellitory of Spain and burnt Alum of each a little quantity, beaten small and into paste with some honey and a little piece thereof put into a hollow tooth or held between the teeth if there be no hollowness in them, stops the defluction of the rheum upon them which causes pains and helps to cleanse the head and void much offensive water."

Joseph Miller recommends the root for incontinence of urine.

Gerard states that the root boiled in wine "being holden in the mouth for a certain space and at sundry times, fasteneth loose teeth." Also: "The juice of Bistort put into the nose prevaileth much against the disease called Polypus."

BITTER APPLE

Citrullus colocynthis, Schrad.
Fam. Cucurbitaceae

Synonyms: Colocynth Pulp, Bitter Cucumber.

Habitat: Ceylon, Persia, Arabia, Syria, Egypt.

Description: Pulp yellowish-white, spongy, very bitter, sometimes containing dark-greenish, oval, flattened seeds, or immature, whitish ones.

Part Used: Pulp of the peeled fruit.

Medicinal Use: Cathartic, irritant, drastic purgative. Seldom used alone, mostly in conjunction with other laxatives and anodynes, such as Aloes, Henbane, etc. Useful in constipation, and in painful menstrual complaints, also in dropsy. As a rule it is taken in pill form.

Preparations: Powdered pulp: Dose, 2–15 gr; Liquid extract: Dose, 5–10 min; Ext. Colocynth. Co. B.P.C.: Dose, 2–8 gr; Pil. Colocynth. et Hyoscy. B.P.C.; Dose, 1 or 2 pills; Pil. Colocynth. Co. B.P.C.: Dose, 1 or 2 pills; Pil. Colocynth. et Hydrarg. B.P.C. 1949: Dose, 1 or 2 pills; Pil. Hydrarg. Subchlor., Colocynth. et Hyoscy. B.P.C. 1949: Dose, 1 pill; Pil. Hydrarg. Subchlor. et Colocynth. B.P.C. 1949: Dose, 1 pill; Tab. Colocynth. et Jalap Co. B.P.C.: Dose, 1–3 tablets.

BITTER ROOT

Apocynum androsaemifolium, Linn.
Fam. Apocynaceae

Synonyms: Dogsbane, Milkweed, Wild Cotton.

Habitat: Mountainous regions of Europe.

Flowering Time: June and July.

Description: Root $\frac{1}{8}$–$\frac{1}{4}$ in. thick, with pale-brown, transversely wrinkled, and cracked bark, half as thick as the white, woody centre, and readily separating from it, with groups of stone cells in the outer bark. Taste, bitter and astringent. The bark of *Apocynum cannabinum* is often sold for it, but has a yellowish wood, is longitudinally wrinkled, and has no groups of stone cells in the outer bark.

Part Used: Root.

Medicinal Use: Emetic, cathartic, tonic, and diuretic. Being a cardiac stimulant it is of great value in cardiac dropsy in doses of 5–15 gr; as a general tonic in dyspepsia in powders of 4 gr three times a day.

Parkinson quotes it as a "soveraine remedy against all poysons . . . and against the biting of a mad dogge." Hence it derives its name Dogsbane.

Preparations: Powdered root: Dose, 4–30 gr; Liquid extract: Dose, 10–30 drops.

Domestic Use: Parkinson writes: "The downe that is found in the cods of these herbes . . . doe make farre softer stuffing for cushions or pillowes or the like than thistle downe, which is much used in some places for the like purposes."

BITTERSWEET

Solanum dulcamara, Linn.
Fam. Solanaceae

Synonyms: Woody Nightshade, Violet Bloom, Scarlet Berry, Felonwood, Felonwort, Dulcamara.

Habitat: A climbing plant growing in hedges. Parkinson writes: "It grew neere unto Bermondsie house on Southwarke side when Gerard wrote thereof, but now is not there to be found."

Flowering Time: July, and the berries ripen in August.

Description: The year-old, greenish-brown shoots, which are the part used, are nearly cylindrical or indistinctly angular, about $\frac{1}{5}$ in. thick, slightly furrowed longitudinally, or sometimes warty and usually cut into short pieces internally hollow or partially filled with pith. The transverse section shows a green layer in the bark and a radiate ring of wood, or more than one ring in older stems. Taste, at first bitter (more so in the spring) and then sweet; odour, unpleasant when fresh, but lost in drying.

Root bark thin, tough externally, blackish or blackish-grey internally, pale-brown fibres of inner bark forming wide wedges. Taste, very astringent, slightly bitter; odour, none.

Parts Used: Twigs, root-bark.

Medicinal Use: Narcotic, resolvent, diuretic. Promotes all secretions and is used in rheumatism, obstinate cutaneous eruptions, scrofula, etc. A decoction is made of 10 dr in 2 pt of boiling water, boiled down to 1 pt, and taken in doses of ½–2 oz with an equal quantity of milk.

Preparation: Liquid extract: Dose, ½–2 dr.

PARKINSON writes: "The country shepheards of Germany, as Tragus reporteth, doth use to hang it [Bittersweet] about their cattells neckes, when they are troubled with the disease they call DIE HYNSCH, which is a swimming in the head, causing them to turn round. . . ."

BITTERSWEET, AMERICAN

Celastrus scandens, Linn.
Fam. Celastraceae

Synonyms: Waxwork, False Bittersweet.

Habitat: North America.

Description: This plant has been confounded with *Solanum dulcamara* or Bittersweet, but is essentially different in appearance and therapeutic action.

Parts Used: Root, bark.

Medicinal Use: Alterative, diuretic, and diaphoretic. Used in liver affections, leucorrhoea, rheumatism, and obstructed menstruation. It is not much used in medicine today.

Preparations: Decoction (1 oz to 1 pt): Dose, 2–4 fl oz three times a day; Solid extract: Dose, 5–10 gr.

BLACKBERRY, AMERICAN

Rubus villosus, Ait.
Fam. Rosaceae

Synonyms: Dewberry, Bramble.

Habitat: This particular variety is a native of the Northern U.S.A., but is also largely cultivated in the British Isles and other European countries.

Description: A low-growing plant in its natural form although frequently trained to fences when cultivated. The stems bear stout prickles and the leaves which are unequally divided are quite distinct from the ordinary Blackberry so well known in this country.

Parts Used: Root, leaves.

Medicinal Use: Astringent, tonic. A valuable remedy for diarrhoea, dysentery, etc. A preparation called Blackberry Cordial contains the properties named above combined with aromatics. The root is the most astringent. The infusion of 1 oz of root or leaves to 1 pt of water is taken in wineglassful doses.

The root bark of *R. trivialis*, Michx., and *R. canadensis*, Linn., are also used in the U.S.A., and the leaves of *R. fructicosus*, Sm., in Europe.

Preparation: Liquid extract: Dose, ½–1 dr.

BLACK CURRANT

Ribes nigrum, Linn.
Fam. Saxifragaceae

Habitat: A well-known British garden plant grown for its fruit.

Description: Leaves palmate, stalked, with scattered, yellow glands on the under surface, about 2 in. in diameter, with three to five pointed, serrate, angular lobes. Odour, characteristic.

Parts Used: Leaves, fruit.

Medicinal Use: Leaves, diuretic, refrigerant, detergent. Very useful in febrile and inflammatory diseases, in hoarseness and affections of the throat. The infusion of 1 oz in 1 pt of boiling water is taken in teacupful doses. The fresh fruit forms an excellent basis for medicated lozenges.

Preparation: Syr. Ribes Nig. B.P.C. (fruit): Dose, ½–1 dr.

Domestic Use: The fruit is used for making jams, jellies, etc. It is also used as a flavouring agent.

BLACK HAW

Viburnum prunifolium, Linn.
Fam. Caprifoliaceae

Synonyms: Stagbush, American Sloe.

Habitat: Eastern and Central U.S.A.

Description: Young bark in thin, quilled pieces, glossy purplish-brown with scattered warts. Old bark greyish-brown, inner surface white and smooth, the thin, corky layer easily separable from the green layer. Fracture, short. Taste, astringent and bitter; odour, slightly valerianic. The root bark is cinnamon-coloured and very bitter.

The bark of a species of *Acer* is sometimes substituted for this bark.

Part Used: Bark of root.

Medicinal Use: Uterine tonic, sedative, nervine, anti-spasmodic. Largely used for preventing miscarriage, in which cases it should be given four or five weeks previous to the expected event. It checks pain and bleeding, and is an excellent remedy for dysmenorrhoea and the after pains of child-birth. The infusion of 1 oz to 1 pt of boiling water is taken in tablespoonful doses.

Preparations: Powdered bark: Dose, 15–30 gr; Elix. Viburn. B.P.C. 1949: Dose, 30–120 min; Elix. Viburn. et Hydrast. B.P.C. 1949: Dose, 30–60 min; Ext. Viburn. B.P.C. 1949: Dose, 3–8 gr; Ext. Viburn. Lig. B.P.C. 1949: Dose, 60–120 min.

BLACK ROOT

Leptandra virginica, Nutt.
Fam. Scrophulariaceae

Synonyms: Culver's Root, Culver's Physic, Physic Root, *Veronica virginica, L.*
Habitat: North America.
Description: Rhizome about $\frac{1}{4}$ in. in diameter, showing stem bases at intervals of $\frac{1}{2}$–$1\frac{1}{2}$ in., blackish-brown, with transverse scars in rings $\frac{1}{8}$–$\frac{1}{4}$ in. apart, and chiefly on the lower surface. Rootlets wiry, brittle, having a short, horny fracture and a white, woody, central cord. Taste, bitterish.
Part Used: Rhizome.
Medicinal Use: Cathartic, diaphoretic, tonic, antiseptic. Used principally for its cathartic effect, as it acts with certainty and without griping. In fevers it is invaluable as a cathartic, purifying the blood and removing all morbid obstructions in a mild natural manner. It is said to act especially on the intestines, and is therefore valuable in chronic constipation and intestinal indigestions. May be advantageously combined with other medicines.
Preparations: Ext. Leptand. (Leptandrin): Dose, $\frac{1}{2}$–2 gr; Powdered Leptandra: Dose, $\frac{1}{4}$–1 dr; Liquid extract: Dose, $\frac{1}{2}$–1 fl dr; Tab. Leptand. Co.: Dose, 1–3 tablets.

BLADDERWRACK

Fucus vesiculosus, Linn.
Fam. Fucaceae

Synonyms: Bladder Fucus, Seawrack, Kelpware, Cutweed.
Habitat: A seaweed common to the British coasts.
Description: Frond flat, forked, blackish, about $\frac{1}{2}$ in. broad and 1 or 2 ft long, with a distinct midrib and oval bladders, usually in pairs. Taste, mucilaginous and saline; odour, like seaweed. *Fucus serratus* has no air vesicles, whilst *Fucus nodosus* has the air vessels single—not in pairs.
Part Used: The dry plant.
Medicinal Use: Deobstruent, antifat. Has been employed with success in obesity. The infusion of 1 oz to 1 pt of boiled water is taken in wine-glassful doses, or better in pill form. It influences the kidneys and acts as an alterative.

Preparations: Liquid extract: Dose, ¼–4 dr; Solid extract: Dose, 15–30 gr. The doses should be gradually increased.

Domestic Use: This and other seaweeds were used in the production of iodine, but this method of production is no longer economical.

There is also prepared a substance called Algin used as a dressing for calico.

BLOOD ROOT

Sanguinaria canadensis, Linn.
Fam. Papaveraceae

Synonyms: Tetterwort, Red Root.

Habitat: North America and Canada.

Description: The rhizome is usually about 2 or more in. long and nearly ½ in. in diameter, reddish brown, and longitudinally wrinkled. Fracture short, transverse section whitish, with numerous small, red resin cells, or sometimes wholly suffused with red. Taste, bitter and acrid; odour, heavy.

Part Used: Rhizome.

Medicinal Use: Stimulant, tonic, expectorant. Of great value in chest diseases, bleeding of the lungs, pneumonia, chronic bronchitis, etc. In whooping cough and croup it acts advantageously, and should be given until vomiting results. As an external remedy the powdered root or tincture acts energetically in cases of fungoid tumours, ringworm, etc. In polypus of the nose it should be used as snuff. Large doses will produce narcotic effects.

Preparations: Powdered root: Dose, 10–30 gr; Tincture: Dose, ½–2 dr; Liquid extract: Dose, 10–30 drops; Solid extract (alc.): Dose, 5–8 gr; Sanguinarin: Dose, ¼–1 gr.

Domestic Use: The North American Indians used Blood Root to stain their bodies. The colouring matter has also been used to stain fabrics.

BLUE FLAG

Iris versicolor, Linn.
Fam. Iridaceae

Synonyms: Water Flag, Poison Flag, Flag Lily, Liver Lily, Snake Lily.

Habitat: A common British garden plant.

Flowering Time: May and June.

Description: Rhizome with annular joints 2 or more in. long, about ¾ in. in diameter, cylindrical, becoming compressed towards the larger end where the cup-shaped stem scar is seen, with numerous rings formed of leaf scars above, and with scars of rootlets below. Fracture short, brownish, the vascular bundles scattered through the central column. Taste, acrid and nauseous; odour, none.

Part Used: Rhizome.

Medicinal Use: Alterative, diuretic, cathartic, stimulant. This is chiefly used for its alterative properties, and enters into many compounds for purifying the blood. It is also valuable in liver complaints, fluor albus, and dropsy. Joseph Miller writes: "The juice of the root is a strong Errhine; being snuff'd up the nostrils it purges the head and clears the brain of their serious phlegmatic Humors."

Preparations: Powdered root: Dose, 20 gr as a cathartic; Liquid extract: Dose, $\frac{1}{2}$–1 dr; Solid extract: Dose, 10–15 gr; Tincture: Dose, 1–3 dr; Irisin or Iridin: Dose, 1–3 gr.

BLUE MALLOW

Malva sylvestris, Linn.
Fam. Malvaceae

Synonyms: Common Mallow, Mauls.

Habitat: A wild British and European plant.

Flowering Time: May and June.

Description: Leaves stalked, roundish, five- to seven-lobed, hairy with stellate hairs, veins prominent below. Flowers mauve-coloured, with dark veins. Calyx with three separate outer bracts. Fruit many-celled, disciform, each cell one-seeded. Taste, mucilaginous; odour, none.

Parts Used: Herb, flowers.

Medicinal Use: Demulcent, mucilaginous, pectoral. The infusion is a popular cure for coughs, colds, etc. Joseph Miller states: "Where Marshmallows are not to be had, this may very well supply its place. A Cataplasm of the leaves applied to the Place, stung by Bees or Wasps, eases the Smart."

Preparation: Liquid extract: Dose, $\frac{1}{2}$–2 dr.

BOLDO

Peumus boldus, Mol.
Fam. Monimiaceae

Synonyms: Boldu, *Boldea fragrans*, C. Gay.

Habitat: Chile.

Description: Leaves oval, shortly stalked, rather thick, rigid and brittle, recurved at the margin, about 2 in. long and $1\frac{1}{4}$ in. wide, rough with points bearing stellate hairs. Taste, slightly lemony; odour, recalling lemon and coriander.

Part Used: Leaves.

Medicinal Use: Diuretic and liver stimulant, antiseptic. Used chiefly in chronic hepatic torpor and dyspepsia. Is also given in catarrh of the bladder, etc. The virtues of the drug seem to be due to an essential oil.

Preparation: Liquid extract: Dose, $\frac{1}{6}$–$\frac{1}{2}$ dr.

BONESET

Eupatorium perfoliatum, Linn.
Fam. Compositae

Synonyms: Thoroughwort, Indian Sage, Feverwort.

Habitat: It grows in most parts of the United States as well as in Europe and Great Britain.

Flowering Time: Late Summer.

Description: Leaves opposite, 4–6 in. long, lanceolate, tapering above to a narrow point, united at their base, crenate at margin, reticulated above, with minute, shining, yellow resin dots beneath. Taste, astringent and persistently bitter; flavour, slightly aromatic.

Part Used: Herb.

Medicinal Use: Diaphoretic, tonic, febrifuge, expectorant, laxative. Will be found a certain remedy in all cases of fever and influenza. In many cases no other medicine will be needed if given in moderate doses frequently. It is largely used by the negroes in the Southern States for this purpose as well as for its tonic effects. Also recommended in catarrh and skin diseases. An infusion of 1 oz to 1 pt of boiling water may be taken in wineglassful doses, hot or cold. For colds and to produce perspiration it should be given hot, and as a tonic, cold.

Preparations: Powdered herb: Dose, 10–20 gr; Liquid extract: Dose:, $\frac{1}{2}$–1 dr; Solid extract: Dose, 5–10 gr; Eupatorin: Dose, 1–3 gr.

BORAGE

Borago officinalis, Linn.
Fam. Boraginaceae

Synonym: Burrage.

Habitat: Great Britain and Europe. It grows in gardens and is found wild in many places, especially near houses.

Flowering Time: June.

Description: Leaves oval, pointed, 3 or more in. long and about 1$\frac{1}{2}$ in. broad, the lower stalked, rough, with stiff, one-celled hairs on the upper surface and on the veins below, the margin entire but wavy. Flowers blue, star-shaped, with central appendages, the anthers forming a cone in the centre. Fruit of four brownish-black nutlets, hollowed at base. Taste of leaves, cucumber-like and saline; odour, none.

Part Used: Leaves.

Medicinal Use: Diuretic, demulcent, emollient, refrigerant. Used in France for fevers and pulmonary complaints. For internal use an infusion is made of 1 oz of leaves to 1 pt of boiling water and taken in wineglassful doses. Externally employed as a poultice for inflammatory swellings.

Dioscorides states that Borage cheers the heart and helps drooping spirits.

Joseph Miller (1723) in *Botanicum Officinale* writes: "The tops are frequently put into wine and cool tankards," a use to which they are still put today.

John Parkinson (1640) speaks of a conserve made of the flowers chiefly used as a cordial to comfort the heart and spirits and therefore good for those that are troubled with "often swounings and passions of the heart." Also, "the ashes boiled in mede or honied water is available against inflammations and ulcers of the mouth and throat."

Preparation: Liquid extract: Dose, $\frac{1}{2}$–1 dr.

BOX

Buxus sempervirens, Linn.
Fam. Buxaceae

Habitat: A native of Europe and Western Asia, but cultivated in Great Britain and U.S.A.

Flowering Time: July and August.

Description: Box is a well-known shrub or tree. It does not usually grow to any size in Britain. The wood is extremely hard, covered with a greyish bark. The small leaves of firm texture are characteristic and keep green throughout the year. The flowers are small, yellowish in colour, and composed of five petals.

Part Used: Leaves.

Medicinal Use: They were at one time used for purifying the blood and for rheumatism but owing to their poisonous nature are seldom used. Joseph Miller does not mention the medicinal use of the leaves but states that chips of wood are sometimes used in a similar manner to Guaiacum and an oil distilled from the wood is used for toothache.

Domestic Use: The hard wood is used for making small household articles and boys' tops.

Biblical References: Isaiah XLI, 19; 2 Esdras XIV, 24.

BOXWOOD, AMERICAN

Cornus florida, Linn.
Fam. Cornaceae

Synonyms: American Dogwood, Flowering Cornel, Dog Tree.

Habitat: Eastern and Central U.S.A.

Flowering Time: April.

Description: Bark in slightly curved pieces averaging about 2 in. long and ½–1 in. wide, greyish and scaly, or, where the outer layer is removed, pale brown and irregularly cracked longitudinally; inner surface pinkish brown, rough, with minute linear prominences. Transverse fracture with somewhat distant medullary rays, and raised groups of stone cells. Taste, astringent, bitter; odour, none.

Parts Used: Bark, root-bark.

Medicinal Use: Tonic, astringent, stimulant. Used with advantage in all fevers, and forms an excellent substitute for Peruvian Bark, also given for headaches and exhaustion. A decoction of 1 oz of bark in 1 pt of water is taken in wineglassful doses.

Preparations: Powdered bark: Dose, ½–1 dr; Liquid extract: Dose, ½–1 dr; Cornin: Dose, 2 gr.

BROOKLIME

Veronica beccabunga, Linn.
Fam. Scrophulariaceae

Synonym: Water Pimpernel.

Habitat: It grows commonly in England and in Europe mostly near water and frequently in beds of watercress.

Flowering Time: June and July. The seed is produced the following month.

Description: Leaves oval, obtuse, stalked, crenate-serrate, opposite, not hairy. Flowers blue, with two stamens, on short, axillary, loose racemes. Fruit two-celled, notched at the apex, roundish. Taste, bitter, slightly acrid; odour, none.

Part Used: Herb.

Medicinal Use: Alterative, diuretic. Is given in scurvy, impurity of blood, etc. An infusion of the leaves of 1 oz to 1 pt of boiling water is taken in wineglassful doses frequently.

Culpeper writes: "Brooklime and water-cresses are often used together in diet-drinks with other things serving to purge the blood and body from all ill humours that would destroy health, and are helpful to the scurvy. They all do provoke the urine and break the stone and pass it away. . . . Being fried with butter and vinegar and applied warm, it helps all manner of tumours, swelling and inflammations."

John Parkinson states: "Farryers do much use it about their horses to take away swellings, to heal the scab, and otherlike diseases in them."

BROOM *Cytisus scoparius*, Linn.
Fam. Leguminosae

Synonyms: Broomtops, Irish Broom. *Spartium scoparium*, Linn., Besom, He-Broom (no flowers), She-Broom (with flowers).

Habitat: British Isles, and temperate Europe.

Flowering Time: April and May.

Description: Stem angular, five-sided, slightly winged, dark green, branching at an acute angle, $\frac{1}{16}$–$\frac{1}{8}$ in. in diameter. Pods flat, blackish, $1\frac{1}{2}$ in. long and $\frac{1}{4}$ in. wide. Flowers yellow, brown when dry, papilionaceous. Taste, bitterish, unpleasant; odour, none.

Part Used: Tops.

Medicinal Use: Diuretic, cathartic. Broom in combination with Agrimony and Dandelion Root is an excellent remedy for dropsy and liver troubles.

Preparations: Liquid extract: Dose, $\frac{1}{2}$–1 dr; Juice: Dose, 1–2 dr; Dec. Scopar. B.P.C. 1949: Dose, 2–4 fl oz; Dec. Scopar. Conc. B.P.C. 1949: Dose, $\frac{1}{4}$–$\frac{1}{2}$ fl oz; Inf. Scopar. Conc. B.P.C. 1949: Dose, 60–120 min; Inf. Scopar. Rec. B.P.C. 1949: Dose, 1–2 fl oz; Sparteinae Sulphate: Dose, 1–2 gr.

BROOM-CORN *Sorghum vulgare*, Pers.
Fam. Graminaceae

Synonyms: Sorghum Seeds, *Sorgum saccharatum*, Moench, Darri, Durra.

Habitat: North-west U.S.A.

Description: Seeds usually white, known in England as Darri, or Durra, about $\frac{1}{8}$ in. in diameter, rounded, slightly compressed, white and starchy within.

Part Used: Seeds.

Medicinal Use: Diuretic, demulcent. The American negroes make a decoction of 2 oz of seeds with 1 qt of water, boiled down to a pint, and take this as a remedy for urinary, bladder, and kidney complaints. This drug is entirely different from Broom (*Cytisus scoparius*) and should not be confounded with it.

Domestic Use: Broom-corn stalks were at one time used for the production of sugar.

BRYONY, BLACK *Tamus communis*, Linn.
Fam. Dioscoreaceae

Synonym: Blackeye Root.

Habitat: Lanes and hedgerows in Great Britain.

Flowering Time: May.

Description: Root nearly cylindrical, 1–$1\frac{1}{2}$ in. in diameter, 3–4 in. long, or more, with scattered, wiry rootlets, blackish-brown externally, whitish within. Usually sold fresh, and, when scraped, yielding a slimy paste. Taste, acrid; odour, slightly earthy. Leaves shiny and heart-shaped. Berries egg-shaped, deep-crimson colour. Flowers green with six petals.

Part Used: Root.

Medicinal Use: Rubefacient, diuretic. The fresh root is scraped and the pulp rubbed into parts affected by gout, rheumatism, or paralysis. It is also reputed as a diuretic.

Preparation: Tincture: 1–5 min.

Black Bryony is a popular remedy for removing discoloration caused by bruises, hence its name—Blackeye Root.

The tincture has a reputation for curing chilblains when applied externally. Joseph Miller states: "A cataplasm of the Root, with vinegar and Cow-dung, helps the gout" and he adds significantly: "It is but rarely used."

BRYONY, WHITE

Bryonia dioica, Jacq.
Bryonia alba., Linn.
Fam. Cucurbitaceae

Synonyms: English Mandrake, Bryonia, Mandragora, Wild Vine, Lady's Seal.

Habitat: Native of Europe, frequent in England but rare in Scotland.

Flowering Time: May to August.

Description: The root is very large, 1–2 ft long or more, branched, and 1–3 in. in diameter, white both externally and internally. The transverse section shows concentric rings and radiating lines of porous, vascular bundles. Taste, acrid and bitter; odour, none. The stems are from 5–6 ft long, slender and branched, channelled, and covered with small rough hairs. The plant climbs by means of curling tendrils. The leaves are large alternate, palmate, with five acute, irregular-toothed lobes. They are rough on both sides and supported by long stalks. The flowers are in small clusters springing from the axils of the leaves. The plant produces a green berry which changes to orange and red.

Part Used: Root.

Medicinal Use: Irritating, hydrogogue, cathartic. Useful in small doses for coughs, influenza, bronchitis, pneumonia. Valuable in cardiac disorders caused by rheumatism or gout, also in malarial and zymotic diseases. Large doses are dangerous.

Barton and Castle in *British Flora Medica* (1845) say the roots of Bryony were exhibited as Mandrakes by imposters who reaped a harvest from the credulity of the common people. These roots they shaped artificially to represent the human form which is commonly found naturally in the Mandragora.

Preparations: Liquid extract: Dose, $\frac{1}{6}$–1 dr; Bryonin: Dose, $\frac{1}{4}$–2 gr.

CULPEPER issues a note of warning when he says: "They are furious, martial plants. The root of Bryony purges the belly with great violence troubling the stomach and burning the liver; and therefore not rashly to be taken. . . ."

This root has in the past frequently been substituted for Mandrake or Mandragora concerning which many superstitions existed. Gerard writes: "There hath been many ridiculous tales brought up of the plant whether of old wives or some runnagate surgeons or physic-mongers, I know not (a title bad enough for them) but sure some one or more that fought to make themselves famous and skilfull above all others were the first broachers of that error I speak of.

"They add further that it is never or very seldom to be found growing naturally, but under a gallos where the matter that hath fallen from the dead body hath given it the shape of a man, and the matter of a woman the substance of a female plant; with many other such doltish dreams. They fable further and affirm that he who would take up a plant thereof must tie a dog thereunto to pull it up; otherwise if a man should do it he should surely die in short space after. Besides many fables of loving matters too full of scurility to set forth in print which I forebear to speak of."

BUCHU

Barosma betulina, Bart. & Wendl.
Fam. Rutaceae

Synonyms: Bucco, *Diosma betulina*.

Habitat: Cape of Good Hope.

Description: The principal variety grown is *Barosma betulina* or Round Buchu. These have a very characteristic rhomboid-obovate outline with a blunt, recurved apex, and are the finest for medicinal use. The next in order of popularity is *Barosma crenulata* or Oval Buchu. The margin of the leaf is crenulated and the apex, although blunt, is not recurved. The third variety, *Barosma serratifolia*, or Long Buchu, is readily recognized by the serrate margin of the leaf and truncate apex. This variety is falling into disuse as it only contains about half the amount of volatile oil compared with the Round or Oval Buchu.

The leaves have a characteristic odour derived from the volatile oil contained in them.

Part Used: Leaves.

Medicinal Use: Diuretic, diaphoretic, stimulant. It exerts a direct effect on the urinary organs, in all affections of which it will be found beneficial. In gravel, inflammation and catarrh of the bladder it is specially useful. The infusion (B.P.C.) of 1 oz of leaves to 1 pt of boiling water is taken in wineglassful doses three or four times a day.

Preparations: Inf. Buchu Con. B.P.C.: Dose, 60–120 min; Inf. Buchu Re. B.P.C. 1949: Dose, 1–2 fl oz; Tinct. Buchu B.P.C. 1949: Dose, 30–60 min; Solid extract Buchu (usually used in pills and tablets): Dose, 5–15 gr; Liquid extract: Dose, ½–1 dr; Barosmin: Dose, 2–3 gr.

BUCKBEAN

Menyanthes trifoliata, Linn.
Fam. Gentianaceae

Synonyms: Bogbean, Marsh Trefoil.

Habitat: It grows in marshy grounds in Great Britain and Europe.

Flowering Time: May and June.

Description: Leaves thin, brittle, with long stalks and three obovate leaflets which are about 2 in. long and 1 in. broad, and entire at the margin. Taste, very bitter; odour, none.

Part Used: Herb.

Medicinal Use: Tonic, deobstruent. A splendid bitter tonic, which will render great service in cases of rheumatism, scurvy, and skin diseases. The infusion of 1 oz to 1 pt of boiling water is taken in wineglassful doses frequently repeated.

Although Joseph Miller recommends the use of this herb for gout, rheumatism, etc., the earlier herbalists did not have a very precise knowledge of its uses.

Preparation: Liquid extract: Dose, 10–40 drops.

Other Uses: Linnaeus states that in Lapland the roots are sometimes fed to cattle, and the powdered roots mixed with flour have been used for human food. The leaves have been used here and elsewhere as a substitute for hops in brewing beer.

BUCKTHORN

Rhamnus cathartica, Linn.
Fam. Rhamnaceae

Synonym: *Baccae Spinae-cervinae.*

Habitat: North Africa, much of Europe.

Description: The berries are used for expressing the juice, with which Syrup of Buckthorn is made. When fresh they are globular, about ⅓ in.

in diameter, with the remains of a calyx beneath; they contain four deeply-grooved seeds, each enclosed in a parchment-like endocarp. The juice, at first greenish, becomes purplish-brown on keeping. Taste, bitter and acrid. Branches of the plant have terminal thorns. Leaves egg-shaped, sharply serrated, and prickly.

Part Used: Berries.

Medicinal Use: Largely used in veterinary practice as a laxative. The juice is expressed from the fresh ripe berries and this is used to make the syrup.

Preparation: Syr. Rham.: Dose, ½–1 dr.

BUCKTHORN, ALDER

Rhamnus frangula, Linn.
Fam. Rhamnaceae

Habitat: Europe, Great Britain, and U.S.A.

Description: Bark in thin, quilled pieces, greenish-black externally, with numerous elongated, whitish, transverse marks (lenticels). When abraded with the nail or a knife a crimson layer appears beneath the epidermis. Inner surface brownish-yellow. Fracture fibrous. Taste, sweetish, then bitter; odour, none. Branches of the plant are thornless. Leaves smooth and entire.

Part Used: Bark.

Medicinal Use: Tonic, laxative, cathartic. The dried seasoned bark, from one to two years old, only should be used, as the freshly-cut bark causes violent griping pains, emesis, and nausea. It is chiefly used as a remedy for chronic constipation, in small doses repeated three to four times daily. The decoction of 1 oz of bark in 1 qt of water boiled down to a pint is taken in tablespoonful doses.

Preparation: Liquid extract: Dose, ½–2 dr.

BUGLE

Ajuga reptans, Linn.
Fam. Labiatae

Synonyms: Common Bugle, Bugula, Middle Confound, Middle Comfrey, Sicklewort, Herb Carpenter.

Habitat: It grows wild generally throughout England, usually in woods.

Flowering Time: It flowers from May to July.

Description: The square stem rising to about 18 in. is smooth on two sides and hairy on the other two. Leaves are opposite, oblong-obovate, and obtuse, slightly toothed at the margin, with hairs on both sides. The flowers are bluish and sometimes ash-coloured. The stamens project from the tubular flower, the upper lip of which is very short. The root is composed of many fibres which spread.

Part Used: Herb.

Medicinal Use: Culpeper states that this plant belongs to Dame Venus and that a decoction of the leaves and flowers in wine ". . . dissolves the congealed blood in those that are bruised inwardly by a fall or otherwise is very effectual for any inward wounds, thrusts or stabs in the body or bowels. . . ."

ANOTHER interesting statement by Culpeper about Bugle is the following: "Many times such as give themselves to drinking are troubled by strange fancies, strange sights in the night time and some with voices . . . Those I have known cured by taking only two spoonfuls of the syrup of this herb after supper two hours, when you go to bed. . . ."

Both Parkinson and Salmon recommended an ointment made "of the leaves of Bugle two parts; of Seaf-heal, Sanicle, and Scabious of each one part, bruised and boiled in Hogs Lard or in a mixture of equal parts of Sheep's Suet and Olive Oil until the herbs are crisp and then strained forth and kept for use." Parkinson adds that he could wish that all the good women and ladies that desire to do good to their own families or their poor neighbours, not to be without this ointment always ready prepared and at hand by them.

In the present day Bugle has to some extent fallen out of use. It is recognized as a bitter, astringent, and aromatic.

Preparation: Infusion of 1 oz to 1 pt of water. Dose, a wineglassful frequently.

BUGLEWEED

Lycopus virginicus, Linn.
Fam. Labiatae

Synonyms: Sweet Bugle, Water Bugle, Gipsywort.

Habitat: Eastern U.S.A.

Description: Stem smooth, obtusely quadrangular. Leaves opposite, not hairy, short stalked, elliptic-lanceolate, and toothed above, but entire and wedge-shaped at the base, gland-dotted beneath. Flowers in axillary clusters, calyx with four ovate, obtuse teeth. Corolla four-lobed, purplish, with only two fertile stamens. Taste, bitter and slightly aromatic; odour, mint-like.

Part Used: Herb.

Medicinal Use: Sedative, astringent, and mild narcotic. Used in coughs. The infusion of 1 oz to 1 pt of boiling water is taken in glassful doses frequently.

Preparations: Liquid extract: Dose, 10–30 drops; Lycopin: Dose, 1–4 gr.

BUGLOSS

Echium vulgare, Linn.
Fam. Boraginaceae

Synonyms: Viper's Bugloss, Blueweed.

It is known as Viper's Bugloss because the seed is shaped like the head of a snake.

Habitat: Grows everywhere. Culpeper writes that the plant with white flowers grows about the castle walls at Lewes in Sussex.

Flowering Time: June and July. The seeds ripen quickly afterwards.

Description: Stems 1–2 ft high, with alternate leaves, both harsh, with rigid, bulbous hairs. Leaves linear, lanceolate, often undulated. Flowers in curved clusters, irregularly tubular, funnel-shaped, blue. Fruit of four small, seed-like pyrenes. Taste, mucilaginous; odour, none.

The common Bugloss, *Lycopsis arvensis*, Linn., has small, wheel-shaped, blue flowers and wavy, toothed leaves which also have rigid hairs with a bulbous base.

Part Used: Herb.

Medicinal Use: Diuretic, demulcent, expectorant. It relieves inflammatory pains, and is used in fevers and nervous complaints. The infusion of 1 oz in 1 pt of boiling water is given in wineglassful to teacupful doses as required.

Gerard writes: "The herbe chewed and the juice swallowed downe is a most singular remedy against poyson and the biting of any venemous beast; and the root so chewed and laid upon the sore workes the same effect."

Culpeper states: "The root and seed is thought to be most effectual to comfort the heart and expel sadness, or causeless melancholy."

Dioscorides says that, if the leaves be held in the hand, no venomous creatures will come near the holder to sting him for that day.

BURDOCK

Arctium lappa, Linn.
Fam. Compositae

Synonyms: Lappa, Lappa minor, Thorny Burr, Beggar's Buttons.

Habitat: A common plant growing in ditches and hedgerows throughout England and Europe.

Flowering Time: June and July.

Description: The root is usually seen in commerce cut up into pieces an inch or more long and about $\frac{3}{4}$ in. in thickness, brownish-grey externally, shrunken and furrowed longitudinally, and whitish internally. The fracture is short and the transverse surface shows a thick bark about a quarter of the diameter of the root, and a central cylinder with a radiate structure, sometimes with cavities containing white remains of tissue. Taste, sweetish and mucilaginous. Fruits, erroneously called seeds, brownish-grey, wrinkled, about $\frac{1}{4}$ in. long and $\frac{1}{6}$ in. in diameter. The leaves are large, rhubarb-like in shape, whitish beneath. Flowerheads globular, with hooked scale-like bracts.

Parts Used: Root, herb, seeds (fruits).

Medicinal Use: Alterative, diuretic, and diaphoretic. It is one of the finest blood purifiers in the herbal system, and should be used in all such cases alone or in conjunction with other remedies. Both root and seed may be taken as a decoction of 1 oz to $1\frac{1}{2}$ pt of water, boiled down to 1 pt, in doses of a wineglassful three or four times a day. The seeds are useful in kidney affections.

Culpeper writes that Venus challenges this herb for her own "and by its leaf or seed you may draw the womb which way you please, either upwards by applying it to the crown of the head . . . or downwards . . . by applying it to the soles of the feet; or if you would stay it in its place, apply it to the navel. . . ."

John Parkinson states: "The juice of the leaves given to drink with old wine doth wonderfully help the bitings of any serpents, as also of a mad dogge"; also: "The leaves being bruised with the white of an egge and laid on any place burnt with fire doth take out the fire, giveth sudden ease and healeth it up afterwards."

Preparations: Root: Liquid extract: Dose, $\frac{1}{2}$–2 dr; Solid extract: Dose, 5–15 gr.

Seed: Liquid extract: Dose, 10–30 drops.

BURNET, GREATER

Sanguisorba officinalis, Linn.
Fam. Rosaceae

Synonyms: Garden Burnet, Salad Burnet.

Habitat: A common garden plant and also growing wild, according to Culpeper "Especially in Huntingdon, in Northamptonshire, in the meadows there; as also near London, by Pancras church and by a causeway-side in the middle of a field by Paddington."

Flowering Time: June and July.

Description: Leaves pinnate, with about thirteen opposite leaflets, rounded at the ends and sharply serrate, the teeth with slender, thickened margins.

Flowerheads purplish, oblong. Taste, astringent; odour, none. Two or three fertile flowers at the top with protruding crimson hairs, with twenty or thirty barren flowers hanging down.

Part Used: Herb.

Medicinal Use: Astringent, tonic. Useful in haemorrhages.

CULPEPER writes of Greater Burnet: "This is an herb the Sun challenges dominion over and is a most precious herb, little inferior to Betony; the continual use of it preserves the body in health and the spirits in vigour; for if the Sun be the preserver of life under God, his herbs are the best in the world to do it by."

BURNET SAXIFRAGE

Pimpinella saxifraga, Linn.
Fam. Umbelliferae

Synonyms: Lesser Burnet, Saxifrage.

Habitat: Various places in England, particularly in Kent.

Flowering Time: June and July.

Description: Root spindle-shaped, brownish, about 8 in. long, often crowned with several hollow stem bases, ringed above, and longitudinally wrinkled and tuberculated below. Fracture short and whitish. Bark thick, with resinous dots in radiating lines, central woody cylinder porous and radiate. Leaves pinnate, with oval, serrate leaflets, nearly smooth or slightly hairy below. White flowers in globular heads with hard, quadrangular calyx tube with netted veins. Taste, cucumber-like; odour, none.

Parts Used: Root, herb.

Medicinal Use: Aromatic, carminative, stomachic. Other uses are very similar to the Greater Burnet.

BURRA GOKEROO

Pedalium murex, Linn.
Fam. Pedaliaceae

Synonym: Barra Gokhru.

Habitat: India.

Description: Fruits pale brown, calyx $\frac{1}{16}$ in. long and $\frac{1}{2}$ in. in diameter at the base, with four angular ridges having a short, straight spine at the base of each, two-celled with four narrow, elongated seeds. Taste, mucilaginous; odour, none.

Part Used: Seeds.

Medicinal Use: Antispasmodic, demulcent, diuretic. Has been used in incontinence of urine, gleet, nocturnal emissions, impotence, and irritation of urinary organs. An infusion (1 in 20) should be taken each day in several doses.

BURR MARIGOLD

Bidens tripartita, Linn.
Fam. Compositae

Synonym: Water Agrimony.
Habitat: Great Britain and Europe.
Description: The flower heads are small and tawny brown seeds numerous with reflexed prickles.
Part Used: Whole plant.
Medicinal Use: Astringent, diaphoretic, diuretic. This plant is particularly useful in dropsy, gout, and haematuria. It has been used with great success in various diseases of the respiratory organs where bleeding has occurred and also in uterine haemorrhage. Dose, Infusion: 1 oz to 1 pt, half-teacupful three or four times a day. The addition of a little Ginger will be helpful.

BUSH TEA

Cyclopia genistoides, Linn.
Fam. Leguminosae

Synonyms: Rooibosch, Boschori-Busch.
Habitat: South Africa.
Description: Reddish-brown stalks from ½–1 in. long, with the aroma and taste of tea. Does not contain caffeine.
Medicinal Use: Sometimes used in South Africa as a substitute for tea where caffeine is not advisable. A mixture of herbs containing Bush Tea is sometimes used for liver and kidney complaints.

BUTCHER'S BROOM

Ruscus aculeatus, Linn.
Fam. Liliaceae

Synonyms: Common Butcher's Broom, Kneeholm, Kneeholy, Pettigree, Sweet Broom.
Habitat: A common British plant. Joseph Miller says: "The plant grows in hedges and Thickets, as in Epping Forest."
Flowering Time: Summer.

Description: Stem erect, much branched. Leaves reduced to minute scales having in their axils egg-shaped cladodes, bearing a small, greenish-white flower in the centre, which forms a round, scarlet berry in September. This is the only British shrub among endogenous plants.

Part Used: Herb (although Joseph Miller states that the only part used is the root).

Medicinal Use: Diaphoretic, diuretic, deobstruent, aperient. Will be found of use in jaundice, gravel, and female obstructions. The decoction is the usual form of administration.

BUTTERBUR

Petasites vulgaris, Desf.
Fam. Compositae

Synonyms: Common Butterbur, *Tussilago petasites.*

Habitat: In low wet grounds and near riversides in Great Britain.

Flowering Time: March before the leaves appear in April.

Description: The rhizome occurs in pieces 2–4 in. long, and about ¼ in. in diameter, of a reddish-brown or purplish-brown colour, furrowed longitudinally, ringed with transverse scars at intervals of about ½ in. The transverse section shows a thin, dark, horny bark, containing dark oil cells and a narrow ring of woody tissue surrounding a large, hard pith. Fracture short. The leaves are sometimes 3 ft broad. Taste, bitterish; odour, none.

Part Used: Root.

Medicinal Use: Cardiac tonic, stimulant, diuretic. Has been in use as a remedy in fevers, asthma, colds, and urinary complaints, gravel, and plague. The decoction is taken warm in wineglassful doses frequently repeated.

Parkinson states: "The decoction of the roote in wine being taken is singular good for those that wheese much and are short winded."

BUTTERNUT

Juglans cinerea, Linn.
Fam. Juglandaceae

Synonyms: White Walnut, Oilnut.

Habitat: U.S.A.

Description: The inner bark, which is the part used, occurs in flat or curved pieces, ⅛–¼ in. thick, but varying in length; it usually has the ends cut off obliquely. Fracture short, having a chequered appearance due to the brown fibres alternating with the white medullary rays and white cellular tissue. Taste, bitter and slightly acrid; odour, feeble.

Part Used: Inner bark.

Medicinal Use: Cathartic, tonic, vermifuge. A gentle purgative, which does not bind after operating. Is also a remedy for worms, especially in children. The solid extract is generally used either in pills or syrup. Four or five pills should be taken at night or a tablespoonful of syrup twice a day. The syrup is made by using ½ oz of extract to 8 oz of simple syrup, beating them well together in a mortar.

Preparations: Liquid extract: Dose, 1–2 dr; Solid extract: Dose, 5–10 gr; Juglandin: Dose, 2–5 gr.

BUTTON SNAKEROOT

Liatris spicata, Willd.
Fam. Compositae

Synonyms: Gay-feather, Blazing Star, Backache Root.

Habitat: U.S.A.

Flowering Time: August.

Description: Rhizome ½ in. or more in diameter, somewhat tuberculate, with several cup-shaped scars. Externally, brownish and slightly wrinkled; internally, whitish, speckled with dark grey dots, very tough. Taste, bitterish, faintly aromatic, somewhat resembling cedar.

The synonym Blazing Star is given because of the beautiful purple flowers produced by this plant.

Part Used: Rhizome.

Medicinal Use: Diuretic, stimulant. It acts kindly on the stomach, and is of value in kidney diseases. Said to be beneficial in Bright's disease, and is used in conjunction with Unicorn Root in menstrual diseases. The infusion of 1 oz to 1 pt is taken in wineglassful doses three to four times daily.

C

CABBAGE TREE

Andira inermis, H., B., & K.
Fam. Leguminosae

Synonyms: *Geoffraeya inermis*, Sw., Jamaica Cabbage Tree, Yellow Cabbage Tree, Worm Bark.

Habitat: West Indies.

Description: In long, flat pieces $\frac{1}{8}$ in. thick, greyish-white and fissured externally, inner surface brownish and striated. Fracture laminated with yellow fibres. Taste, mucilaginous, bitter; odour, slight but disagreeable.

Part Used: Bark.

Medicinal Use: Febrifuge, cathartic, vermifuge. Has proved an effectual anthelmintic. The infusion of 1 oz in 1 pt of water may be taken in tablespoonful doses three to four times a day. Any unpleasant action may be obviated by Castor Oil, Lemon Juice, or Warm Water.

Preparation: Liquid extract: Dose, $\frac{1}{4}$–1 dr.

CACAO

Theobroma cacao, Linn.
Fam. Sterculiaceae

Synonyms: Cocoa, Chocolate Tree.

Habitat: Cultivated in most tropical countries.

Description: Seeds oval, oblong compressed, $\frac{3}{4}$ in. or more long, husk thin and papery. Seed breaking up into angular fragments under pressure, due to the presence of the inner seed coat between the folds of the cotyledons. Taste and odour well known.

Part Used: Seeds.

Medicinal Use: Nutritive, stimulant, diuretic. In the household, cocoa as well as chocolate is a well-known nutritive beverage. These preparations are however seldom used as medicine, although chocolate is an agreeable and convenient base for lozenges of nauseous or bitter drugs, such as Calomel, Santonin, etc. The cocoa-butter, expressed from the seeds, forms a hard, bland article, much used in suppositories, lip salves, pomades, etc. Another constituent of the seeds is Theobromine, which resembles Caffeine in its stimulant and diuretic action.

Preparation: Ol. Theobrom. B.P.

CAJUPUT

Melaleuca leucadendron, Linn.
Fam. Myrtaceae

Synonyms: Cajeput, White Tea Tree, Swamp Tea Tree, Broad-leaved Tea Tree, White-wood, *Melaleuca Cajuputi*, Roxb.

Habitat: East Indies.

Description: The tree from which the oil is obtained is large with a crooked trunk. The oil is distilled abroad from the fresh leaves and twigs. As imported into this country, it is of a greenish colour, due to contamination with copper when originally distilled. In order to comply with the description in the B.P.C. the oil has to be re-distilled in this country, when it appears colourless or pale yellow. The odour recalls that of Camphor and Eucalyptus.

Part Used: Oil.

Medicinal Use: Stimulant, antispasmodic, diaphoretic. The natives of the Molucca Islands, where the tree grows, esteem it very highly as a remedy for all kinds of pains, internal and external. It may be employed with advantage in lotions for rheumatic affections, toothache, neuralgia, sprains, and bruises. Internally, it may be taken on sugar in doses of 1–10 drops as a valuable diffusive stimulant in colics, spasms, flatulence, and hiccough.

Preparations: Ol. Cajuput. B.P.C.: Dose, 1–3 min; Sp. Cajuput. B.P.C. 1949: Dose, 5–30 min; Ung. Methyl. Salicyl. Co. B.P.C.

CALABAR BEAN

Physostigma venenosum, Balf.
Fam. Leguminosae

Synonyms: Ordeal Bean, Chopnut.

Habitat: Gulf of Guinea and West Coast of Africa.

Description: The plant is similar in some ways to the Scarlet Runner Bean but grows to a height of some 50 ft. The seeds are dark-brownish or blackish-brown, $1–1\frac{1}{4}$ in. long, $\frac{5}{8}$ in. broad, $1\frac{1}{2}$ in. thick, oblong with rounded ends, or slightly kidney-shaped, the hilum extending along the whole convex side. Cotyledons white, turning yellow when touched with strong potash solution. They are poisonous. The tribes of tropical West Africa at one time used them on persons accused of witchcraft, compelling them to undergo the ordeal of swallowing them.

Part Used: Ripe seeds.

Medicinal Use: Sedative, myotic. It allays extreme nervous irritation, but should be given with great care, and only under medical advice, as large doses have a poisonous effect. Mostly used in combination with Prickly Ash or Belladonna. Its chief use is in eye diseases as a local myotic. Produces contraction of the pupil.

Preparations: Liquid extract: Dose, 1–3 min; Physostigmine Salicylate B.P.: Dose, $\frac{1}{100}-\frac{1}{50}$ gr.

CALAMINT

Calaminta officinalis, Moench
Fam. Labiatae

Synonyms: Common Calamint, Basil Thyme, *Calamintha menthifolia*, Host., Mountain Mint.

Habitat: A common plant found in Great Britain and Europe.

Flowering Time: July and August.

Description: Leaves broadly ovate, slightly serrate, stalked. Flowers pale purple. Calyx with upper teeth triangular, erect, fringed with hairs, lower teeth longer, awl-shaped. Taste, aromatic; odour, mint-like.

Part Used: Herb.

Medicinal Use: Diaphoretic, expectorant. Usually used in the form of a decoction or syrup.

Etmuller states: "In asthma and shortness of breath it is no common remedy, especially if boiled in oxymel . . ." It has also been used to apply to parts of the body that are bruised or suffer from rheumatic pains.

CALAMUS

Acorus calamus, Linn.
Fam. Araceae

Synonyms: Sweet Flag, *Calamus aromaticus*, Sweet Sedge.

Habitat: It grows freely on the banks of rivers in the British Isles and in Europe.

Flowering Time: July and August.

Description: Rhizome about $\frac{3}{4}$ in. in diameter, pale fawn-coloured, longitudinally wrinkled, with numerous oblique transverse leaf scars above, crowded in the part near the stem with small, circular root scars underneath. Fracture whitish, short, and finely porous, with scattered woody bundles visible when the section is wetted. Taste, aromatic, pungent, and bitter; odour, sweet and aromatic. The peeled rhizome is usually angular and often split, and is less aromatic.

Part Used: Rhizome.

Medicinal Use: Aromatic, carminative, and stomachic. Useful in flatulence, wind, colic, ague, and dyspepsia, etc. Is often added to tonic medicines. The root may be chewed in dyspepsia, or an infusion of 1 oz to 1 pt of boiling water may be taken freely in doses of a teacupful. An old remedy for ague. The use of this rhizome in medicine was known to the ancient Greek and Arabian doctors.

Thomson recommends it for infants' colic combined with magnesia and chalk.

The fresh candied root was used by the Indians and Turks for dyspepsia.

Preparations: Liquid extract: Dose, 15–60 drops; Powdered root: Dose, $\frac{1}{4}$–1 dr.

Biblical References: Exodus XXX, 23; Solomon IV, 14; Isaiah XLIII, 24; Ezekiel XXVII, 19. Isaiah refers to Calamus as Sweet Cane.

CALOTROPIS

Calotropis procera, Brown
Calotropis gigantea, Ait.
Fam. Asclepiadaceae

Synonyms: Mudar Bark, *Asclepias procera*, Willd.

Habitat: India.

Description: The bark occurs in irregular short pieces, slightly quilled or curved, and from ⅛–⅕ in. thick, and ¾ in. or more in width. Externally greyish yellow, soft and spongy; internally, yellowish-white and smooth, or finely striated. Fracture short, yellowish-white. Taste, acrid and bitter,

Part Used: Bark.

Medicinal Use: Used as a local remedy in India for elephantiasis, leprosy, and chronic eczema. Internally for diarrhoea and dysentery.

Preparations: Powdered bark: Dose, 3–10 gr as expectorant, ½–1 dr as emetic; Tincture (1 in 10): Dose, ½–1 dr.

Domestic Use: The stems of *Calotropis gigantea* provide a fibre which is spun into fine thread for sewing and weaving.

CALUMBA

Jateorhiza palmata, Miers
Fam. Menispermaceae

Synonyms: *Cocculus palmatus*, D.C., Colombo.

Habitat: East Africa and the localities of the Zambezi. Introduced into Europe in the seventeenth century.

Description: Root in circular sections about 1½–2½ in. in diameter and ¼ in. or more in thickness, the centre usually depressed. Bark thick, outer surface greyish-brown, transverse section yellowish, rather darker in the bark, vascular bundles in radiating lines. Fracture short and mealy. Taste, mucilaginous, very bitter; odour, slight.

Part Used: Root.

Medicinal Use: Tonic, febrifuge. A bitter tonic, without astringency. Valuable in all cases of dyspepsia, weakness of stomach, etc. An infusion of 1 oz in 1 pt of cold water may be taken in two tablespoonful doses three to four times a day.

Preparations: Powdered root: Dose, 10–30 gr; Liquid extract: Dose, 10–30 min; Inf. Calumb. B.P.C. 1949: Dose, ½–1 fl oz; Inf. Calumb. Conc. B.P.C. 1949: Dose, 30–60 min; Inf. Calumb. Rec. B.P.C. 1949: Dose, ½–1 fl oz; Tinct. Calumb. B.P.C. 1949: Dose, 30–60 min; Solid or Powdered extract: Dose, 2 gr.

CAMPHOR

Cinnamomum camphora, T. Nees & Eberm.
Fam. Lauraceae

Synonyms: Gum Camphor, Laurel Camphor, *Laurus camphora*, Linn., *Camphora officinarum*, Nees, Camphire.

Habitat: Central China and Japan.

Description: A colourless, crystalline, translucent mass with a characteristic odour. There are several varieties of camphor. It is imported in small, square pieces usually weighing about ¼ oz and also as Camphor Flowers. It is readily soluble in spirit of wine, to a less extent in warm, fixed oils and in water sufficiently to flavour it strongly. It floats in water.

Camphor is obtained from large trees indigenous to Formosa by passing steam through the chipped wood. The distillate contains Camphor, which is separated and resublimed, leaving an essential oil of Camphor. From this oil, Safrol is obtained by fractional distillation.

Medicinal Use: Sedative, anodyne, antispasmodic, diaphoretic, anthelmintic. Internally, Camphor is used in colds, chills, and in diarrhoea from colds. In all inflammatory affections, fevers, and hysterical complaints, it will be found of great value. It acts beneficially in gout, rheumatic pains, and neuralgia, and is highly valued in all irritations of the sexual organs. Large doses should be carefully avoided, as they cause vomiting, palpitation, and convulsions. Externally, it can be safely applied in all cases of inflammations, bruises, sprains, etc.

Joseph Miller writes: "Some people hang it in a silk bag, about the neck, to cure agues."

Preparations: Dose of Camphor, 2–5 gr; Aq. Camph. B.P.: Dose, ½–1 fl oz; Aq. Camph. U.S.P.; Aq. Camph. Conc. B.P.C. 1949: Dose, 5–15 min; Chloral Camph. B.P.C. 1949; Cret. Camph. B.P.C. 1949; Linct. Opii Camph. Co. B.P.C. 1949: Dose, 30–120 min; Lin. Camph. B.P.; Lin. Camph. U.S.P.; Lin Camph. et Sapon. U.S.P.; Lin. Camph. Ammon. B.P.; Lin. Chlorof. B.P.C. 1949; Lin. Chlorof. U.S.P.; Neb. Eucalyp. Co. B.P.C.; Neb. Menthol et Thymol Co. B.P.C.; Phenol c. Camph. B.P.C. 1949; Pig. Chloral. Co. B.P.C. 1949; Sp. Camph B.P.C.: Dose, 5–30 min; Syr. Opii Camph. B.P.C. 1949: Dose, 30–60 min; Tinct. Opii Camph. Conc. B.P.C.: Dose, 4–8 min; Tinct. Opii Camph. B.P.: Dose, 30–60 min; Tinct. Opii Camph. U.S.P.: Dose, 1 fl dr; Ung. Camph. Dur. B.P.C. 1949; Ung. Capsic, Co. B.P.C. 1949.

Biblical References: Song of Solomon I, 14, IV, 13.

CANADIAN HEMP

Apocynum cannabinum, Linn.
(and other species)
Fam. Lauraceae

Synonyms: Black Indian Hemp, *Apocynum pubescens*, Brown.

Habitat: U.S.A. and Canada.

Description: Root $\frac{1}{4}$ in. or more in diameter, rarely branched, longitudinally wrinkled, sometimes fissured transversely, pale brown externally. Bark thick, whitish, with central, porous, radiate wood, and often a small, central pith. Fracture short. Taste of the bark, permanently bitter, disagreeable; odour, none.

Parts Used: Root and rhizome.

Medicinal Use: Diaphoretic, diuretic, expectorant, emetic. Valuable in cardiac dropsy, and recommended favourably in intermittent and remittent fevers. Is also used in amenorrhoea and leucorrhoea. A decoction of 1 oz in 1 pt of water is taken in tablespoonful doses or more. As an emetic give 10–30 gr of Powdered Root.

Preparations: Powdered root: Dose, 1–5 gr; Liquid extract: Dose, 1–5 min; Tinct. Apocyn.: Dose, 5–10 min; Apocynin: Dose, $\frac{1}{2}$–1 gr.

CANCHALAGUA

Erythraea chilensis, Pers.
Fam. Gentianaceae

Habitat: Pacific Coast of America.

Description: Closely resembles Centaury, but is more branched and has linear leaves and distinctly stalked flowers.

Part Used: Herb.

Medicinal Use: Bitter, tonic, stimulant. An excellent general tonic and stimulant. May be used in dyspepsia and all complaints of digestion. The infusion of 1 oz to 1 pt of boiling water is taken in wineglassful doses.

Preparation: Liquid extract: Dose, $\frac{1}{2}$–1 dr.

CANELLA

Canella alba, Murr.
Fam. Canellaceae

Synonyms: White Cinnamon, West Indian Wild Cinnamon.

Habitat: The Bahamas.

Description: Bark fawn-coloured externally, chalky white on inner surface, in quilled pieces $\frac{1}{4}$–$1\frac{1}{2}$ in. in diameter. Transverse fracture short, whitish, with numerous bright, orange-yellow dots composed of resin cells. Taste, biting, aromatic, slightly recalling that of cinnamon; odour, aromatic.

The thick, ash-grey cork is removed by gentle beating, when the bark is loosened.

Part Used: Bark.

Medicinal Use: Aromatic, stimulant, tonic. Useful in enfeebled conditions of the stomach and intestines. Generally given in combination with other stomachics. Dose, 10–40 gr.

Preparation: Pulv. Aloes et Canella (Hiera Picra): Dose, 3–10 gr.

Domestic Use: It is used by the natives as a condiment.

CARAWAY

Carum carvi, Linn.
Fam. Umbelliferae

Synonyms: Caraway Seed, Caraway Fruit, Alcaravea.

Habitat: Common in Europe and Asia. Cultivated in N. Africa, and occasionally in Great Britain.

Description: The fruit, wrongly called seed, is too well known to need description. The quality varies. English caraways are brighter brown and cleaner, and are the best. Dutch are darker coloured, Mogador are light brown, but longer. The fruit should be free from stalks and dirt.

Part Used: Fruit.

Medicinal Use: Carminative, stimulant. Used in children's ailments, flatulence, and stomachic derangements.

Preparations: Powdered seeds: Dose, 10–30 gr; Liquid extract: Dose, 5–30 min; Ol. Cari B.P.C.: Dose, 1–3 min; Aq. Cari Conc. B.P.C.: Dose, 5–15 min; Aq. Cari Dest.: Dose, $\frac{1}{2}$–1 fl oz; Conf. Piper.: Dose, 1–2 dr; Tinct. Cardam. Arom. B.P.C.: Dose, 2–10 min.

Domestic Use: Caraway is used as a flavouring and also in seedcakes.

CARDAMOM

Elettaria cardamomum, Maton
var. *minuscula*, Burkill
Fam. Zingiberaceae

Synonyms: Mysore Cardamom Seed, Malabar Cardamom.

Habitat: Malabar Coast, Ceylon.

Description: Fruits ovoid or oblong, more or less triangular, longitudinally furrowed, varying in length from $\frac{2}{5}$–$\frac{4}{5}$ in., or, in bleached samples, the angles are rounded and the surface smooth. The fruits should yield 75 per cent of seeds. Seeds from ripe capsules are sold as split seeds, being broken in the process of extraction. The unbroken fruits are gathered before quite ripe, so as not to split open in drying.

Parts Used: Fruits, seeds.

Medicinal Use: Carminative, stomachic. A warm, grateful aromatic, chiefly employed in flatulence or as a flavour. The fruits should be crushed for use, and the infusion of 2 oz to 1 pt of boiling water taken in wine-glassful doses.

Preparations: Powdered fruits: Dose, 10–30 gr; Liquid extract: Dose, 5–30 min; Ol. Cardamom B.P.C. 1949: Dose, $\frac{1}{2}$–3 min; Pulv. Cinnam. Co. B.P.C. 1949: Dose, 10–60 gr; Tinct. Cardam. Arom. B.P.C.: Dose, 2–10 min; Tinct. Cardam. Co. B.P.: Dose, 30–60 min; Tinct. Cardam. Co. U.S.P.: Dose, 1 fl dr.

CAROBA

Jacaranda procera, Spreng.
Fam. Bignoniaceae

Synonyms: Carob Tree, Caaroba, *Jacaranda caroba*, D.C., *Bignonia caroba*, Vell.

Habitat: South America and South Africa.

Description: Leaflets leathery, lanceolate, tapering below, obtuse at the apex, about $2\frac{1}{2}$ in. long and 1 in. broad, minutely pitted on both surfaces, midrib prominent below, depressed above, veins spreading. Taste, bitterish; flavour, tea-like; odour, none.

Part Used: Leaves.

Medicinal Use: Alterative, diaphoretic, diuretic. It appears to have a sedative effect upon the nervous system but is rarely used. Dose, 15–60 gr.

CASCARA AMARGA

Picramnia antidesma, S.W.
(and other species)
Fam. Simarubaceae

Synonym: West Indian Snakewood.

Habitat: Mexico, Central America, and Panama.

Description: Bark in small fragments less than 1 in. long and about $\frac{1}{4}$ in. wide and $\frac{1}{8}$ in. thick, externally greyish, internally deep brown, inner surface nearly smooth. Transverse fracture short, showing numerous white dots, due to groups of stone cells. Taste, at first astringent, then bitter; flavour, earthy.

Part Used: Bark.

Medicinal Use: Bitter tonic. Said to have distinctly alterative properties.

Preparation: Liquid extract: Dose, 20–40 min.

CASCARA SAGRADA *Rhamnus purshiana*, D.C.
Fam. Rhamnaceae

Synonyms: Sacred Bark, Chittem Bark.

Habitat: California and British Columbia.

Description: Bark in quilled or curved pieces about ¾ in. wide and $\frac{1}{16}$ in. thick, purplish-brown, furrowed longitudinally with transversely linear marks (lenticels), sometimes silvery grey with lichens. The inner surface is transversely wrinkled and longitudinally striated, reddish-brown. Transverse fracture pale or dark brown, according to age. Taste, persistently bitter or nauseous; odour, leather-like. Specimens with dark-brown fracture, indicating its having been kept, are to be preferred, as recent bark sometimes causes griping. Collected in the spring and early summer.

Part Used: Bark. It should be kept for at least a year after being shipped before use.

Medicinal Use: Laxative, tonic. Largely used for habitual constipation, dyspepsia, and digestive complaints, also in the treatment of piles. For chronic constipation a first dose of ½ or 1 teaspoonful at bedtime should be taken, followed by doses of 5–10 drops before each meal.

Preparations: Powdered bark: Dose, 20–40 gr; Elix. Casc. Sagr. B.P.: Dose, 30–60 min; Emuls. Paraff. Liq. c. Casc. Sagr. B.P.C. 1949: Dose, ¼–1 fl oz; Ext. Casc. Sagr. Liq. B.P.: Dose, 30–60 min; Fldext. Casc. Sagr. U.S.P.: Dose, 15 min; Ext. Casc. Sagr. Sicc. B.P.: Dose, 2–8 gr; Ext. Casc. Sagr. U.S.P.: Dose, 5 gr; Mist. Casc. B.P.C. 1949: Dose, ½–1 fl oz; Mist. Casc. et Bellad. B.P.C.: Dose, ½ fl oz; Mist. Casc. et Bellad. pro Infant. B.P.C.: Dose, 60–120 min; Pil. Casc. Bellad. et Nuc. Vom. B.P.C. 1949: Dose, 1–3 pills; Syr. Casc. Aromat. B.P.C. 1949: Dose, 30–120 min; Syr. Fic. Co. B.P.C.: Dose, 30–120 min; Tab. Casc. Sagr. B.P.C. 1949: Dose, 2–8 gr; Tab. Casc. Sagr. U.S.P.: Dose, 5 gr; Tab. Casc. Sagr. Co. B.P.C.: Dose, 1 or 2 tablets.

CASCARILLA *Croton eleuteria*, Benn.
Fam. Euphorbiaceae

Synonym: Sweet Wood Bark.

Habitat: Bahamas. Imported into Europe in the seventeenth century.

Description: The bark occurs in short, quilled pieces, up to ½ in. in diameter, usually with chalky, more or less cracked, white surface, with black dots due to the fruit of lichens. Transverse fracture reddish-brown. Taste, aromatic, bitter. Fragrant when burnt, whence its use in fumigating pastilles and tobacco.

Medicinal Use: Stimulant, aromatic, tonic. Used in dyspepsia, flatulence, and diarrhoea; in convalescence from acute diseases and to prevent vomiting. Often combined with Cinchona, when this causes nausea. The infusion of 1 oz to 1 pt of boiling water is taken in doses of a tablespoonful to a wineglassful as required.

Preparations: Powdered bark: Dose, 20–40 gr; Liquid extract: Dose, ½–1 dr; Inf. Cascaril. Conc.: Dose, ½–1 dr; Inf. Cascaril. Rec.: Dose, ½–1 fl oz; Tinct. Cascaril. B.P.C. 1949: Dose, 30–60 min.

CASHEW NUT

Anacardium occidentale, Linn.
Fam. Anacardiaceae

Synonyms: *Cassuvium pomiferum*, East Indian Almonds.

Habitat: West Indies, Tropical America.

Description: Fruit kidney-shaped, smooth, greyish, about 1 in. long, ½ in. broad and thick. The thick shell is porous and contains a dark, acrid oil, dangerous to very sensitive skins. The nuts are roasted to obtain the kernels, which are edible when thus obtained.

Part Used: Nut.

Medicinal Use: Nutritive. The roasted kernels are edible and of agreeable flavour. The fresh juice of the shell is acrid and corrosive, and the West Indian negroes use it for warts, corns, etc. The tree-bark has proved efficient in certain malarial fevers not yielding to treatment by Quinine.

CASSIA

Cinnamomum cassia, Blume
Fam. Lauraceae

Synonyms: Chinese Cinnamon, *Cassia lignea*, Casia Bark.

Habitat: China.

Description: The bark is in bull-brown quilled pieces: sometimes remains of the epidermal layer are present. Quills not so thin are rarely inserted inside one another as in cinnamon. Taste and odour, aromatic, similar to Cinnamon, but distinct. The Oil of Cinnamon of the U.S.P. is the volatile oil distilled from the leaves and twigs of this plant. This is known as Oil of Cassia in the B.P.C.

CASSIA BUDS are probably obtained from the same plant and allied species and consist of the immature fruits. They are used for the same purposes as the bark.

Part Used: Bark.

Medicinal Use: Tonic, stomachic, carminative. Used for domestic purposes and as a substitute for Ceylon Cinnamon in medicine.

Biblical References: Exodus XXX, 24; Psalms XLV, 8.

CASSIA PODS

Cassia fistula, Linn.
Fam. Leguminosae

Synonym: Pudding Stick.

Habitat: East and West Indies and Egypt.

Description: Cassia Pods are the ripe fruits, attaining a length of $1\frac{1}{2}$–2 ft. The interior is divided into compartments by transverse sections about 5 mm apart. A thin layer of black fruit pulp fills the cavity. As the fruit ripens the pulp contracts and the seeds rattle when shaken. The tree is 20–30 ft high and is easily recognized by the hanging racemes of brilliant yellow, fragrant flowers.

Part Used: Pulp.

Medicinal Use: A pleasant fruit laxative.

Joseph Miller states: "The pulp of Cassia is a gentle, soluble medicine, pleasant to take and purges very gently, without gripings. . . ."

It is usually used compounded with other laxatives as, for example, Senna.

Preparations: Cass. Pulp B.P.C.: Dose, 60–120 gr; Conf. Senn. B.P.C.: Dose, 60–120 gr.

CASTOR OIL PLANT

Ricinus communis, Linn.
Fam. Euphorbiaceae

Synonyms: Castor Oil Bush, Palma Christi.

Habitat: Native of India but cultivated in many tropical countries.

Description: The three principal varieties of oil met with are the French, Italian, and English. Of these the Italian has the least taste.

The seed from which the oil is expressed is poisonous, but the poisonous ingredients are left behind in the cake after pressing.

Part Used: Oil expressed from the seeds.

Medicinal Use: Cathartic, purgative. From its mildness of action this is especially adapted for young children and child-bearing women, and may be used in cases of constipation, colic, and in diarrhoea due to slow digestion. It is also used for removing worms after other suitable remedies have been administered. Externally, it has been recommended for itch, ringworm, and cutaneous complaints. The nauseous taste can be covered by Lemon Oil, Sassafras Oil, and other essential oils, or Castor Oil may be administered in fresh or warmed milk. The Canary Island women use the fresh leaves as an application to the breasts in order to increase the secretion of milk.

Preparations: Ol. Ricin. B.P.: Dose, 60–240 min; Ol. Ricin. U.S.P.: Dose, 4 fl dr; Crem. Zinc Oxid. et Ol. Ricin. B.P.C. 1949: Emuls. Ol. Ricin.: Dose, 1–2 fl oz; Mist. Ol. Ricin.: Dose, 1–2 fl oz; Ol. Ricin. Arom.: Dose, 1–8 fl dr; Ol. Ricin. Sulphat. B.P.C.

CATECHU, BLACK

Acacia catechu, Willd.
Fam. Leguminosae

Synonyms: Cutch, *Catechu nigrum*.

Habitat: India and Burma.

Description: Two substances are sold under the name of Catechu. The one in black, shining pieces or cakes, sometimes with the remains of a leaf on the outside, derived from *Acacia catechu*, which is known as Cutch or Black Catechu, and a second in dark or pale brown cubes with a dull, powdery fracture, or sometimes in lozenge form, which is known as *Terra japonica*, or Gambier, or Pale Catechu (q.v.).

Part Used: Extract from leaves and young shoots.

Medicinal Use: Astringent. Is used in chronic diarrhoea, chronic catarrh, and chronic dysentery. Useful for arresting excessive mucous discharges, and for checking haemorrhages. Recommended as a local application in relaxed sore throat, sponginess of gums, etc.

Preparation: Powdered Catechu: Dose, 5–15 gr.

CATECHU, PALE

Uncaria gambier, Roxb.
Fam. Rubiaceae

Synonyms: *Terra japonica*, Gambier, *Ourouparia gambir*, Baillon.

Habitat: India and Burma.

Description: The leaves and shoots are boiled in water and the strong decoction poured into wooden trays. When it is set it is cut into cubes and dried.

Medicinal Use: Largely the same as Black Catechu.

Preparations: Powder: Dose, 5–15 gr; Mist. Cret. Aromat. c. Opio. B.P.C.: Dose, $\frac{1}{2}$–1 fl oz; Mist. Cret. c. Catech. B.P.C. 1949: Dose, $\frac{1}{2}$–1 fl oz; Mist. Cret. c. Catech. pro Infant. B.P.C. 1949: Dose, 60–120 min; Tinct. Catech. B.P.C.: Dose, 30–60 min; Catechu Lozenges.

Domestic Use: It is largely used in the tanning industry.

CATNEP

Nepeta cataria, Linn.
Fam. Labiatae

Synonyms: Catmint, Nep.

Habitat: A common garden plant in England.

Flowering Time: July.

Description: Stem opaque, hairy, grey. Leaves stalked, cordate-ovate, pointed, incise-serrate, whitish, hairy beneath. Flowers white, dotted with crimson, two-lipped, upper lip straight, calyx tubular, lower stamens shortest, arranged in short, dense, branched spikes. Taste and odour mint-like but characteristic.

The stem and leaves are rendered so white by the down that an old English simile is, "As white as Nep."

Part Used: Herb.

Medicinal Use: Carminative, tonic, diaphoretic, refrigerant. As it produces free perspiration it is very useful in colds, etc. The infusion of 1 oz to 1 pt of boiling water may be taken by adults in doses of 2 tablespoonfuls, by children in 2 or 3 teaspoonfuls frequently, to relieve pain and flatulence.

Culpeper states: "The green herb, bruised and applied to the part for two or three hours, easeth the pain arising from piles. The juice also, being made up into an ointment, is effectual for the same purpose. Washing the head with a decoction thereof taketh away scabs; and may be used to the like effect on other parts of the body." Some of the old herbalists recommend the use of the herb against barrenness.

CATNEP gets its name from the liking of cats for this plant. It is said that when it starts to wither they will roll themselves in it and chew it. There is an old belief that it makes cats "frolicsome, amorous and full of battle." There is also an ancient saying that "if the root be chewed it will make the most quiet person fierce and quarrelsome."

CAYENNE

Capsicum minimum, Roxb.
Capsicum frutescens, Linn.
Fam. Solanaceae

N.B. The only Capsicums recognized in the B.P.C. are the above.

Synonyms: African Pepper, Guinea Pepper, Bird Pepper, Chillies, *Capsicum fastigiatum*, Blume, Red Pepper.

Habitat: Sierra Leone, Zanzibar, Nyasaland, Madagascar, Japan, and Tropical America.

Description: The fruit varies much in colour, size, and pungency. The most pungent are those of Sierra Leone, but the colour is yellowish-red. Japanese are bright red and longer, but less pungent. Birdseye Cayenne are small, bright, Japanese pods of equal size. These are the most expensive, owing to the cost and care in collection. Zanzibar Chillies often have the stalks attached. Other varieties: Paprika, Hungarian, *C. tetragonum* and *C. annuum*, var. *longum*; Bombay (large), *C. annuum*, Linn.; Spanish Bird Pepper, *C. annuum* var. *grossum*. Of these varieties the one of greatest interest is the Hungarian Paprika, which is grown in very large quantities.

It is used as a bird food to improve the plumage of canaries. It is also largely used as a food spice and more recently its medicinal value has been brought to notice by Prof. Dr. Szent Gyorgyi, who has pointed out that Paprika is the richest source of vitamin C.

Part Used: Fruit.

Medicinal Use: Stimulant, tonic, carminative, rubefacient. The purest and most certain stimulant in herbal *materia medica.* Produces natural warmth and equalizes the circulation. Persons exposed any length of time to cold and damp may ward off disease by taking pills made of pure Cayenne, and a cold may generally be removed by one or two doses of the powder taken in warm water. Cayenne enters into many of the compounds of the herbal practice, and is one of the most important remedies.

Preparations: Emp. Bellad. et Capsic. B.P.C.; Emp. Capsic. B.P.C.; Gossyp. Capsic. B.P.C.; Oleores. Capsic. B.P.C.: Dose, $\frac{1}{100}$–$\frac{1}{80}$ gr; Tel. Carbas. et Gossyp. Capsic. B.P.C.; Tinct. Capsic. B.P.C.: Dose, 5–15 min; Tinct. Capsic. fort: Dose, 1–3 min; Ung. Capsic. B.P.C.; Ung. Capsic. Co. B.P.C. 1949; Capsicum Powder: Dose, $\frac{1}{2}$–2 gr.

CEDRON

Simaba cedron, Planch.
Fam. Simarubaceae

Synonym: Cedron Seeds.

Habitat: Central America.

Description: The Cedron Seeds of commerce consist of the separated cotyledons; these are flattened on one side and convex on the other, and are of a greyish-yellow tint about 1$\frac{1}{2}$ in. long and $\frac{1}{2}$–$\frac{3}{4}$ in. in diameter. Fracture short and yellowish. Taste, very bitter; odour, recalling that of coconut.

Part Used: Seeds.

Medicinal Use: Febrifuge, bitter, tonic, antispasmodic, sedative. The seeds are intensely bitter and have been employed in malarial complaints and in dyspepsia. The dose of the powdered seeds is 1–10 gr, and the infusion of 1 oz in 1 pt of boiling water may be given in doses of a tablespoonful three to four times a day.

CELANDINE

Chelidonium majus, Linn.
Fam. Papaveraceae

Synonyms: Garden Celandine, Greater Celandine. (Must not be confused with Lesser Celandine which is an entirely different plant known commonly as Pilewort, q.v.)

Habitat: A common garden plant found in England and in Europe. It also grows wild on waste ground.

Flowering Time: May.

Description: Leaves pinnate, green above, greyish below, 6–12 in. long and 2–3 in. wide. Leaflets opposite, deeply cut, with rounded teeth. Leaf-stalk flat above, convex beneath, with recurved hairs, exuding a saffron yellow juice when fresh and broken. The flowers are yellow, consisting of four small petals set in a calyx of two hollow parts. The black shining seeds are contained in narrow pods. Taste, acrid, bitter, and caustic; odour disagreeable.

Part Used: Herb.

Medicinal Use: Alterative, diuretic, purgative. Used in jaundice, scrofulous diseases, eczema, etc. The infusion of 1 oz of herb to 1 pt of boiling water is taken in wineglassful doses. The fresh juice makes an excellent application for corns and warts.

Joseph Miller writes: "Outwardly it is used for sore eyes, to dry up the rheum and take away specks and films as also against Tetters, and Ring-worms and scurfy breakings out."

Culpeper states that the root if chewed in the mouth helps toothache.

John Parkinson (1640) writes: "Matthiolus saith that if the green herb be worn in their shoes that have the Yellow Jaundice so as their bare feet tread thereon it will help them of it."

Preparation: Liquid extract: Dose, $\frac{1}{2}$–1 dr.

CELERY

Apium graveolens, Linn.
Fam. Umbelliferae

Synonym: Smallage.

Habitat: Southern Europe. It is cultivated in the British Isles, India, and U.S.A. The wild variety grows in marshy places and has an unpleasant odour which is not present in the cultivated varieties.

Description: Celery is a well-known plant needing no description. The seeds, which are principally used in medicine, are very small, $\frac{1}{25}$ in. long, ovate, plano-convex, brown, with five paler, longitudinal ribs. Taste and odour that of celery.

Parts Used: Seeds and stems.

Medicinal Use: Carminative, diuretic, tonic, and aphrodisiac. Used as a flavour and a tonic in combination with other drugs such as Coca, Kola, Damiana, etc. It is recommended as excellent in rheumatism. Culpeper recommends the use of the seed, plant, and roots for various complaints, but today it is the seed that is usually used.

Preparations: Liquid extract: Dose, 5–20 min.

Essential oil: Dose, $\frac{1}{2}$–2 drops.

Powdered seeds: Dose, 20–60 gr.

Domestic Use: The stems of Celery are a very well-known food. They should be collected after the frost has been on them.

CENTAURY

Erythraea centaurium, Pers.
Fam. Gentianaceae

Synonyms: Century, Centory, Feverwort.

Habitat: Fields, pastures, and woods in England and Europe.

Flowering Time: July.

Description: Stem 8–12 in. high, with opposite, lanceolate-ovate leaves, having 3–5 longitudinal ribs, hairless, and entire at the margins. Flowers pink, with twisted anthers. Taste, bitter; odour, slight, disappearing when dried.

Parts Used: Herb, leaves.

Medicinal Use: Aromatic, bitter, stomachic, tonic. Should be given in conjunction with Barberry Bark in cases of jaundice. Is used extensively in dyspepsia. The dose of the infusion of 1 oz to 1 pt of boiling water is a wineglassful.

Culpeper places this herb under the dominion of the sun "as it appears that their flowers open and shut as the Sun either sheweth or hideth his face." He also writes "The herb is so safe you cannot fail in the using of it. Take it inwardly only for inward diseases, and apply it outwardly for outward complaints; it is very wholesome, but not pleasant to the taste."

Preparation: Liquid extract: Dose, ½–1 dr.

CHAMOMILE

Anthemis nobilis, Linn.
Fam. Compositae.

Synonyms: Roman Chamomile, Double Chamomile.

Habitat: Cultivated to a small extent in England but to a larger extent in Belgium and France.

Flowering Time: Early summer.

Description: Flowers, double, i.e. consisting entirely of ligulate florets, about ½ in. in diameter, leaving, when pulled off, a conical, solid receptacle, covered with lanceolate, membraneous scales (paleae). Leaves pinnately divided into short and hairy leaflets. Taste, aromatic and very bitter. In English Chamomile Flowers a few of the central florets are tubular. Wild Chamomile Flowers, having only an outer row of ligulate florets, are known as Scotch Chamomiles.

Parts Used: Flowers, herb.

Medicinal Use: Stomachic, antispasmodic, tonic. An old-fashioned but extremely efficacious remedy for hysterical and nervous affections in women. Also used as an emmenagogue. The flowers combined with crushed poppy-heads make a good poultice for allaying pains, when other means have failed. As a lotion it is also excellent for external application in toothache, earache, neuralgia, etc. The herb and flowers are equally valuable. The dose of the infusion of 1 oz to 1 pt of boiling water is a tablespoonful to a wineglassful. The herb is also used in the manufacture of herb beers. As a tonic the Powdered Flowers may be used in doses of ½–1 dr three times a day.

CULPEPER writes of Chamomile: "Nichessor saith the Egyptians dedicated it to the Sun because it cured agues; and they were like enough to do it, for they are the most superstitious people in their religion I ever read of."

Preparations: Dec. Papav. et Anthem. Forte; Ext. Anthem.; Dose 2–8 gr; Ext. Anthem. Liq.: Dose, ½–1 dr; Ol. Anthem. B.P.C. 1949: Dose, ½–3 min (this is the oil distilled from the flowers).

CHAMOMILE, GERMAN

Matricaria chamomilla, Linn.
Fam. Compositae

Synonyms: Single Chamomile, Pin Heads.
Habitat: Growing wild in many parts of Europe and the British Isles.
Flowering Time: Early summer.
Description: The flower heads are much smaller than the preceding, and have only one row of ligulate florets, which are usually bent backwards when dry. The receptacle is conical and hollow, and has no membranous bracts on it. Taste, bitter and aromatic; odour, like the preceding, but weaker. The florets readily fall off.
Part Used: Flowers.
Medicinal Use: Carminative, sedative, tonic. It is an excellent remedy in children's ailments. It acts as a nerve sedative and also as a tonic upon the gastro-intestinal canal. Useful during dentition, in cases of earache, neuralgic pains, stomach disorders, and infantile convulsions. The infusion of ½ oz to 1 pt of boiling water may be given freely in teaspoonful doses to children. Also used externally as a fomentation.
Preparations: Liquid extract: Dose, ¼–1 dr; Powder: Dose, 2–4 dr.

CHAULMOOGRA

Taraktogenos kurzii, King
Fam. Flacourtiaceae

Synonyms: Chaulmugra, Chaulmogra. These seeds were for some years supposed to be the produce of *Chaulmoogra odorata*, Roxb., but it has since been shown that the seeds of that plant are quite different.

Habitat: Malay Peninsula, India, Assam.

Description: Seeds greyish, about 1 in. long and $\frac{5}{8}$ in. in diameter, irregularly angular with rounded ends. Kernel (albumen) oily, enclosing two thin, heart-shaped, three-veined cotyledons with a straight radicle. Taste, somewhat acrid; odour, disagreeable.

Varieties: Chaulmoogra Oil has now been almost entirely replaced by Hydnocarpus Oil, which is official in the B.P. This is derived from *Hydnocarpus wightiana*, Blume. The oil has similar properties to those of Chaulmoogra and the dose is the same.

The ethyl esters of Hydnocarpus are also official in the B.P., and are preferred for injections in cases of leprosy. The doses are the same as for Oil of Chaulmoogra.

Part Used: Seeds. Oil expressed from the seeds.

Medicinal Use: Sedative, febrifuge, dermatic. The seeds may be given internally, when powdered and made into pills, in doses of 3–6 gr. The oil expressed from the seeds has been much praised as an internal and external remedy in scrofulous, and rheumatic skin affections. It has proved itself a valuable agent in stiffness of joints and cutaneous eruptions such as eczema and psoriasis. The best form is the ointment made of 1 part of oil to 4 of base. For internal administration the oil is administered in the form of an emulsion with almonds or milk.

Preparation: Oil: Dose, 5–15 min gradually increasing to 60 min when given by the mouth, or 30 min gradually increasing to 75 min by subcutaneous and intramuscular injection.

CHEKEN

Eugenia chequen, Mol.
Fam. Myrtaceae

Synonyms: Chekan, Chequen, *Myrtus cheken*, Spreng.

Habitat: Chile.

Description: Leaves leathery, ovate, $\frac{5}{8}$–1 in. long, $\frac{1}{4}$–$\frac{1}{2}$ in. wide, and entire at the margins, very shortly stalked with numerous minute, round, translucent oil cells. Twigs with opposite leaf scars. Taste, astringent and bitter; flavour, aromatic, recalling that of bay leaves; odour, very slight.

Part Used: Leaves.

Medicinal Use: Diuretic, expectorant, tonic. Is reputed to be a valuable remedy in catarrhal disorders of respiratory organs. Dr. Murrell, of London, claimed it to be excellent in winter coughs of elderly persons.
Preparation: Liquid extract: Dose, 1–2 dr.

CHERRY-LAUREL

Prunus laurocerasus, Linn.
Fam. Rosaceae

Habitat: It is a native of Russia but has now been cultivated in most countries with a temperate climate. It is mentioned as being a garden shrub in England by Gerard in 1597. He calls the plant Cherry-bay.
Description: Leaves leathery, shining, about 5–6 in. long by 1½–2 in. wide, oblong, lanceolate, pointed, and serrate at the margins. At the back of the leaf there are two or three dot-like glands close to the midrib near the base. Odour, when the fresh leaves are bruised, like that of oil of bitter almonds, owing to the presence of minute quantities of prussic acid.
Part Used: Leaves.
Medicinal Use: Sedative. Mostly used to produce cherry-laurel water, and as such, of value in cough, whooping cough, and asthma, as an addition to other medication. Also useful in dyspepsia, indigestion, etc.
Preparation: Aq. Laurocer. B.P.C. 1949: Dose, 30–120 min.

CHERRY STALKS

Prunus avium
(and other species)
Fam. Roseaceae

Description: Fruit stalks about 1¾ in. long and $\frac{1}{24}$ in. in thickness, enlarged at one end. The stalks of various species are collected indifferently, viz. *P. cerasus*, Linn., and *P. duracina*, Sweet, i.e. of the red, black, and white or Bigarreau cherries. Taste, bitter and astringent.
Medicinal Use: They are rarely used now but at one time were considered a good astringent tonic.

CHESTNUT

Castanea sativa, Mill.
Fam. Fagaceae

Synonyms: *Castanea dentata*, Borkh., *Castanea vulgaris*, Lam., Sweet Chestnut, Spanish Chestnut.
Habitat: A tree found in Great Britain, Europe, and America.
Description: Leaves leathery, about 6–8 in. long, and 2½ in. broad, oblong, lanceolate, feather-veined, margins with distinct, sharp-pointed, spreading

teeth. In the American form of the tree (Castanea dentata) the teeth are curved forward. Taste, astringent; odour, none.

Part Used: Leaves.

Medicinal Use: Tonic, astringent. In some places chestnut leaves are used as a popular remedy in fever, ague, etc. Their reputation, however, rests upon their remarkable efficiency in paroxysmal or convulsive coughs, whooping coughs, and other irritable and excitable conditions of the respiratory organs. The infusion of 1 oz of leaves in 1 pt of boiling water is administered in tablespoonful to wineglassful doses, repeated three to four times daily.

Domestic Use: The old herbalists do not mention the use of the leaves, but the nut itself is frequently mentioned as a food and as a stuffing for poultry, a use to which it is frequently put today.

Biblical References: Genesis XXX, 37; Ezekiel XXXI, 8.

CHICKWEED

Stellaria media, Cyrill.
Fam. Caryophyllaceae

Synonyms: *Alsine media*, Linn., Starweed, Star Chickweed.

Habitat: A common weed in England. As Joseph Miller says: "It grows everywhere in moist places and in gardens too frequently."

Flowering Time: It flowers and seeds all through the summer months.

Description: Stem jointed, with a line of hairs down one side only. Leaves ovate, about $\frac{1}{2}$ in. long by $\frac{1}{4}$ in. broad with flat stalks below, stalkless above. Flowers singly in the axils of the upper leaves, petals white and narrow, shorter than the calyx. Taste, slightly saline; odour, none.

Part Used: Herb.

Medicinal Use: Demulcent, refrigerant. The fresh leaves have been used as poultice to indolent ulcers, with most beneficial results. Has also been employed as an application in ophthalmia and as an ointment in cutaneous diseases. An infusion of 1 oz to 1 pt of boiling water taken in wineglassful doses at intervals during the day is good for scurvy and kidney disorders.

Gerard adds: "Little birds in cages (especially Linnets) are refreshed with the lesser Chickweed when they loath their meat. . . ."

Culpeper writes: "Boil a handful of Chickweed and a handful of red rose leaves dried in a quart of muscadine until a fourth part be consumed; then put to them a pint of oil of trotters or sheep's fat; let them boil a good while, still stirring them well; which being strained, anoint the grieved place therewith, warm against the fire, rubbing it well with one hand; and bind also some of the herb to the place and, with God's blessing it will help in three times dressing."

CHICORY

Cichorium intybus, Linn.
Fam. Compositae

Synonym: Succory.

Habitat: A vegetable garden plant in this country. Grown commercially in Europe and to a lesser extent in England.

Description: Root brownish, with tough, loose, reticulated, white layers surrounding a radiate woody column. Often crowned with remains of the stem. Taste, bitter, mucilaginous; odour, none.

Part Used: Root.

Medicinal Use: Tonic, diuretic, laxative. A decoction of 1 oz of the root to 1 pt of boiling water taken freely has been found effective in jaundice, liver enlargements, gout, and rheumatic complaints.

Domestic Use: The leaves are sometimes used in salad, but more frequently the Garden Endive (*Cichorium endiva*) is used for this purpose. The root, roasted and ground, is used in coffee mixtures.

CHINA

Smilax china, Linn.
Fam. Liliaceae

Habitat: Native of Japan, but growing in China and various other Eastern countries.

Description: Tubers cylindrical, somewhat flattened sometimes, 4–6 in. long and 1 or 2 in. in thickness, with short knotty branches, and a rusty, shining bark. Internally, of a pale fawn colour. Taste, insipid; odour, none.

Part Used: Root.

Medicinal Use: Alterative. Used occasionally as a substitute for Sarsaparilla and for similar purposes.

CHIRETTA

Swertia chirata, Buch.-Ham.
Fam. Gentianaceae

Synonyms: Brown Chirata, White Chiretta, Chirayta, *Ophelia chirata*, Griseb.

Habitat: Northern India.

Description: Stems brown or purplish, $\frac{2}{10}-\frac{3}{10}$ in. thick, cylindrical below, quadrangular upwards, containing a large pith. Leaves opposite, entire with three to seven longitudinal ribs. Capsules, one-celled, two-valved. Taste, intensively bitter; odour, none.

GREEN CHIRETTA, derived from *Andrographis paniculata*, Ness. (Fam. Acanthacae), has an equally bitter but not an earthy taste.

Part Used: Entire plant.

Medicinal Use: Bitter tonic. May be used wherever a tonic is required. The dose of the infusion of $\frac{1}{2}$ oz to 1 pt of water is half to one wineglassful.

Preparations: Powdered plant: Dose, 5–30 gr; Liquid extract: Dose, $\frac{1}{2}$–1 fl dr; Solid extract: Dose, 4–8 gr; Inf. Chirat. Conc. B.P.C. 1949: Dose, 30–60 min; Inf. Chirat. Rec.: Dose, $\frac{1}{2}$–1 fl oz; Tinct. Chirat.: Dose, $\frac{1}{2}$–1 dr.

CICELY, SWEET

Myrrhis odorata, Scop.
Fam. Umbelliferae

Synonyms: Smoother Cicely, Sweet Chervil, Great Chervil.

Habitat: A common British garden plant.

Description: Leaves large, tripinnate, leaflets hairy on the veins below and on the margins, leafstalks with spreading hairs. Leaflets ovate lanceolate, usually with white splashes near the base of the larger ones. Taste, sweet anise-like. Root whitish, $\frac{1}{2}$–$1\frac{1}{2}$ in. broad, with small central columns and radiate structure, the medullary rays curved in the bark. *Osmorhiza longistylis*, D.C., yields American Sweet Cicely.

Parts Used: Root, herb.

Medicinal Use: Carminative, stomachic, expectorant. The fresh root may be eaten freely. It is found useful in coughs and flatulence; also as a gentle stimulant in indigestion and stomachic complaints. The dried root is best used in the form of a decoction, and the herb in an infusion. An infusion of the herb gives good results for anaemia and is a splendid tonic for young girls.

Cicely Root and Angelica were used to prevent infection in the time of the plague.

CINCHONA

Cinchona calisaya, Weddell
Cinchona ledgeriana, Moens.
Cinchona officinalis, Linn.
Cinchona succirubra, Pav.
Fam. Rubiaceae

Official varieties are obtained from the above and from hybrids of *C. calisaya* or *C. ledgeriana* with *C. officinalis* or *C. succirubra*.

Synonyms: Peruvian Bark, Jesuit's Bark.

Habitat: The chain of the Andes. It is now cultivated in India and Java.

Description: *C. Calisaya* generally occurs in quills marked with white patches. Broad, longitudinal fissures with regular, transverse cracks about

6–12 mm apart. The outer cork layer frequently exfoliates. Rich in quinine.

C. ledgeriana, considered to be a variety of *C. calisaya*, is cultivated in Java, for quinine: usually occurs in single, sometimes double, quills which exhibit light grey patches of lichen. Has numerous longitudinal fissures and transverse cracks. Rich in quinine.

C. officinalis occurs in narrow quills, with numerous longitudinal and transverse cracks, giving a characteristic roughness to the back. Rich in quinine.

C. succirubra occurs in two forms. Flat from S. America; quills from Java. The flat red bark has longitudinal ridges and bright red warts, the inner surface being distinctly red. Succirubra quills are generally large. Outer surface reddish-brown colour with grey lichens attached. Generally strongly wrinkled with reddish warts. Rich in cinchonidine.

C. lancifolia, or Carthagena or Columbian Bark, occurs in single quills and flat pieces. The bark easily splinters and has numerous patches of silvery cork. Poor in quinine.

These barks with the exception of the last named are described in the *British Pharmaceutical Codex* and a standard of not less than 6 per cent total alkaloids is laid down.

Medicinal Use: Antiperiodic, febrifuge, tonic, astringent. Useful in all febrile and typhoid conditions, and in remittent and intermittent fevers. As a general tonic it is much esteeemed, and finds extensive use in the treatment of neuralgia, dyspepsia, and debility. With many persons over-doses produce headache, giddiness, and imperfect hearing.

Preparations: Powdered bark: Dose, 5–15 gr; Dec. Cinchon. Conc. B.P.C. 1949: Dose, 60–120 min; Ext. Cinchon. B.P.C.: Dose, 2–8 gr; Ext. Cinchon. Liq. B.P.C.: Dose, 5–15 min; Inf. Cinchon. Acid Conc. B.P.C. 1949: Dose, 30–60 min; Inf. Cinchon. Acid Rec. B.P.C. 1949: Dose, $\frac{1}{2}$–1 fl oz; Tinct. Cinchon. B.P.C. 1949: Dose, 30–60 min; Tinct. Cinchon. Co. B.P.C. 1949: Dose, 30–60 min; Quinine B.P.C. (alkaloid): Dose, 1–10 gr; and the various salts of quinine, Totaquina B.P.: Dose, 5–10 gr (mixture of alkaloids); salts of Cinchonine and Cinchonidine.

IN the year 1638 the wife of the Viceroy of Peru, Count of Cinchon, was attacked with fever and her physician on her recommendation treated her with the powdered bark and she was cured. Upon her recovery she proceeded to make the cure widely known and hence the name Cinchona.

CINERARIA MARITIMA

Senecio maritimus, Linn.
Fam. Compositae

Synonym: Dusty Miller.

Habitat: Native of West Indies but introduced into other countries, including England and U.S.A.

Description: Leaves 5–8 in. long and about 2–2¼ in. wide, pinnately divided, segments about three lobed, white with a dense white coating of hairs beneath. Flowerheads yellow, about ⅜ in. in length.

Part Used: Sterilized juice of the plant.

Medicinal Use: The sterilized juice of the plant is employed for the treatment of capsular and lenticular cataract of the eye. Its use is recommended before resorting to an operation. It should be applied to the eye by means of a medicine dropper.

CINNAMON

Cinnamomum zeylanicum, Nees
Fam. Lauraceae

Habitat: Native of Ceylon, but cultivated in other Eastern countries.

Description: In pale-brown, thin quills, several rolled in one another. Quills usually ⅜–⅝ in. in width, but not exceeding 1/16 in. in thickness. Taste, sweet, pungent, and aromatic; odour, characteristic.

Varieties: Saigon Cinnamon, derived from *Cinnamomum laureirii*, Nees, is official in the U.S.P. It appears in thin greyish brown quills, warty. It is sweeter and stronger than Ceylon Cinnamon. For *Cinnamomum cassia*, see Cassia.

Cinnamon Leaf Oil is distilled in Ceylon and imported into this country, but is not official. It serves as a cheaper variety of oil, but contains less cinnamic aldehyde than that from the bark. Oil of Cinnamon in the United States is distilled from *Cinnamomum cassia* and is known in Great Britain as Oil of Cassia.

Parts Used: Bark and the oil distilled from the bark and leaves.

CINNAMON was valued in the East as a spice for use in the temples where burnt offerings were made, in order to counteract the objectionable smell that resulted.

Medicinal Use: Aromatic, astringent, stimulant, carminative. A fragrant cordial especially useful for weakness of the stomach and diarrhoea. Checks nausea and vomiting. Generally combined with other remedies.

Preparations: Powdered Bark: Dose, 5–20 gr; Aq. Cinnam. Dest. B.P.C.: Dose, ½–1 fl oz; Aq. Cinnam. Conc. B.P.: Dose, 5–15 min; Pulv. Cinnam. Co. B.P.C. 1949: Dose, 10–60 gr; Tinct. Cinnam. B.P.C. 1949: Dose, 30–60 gr; Tinct. Lavand. Co. B.P.C. 1949: Dose, 30–60 gr; Ol. Cinnam. B.P.: Dose, 1–3 min; Elix. Quinin. Ammon. et Cinnam. B.P.C. 1949: Dose, 30–60 min; Sp. Cinnam. B.P.C. 1949: Dose, 5–20 min; Tinct. Cardam. Aromat. B.P.C.: Dose, 2–10 min.

Domestic Use: Cinnamon is used as a flavouring agent.

Biblical References: Exodus XXX, 23; Song of Solomon LV, 14; Proverbs VII, 17; Ecclesiasticus XXIV, 15; Revelation XVIII, 13.

CLARY

Salvia sclarea, Linn.
Fam. Labiatae

Synonyms: Clarry, Cleareye, Christ's Eye.

Of the last synonym Culpeper says: "I could wish for my soul, blasphemy, ignorance, and tyranny were ceased among physicians, that they may be happy, and I joyful."

Habitat: It grows commonly in this country both in gardens and wild. Culpeper states that "you may find it plentifully if you look in the fields near Grays Inn and Chelsea."

Flowering Time: From June to August.

Description: Leaves large, heart-shaped, pointed, wrinkled, covered with velvety hairs. Flowers blue or white, with large membraneous bracts longer than the calyx. Taste, warm and aromatic, slightly bitter; odour, aromatic, recalling that of Tolu.

Part Used: Herb (and at one time the seeds).

PARKINSON writes: "The fresh leaves fried in butter, being first dipped in a batter of flour, eggs and a little milk served as a dish to the table is not unpleasant to any. . . ." Also: "Some brewers of ale and beer do put it into their drink to make it more heady, fit to please drunkards who thereby become either dead drunke or foolish drunke or madde drunke."

Medicinal Use: Antispasmodic, balsamic. This plant has been used both fresh and dry. Mostly employed in disordered states of digestion as a stomachic. It has also been of service in kidney diseases with good results. The mucilage of the seeds has been used in ophthalmic disorders. The old herbalists considered a decoction of the herb to be most efficacious in any complaint of the eyes.

Parkinson (1640) writes: "The seed thereof is used to be put into the eyes to clear them from any moates or other such like things are gotten within the liddes to offend them." Several of the other ancient herbalists say the same.

John Hill, M.D. (1761), explains: "As soon as the seed is put in the warmth and moistures of the eye operating upon its own substance, cover it with a thick and tough mucilage; as it continues moving in the eye this entangles the little substances which had got in by accident and occasioned the pain; and brings them out with it."

CLIVERS

Galium aparine, Linn.
Fam. Rubiaceae

Synonyms: Cleavers, Goosegrass, Hayriffe, Erriffe, Burweed, Goosebill.

Habitat: A wild plant growing in hedges and ditches throughout the country. Culpeper says: "It is also an inhabitant in gardens that it ramps upon and is ready to choak what ever grows near it."

Flowering Time: June and July.

Description: Stem quadrangular. Leaves lanceolate, about ½ in. long and ¼ in. broad, in rings of six, with backward bristly hairs at the margins. Fruit nearly globular, about ⅛ in. in diameter, covered with hooked bristles. Taste, slightly saline; odour, none.

Part Used: Herb.

Medicinal Use: Aperient, diuretic, tonic, alterative. Should be given in obstruction of urinary organs, suppression of urine, gravelly deposits, etc. Acts as a solvent of stone in the bladder. The infusion, hot or cold, of 1 oz to 1 pt of water is taken frequently in wineglassful doses.

Besides the frequent reference in old herbals to the use of this herb as a remedy against the bites of venomous creatures, Gerard states: "Women do usually make a pottage of Clevers with a little mutton and otemeale, to cause lanknesse and keep them from fatnesse."

Culpeper writes: "It is a good remedy in the Spring, eaten (being first chopped small and boiled well) in water-gruel, to cleanse the blood and strengthen the liver, thereby to keep the body in health, and fitting it for that change of season that is coming."

Preparation: Liquid extract: Dose, ½–1 dr.

CLOVES

Eugenia caryophyllus (Spreng.), Sprague.
Fam. Myrtaceae

Synonyms: Clavos, *Eugenia caryophillata*, Thunb.

Habitat: Native of the Molucca Islands. Introduced into Zanzibar, Pemba, Penang, Amboyna, and Madagascar. The world's supplies now come from these places.

Description: The Clove tree is an evergreen, producing brown flowerbuds, nailshaped, the lower portion consisting of calyx tube enclosing in its upper half the ovary filled with minute ovules. Calyx teeth four, surrounded by the unopened globular corolla of four concave, overlapping petals. Stamens numerous. Taste, hot; flavour, that of cloves. On pressing the calyx tube with the finger-nail, oil should exude.

Parts Used: Unexpanded flower buds and the oil distilled from them.

Medicinal Use: Stimulant, aromatic, carminative. A warm, stimulating aromatic, used chiefly in combination with other remedies.

Preparations: Inf. Caryoph. Conc. B.P.C.: Dose, 30–60 min; Inf. Caryoph. Rec. B.P.C. 1949: Dose, ½–1 fl oz; Ol. Caryoph. B.P. and U.S.P.: Dose, 1–3 min.

From the oil are made: Eugenol B.P.C. and U.S.P.: Dose, 1–3 min; and Iso-Eugenol. Both are used largely in perfumery. From Eugenol is produced Vanillin B.P.C. and U.S.P.

Domestic Use: Cloves are used as a spice and flavouring agent.

CLUBMOSS

Lycopodium clavatum, Linn.
Fam. Lycopodiaceae

Synonyms: Lycopodium, Lycopodium Seed, Vegetable Sulphur.

Habitat: Central and Northern Europe and the northern parts of Great Britain. It also grows in many other parts of the world.

Description: Stem woody, slender, elongated, with a few lateral, forked branches, and a few scattered, whitish roots below. Leaves crowded and scale-like, hair-tipped. Spore cases in spikes borne on erect, forked, club-shaped branches, at right angles to the prostrate stem, spores somewhat triangular, yellow, forming a mobile powder which floats on water without being wetted.

Part Used: Plant and spores.

Medicinal Use: Sedative, emollient. Lycopodium has long been utilized for dusting over pills and the making of fireworks. Lately it has come into prominence as a remedy for internal use in urinary disorders, and has rendered a good service in the treatment of spasmodic retention of urine in children, catarrhal cystitis, and in chronic kidney diseases, causing pain in kidneys, ureters, and bladder, and associated with rheumatic symptoms. It is efficient as a gastric sedative in indigestion, dyspepsia, and catarrhal gastritis. Dose, 10–60 gr.

COCA

Bolivian: *Erythroxylum coca*, Lam.
Peruvian: *Erythroxylum truxillense*, Rusby
Fam. Erythroxylaceae

Habitat: Peru, Bolivia, cultivated in Java and Formosa.

Description: Bolivian or Huanuco: Leaves are brownish green, oval, thin but tough, nearly 2 in. long and 1 in. wide, with two lines on the under-surface parallel to the midrib, margins entire, apex rounded, a faint projecting line occurring on the upper surface of the midrib. Peruvian leaves, derived from *Erythroxylum truxillense*, Rusby, are green, oblanceolate, and very brittle, but tapering below; about $1\frac{1}{2}$ in. long and $\frac{1}{2}$ in. broad in the upper half without any projecting line on the midrib.

Java Coca (*E. trux*) is exported in the form of a coarse powder and is generally used for the manufacture of Cocaine.

Part Used: Leaves.

Medicinal Use: A powerful nerve stimulant and anodyne. Coca prevents fatigue, and the leaves are chewed by the South American natives to enable them to perform feats of endurance. Is also used in the treatment of asthma and as an aphrodisiac and a general nerve tonic. The leaves contain an alkaloid, Cocaine, which is used as an anaesthetic. The distribution and use of this drug is controlled by the Dangerous Drugs Act.

Preparations: Ext. Cocae Liq. (miscible): Dose, $\frac{1}{2}$–1 dr; Ext. Cocae Liq. B.P. 1898: Dose, $\frac{1}{2}$–1 dr; Ext. Cocae B.P.C. 1923: Dose, 2–10 gr; Elixir Cocae: Dose, 1–4 dr.

COCCULUS INDICUS

Anamirta paniculata, Colebr.
Fam. Menispermaceae

Synonyms: Fish Berries, Indian Berries, Levant Berries, Hockle Elderberry.

Habitat: East Indies.

Description: Fruits roundly kidney-shaped $\frac{4}{10}$–$\frac{5}{10}$ in. long, blackish, containing a horse-shoe-shaped seed. Fruitshell tasteless, seed bitter and oily. The seeds stupefy fish when thrown into water.

Part Used: Berries or seeds.

Medicinal Use: Stimulant, parasiticide. Though very poisonous, it has occasionally been given internally for similar purposes as Nux Vomica and its preparations. As an ingredient of an ointment it has been used in obstinate skin diseases, such as barber's itch, etc.

Preparations: Fluid extract: Dose, $\frac{1}{4}$–1 min; Picrotoxin B.P.

COCILLANA

Guarea rusbyi, Rusby
Fam. Meliaceae

Synonyms: Huapi Bark, *Sycocarpus rusbyi, Guarea trichilioides.*

Habitat: Eastern Andes.

Description: The bark occurs in flat or curved pieces of varying size, the outer surface fissured and grey-brown in colour. Where the cork has been removed, it shows an orange-brown colour. Inner surface brown and strongly striated longitudinally. Odour, characteristic; taste, astringent and slightly nauseous.

Part Used: Bark.

Medicinal Use: Expectorant. Resembles Ipecacuanha in action. Used in bronchitis, bronchial pneumonia, phthisis.

Preparations: Powdered bark: Dose, 8–15 gr; Ext. Cocillan. Liq. B.P.C.: Dose, 5–15 min; Syr. Cocillan. Co. B.P.C. 1949: Dose, 30–60 min.

COFFEE

Coffea arabica
Fam. Rubiaceae

Synonym: Caffea.

Habitat: Arabia. It is cultivated in many tropical countries.

Description: The seeds are oval concave on one side, flat on the other, greenish-grey, with central longitudinal furrow. Caffeine occurs in commerce in silky white crystals.

Part Used: Kernel of the dried ripe seed.

Medicinal Use: Stimulant, anti-narcotic, anti-emetic. As a beverage Coffee is well known and is often used in domestic practice as a remedy in headache and as a general stimulant. When taken in excess it produces unpleasant heart symptoms. As a medicinal agent the beverage made from roasted seeds may be used, or the Caffeine, where a heart stimulant is needed. In narcotic poisoning it forms a valuable adjunct, as it dispels stupor and drowsiness, and is also used in cases of alcohol habit. Possessing decided diuretic properties it can be employed with advantage in gout, rheumatism, and gravel. Dropsies of cardiac origin are also benefited by it.

Preparations: Coff. Praep. B.P.C.; Dec. Coff. Praep. B.P.C. 1949.

Caffeine B.P. may be prepared from Coffee. It is also manufactured synthetically. From Caffeine its various salts are made, and these enter into a number of preparations in the B.P. and B.P.C. Dose of Caffeine B.P. is 5–10 gr.

CULPEPER has this to say about Coffee: ". . . they do prepare it to make a coffee-liquor with, it then stinks most loathsomely, which is an argument of some Saturnine quality in it: the propugners of this filthy drink affirm it causes watchfulness . . . they also say it makes them sober when they are drunk. . . ."

COHOSH, BLACK

Cimicifuga racemosa, Nutt.
Fam. Ranunculaceae

Synonyms: Black Snakeroot, Bugbane, Rattleroot, Rattleweed, Squawroot, *Actaea racemosa*, Linn., *Macrotys actaeoides*, Rafin.

Habitat: United States and Canada. Introduced into England about 1860.

Description: Rhizome thick, hard, and knotty, with short lateral branches, cylindrical, compressed, marked with transverse leaf scars. Transverse section horny, enclosing a ring of woody tissue within a hard, thick bark. Rootlets, when present, show on transverse section the woody tissue like a Maltese cross. Taste, bitter and acrid, and rather astringent; odour, disagreeable.

Part Used: Rhizome.

Medicinal Use: Astringent, diuretic, emmenagogue, alterative. In small doses useful in children's diarrhoea. In paroxysms of consumption it gives relief by allaying the cough, reducing rapidity of pulse, and inducing perspiration. Is specially recommended in cases of obstructed menses. In whooping cough its action is very highly spoken of. Frequently employed as a remedy for rheumatism. Said to be a specific in St. Vitus's Dance of children. Overdoses produce nausea and vomiting.

Preparations: Liquid extract B.P. 1898: Dose, 5–30 drops; Tincture: Dose, ½–1 dr; Cimicifugin or Macrotin: Dose, 1–6 gr; Powdered extract: Dose, 4 gr; Solid extract: Dose, 1–3 gr.

COHOSH, BLUE

Caulophyllum thalictroides, Mich.
Fam. Berberidaceae

Synonyms: Papoose Root, *Leontice thalictroides*, Linn., Squawroot.

Habitat: United States of America.

Description: Rhizome brownish grey, about 4 in. long and $\frac{1}{4}$–$\frac{3}{8}$ in. thick, and knotty with short branches, with numerous, crowded, concave stem-scars, on the upper side; furnished below with long, pale-brown, tough rootlets about $\frac{1}{25}$ in. thick; internally whitish, with narrow, woody rays. Taste, sweetish, then bitter and acrid; nearly inodorous.

Part Used: Rhizome.

Medicinal Use: Diuretic, antispasmodic, vermifuge, and emmenagogue. Very efficacious in rheumatic affections and female complaints. The Indian women use it largely to expedite parturition and to induce menstruation.

Preparations: Ext. Cauloph. Liq.: Dose, 10–30 min; Liq. Cauloph. et Pulsat.: Dose, 1–2 dr; Liq. Cauloph. et Pulsat. Co.: Dose, 1–2 dr; Solid extract: Dose, 5–10 gr; Caulophyllin: Dose, 2–5 gr; Powdered root: Dose, 5–30 gr.

COLCHICUM

Colchicum autumnale, Linn.
Fam. Liliaceae

Synonyms: Meadow Saffron, Naked Ladies.

Habitat: North Africa and Europe, and in some localities in the British Isles.

Flowering Time: September.

Description: The corm or root is usually solid in transverse slices, notched on one side, and somewhat reniform in outline, white and starchy internally. The corms are collected in the early summer and cut into thin slices. Taste, sweetish, then bitter and acrid. Produces a pale-purple flower in the autumn.

The seeds are dull brown, nearly spherical, finely pitted, with a crest-like appendage at the hilum, very hard and horny, with a minute embryo. Taste, bitter and acrid; odour, none. A good sample of the seeds and corms yields about 0·5 per cent Colchicine.

Parts Used: Corms, seeds.

Medicinal Use: Antirheumatic, cathartic, emetic. Its reputation rests largely upon its value in acute gouty and rheumatic complaints. Mostly used in conjunction with some alkaline diuretic. Also given in pill form. Overdoses cause violent purging, etc.

Gerard states: "The roots of all sorts of Mede Saffrons are very hurtful to the stomacke, and being eaten they kill by choaking as Mushromes do according to Dioscorides; whereupon some have called it Colchicum strangulatorium."

Preparations: From Corm: Ext. Colch. Sicc. B.P.C. 1949: Dose, $\frac{1}{6}$–$\frac{1}{2}$ gr; Powdered Corm: Dose, 2–5 gr; Pil. Colch. et Aloes: Dose, 1–4 pills; Pil. Colch. et Hydrarg.: Dose, 1–3 pills; Pil. Colch. et Hydrarg. Co.: Dose, 1 or 2 pills; Ext. Colch. Liq. B.P.; Mist. Colch. B.P.C.: Dose, $\frac{1}{2}$ fl oz; Mist. Colch. et Sod. Sal. B.P.C.: Dose, $\frac{1}{2}$ fl oz; Tinct. Colch. B.P.: Dose, 5–15 min; Vin. Colch.: Dose, 10–30 min; Powdered Seeds: Dose, 2–5 gr.

From Corm and Seeds the alkaloid Colchicine is prepared: Dose, B.P. $\frac{1}{120}$–$\frac{1}{60}$ gr; U.S.P. $\frac{1}{120}$ gr; Tab. Colchicin. B.P.C. and U.S.P.

COLOPHONY

Pinus palustris, Mill.
Pinus taeda, Linn.
(and other species)
Fam. Pinaceae

Synonyms: Amber Resin, Rosin.

Habitat: U.S.A.

Description: Colophony Resin is the residue left after the distillation of Turpentine. Resin varies in colour from pale yellow to brown, and appears in brittle masses. For medicinal purposes, the pale resin is preferred.

Medicinal Use: Used principally in ointments and plasters. The ointment is used in cases of boils and ulcers as a stimulant.

Preparations: Emp. Plumb. et Coloph. in Mass, B.P.C.; Emp. Plumb. et Sap. in Mass B.P.C.; Resin Carbolisat. B.P.C. 1949; Ung. Coloph. B.P.C. (previously Ung. Resinae B.P. 1914).

Domestic Use: It is used in the arts. Colophony is used also to apply to the bow of the violin.

COLTSFOOT

Tussilago farfara, Linn.
Fam. Compositae

Synonyms: Coughwort, Horsehoof, Foal's Foot, Bull's Foot.

Habitat: A common wild plant in Europe and the British Isles, growing by brooks and rivers and in wet places.

Flowering Time: Early spring. The flowers fade before the appearance of the leaves.

Description: Leaves hoof-shaped with angular teeth on the margins, about 4 in. in diameter, long-stalked, green above, coated with matted, long white hairs, beneath and on the upper surface when young. Taste, mucilaginous, bitterish, and slightly astringent. The leaves appear much later than the bright yellow flowers.

Parts Used: Leaves, flowers.

Medicinal Use: Demulcent, expectorant. This is one of the most popular of cough remedies, and is generally given in conjunction with one or two other herbs possessing pectoral qualities, such as Horehound, Marshmallow, Ground Ivy, etc. A decoction is made of 1 oz of leaves in 1 qt of water boiled down to 1 pt, and is taken in teacupful doses sweetened. The dried leaves have been used for smoking in pulmonary complaints.

Preparations: Leaves: Liq. ext.: Dose, ½–1 dr; Solid Ext.: Dose, 5–10 gr.
Flowers: Ext. Tussilag. Liq.: Dose, 10–30 min; Syr. Tussilag.: Dose, ½–2 dr.

COLUMBO, AMERICAN

Frasera carolinensis, Walt.
Fam. Gentianaceae

Synonyms: *Frasera walteri*, *Frasera canadensis*.

Habitat: U.S.A. and Canada.

Description: Root in pieces 3–4 in. long and about ½–1 in. thick, often split longitudinally, the thick bark overlapping on the edges, pale brownish-grey and transversely wrinkled externally above and longitudinally below. Transverse section pale yellowish brown or fawn colour. Fracture short and rather spongy. Taste, sweetish then bitter; flavour resembling Gentian.

Part Used: Root.

Medicinal Use: Tonic, stimulant. This drug is a gentle stimulant and may be serviceable in all cases where a bitter tonic is required, as it gives tone to the whole system and is reputed to relieve obstinate constipation. The infusion may be taken in doses of a wineglassful three to four times a day. The dose of the powder is from 20–60 gr. It is sometimes used as a substitute for Calumba Root.

Preparation: Fraserin: Dose, 1–3 gr.

COMBRETUM

Combretum sundaicum, Miq.
Fam. Combretaceae

Synonyms: Opium Antidote, Jungle Weed.

Habitat: China.

Description: Leaves 4–5 in. long and about 2½ in. broad, with 8–10 lateral spreading nerves, perforated in the axils, surface minutely scaly on the young leaves. Taste, slightly astringent and tea-like; odour, none.

Part Used: Herb.

Medicinal Use: It has been used in China for treatment of the Opium habit but its action is uncertain. Other species of the same plant have been used to poison arrows.

COMFREY

Symphytum officinale, Linn.
Fam. Boraginaceae

Synonyms: Blackwort, Nipbone, Knitbone, Consolida.
Habitat: It grows by riversides and in moist places throughout the country.
Flowering Time: June or July.
Description: The plant has large, hairy or prickly leaves at the base growing smaller the higher they are on the stalk, which is hollow and hairy and growing to about 3 ft in height, bearing at the top spikes of white flowers. The root is brownish black, deeply wrinkled, and is seen in commerce in pieces 3–6 in. long and $\frac{1}{2}$–$\frac{3}{4}$ in. thick, greyish and horny internally. Fracture short. Transverse section showing a thick bark, short wood bundles, and broad medullary rays. Taste, sweetish, mucilaginous, and faintly astringent; odour, none.
Parts Used: Root, leaves.
Medicinal Use: Demulcent, astringent. Is very highly esteemed as a remedy in all pulmonary complaints, and hemoptysis, and forms an ingredient in a large number of herbal preparations. Wherever a mucilaginous medicine is required this may be given. Has been used of late by the medical profession as a poultice to promote healing of obstinate ulcerous wounds. A decoction is made by boiling $\frac{1}{2}$–1 oz of crushed root in 1 qt of water or milk. Dose, a wineglassful. The leaves are preferably taken as an infusion prepared in the usual manner. Comfrey leaves subdue every kind of inflammatory swelling when used as a fomentation. The synonym Consolida has arisen because of its reputation to knit together broken bones and flesh. Culpeper states that: ". . . if they (the roots) be boiled with dissevered pieces of flesh in a pot, it will join them together again." Also: "The roots of Comfrey taken fresh, beaten small and spread upon leather, and laid upon any place troubled with the gout doth presently give ease of the pains. . . ."
Preparation: Liquid extract: Dose, $\frac{1}{2}$–2 dr.

CONDURANGO

Marsdenia condurango, Nichols.
Fam. Asclepiadaceae

Synonyms: *Gonolobus condurango* (Triana), Eagle-vine.
Habitat: Ecuador.
Description: In quilled pieces 2–4 in. long, about $\frac{1}{2}$ in. in diameter, and $\frac{1}{12}$–$\frac{1}{4}$ in. thick. Outer surface brownish grey, with scattered warts of the

same colour. Transverse fracture yellowish white, granular, with scattered, fine silky fibres. Taste, bitter and somewhat acrid, and faintly aromatic.

Part Used: Bark.

Medicinal Use: Alterative, stomachic, aromatic.

Preparations: Powdered bark: Dose, $\frac{1}{4}$–1 dr; Liquid extract: Dose, $\frac{1}{2}$–1 dr.

CONTRAYERVA

Dorstenia contrayerva, Linn.
and other varieties of *Dorstenia*
Fam. Moraceae

Habitat: Mexico, West Indies, Peru.

Description: Rhizome about 1–1$\frac{1}{2}$ in. long and $\frac{3}{8}$ in. thick reddish brown, rough with leaf scars, nearly cylindrical, tapering suddenly at the end into a tail-like root furnished with numerous curled, wiry, reddish-brown rootlets, and 2–3 in. long. Transverse section horny, showing a thick bark, narrow, interrupting ring of wood, and a large horny pith. Taste, slightly aromatic, becoming acrid on mastication, causing a flow of saliva; odour not unpleasant.

Part Used: Rhizome.

Medicinal Use: Diaphoretic, stimulant. These properties make it a good remedy in typhus fever, dysentery, and skin diseases. The powder is taken in doses of 30 gr, but the infusion of 1 oz in 1 pt of boiling water is the best form of administration.

Joseph Miller describes this root as cordial and alexipharmic. It is said by him to resist the bites of venomous creatures. The name Contrayerva in Spanish signifies counter-poison or antidote.

COOLWORT

Tiarella cordifolia, Linn.
Fam. Saxifragaceae

Synonym: Mitrewort.

Habitat: America.

Description: Leaves with long, slender stalks, heart-shaped, 2$\frac{1}{2}$–4$\frac{1}{2}$ in. wide, radiate veined with 5–12 sharp lobes, which are irregularly toothed, the teeth having sharp points. Taste, faintly astringent; inodorous.

Part Used: Herb.

Medicinal Use: Diuretic, tonic. In cases of gravel, suppression of urine, and most complaints affecting the urinary organs, it is very useful. In dyspepsia and liver disorders it acts as a tonic and counteracts the acidity of the stomach. The infusion of 1 oz to 1 pt of boiling water is taken frequently in doses of a wineglassful.

COPAIBA

Copaifera langsdorffii, Desf.
and other species
Fam. Leguminosae

Synonyms: Copaiva, Capivi, Balsam Copaiva, Balsam Capivi.

Habitat: Brazil and north of S. America.

Description: The tree from which it is obtained is described as reaching 100 m in height. It is tapped to obtain the oleoresin, which differs much in appearance and fluidity. The Para kind is yellowish and comparatively fluid. The Maracaibo and Maranham varieties are thicker and fluorescent, and of a redder tint. The former contains more volatile oil, from 60–90 per cent, the latter more resin and only 40 per cent of oil. The thinner kinds are usually preferred in this country, the thicker in Germany.

Part Used: Oleoresin.

Medicinal Use: This drug was introduced into Europe in the seventeenth century. The action is stimulant, diuretic, cathartic. Used in excessive mucous discharges, as in gleet, leucorrhoea, chronic catarrh of bladder, etc. On account of taste is generally given in pill or capsule form, mostly in combination with alkalines or Santal Oil, Cubebs, etc. Dose, B.P.C. 1949, 10–30 min.

Preparations: Ol. Copaib.: Dose, 5–20 min; Liq. Copaib.: Dose, 1–2 dr; Liq. Copaib. Buchu et Cubeb.: Dose, 1–2 dr; Liq. Copaib. Buchu et Cubeb. c. Ol. Santal: Dose, 1–2 dr; Liq. Copaib. et Ol. Santal: Dose, 1–2 dr.

CORIANDER

Coriandrum sativum, Linn.
Fam. Umbelliferae

Habitat: Temperate Europe, Africa, Malta, and India.

Flowering Time: July and August.

Description: The fruits are globular, about $\frac{1}{8}$ in. in diameter with fine longitudinal ridges, separable into two halves (mericarps), each of which is concave internally and shows two brown, longitudinal oil cells (vittae). Taste, aromatic; odour, when crushed, characteristic. Unripe fruits have a fetid odour, resembling rubber.

Part Used: Fruit.

Medicinal Use: Stimulant, carminative. Mostly used as a flavouring and to prevent griping.

Preparations: Powdered fruit: Dose, 5–15 gr; Liquid extract: Dose, 5–30 min; Ol. Coriand. B.P.: Dose, 1–3 min; Sp. Aurant. Co. B.P.C.

Biblical References: Exodus XVI, 31; Numbers XI, 7.

CORN ERGOT

Ustilago maydis, Léveillé
Fam. Ustilaginaceae

Synonyms: Cornsmut, Cornbrand, Ustilago.

Description: A blackish powder in irregular, globose masses, somewhat lobed, and sometimes 6 in. or more in thickness. Powder consisting of innumerable fungus spores, with portions of the blackish, enclosing membrane. The spores are rounded, with a rough surface, as seen under the microscope. Taste, unpleasant; odour, heavy. It should be kept dry, and obtained fresh every year. The name Cornsmut is more applicable, as the name Ergot is applied to a solid form of fungus mycelium (*see* Ergot).

Part Used: Fungus.

Medicinal Use: Emmenagogue, parturient. A favourite remedy of Dr. Ellingwood in labour, post-partum haemorrhages, and haemorrhages of lungs, bowels, etc. Useful in spermatorrhoea, amenorrhoea, dysmenorrhoea, and other menstrual derangements. Dose, 1–20 gr.

Preparation: Liquid extract: Dose, $\frac{1}{2}$–2 dr.

CORNFLOWER

Centaurea cyanus, Linn.
Fam. Compositae

Synonyms: Bluebottle, Blueblow, Hurtsickle, Bluet (French). According to Culpeper it is called Hurtsickle because it turns the edges of the sickles that reap the corn.

Habitat: This plant grows wild, particularly in cornfields, but not in fields of peas or beans. It is also cultivated in gardens.

Flowering Time: It flowers from the beginning of May to the end of August.

Description: The flower heads are globular with closely overlapping fringed scales and florets. The florets are usually bright blue but other colours have been cultivated. They are tubular and the outer ones trumpet-shaped and seven-lobed.

Part Used: Flowers.

Medicinal Use: Today the Cornflower is rarely used in medicine except on occasions as a tonic and stimulant, although the ancient herbalists gave it many uses including its application to the bites of venomous beasts. A preparation known as *Eau de Casselunette* (break-spectacle water) used to be made from the flowers and many years ago appeared in the Parisian Codex. It was said to be an excellent remedy for the inflammation of the eyes and for dimness of eyesight.

Domestic Use: An ink was at one time prepared from the juice of the flowers to which alum was added. A similar preparation was used for dyeing cloth but it was found not to be permanent.

CORN SILK

Zea mays, Linn.
Fam. Graminaceae

Synonym: *Stigmata maidis.*

Description: Fine, silky, yellowish threads about 6 in. long and $\frac{1}{20}$ in. in diameter, finely hairy, consisting of the stigmas from the female flowers of maize. Taste, sweetish; odour, none.

Part Used: Flower pistils of Maize.

Medicinal Use: Demulcent, diuretic. Recommended as a valuable remedy in many urinary troubles, bladder affections, etc. Especially useful in purulent decomposition of urine in the bladder. The infusion of 2 oz in 1 pt of boiling water is a most active preparation, and should be freely taken.

Preparation: Liquid extract: Dose, $\frac{1}{2}$–2 dr.

CORSICAN MOSS

Alsidium helminthocorton, Kütz.
Fam. Fucaceae

Synonym: *Fucus helminthocorton*, Linn.

Habitat: North Atlantic.

Description: In tangled tufts of slender, brownish-white, cylindrical threads, showing under the microscope transverse series of small, oblong cells which give it a striated appearance. Taste, saline; odour, that of seaweed.

Medicinal Use: Anthelmintic, vermifuge. Acts very powerfully on lumbricoid intestinal worms. The dose is from 10–60 gr taken with honey, treacle, syrup, or made up as an infusion.

COTO

Various species of *Nectandra*
Fam. Lauraceae

Synonym: Paracoto.

Habitat: Bolivia.

Description: Genuine Coto Bark is no longer to be met with in commerce. Paracoto Bark, which is now very rare in commerce, occurs in curved, thick pieces 4–6 in. or more long, and about 2½ in. wide, and ½–¾ in. thick, of a full brown colour, a more or less corky outer surface, sometimes with patches of whitish epidermis, and a rough, coarsely striated inner surface. The transverse section shows numerous small groups of stone cells. Taste, hot and biting; flavour aromatic. The edges of the section, both transverse and longitudinal, if kept in a bottle, become coated with a fine, whitish, crystalline efflorescence.

Part Used: Bark.

Medicinal Use: Antiseptic, astringent. Used with good results in intestinal catarrh, diarrhoea, and dysentery. A decoction of 1 oz of bark in 1 pt of boiling water may be taken in tablespoonful doses or more as required.

Preparations: Powdered bark: Dose, 1–8 gr; Ext. Coto Liq.: Dose, 5–15 min; Tinct. Coto: Dose, 10–30 min.

COTTON ROOT

Gossypium herbaceum, Linn.
(and other species)
Fam. Malvaceae

Habitat: Greece, Turkey, Sicily, and Malta.

Flowering Time: June.

Description: In flexible or quilled strips, brownish yellow externally with faint, longitudinal ridges or meshes, circular black dots or short transverse lines and brownish-orange spots where the epidermal surface is abraded. Inner surface whitish, with a silky lustre. Inner bark of long, tough fibres, separable in papery layers. Taste, faintly acrid and astringent.

Part Used: Bark of root.

Medicinal Use: Emmenagogue, parturient, oxytocic. Said to contract the uterus in a more effective and safe manner than ergot. Used in cases of difficult or obstructed menstruation. It seems especially useful in sexual lassitude. An infusion of 2 oz to 1 pt of boiling water is taken in wineglassful doses.

Preparations: Dec. Gossyp. Cort.: Dose, ½–2 fl oz; Ext. Gossyp. Cort. Liq.: Dose, ½–1 dr; Tinct. Gossyp. Cort.: Dose, ½–1 dr; Solid extract: Dose, 15–20 gr; Ol. Gossyp. Sem. B.P.C. 1949 (Cottonseed Oil).

COUCHGRASS

Agropyron repens, Beauv.
Fam. Graminaceae

Synonyms: Twitchgrass, Quickgrass, *Triticum repens*, Linn., and erroneously Dog's Grass, Agropyrum.

Habitat: It grows in many parts of the world and as Joseph Miller states ". . . and is too frequent in gardens, whence it is hard to extirpate it."

Description: Rhizome slender, tubular, about $\frac{1}{10}$ in. in diameter, stiff, shining pale yellow, smooth, with nodes at intervals of about an inch. It is met with in commerce, cut up into short lengths of $\frac{1}{8}$ and $\frac{1}{4}$ in. and dried. Taste, slightly sweet; odour, none.

SUBSTITUTES. The rhizome of *Cynodon dactylon*, or Dog's Grass, is frequently imported into England as *Triticum repens*. This contains abundance of starch, which may easily be detected by boiling and adding Tincture of Iodine, giving the usual black solution. The root is white and almost solid.

Part Used: Rhizome.

Medicinal Use: Diuretic, demulcent, aperient. Used in urinary and bladder complaints, cystitis, nephritis, etc. Also recommended in gout and rheumatism. The infusion, made from 1 oz in 1 pt of boiling water, is taken in wineglassful doses seveıal times daily for feverishness, etc.

Preparations: Dec. Agropyr.: Dose, $\frac{1}{2}$–2 fl oz; Ext. Agropyr. Liq.: Dose, 1–2 dr.

COWHAGE

Mucuna pruriens, D.C.
Fam. Leguminosae

Synonyms: Cowage, Cowitch, *Dolichos pruriens*, Linn.

Habitat: India, Africa, South America.

Description: The hairs of the pod are brownish, about $\frac{1}{10}$ in. long, and consist of a conical, sharply-pointed cell, about $\frac{1}{40}$ in. in diameter, barbed at the apex. Considerable caution should be used in handling this drug, as the hairs are extremely irritating to the skin.

Part Used: The hairs on the pods.

Medicinal Use: Anthelmintic, rubefacient. In doses of $\frac{1}{2}$–1 teaspoonful in honey, syrup, etc., it expels intestinal worms. In the form of an ointment it acts similarly to Croton Oil, producing no inconvenience.

Preparation: Dose of Powdered Cowhage, 10–60 gr.

COWSLIP

Primula veris, Linn.
Fam. Primulaceae

Synonym: Paigles, Peagles.
Habitat: A common wild flower in the woods in all parts of Great Britain.
Flowering Time: April and May.
Description: The corolla, which is the part used, is tubular and yellow and about $\frac{1}{2}$ in. across, but becomes green on drying; it is dilated near the throat, where it is folded and spotted with yellowish orange. The corolla is five-lobed and about $\frac{1}{2}$ in. in width. Taste, sweetish; odour, recalling that of apricots.
Part Used: Flower.
Medicinal Use: Sedative, antispasmodic. Useful in restlessness, insomnia, etc. *See also* Primrose.

Gerard writes: "An unguent made with the juice of Cowslips and oil of Linseed, cureth all scaldings or burnings with fire, water or otherwise."

CRAMP BARK

Viburnum opulus, Linn.
Fam. Caprifoliaceae

Synonyms: High Cranberry, Guelder Rose, Snowball Tree.
Habitat: Europe, Great Britain and America.
Description: A large bush growing to the height of 10 ft. The bark is thin, $\frac{1}{50}$–$\frac{1}{12}$ in. thick, in curved pieces, greyish brown externally, with scattered brownish warts (lenticels), faintly cracked longitudinally, inner surface pale brown, laminate. Fracture tough, with flat splinters. Taste, bitterish, slightly astringent.
Part Used: Bark.
Medicinal Use: Antispasmodic, nervine. As its name implies, it is very effectual in cases of cramp, convulsions, and spasms of all kinds and is held in high esteem by all who employ it. It is chiefly used in combination as a tincture, but may be given as a decoction by using $\frac{1}{2}$ oz in 1 pt of water. Dose, a tablespoonful to a wineglassful as required.
Preparations: Liquid extract: Dose, $\frac{1}{2}$–2 dr; Viburnin: Dose, 1–3 gr.

CRANESBILL, AMERICAN

Geranium maculatum, Linn.
Fam. Geraniaceae

Synonyms: Alumroot, Storksbill, Wild Geranium.
Habitat: U.S.A.
Description: Root about $1\frac{1}{2}$–2 in. long, $\frac{1}{4}$–$\frac{3}{8}$ in. thick, dull brown, hard, knotty, with small protuberances. Fracture short, pale brown or reddish,

with white dots. Taste, very astringent; odour, none. Cranesbill Herb (English) is the *Geranium dissectum*, Linn., and has similar properties to *G. maculatum*. The flowers of the English herb are blue and the petals drop off easily, the stem, 2–3 ft high, is swollen at the joints, and the seed pod, long, sharp, pointed, looking like a crane's bill.

Parts Used: Root, herb.

Medicinal Use: Styptic, astringent, tonic. The root possesses the greater astringency. The infusion of 1 oz of herb in 1 pt of boiling water is useful in infantile cholera, diarrhoea, etc. Adult dose, a wineglassful as required. The fluid extract of the root may be used to stop internal or external bleeding. It has a tonic and astringent action on the kidneys. An injection for leucorrhoea (whites) and for flooding is prepared by pouring a pint of boiling water upon 1 oz each crushed Cranesbill and Beth Root. The clear liquid is injected twice a day.

Preparations: Liquid extract: Dose, $\frac{1}{2}$–1 dr; Geranin: Dose, 1–3 gr.

CRAWLEY

Corallorhiza odontorhiza, Nutt.
Fam. Orchidaceae

Synonyms: Coral Root, Dragon's Claw, Chicken Toe.

Habitat: U.S.A.

Description: This is a parasitic, leafless herb. The rhizome appears in small brown, coral-like, branched pieces, about 1 in. long and $\frac{1}{12}$ in. in thickness, with minute warts and transverse scars. Fracture short, greyish, horny. Taste, sweetish then bitter; odour, strong and peculiar when fresh. Very liable to attacks of mites if kept long.

Part Used: Rhizome.

Medicinal Use: Diaphoretic, sedative, febrifuge. Of great value in the treatment of all fevers, pleurisy, etc., and may be relied upon in all cases to bring on free perspiration. As a warm infusion of 1 oz to 1 pt of boiling water, it may be taken as hot as bearable in doses of a small teacupful until perspiration is produced.

Preparation: Liquid extract: Dose, 15–30 drops.

CROSSWORT

Galium cruciata, Linn.
Fam. Rubiaceae

Synonyms: Yellow Bedstraw, Common Crosswort.

Habitat: Culpeper says: "It groweth in many moist grounds, as well as untilled places about London, in Hampstead church-yard, at Wye in Kent and sundry other places." It is in fact a common wild plant in the British Isles and Europe.

Flowering Time: May.

Description: Stem slender, about 1–2 ft long. Leaves, four in a whorl, elliptic, oblong, hairy. Flowers, yellow, in small clusters, about eight together in the axils of the upper leaves.

Part Used: Herb.

Medicinal Use: Principally it is used made into a salve for wounds. Culpeper writes: "It is a singular good wound herb, and is used inwardly not only to stay bleeding of wounds, but to consolidate them, as it doth outwardly any green wound which it quickly drieth up and healeth."

CROTON SEEDS

Croton tiglium, Linn.
Fam. Euphorbiaceae

Synonyms: Tiglium, *Tiglium officinale*, Klotsch.

Habitat: Malabar Coast. Indian Archipelago.

Description: Yellowish or reddish-brown, rather viscid oil. Taste, burning acid; odour, unpleasant. It should be classed with the poisons, as a dose of more than one drop internally is liable to prove dangerous. It can be separated by alcohol into a purgative portion which is not vesicatory, the portion soluble in alcohol containing the vesicatory and dangerous principle. The outer, brown layer of the seeds is easily removed, leaving a hard, black coat. The seeds generally have a mottled appearance.

Part Used: Oil expressed from the seeds.

Medicinal Use: Irritant, rubefacient, cathartic. Its action is prompt, and it frequently induces catharsis within an hour after taking. The smallness of the dose makes it valuable where large quantities of medicine cannot be tolerated. It is frequently used with Castor Oil or it may be administered in capsules or pills. The dose is ½–1 min. Externally Croton Oil is used for its counter-irritating and vesicant effects.

Preparation: Lin. Croton.

CUBEB

Piper cubeba, Linn.
Fam. Piperaceae

Synonym: Tailed Pepper.

Habitat: Java, Southern Borneo, and Sumatra.

Description: The fruit resembles black pepper in size and colour, but always tapers suddenly below into a stalk, and the taste is not pungent but warm, aromatic, and rather turpentiney. The seed has a minute embryo in a small cavity at the apex. If genuine, the crushed fruit turns crimson with strong sulphuric acid. A spurious kind, with a nutmeg odour, does not give this colour and is liable to produce poisonous symptoms.

Part Used: Unripe fruit.

Medicinal Use: Aromatic, diuretic, expectorant. A valuable remedy in cases of gleet, catarrh, and internal inflammations. Also used in coughs, bronchitis, and lung troubles generally. Has a stimulating effect upon the mucous membranes. The oil is generally given in capsule form and in combination with Copaiba, Santal Oil, etc. The fruit contains about 15 per cent of volatile oil.

Preparations: Powdered fruits: Dose, ½–1 dr; Ext. Cubeb Liq.: Dose, ½–1 dr; Oleores. Cubeb B.P.C. 1949: Dose, 5–30 min; Ol. Cubeb. B.P.C. 1949: Dose, 5–20 min; Tinct. Cubeb.: Dose, ½–1 dr; Cubeb. Bronchial troches.

CUCKOOPINT

Arum maculatum, Linn.
Fam. Araceae

Synonyms: Starchwort, Ramp, Lords and Ladies, Wake-Robin.

Habitat: Widely distributed over Europe and the British Isles.

Description: The plant consists of a one-leafed, erect, and pointed spathe, convolute at the base. The flower is enclosed in the spathe. Inside the spathe grows a club-shaped spadix of purple or buff colour, the lower part of which bears the flowering organs. The root, which is used medicinally, is ovoid and about the size of a hazel nut, showing annular scars left by the leaf basis and scars of rootlets below. The taste is acrid; odour, none.

Part Used: Root.

Medicinal Use: Diaphoretic, expectorant. It is a remedy internally and locally for a sore throat. The dose is 10–30 gr of the powdered root. Large doses produce gastric inflammation, and fatal effects have been recorded. At one time this root was official in the Dublin *Pharmacopoeia.*

Dioscorides states that the leaves are also used, but they must be eaten after they are dried and boiled. He further states that the root has a peculiar virtue against the gout "being laid on stamped with cow's dung."

Gerard writes: "Bears, after they have lain in their dens 40 days without any manner of sustenance but what they get with licking and sucking their own feet, do, as soon as they come forth eat the herb Cuckoo-pint; through the windy nature thereof, the hungry gut is opened and made fit again to receive sustenance; for by abstaining from food for so long a time the gut is shrunk and drawn close together, that in a manner it is quite shut up."

Gerard also states that "the most pure white starch is made from the roots of Cuckoo-pint; but most hurtful to the hands of the laundress that hath the handling of it, for it choppeth, blistereth and maketh the hands rough and rugged and withall smarting." The starch thus obtained was used to starch the lawn ruffs worn in the days of Queen Elizabeth.

CUDWEED

Gnaphalium uliginosum, Linn.
Fam. Compositae

Synonyms: Cottonweed, Cotton Dawes.

Habitat: It is a common plant growing chiefly in barren places in all parts of the country.

Flowering Time: June and July. The seeds ripen in August.

Description: Stems and underside of leaves white, downy, with appressed woolly hairs. Leaves linear, about $1\frac{1}{4}$ in. long and $\frac{1}{5}$ in. wide, not hairy above. Flowerheads in a corymb. Phyllaries linear, tapering, chaffy. Receptacle not hairy.

Part Used: Herb.

Medicinal Use: Astringent. An excellent remedy for quinsy. The infusion of 1 oz to 1 pt of boiling water should be taken internally in wineglassful doses, but also used as a gargle.

Gerard writes: "Gnaphalium boyled in strong lee, cleanseth the haire from nits and lice; also the herb being laid in ward-robes and presses keepeth apparell from moths. The fume or smoke of the herbe dried and taken with a funnell, being burned therein and received in such manner as we used to take tobacco that is with a crooked pipe made for the same purpose by the Potter, prevaileth against the cough of the lungs, the great ache or paine of the head and cleanseth the breast and inward parts."

Culpeper reports: "Pliny saith, the juice of the herb taken in wine and milk is a sovereign remedy against the mumps and quinsey . . . whosoever shall so take it shall never be troubled with that disease again."

According to Joseph Miller, Cudweed was so named because "It is given to cattle that have lost the ruminating faculty. . . ."

Preparation: Liquid extract: Dose, $\frac{1}{2}$–1 dr.

CUMMIN

Cuminum cyminum, Linn.
Fam. Umbelliferae

Habitat: Indigenous to the Upper Nile. Cultivated along the Mediterranean coast and in India.

Description: Oblong cremocarps, light brown in colour. Each mericarp has five prominent ribs and four secondary ones. Odour and taste somewhat like aniseed but less sweet.

Part Used: Fruits.

Medicinal Use: Carminative. Used frequently in veterinary medicines.

Domestic Use: In the Middle Ages Cummin was used as a spice.

Biblical References: Isaiah XXVIII, 25, 27, 28; Matthew XXIII, 23.

CUP MOSS

Clandonia pyxidata, Fries

Synonym: Chin Cups.
Habitat: It grows in the British Isles and Europe on barren ground.
Description: The scyphi or wineglass-shaped portions of the plant are used. They are greyish white, about 1 in. long, with a hollow stem $\frac{1}{16}$–$\frac{1}{8}$ in. in diameter, and a terminal cup about $\frac{1}{4}$ in. wide; the scyphi are sometimes proliferous. Taste, mucilaginous and slightly sweet; odour, none. The plant is erroneously called a moss, as it belongs to the group of lichens.
Part Used: Plant.
Medicinal Use: Expectorant. Is excellent for children's coughs and whooping coughs. A decoction is made of 2 oz to 1 pt of water sweetened with honey.

Joseph Miller writes: "The moss is reckon'd a specific against the Hooping or Chin-Cough in children, being given in a decoction sweetened with sugar or some pectoral Syrup."

CUP-PLANT

Silphium perfoliatum, Linn.
Fam. Compositae

Synonyms: Indian Cup-plant, Ragged Cup.
Habitat: India.
Description: Rhizome cylindrical, crooked, elongated, pitted and rough, with small roots; the transverse section exhibits large resin cells.
Part Used: Rhizome.
Medicinal Use: Tonic, diaphoretic, alterative. As a general restorative, it has been found useful, also in fevers and spleen and liver affections. The decoction of the powdered root may be given in wineglassful doses.

D

DAMIANA

Turnera diffusa, Willd.
var. Aphrodisiaca, Urb.
Fam. Turneraceae

Habitat: Indigenous to Texas and Mexico. It is also found in other parts of sub-tropical America and Africa.

Description: Leaves alternate, linear, wedge-shaped, shortly stalked, hairy, about $\frac{3}{4}$–1 in. long and $\frac{1}{8}$–$\frac{1}{4}$ in. broad, with a few serrate teeth, having recurved margins. Taste, bitter, aromatic, with a fig-like flavour.

Part Used: Leaves.

Medicinal Use: Aphrodisiac, diuretic, tonic.

Preparations: Ext. Damian: Dose, 5–10 gr; Ext. Damian. Liq.: Dose, $\frac{1}{2}$–1 dr; Mist. Damian. Co.: Dose, 1–2 dr.

DAMIANA is very largely prescribed on account of its aphrodisiac qualities, and there is no doubt that it has a very great general and beneficial action on the reproductive organs. It also acts as a tonic to the nervous system.

DANDELION

Taraxacum officinale, Wiggers.
Fam. Compositae

Synonyms: *Taraxacum dens-leonis*, Desf., *Leontodon taraxacum*, Linn.

Habitat: Widely distributed over most of the world as a troublesome weed.

Flowering Time: Early summer and then for most of the year.

Description: The Dandelion plant is so well known it needs no description. The root is collected in the autumn.

Parts Used: Root and leaves.

Medicinal Use: Diuretic, tonic, and slightly aperient. It is chiefly used in kidney and liver disorders, and is perhaps one of the most generally prescribed remedies. It may be given in any form, but its beneficial action is best obtained when combined with other agents.

Preparations: Ext. Tarax.: Dose, 5–15 gr; Ext. Tarax. Liq. B.P.C. 1949: Dose, ½–1 dr; Succ. Tarax. B.P.C. 1949: Dose, 1–2 dr.
Domestic Use: The young leaves are used in salads.

A PLEASANT way of taking dandelion is in the form of a substitute for coffee. The roasted roots are ground and used as ordinary coffee, giving a beverage tasting much like the original article, and which certainly possesses most beneficial properties in cases of dyspepsia, gout, and rheumatism.

DEER'S TONGUE

Liatris odoratissima, Willd.
Fam. Orchidaceae

Synonyms: Vanilla Leaf, Wild Vanilla, *Trilisia odoratissima*, Cass.
Habitat: America.
Description: Leaves varying in size from the base of the plant upwards. Root leaves fleshy, 4–10 in. long, obovate-lanceolate, tapering below into a flattened stalk. Stem leaves oblong, clasping the stem at their base. The dried leaves have a strong odour of new-mown hay.
Part Used: Leaves.
Medicinal Use: Diuretic, stimulant, tonic.
Domestic Use: Owing to the sweet smell of the leaves, they are used in sachets and as a flavouring to tobacco.

DEVIL'S BIT

Scabiosa succisa, Linn.
Fam. Compositae

Synonym: Ofbit.
Habitat: It grows in meadows and fields in many parts of Great Britain.
Flowering Time: August.
Description: Leaves opposite, stalked, oval, lanceolate, with scattered one-celled glands. Florets purplish, with four lobes. Receptacle hairy. Stems often purplish.

Culpeper says: "The root was longer until the devil bit it away, envying its usefulness to mankind."

Part Used: Herb.
Medicinal Use: Diaphoretic, demulcent, febrifuge. Makes a useful tea for coughs, fevers, and internal inflammations. This remedy is generally given in combination with others. The infusion of 1 oz to 1 pt of boiling water is taken in wineglassful doses, frequently repeated.

Culpeper writes: "The herb (All that the devil hath left of it) being boiled in wine and drank is very powerful against the plague and all pestilential diseases and fevers, poisons also, and the bitings of venemous beasts. It helps those that are inwardly bruised by any casualty or outwardly by falls or blows. . . ."

DILL

Anethum graveolens, Linn.
Fam. Umbelliferae

Synonyms: Dill Seed, Dill Fruit, *Peucedanum graveolens*, Benth.

Habitat: Indigenous to the Mediterranean districts and South Russia. Cultivated in England and Europe.

Flowering Time: July and August.

Description: Fruits oval, compressed, winged, about $\frac{1}{10}$ in. wide, with three longitudinal ridges on the back, and three dark lines or oil cells (vittae) between them, and two on the flat surface. Taste, aromatic, resembling caraway, but distinct. Indian Dill Seed is narrower and more convex, with paler, more distinct ridges, and narrower wings. The essential oil it contains is not identical with that of European Dill.

Part Used: Dried ripe fruit.

Medicinal Use: Carminative, stomachic. In children's complaints, such as flatulence, disordered digestion, etc., it is an excellent remedy, mostly given in the form of Dillwater. The oil may also be administered in doses of 1–5 drops on sugar.

Preparations: Aq. Aneth. Conc. B.P.: Dose, 5–15 min; Aq. Aneth. Dest. B.P.C. 1949: Dose, $\frac{1}{2}$–1 dr; Ol. Aneth. B.P.: Dose, 1–3 min.

DODDER

Cuscuta epithymum, Murr.
Fam. Convolvulaceae

Synonyms: Lesser Dodder, Dodder of Thyme, Hell-weed, Devil's Guts.

Habitat: A parasite growing in most parts of the world.

Description: Stem thread-like, curled and twisted, without leaves, but with small, globular clusters of flowers, about $\frac{1}{6}$–$\frac{1}{4}$ in. in diameter at intervals. Taste, saline and slightly acrid; odour, none.

Part Used: Herb.

Medicinal Use: Hepatic, laxative. Has been used in urinary complaints, kidney, spleen, and liver diseases.

Culpeper writes: "All Dodders are under Saturn. Tell me not of physicians crying up Epithymum, or that Dodder which grows upon

Thyme . . . he is a physician indeed, that hath wit enough to choose the Dodder according to the nature of the disease and humour peccant. We confess Thyme is the hottest herb it usually grows upon; and therefore that which grows upon Thyme is hotter than that which grows upon cold herbs; for it draws nourishment from what it grows upon, as well as from the earth where its root is, and thus you see old Saturn is wise enough to have two strings to his bow."

DOG-ROSE

Rosa canina, Linn.
Fam. Rosaceae

Synonyms: Wild Briar, Hip Tree, Cynosbatos.

Habitat: Europe and parts of Asia, North Africa, British Isles.

Flowering Time: June. The hips are ready for gathering at the end of September.

Description: Fruits oval, fleshy, hollow, scarlet when fresh, blackish when dried, with remains of the calyx teeth at the apex, seeds angular, whitish, densely covered with hairs. Taste of fruit, sweetish and acidulous.

Part Used: The ripe fruit.

Medicinal Use: Hips contain invert sugar, Citric Acid, Malic Acid, and from 0·4–1·0 per cent of Ascorbic Acid (Vitamin C). The latter makes it suitable for infants and children specially when undernourished or bottle fed. It is usually given in the form of a syrup.

A conserve made from the ripe fruit was at one time official. It makes an excellent material for binding pill masses.

Preparations: Conf. Ros. Can.; Syr. Ros. Can.

Biblical References: Judges VIII, 7; Isaiah V, 6, XXVII, 4, XXXII, 13, LV, 13; Ezekiel II, 6; Micah VII, 4. In two passages the original word means both scorpion and briar and it is almost certain that the passages should read ". . . but I will chastise you with scourges of briars."

DRAGON'S BLOOD

Daemonorops propinquus, Becc.
(and other species)
Fam. Palmae

Synonyms: *Sanguis draconis*, *Daemonorops draco*, Blume.

Habitat: Malaya, Sumatra.

Description: The plant produces small fruits the size of a cherry covered with scales from which exudes a red resin. This is mixed with water and melted, and is then poured into a cloth and pressed. The rounded mass or pudding bears the impress of the cloth and is known as lump Dragon's Blood. Sometimes it is imported in sticks wrapped in leaves and is called Reed, or in tears known as Zanzibar and Singapore Drop Dragon's Blood.

Part Used: Resin.

Medicinal Use: Astringent. It has been used for diarrhoea and dysentery, but is not much used in medicine today.

Domestic Use: As a colouring agent in varnishes and stains.

DWARF ELDER

Sambucus ebulus, Linn.
Fam. Caprifoliaceae

Synonyms: Danewort, Wallwort, Ground Elder.

Habitat: Europe and the British Isles. Parkinson writes: ". . . where if it be gotten into a ground it will so creepe and runne therein, that it will hardly be gotten forth." It is a troublesome weed.

Flowering Time: July. The fruit ripens in September.

Description: Leaves pinnate, leaflets longer than those of the common Elder, often with small stipulets at their base. Flowers white with pink anthers, stem not woody. In the United States the name of Dwarf Elder is given to a different plant, viz. *Aralia hispida*, Vent., Fam. Araliaceae.

Part Used: Leaves.

Medicinal Use: Expectorant, diuretic, diaphoretic, purgative. It is said to be very efficacious in dropsy. Dose, of the decoction: a wineglassful three or four times a day.

DYER'S GREENWEED

Genista tinctoria, Linn.
Fam. Leguminosae

Synonyms: Greenweed, Dyer's Weed, Dyer's Broom, Woadwaxen.

Habitat: Europe. Cultivated in Great Britain and U.S.A.

Flowering Time: June and July.

Description: Stems almost unbranched, about 6–8 in. long, angular, with erect linear-lanceolate, sessile, hairless leaves, about $\frac{3}{4}$ in. long and $\frac{3}{16}$ in. broad. Flowers, yellow, papilionaceous, in spikes terminating the stem. Taste, bitter; odour, none.

Parts Used: Twigs, leaves.

Medicinal Use: Diuretic, cathartic, emetic. This plant has been successfully used as a remedy in dropsical affections; also in gout, rheumatism, and in albuminuria. The decoction may be given in wineglassful doses three to four times daily.

Domestic Use: A yellow dye has been made from the flowers.

E

ECHINACEA

Echinacea angustifolia, D.C.
Fam. Compositae

Synonyms: Black Sampson, Coneflower.

Habitat: Native to the prairie regions of America, west of Ohio.

Description: A perennial herb not growing to any great height. The dried rhizome is greyish-brown externally, more or less twisted, furrowed longitudinally, $\frac{1}{4}$–$\frac{1}{2}$ in. in diameter. The transverse section shows a thin, brown bark, a yellowish, porous wood in narrow wedges, with numerous slender, black fibres which give a greyish appearance to the broken surface. Taste, slightly aromatic, bitterish, with a tingling sensation like Pellitory Root; odour, none.

Part Used: Rhizome.

Medicinal Use: Alterative, antiseptic. Useful in all diseases due to impurities in blood, such as boils, carbuncles, gangrene, etc., internally and externally. Is a good appetizer and improves digestion. Used in fermentative dyspepsia. Of special importance in typhoid and other fevers.

Preparation: Liquid extract: Dose, $\frac{1}{2}$–1 dr.

ELDER

Sambucus nigra, Linn.
Fam. Caprifoliaceae

Synonyms: Black Elder, European Elder.

Habitat: Europe and the British Isles, growing frequently in hedges.

Flowering Time: May. The berries ripen in September.

Description: Bark light grey, soft and corky externally, with wide fissures, inner surface white and smooth. The transverse fracture shows a pale brown, outer portion in thin layers and a thinner, white, finely-radiate inner portion. Taste, sweetish at first, then bitter and nauseous. The flowers are wheel-shaped, small, with five oval, obtuse segments, pale yellow when fresh, becoming of a pale brownish-yellow when dried. Taste, mucilaginous; odour, slight, but characteristic.

Parts Used: Bark, flowers, berries.

Medicinal Use: Alterative, diuretic. An infusion of 1 oz of bark or flowers in 1 pt of water is taken in wineglassful doses. Has been successfully employed in epilepsy. Elderberry wine or juice taken hot is an old English remedy for colds. A mixture of Elder flowers and Peppermint taken as an infusion has long been known as a remedy for influenza.

ELECAMPANE

Inula helenium, Linn.
Fam. Compositae

Synonyms: Scabwort, Aunée (Fr.).

Habitat: Temperate Europe and Asia. Cultivated for medicinal use in some European countries. It is also cultivated in Great Britain.

Flowering Time: June and July.

Description: Roots light grey, hard, horny, in cylindrical pieces of varying length, usually $\frac{1}{3}$–$\frac{3}{4}$ in. in thickness, often attached to large sections of the crown of the root. The fracture is short, the transverse section shows a radiate structure, with numerous dark oil cells. Taste, aromatic, bitter, and acrid; the odour recalls that of Orris Root and Camphor. The root resembles that of Belladonna in colour and shape, but does not show a white surface when the epidermis is scraped as in Belladonna.

The plant is similar in appearance to Horseradish.

Part Used: Root.

Medicinal Use: Diaphoretic, diuretic, expectorant. Is used principally in combination with other remedies for cough, and pulmonary disorders generally. It is also alterative and tonic. The decoction of 1 oz to 1 pt of boiling water is taken in wineglassful doses.

Culpeper writes: "The distilled water of the leaves and roots together is very profitable to cleanse the skin of the face or other parts from any morphew spots or blemishes."

Preparations: Powdered root: Dose, $\frac{1}{2}$–1 dr; Liquid extract: Dose, $\frac{1}{2}$–1 dr; Inulin: Dose, 1–3 gr.

ELM

Ulmus campestris, Sm.
Fam. Ulmaceae

Synonyms: Common Elm, Field Elm.

Habitat: A common tree in Europe and the British Isles.

Flowering Time: Early spring, before the leaves appear.

Description: The inner bark only is used, deprived of the corky layer; it is in thin strips $\frac{1}{10}$–$\frac{1}{8}$ in. in thickness, externally of a rusty-brown colour, and paler on the inner surface. Fracture laminate and fibrous. Taste, mucilaginous, astringent, and faintly bitter; odour, none.

Part Used: Bark.

Medicinal Use: Astringent, demulcent, diuretic. Both Parkinson and Culpeper say that the bark ground with brine until it comes to the form of a poultice and laid on the place pained with the gout, gives great ease.

Biblical Reference: Hosea IV, 13.

EMBELIA

Embelia ribes, Burm.
Fam. Myrsinaceae

Habitat: India.

Description: The small, globular fruits are about the size of white pepper, reddish-brown, striated longitudinally, with a small beak at the apex. The single seed is horny with a mildewed appearance, due to a minute, crystalline powder; at the base it has a cup-like hollow. Taste, astringent and aromatic; odour, imperceptible. The above description applies to *Embelia robusta*, which is always supplied in commerce under the name of *E. ribes*. The latter is not striated longitudinally.

Part Used: Fruit.

Medicinal Use: Taenicide, carminative, diuretic. Used by the East Indian natives in dyspepsia and rheumatic affections; but its reputation is due to its action of expelling tapeworms. The fruits (commonly known as seeds) in powder are given in doses of 1–3 teaspoonfuls, with milk, upon an empty stomach, and followed by a purgative.

Preparations: Powdered fruit: Dose, 1–4 dr; Liquid extract: Dose, 1–4 dr.

EPHEDRA

Ephedra sinica, Stapf.
Ephedra equisetina, Bunge.
and *Ephedra gerardiana*, Wall. (Indian)
Fam. Ephedraceae

Synonym: Ma Huang.

Habitat: Northern China. The last named is a native of India.

Description: Slender, aerial, green stems jointed in cane-like branches of about 20 tufts about 6 in. high. Leaves reduced to sheaths surrounding the stems, which terminate in a sharp, recurved point with rough internodes.

Part Used: Stems.

Medicinal Use: Has been used in China since ancient times for asthma and hay fever. Chief constituent, an alkaloid, Ephedrine, which may be administered by the mouth or hypodermically.

Preparations: Ext. Ephed. Liq.: Dose, ¼–1 dr; Ephedrine B.P. (alkaloid); Ephed. Anhydros B.P.C. 1949; Ephed. Hydrochlor. B.P.: Dose, ¼–1 gr.

From Ephed. Hydrochlor. B.P. are made the following: Elix. Ephed. Hydrochlor. B.P.C.: Dose, 30–120 min; Elix. Caffein Iod. et Ephed.: Dose, 30–60 min; Mist. Bellad. et Ephed. pro Infant. B.P.C.: Dose, 60–120 min; Mist. Stramon. et Ephed. pro Infant. B.P.C. 1949: Dose, 60–120 min; Neb. Ephed. Aquos. B.P.C.; Tab. Ephed. Hydrochlor. B.P.

Ephedrine, Ephedrine Hydrochloride, Ephedrine Sulfate, and Ephedrine Sulfate Tablets are official in the U.S.P.

ERGOT

Claviceps purpurea, Tul.
Fam. Hypocreaceae

Synonyms: Ergot of Rye, Smut of Rye, Spurred Rye, *Secale cornutum*, Nees.

Description: The hard mycelium of the fungus known in commerce as Ergot, and formed at the expense of the grains of Rye, is purplish externally, $\frac{1}{3}$–$1\frac{1}{2}$ in. long, and $\frac{2}{16}$–$\frac{3}{16}$ in. in diameter, cylindrical, compressed, tapering, with rounded ends, and with a longitudinal fissure down each side. Fracture short and horny. Interior whitish, with a purple tinge towards the outside. Odour, disagreeable. Good Ergot should be brittle and show no signs of mites. It requires to be kept chemically dry, preferably in bottles having quicklime in a hollow stopper. The Spanish is larger than the Russian, and is more esteemed.

Part Used: Fungus.

Medicinal Use: Emmenagogue, haemostatic, uterine stimulant. Largely used in menstrual disorders, as in leucorrhoea, dysmenorrhoea, amenorrhoea, for its stimulating action. Also an admirable remedy in haemorrhage, flooding, intestinal bleeding, etc. Of value in spermatorrhoea, and enlarged prostate.

Preparations: Ext. Ergot. B.P.C. 1949: Dose, 1–3 gr; Ext. Ergot. Liq. B.P.C.: Dose, 10–20 min; Ergot. Praep. B.P.C.: Dose, $2\frac{1}{2}$–8 gr, from which is made Tab. Ergot. B.P.C.

The alkaloid Ergotamine is used for preparing Ergotam. Tart. B.P. and U.S.P.; Ergotox. Aethanosulph. B.P.C. 1949; Tab. Ergotamin. Tart. B.P.C. 1949 and U.S.P.

The Alkaloid Ergometrine is used to produce Ergometrin Maleas B.P. and U.S.P.; Inj. Ergomet. Maleat. B.P. and U.S.P.; Tab. Ergomet. Maleat. B.P. and U.S.P.

ERYNGO

Eryngium campestre, Linn.
Fam. Umbelliferae

Synonyms: Eringo, Sea Holly.

Habitat: It grows mainly on sandy soil near the sea in Great Britain and Europe. Gerard reports: "I found it growing at Whitstable in Kent, at Rie and Winchelsea, in Sussex and in Essex, at Landamer landing at Harwich, and upon Langtree Point. . . ."

Flowering Time: July.

Description: Root 2–4 in. long or more, transversely wrinkled, blackish-brown, crowned with the bristly remains of leaf-stalks, sometimes branched above. Fracture spongy, and coarsely fibrous, with a small, radiate, yellow centre. Taste, sweetish, mucilaginous; odour, none. The root of a similar plant, *Eryngium maritimum*, is also sold under the name of Eryngo Root.

Part Used: Root.

Medicinal Use: Diaphoretic, diuretic, expectorant. It is mostly used in uterine irritation, bladder diseases, painful micturition, with frequent and ineffective attempts to empty the bladder. Culpeper quotes an external use thus: "If the roots be bruised, and boiled in old hog's grease, or salted lard, and broken bones, thorns, etc., remaining in the flesh, they do not only draw them forth, but heal up the place again, gathering new flesh where it was consumed."

ETERNAL FLOWER

Helichrysum stoechas, D.C.
Fam. Compositae

Synonyms: *Gnaphalium stoechas*, Linn., *Gnaphalium citrinum*, Lam., *Stoechas citrina*, Goldilocks.

Habitat: A garden plant in Europe and the British Isles.

Flowering Time: August.

Description: Stem shrubby. Leaves linear, revolute at the margins, whitish, tomentose beneath and sometimes above. Flowerheads arranged in a crowded corymb, ovate, shortly stalked, with the outer scales of the involucre yellow and shining, ovate, rather acute. Taste, warm, pungent, bitterish; odour, when rubbed, agreeable.

Part Used: Tops.

Medicinal Use: Expectorant, deobstruent. Used in colds. Not very often used in medicine today.

Domestic Use: Because the dried flowers retain their colour they are used in Pot-Pourri.

EUCALYPTUS

Eucalyptus globulus, Labill.
Fam. Myrtaceae

Synonym: Blue Gum Tree.

Habitat: Victoria and Tasmania. It is cultivated in S. Europe.

Description: The leaves are tough, leathery, greyish green, scimitar-shaped (or, more rarely, when obtained from the younger leaves or shoots, ovate and stalkless), 4–6 in. long and about 1–1½ in. wide in the centre, shortly stalked and rounded at the base, with numerous transparent oil dots. Taste, aromatic and cooling; flavour, characteristic, somewhat camphoraceous.

Eucalyptus Oil is distilled from several varieties of Eucalyptus in addition to *E. globulus*, amongst these being *E. polybractea* and *E. dumosa*.

A citron-scented Eucalyptus is obtained from *E. maculata*, var. *citriodora*, Hook, in Queensland.

Parts Used: Leaves and the oil distilled from them.

Medicinal Use: Antiseptic, antispasmodic, stimulant. An Australian household remedy for many diseases and complaints. In England the oil is the preparation best known and most largely used. Its efficacy depends chiefly upon its antiseptic properties, which are extremely potent, though quite safe. In all fevers and febrile conditions the oil may be used freely externally and internally. It may be inhaled for asthma, diphtheria, sore throat, etc.

As a local application for ulcers, etc., 1 oz should be added to 1 pt of lukewarm water. Its effect is stimulating, antiseptic, and corrective. For local injections, ½ oz to 1 pt is sufficient. Physicians report not only quick healing follows, but all offensive odours cease immediately. In this connexion it is most valuable as a local application in growths and wounds. Internally the Fluid Extract is used in scarlet, typhoid, and intermittent fevers, and the oil is often applied to the body freely at the same time. In croup and spasmodic throat troubles it may be used in a similar way.

Preparations: Tinct. Eucalyp.: Dose, ¼–2 fl dr; Ol. Eucalyp. B.P.: Dose, 1–3 min; Ol. Eucalyp. U.S.P.; Dose, 8 min; Eucalyptol B.P.C. and U.S.P.: Dose, 1–3 min; Lin. Methyl. Sal. et Eucalyp. B.P.C.; Ung. Eucalyp. B.P.C. 1949; Vap. Menthol et Eucalyp. B.P.C.; Narist. Menthol et Thymol B.P.C.; Neb. Eucalyp. Co. B.P.C.

EUCALYPTUS KINO

Eucalyptus rostrata, Schlecht.
(and other species)
Fam. Myrtaceae

Synonyms: Kino Eucalyptus, Gum Eucalyptus, Red Gum.

Habitat: Madras and Ceylon.

Description: Dark, reddish brown, irregular pieces somewhat dusty. Taste, astringent; adheres to the teeth and colours the saliva red.

Part Used: The juice of the tree dried in the sun.

Medicinal Use: Astringent and tonic. Employed with benefit in all affections of the mucous membrane of the stomach and bowels, and is a valuable remedy in cases of chronic dysentery and diarrhoea. Also used in the form of a gargle or lozenge for the tonsils and throat.

Preparations: Powdered gum: Dose, 5–20 gr; Ext. Kino Eucalypt. Liq.: Dose, ½–1 dr; Tinct. Kino Eucalypt. 1949: Dose, 15–40 min; Troch. Kino Eucalypt. B.P.C. 1949: Each lozenge contains 1 gr.

EUPHORBIA

Euphorbia hirta, Linn.
Fam. Euphorbiaceae

Synonyms: Asthma-weed, Catshair, *Euphorbia pilulifera*.

Habitat: India and other tropical countries.

Description: Stem slender, cylindrical, with bristly hairs and opposite leaves, which are lanceolate, about $\frac{3}{4}$ in. long and $\frac{3}{8}$ in. wide, and toothed at the margin. Flowers very small, in dense, round clusters in the axils of the leaves. Seeds very small, reddish, oblong, angular, with a wrinkled surface. Taste, bitter; odour, none.

Part Used: Herb.

Medicinal Use: Anti-asthmatic pectoral. In Australia it is much esteemed as a remedy for coughs, bronchial and pulmonary disorders, but more especially for the prompt relief it affords in paroxysmal asthma. The infusion of $\frac{1}{2}$ oz in 1 pt of boiling water is taken in tablespoonful doses.

Preparations: Tincture 1 in 5: Dose, 10–30 min; Ext. Euphorb. Liq. B.P.C..: Dose, 2–5 min; Ext. Euphorb,: Dose, 1–2 gr; Syr. Cocillan. Co. B.P.C. 1949: Dose, 30–60 min.

EUPHORBIUM

Euphorbia resinifera, Berg.
Fam. Euphorbiaceae
(dried latex of the above plant)

Synonym: Gum Euphorbium.

Habitat: Native of Morocco, and grows near the Atlas mountains.

Description: The plant itself has fleshy quadrangular stems, covered in spines and resembles a Cactus. The latex is collected by making incisions in the stems and allowing the milky juice to harden by exposure. The dried latex, known as Euphorbium, appears in irregular pieces of a dull yellowish or brownish hue and waxy surface, usually about $\frac{1}{2}$ in. in diameter, often perforated where it has formed around the spines of the fleshy plant. Taste, extremely acrid and persistent. The dust excites violent sneezing and is dangerous to inhale.

Part Used: Dried latex.

Medicinal Use: It is employed as a drastic purgative, but is not now used internally to any extent. It was known to the ancient herbalists and Pliny mentions its drastic purging quality.

Commercial Use: In anti-fouling compositions for ships.

EVENING PRIMROSE

Oenothera biennis, Linn.
Fam. Onagraceae

Synonyms: Tree Primrose, Sun Drop.

Habitat: U.S.A. Cultivated in British and European gardens.

Description: Leaves oblong, lanceolate, 3–5 in. long and 1 in. or more wide, pointed, nearly entire at the margins, and furnished with short hairs. Taste, mucilaginous and slightly astringent; odour, none.

Parts Used: Leaves, bark.

Medicinal Use: Astringent, sedative. This drug has been tested in various directions, and Professor Scudder employed it with success in the treatment of gastro-intestinal disorders of a functional origin. It has also proved of service in dyspepsia, hepatic torpor, and in female disorders associated with pelvic fullness. It is also recommended for whooping cough and spasmodic asthma. The dose ranges from 5–30 gr.

Preparation: Liquid extract: Dose, ½–1 fl dr.

EYEBRIGHT

Euphrasia officinalis, Linn.
Fam. Scrophulariaceae

Habitat: A wild plant growing in meadows and grassy places in England and Europe.

Flowering Time: July.

Description: Stems about 4–6 in. long, often branched below. Leaves opposite below, alternate above, about ⅓ in. long and ¼ in. broad, lanceolate or nearly rhomboid above, with four to five teeth on each side. Flowers small, axillary, whitish, two-lipped, with a yellow throat and four stamens. Taste, saline, bitter, and slightly astringent.

Part Used: Herb.

Medicinal Use: Slightly tonic, astringent. It is employed principally as a remedy in diseases of the sight, weakness of the eye, ophthalmia, etc. Combined with Golden Seal it makes a most excellent lotion for general disorders of the eyes.

Culpeper writes: "If the herb was but as much used as it is neglected, it would half spoil the spectacle makers' trade; and a man would think, that reason should teach people to prefer the preservation of their natural before artificial spectacles; which that they may be instructed how to do, take the virtues of Eyebright as follows—

> The juice or distilled water of the Eyebright taken inwardly in white wine or broth or dropped into the eyes for divers days together, helps all infirmities of the eyes that cause dimness of sight."

Parkinson reports that Arnoldus de Villa nova in his Book on wines "much commendeth the wine made with Eyebright put into it when it is new made and before it worke (Which because we cannot make in our land, I could wish that the Eyebright might be tunned up with our strong beere in the same manner. . . .) to helpe the dimnesse of sight, and saith that the use thereof restored old men's sight to read small letters without spectacles that could hardly read great ones with their spectacles before. . . ."

Preparation: Liquid extract: Dose, 1 dr.

F

FENNEL *Foeniculum vulgare*, Mill.
Fam. Umbelliferae

Synonym: Hinojo.

Habitat: Countries bordering the Mediterranean, but also growing wild in most parts of Europe and the British Isles. It is also cultivated in Europe.

Flowering Time: June.

Description: The fruit is about $\frac{4}{10}$ in. long and $\frac{1}{10}$ in. broad, oblong, cylindrical, and slightly curved. Each half-fruit has four longitudinal ridges, the two lateral thicker than the dorsal. Taste, sweetish, aromatic; odour, similar. The colour varies from greenish to brownish, but the greenish are most esteemed. Indian and German Fennel are usually rather smaller and straighter, and not quite so rounded at the ends. Persian and Japanese Fennel are the smallest, and have a sweeter taste, resembling anise. Roumanian Seeds are dark and unfitted for use in Compound Liquorice Powder.

Part Used: Fruit.

Medicinal Use: Stimulant, carminative, stomachic. Generally added to other medicines for flavouring purposes and used as a carminative, and as such it forms part of the well-known Compound Liquorice Powder.

Preparations: Aq. Foenic. Conc.: Dose, 5–15 min; Aq. Foenic. Dest.: Dose, $\frac{1}{2}$–1 fl oz; Aq. Foenic. U.S.P.; Liquid extract: Dose, 5–30 min; Ol. Foenic. B.P.C. 1949 and U.S.P.: Dose, $\frac{1}{2}$–3 min; Pulv. Glycyrrh. Co. B.P.: Dose 60–120 gr.

Domestic Use: In Europe the young shoots are used as a vegetable.

FEVERBUSH *Garrya fremontii*, Torr.
Fam. Cornaceae

Synonyms: Skunkbush, California Feverbush.

Habitat: California, Oregon.

Description: Leaves short stalked, 1–3 in. long and nearly as broad, leathery, greyish green, entire at the margins, often with a point at the apex. Taste, bitter; odour, slight.

Part Used: Leaves.

Medicinal Use: Tonic, bitter, antiperiodic. The leaves are used in California as a substitute for Peruvian Bark and for similar purposes. The dose is 10–30 gr of the powder.

FEVERFEW *Chrysanthemum parthenium*, Bernh.
Fam. Compositae

Synonyms: *Pyrethrum parthenium*, Sm., Featherfew, Featherfoil.
Habitat: It grows wild in many parts of Europe and the British Isles.
Flowering Time: June and July.
Description: Stem finely furrowed, hairy. Leaves alternate, downy, with short hairs, or nearly smooth, about $4\frac{1}{2}$ in. long and 2 in. broad, bipinnatifid, with serrate margins, the leaf stalk flattened above, and convex beneath. Taste, bitter, nauseous; odour resembling that of tansy.
Part Used: Herb.
Medicinal Use: Aperient, carminative, bitter. It is largely used to promote the menses, expel worms, and in hysterical conditions. As an infusion of 1 oz to 1 pt of boiling water, it is taken frequently in doses of half a teacupful.

Culpeper states: "The powder of the herb taken in wine with some Oxymel purges both choler and phlegm and is available for those that are short winded, and are troubled with melancholy and weariness, or sadness of spirits." He also recommends it as "an especial remedy against opium when taken too liberally."
Preparation: Liquid extract: Dose, 1–2 dr.

FIG *Ficus carica*, Linn.
Fam. Moraceae

Habitat: Asia Minor and Syria. Cultivated in most Mediterranean countries. It is also cultivated in England but the fig does not always ripen.
Description: The fleshy inflorescence, or syconus, called a fig, contains the minute ovaries or so-called seeds, each of which is the result of one of the single female flowers with which the cavity is filled. The male flowers occupy the minute tabular orifice at the apex of the fig.
Part Used: Fleshy inflorescence (so-called fruit).
Medicinal Use: Nutritive, emollient, demulcent, laxative. The fresh and dried fruits are used in constipation, and they form part of the official confection of Senna. Roasted figs have a place in domestic practice as a poultice for gumboils, boils, and carbuncles. A poultice of dried figs in milk is said to remove unpleasant odours from ulcers.
Preparations: Syr. Fic. Co. B.P.C.: Dose, 30–120 min; Conf. Senn. B.P.C.: Dose, 60–120 gr; Conf. Senn. et Sulphur B.P.C. 1949: Dose, 60–120 gr.
Biblical References: Genesis III, 7; Numbers XIII, 23, XX, 5; Deuteronomy VIII, 8; Judges IX, 10 and 11; 1 Samuel XXV, 18, XXX, 12; I Kings IV, 25; 2 Kings XVIII, 31, XX, 7; 1 Chronicles XII, 40; Nehemiah XIII, 15; Psalm

cv, 33; Proverbs xxvii, 18; Song of Solomon ii, 13; Isaiah xxxiv, 4, xxxvi, 16; xxxviii, 21; Jeremiah v, 17, viii, 13, xxiv, 1, 2, 3, 5, 8, xxix, 17; Hosea ii, 12, ix, 10; Joel i, 7, 12, ii, 22; Amos iv, 9; Micah iv, 4; Nahum iii, 12; Habakkuk iii, 17; Haggai ii, 19; Zechariah iii, 10; Matthew vii, 16, xxi, 19, 20, 21, xxii, 32; Mark xiii, 28; Luke vi, 44, xiii, 6, xxi, 29; John i, 48, 50; James iii, 12; Revelation vi, 13.

FIGWORT

Scrophularia nodosa, Linn.
Fam. Scrophulariaceae

Synonyms: Rosenoble, Throatwort, Carpenter's Square, Scrofula Plant.
Habitat: A European and British wild plant.
Flowering Time: June.
Description: The herb has a square stem, opposite, stalked leaves, 4–5 in. long and 1½–2 in. broad, rounded, but unequal at the base and tapering to a point above, margins sharply but unequally serrate, the veins and veinlets prominent beneath and depressed above. Taste, bitter; odour, narcotic. The knotty rhizome and acutely-pointed leaves distinguish this from the water figwort (*S. aquatica*).
Part Used: Herb.
Medicinal Use: Diuretic, depurative, anodyne. This is called the Scrofula Plant, on account of its great value in all cutaneous eruptions, abscesses, wounds, etc. The leaves should be applied as a poultice, and an infusion of 1 oz to 1 pt of boiling water, taken internally in half-wineglassful doses.

Culpeper states: "Venus owns the herb, and the Celestial Bull will not deny it; therefore a better remedy cannot be for the King's Evil, because the Moon that rules the disease is exalted there."
Preparation: Liquid extract: Dose, 1–2 dr.

FIVE-LEAF-GRASS

Potentilla reptans, Linn.
Fam. Rosaceae

Synonyms: Cinquefoil, Fivefinger.
Habitat: A common wild plant growing in hedges.
Flowering Time: All the summer.
Description: Stem slender, creeping, with internodes 2–4 in. long or more, leafstalks 1–2 in. long, with five leaflets, the central one free, the two lateral joined near the base, obovate-obtuse, bluntly serrate, about 2 in. across and 1½ in. long, with scattered hairs on the veins and margins, veins prominent below. Taste, astringent; odour, none.
Parts Used: Herb, root.

Medicinal Use: Astringent, febrifuge. The infusion of 1 oz of herb in 1 pt of boiling water is used in wineglassful doses for diarrhoea, looseness of bowels, etc. Externally, as an astringent lotion.

According to Gerard: "The leaves are used among herbes appropriate for the same purpose to cure ruptures and burstings. The juyce of the roots while they be young and tender is given to be drunke against the diseases of the liver and lungs and all poyson."

Joseph Miller recommends the use of the root in the form of a gargle ". . . for sore mouths and ulcerated gums and to fasten loose teeth."

FLEABANE

Erigeron canadense, Linn.
Fam. Compositae

Synonyms: Canada Fleabane, Coltstail, Prideweed.

Habitat: There are several varieties of this plant growing in diverse places as far apart as America and Europe. In America it is a troublesome weed which gets amongst the Peppermint crops.

Flowering Time: June, July, and August.

Description: Stem unbranched, leaves oblanceolate, and short-stalked below, with five teeth, upper becoming linear and entire, usually 1–2 in. Flower heads, numerous, bell-shaped, about $\frac{1}{6}$ in. long and broad, whitish, shorter than the involucre, receptacle naked, fruits (achenes) flat, with fine, bristly pappus. Taste, astringent, aromatic, and bitter; odour, slight.

Parts Used: Herbs, seeds.

Medicinal Use: Astringent, diuretic, tonic. Considered efficient in diarrhoea, gravel, and in many kidney affections. The infusion is very serviceable in such cases, given in doses of a wineglassful to a teacupful. It owes its virtues to a volatile oil.

The herb is mentioned by Gerard, Parkinson, and others. Parkinson writes, talking of the leaves: "Galen saith . . . they are hot and dry in the third degree and therefore warmeth any place whereunto they are applied, whether used of themselves or boyled in oyle and anoynted . . . bound to the forehead is a great helpe to cure one of the frensie." He goes on to say that "If either Goats or Sheepe eate hereof it will kill them by any extremity of thirst."

Preparations: Oil: Dose, 2–5 drops; Liquid extract: Dose, $\frac{1}{2}$ dr.

FLUELLIN

Linaria elatine, Mill.
Fam. Scrophulariaceae

Habitat: A wild plant in Europe and Great Britain. Culpeper states: "They grow in the borders and other parts of corn-fields and fertile grounds, specially near Southfleet in Kent and at Buckworth, Hamerton, Rickmansworth in Huntingdonshire. . . ."

Flowering Time: June and July.

Description: A many-branched and partly-recumbent plant. Leaves round or oval and somewhat pointed and of a greyish-green colour. The flowers resemble Toad Flax and are yellow in colour.

Part Used: Herb.

Medicinal Use: Astringent. Recommended for internal bleeding, profuse menstruation, and bleeding of the nose. It consolidates and strengthens. The infusion (1 oz to 1 pt) may be taken internally or applied to wounds.

Culpeper describes it as a lunar herb and says: "The leaves bruised and applied with barley-meal to watering eyes that are hot and inflamed by defluxions from the head, helpeth them exceedingly."

FOENUGREEK

Trigonella foenum-graecum, Linn.
Fam. Leguminosae

Synonym: Fenugreek.

Habitat: N. Africa, India.

Description: The words *foenum-graecum* mean Greek hay and arise because of the appearance of the plant which has long slender stems. The seeds as they appear in commerce are brownish yellow, about $\frac{1}{8}$ in. long, oblong rhomboid, with a deep furrow almost dividing the seeds into two unequal lobes. Taste, recalling that of celery or lovage; odour, similar.

Part Used: Seeds.

Medicinal Use: Emollient. Used externally as a poultice in abscesses, boils, carbuncles, etc. Internally a decoction of 1 oz of seeds in 1 pt of water is used in inflamed conditions of stomach and intestines. Its chief use is as an ingredient in cattle and horse condiments.

Gerard says: "It is good to wash the head with the decoction of the seed, for it taketh away the scurfe, scales, nits, and all other suchlike imperfections."

Domestic Use: It is an ingredient in curry powders.

FOOL'S PARSLEY

Aethusa cynapium, Linn.
Fam. Umbelliferae

Synonyms: Dog Parsley, Dog Poison.

Habitat: A wild plant in Europe and Great Britain.

Flowering Time: July to September.

Description: Leaves resembling those of Hemlock, but smaller, and the ultimate segments have brown points. The distinguishing mark for Fool's

Parsley is a tag of three long, slender stripes hanging down at the base of each cluster of flowers.

Part Used: Herb.

Medicinal Use: Stomachic, sedative. In gastro-intestinal troubles of infants, this has been found very useful, also in cholera infantum, convulsions, and summer diarrhoea. Fool's Parsley has sometimes been mistaken for ordinary Parsley with unfortunate results. It should at all times be taken with caution. There are cases cited where Fool's Parsley has been eaten and caused pain and hardness in the stomach, giddiness, confusion of vision, and vomiting.

FOXGLOVE

Digitalis purpurea, Linn.
Fam. Scrophulariaceae

Synonym: Purple Foxglove. According to Prior, *Popular Names of British Plants* (1870), the name Foxglove is derived from the Anglo-Saxon, Foxes-glew, an ancient musical instrument with hanging bells.

Habitat: Europe, the British Isles.

Flowering Time: May and June.

Description: Root leaves 8 or 9 in. long or more, and 3–4 in. broad, tapering below into a winged stalk, the veins running down into the winged parts; vein at an acute angle to the midrib, prominent beneath and depressed on the upper surface giving the leaf a reticulated surface. Hairs short, forming a densely velvety surface below, but more scattered above, those on the leafstalks long and silky. The margins irregularly crenate. Taste, very bitter; odour of the dried leaves, tea-like.

Part Used: Leaves.

Medicinal Use: Cardiac tonic, sedative, diuretic. Used in cardiac complaints arising from kidney diseases; also in dropsy and urinary suppression. Owing to its cumulative action it should be used with great care. The infusion of 1 dr in 1 pt of boiling water is taken in teaspoonful to table-spoonful doses.

Gerard had not a high opinion of the use of this drug, saying: "The Fox-gloves, in that they are bitter, are hot and dry, with a certaine kinde of clensing qualitie joyned therewith; yet they are of no use, neither have they any place amongst medicines, according to the Antients."

Digitalis is a poison and should be used only under medical advice.

Preparations: Digit. Praep. B.P.: Dose, $\frac{1}{2}$–$1\frac{1}{2}$ gr; Digit. Pulverat. B.P.; Inf. Digit. Rec. B.P.C. 1949: Dose, Single administration, 1–4 fl oz; Repeated administrations, 90–300 min; Pil. Digit. Co. B.P.C.: Dose, 1 or 2 pills; Tab. Digit. Co. B.P.C.: Dose, 1 or 2 tablets; Tab. Digit. Praep. B.P. and U.S.P.; Tinct. Digit. B.P. and U.S.P.: Dose,

5–15 min; Digitalin B.P.C.: Dose, Single administration, ½–1 gr; Repeated dose, $\frac{1}{16}$–$\frac{1}{5}$ gr. subcutaneous injection; Inj. Digit. U.S.P.; Cap. Digit. U.S.P.; Digitoxin B.P.C.: Dose, $\frac{1}{600}$–$\frac{1}{60}$ gr; Digitoxin U.S.P.: Dose, $\frac{1}{600}$ gr; Inj. Digitox. B.P. and U.S.P.; Tab. Digitox. B.P. and U.S.P.

FRINGETREE

Chionanthus virginica, Linn.
Fam. Oleaceae

Synonyms: Old-man's Beard, Snowdrop Tree.

Habitat: Southern U.S.A.

Description: The root bark occurs in irregular, quilled pieces 2–3 in. long and about ⅛ in. thick, externally dull brown with irregular concave scars, the inner surface quite smooth and bright buff. The transverse fracture short, pale-buff colour, dense; the inner layer with projecting bundles of stone cells. Taste, very bitter; odour, none.

Part Used: Rootbark.

Medicinal Use: Alterative, diuretic, tonic. Used in bilious and typhoid fevers. Is prompt and efficacious in liver derangements, and also in jaundice and gall-stones. In female disorders, useful in conjunction with Pulsatilla and other remedies. The infusion of 1 oz to 1 pt of boiling water is taken in tablespoonful to wineglassful doses. Externally this is used as a lotion or injection.

Preparations: Liquid extract: Dose, 5–30 drops; Chionanthin: Dose, 1–3 gr.

FROSTWORT

Helianthemum canadense, Michx.
Fam. Cistaceae

Synonyms: Rock Rose, Frostweed, *Cistus canadensis*, Linn.

Habitat: Europe, Great Britain, and U.S.A.

Flowering Time: In Britain, July and August.

Description: Twigs, slender, purplish-brown, with opposite leaf scars. Leaves linear, oblong, about ⅜–⅝ in. long, greyish-green, due to a whitish covering of tufted hairs; fertile, apetalous flowers in small clusters. Fruit small, ovate, triangular, brown, polished, containing a few dull-brown, angular seeds. Taste, astringent and bitter; odour, none.

Part Used: Herb.

Medicinal Use: Alterative, tonic, astringent. Internally it is used as a cure for scrofula. The infusion of 1 oz to 1 pt of boiling water is taken freely in doses of a wineglassful. Also used externally as a wash for ulcers, etc.

Gerard writes: "Pliny writeth the Helianthemum growes . . . in the mountains of Cicilia neere the sea; saying further, that the wise men of these countries and the Kings of Persia do anoint their bodies herewith, boiled with Lion's fat, a little Saffron and Wine of Dates, that they may seem faire and Beautiful. . . ."

Preparation: Liquid extract: Dose, ½–1 dr.

FUMITORY

Fumaria officinalis, Linn.
Fam. Fumariaceae

Synonym: Earth Smoke (probably derived from the appearance of the foliage on a dewy summer morning, or as some suppose, due to its smoky smell).

Habitat: It is supposed to have originally been introduced from Asia or Greece, but is now a common plant to be found in cultivated fields and by the hedges in Europe and the British Isles.

Flowering Time: Throughout the summer.

Description: Stems angular. Leaves twice pinnate, the ultimate segments linear, obtuse or pointed, not hairy. Flowers slender, pink, in short spikes, irregular, with two bundles of three stamens each. Fruit, globular, depressed, containing one seed. Taste, bitter, saline and somewhat unpleasant.

Part Used: Herb.

Medicinal Use: Slightly tonic, diuretic, aperient. Used mainly in stomach derangements, liver complaints and skin affections. The infusion of 1 oz to 1 pt of water may be freely taken in doses of a wineglassful every three hours.

Gerard writes: "Dioscorides affirmeth that the juice of Fumitory, of that which groweth among Barley, with gum Arabic, doth take away unprofitable hairs that prick the eyes, growing upon the eye lids, the hairs that prick first plucked away, for it will not suffer others to grow in their place."

Culpeper writes: "The juice of the Fumitory and Docks mingled with vinegar and the places gently washed therewith, cures all sorts of scabs, pimples, blotches, wheals and pushes which arise on the face or hands or any other part of the body."

John Hill, M.D. (1756), says: "Some smoke the dried leaves in the manner of tobacco for disorders of the head with success."

Preparation: Liquid extract: Dose, ½–1 dr.

G

GALANGAL

Alpinia officinarum, Hance
Fam. Zingiberaceae

Synonyms: Galanga, East Indian Root, Lesser Galangal.
Habitat: Island of Hainan and the coast of S.E. China.
Description: It is a flag-like plant. The rhizome is dark reddish-brown, cylindrical, about $\frac{1}{2}$–$\frac{3}{4}$ in. in diameter and $1\frac{1}{2}$–3 in. long, marked at short intervals with raised rings or scars of leaf bases. Fracture hard and tough. The transversely cut surface is paler than the outside with a darker, central column. Taste, pungent and spicy; odour, agreeable, recalling that of ginger. Greater Galangal, imported from Java, is larger and paler and is less pungent, the botanical origin being *Alpina galanga*, Willd.
Part Used: Rhizome.
Medicinal Use: Carminative, stimulant. Is specially useful in dyspepsia, preventing fermentation and removing flatulence. The decoction of 1 oz in 1 pt of boiling water may be taken in tablespoonful to wineglassful doses. The powder is used as a snuff. It is sometimes used in cattle medicines.
Preparations: Powdered root: Dose, $\frac{1}{4}$–$\frac{1}{2}$ dr; Liquid extract: Dose, $\frac{1}{2}$–1 dr.
Domestic Use: Galangal has been used as a spice. In Russia it is said to be taken by the Tartars in tea.

GALBANUM

Ferula galbaniflua, Boiss. & Buhse
(and other species)
Fam. Umbelliferae

Synonym: Gum Galbanum.
Habitat: Persia and the Levant.
Description: The gum-resin is usually formed of an agglomeration of tears, some of which are translucent, and some pale bluish-green, and which are intermixed with transverse sections of the root (Levant), or mixed with fruits and stalks (Persian). The finest kind, not often obtainable, occurs in friable masses of loosely agglomerated, yellowish or brownish, small tears, opaque and yellowish white internally, with a slight musky as well as turpentiney odour, the latter odour prevailing in the commoner kind. A piece of Galbanum immersed in water will give a blue fluorescence if a drop of liquid ammonia is added, indicating the presence of umbelliferone.

Part Used: Gum-resin.

Medicinal Use: Stimulant, resolvent. It has been used internally in hysteria, rheumatism, chronic affections of mucous air passages, and is given in doses of 10–30 gr, mostly in emulsion. Externally it forms part of plasters and ointments.

Preparation: Pil. Galban. Co.: Dose, 1–2 pills.

Biblical Reference: Galbanum is mentioned once in the Bible along with other ingredients for making incense: Exodus xxx, 34.

GALE, SWEET

Myrica gale, Linn.
Fam. Myrticaceae

Synonyms: Dutch Myrtle, Bog Myrtle.

Habitat: Mediterranean countries, but cultivated in many others.

Description: Stem shrubby. Leaves leathery, lanceolate-obovate, about 1 in. long and $\frac{1}{2}$ in. wide, furnished with small resinous glands. Taste, aromatic, astringent; odour, pleasant, distinctive, recalling that of bay leaves.

Part Used: Shrub.

Medicinal Use: Aromatic, astringent.

GALLS

Quercus infectoria, Olivier
Fam. Fagaceae

Synonyms: Nutgalls, Blue Galls, *Gallae ceruleae*, Oak Galls.

Habitat: Turkey, Greece, and Syria.

Description: Galls are formed as a result of the bark being punctured by an insect for the laying of eggs, after which an excrescence grows. The plant itself is of the oak family but rarely grows to more than a shrub.

The Aleppo or Turkey Oak Galls are spherical from $\frac{4}{10}$–$\frac{8}{10}$ in. in diameter, smooth, in an irregular zone, bluish or olive green and heavy if the insect has not escaped, but perforated near the middle with a round hole, and yellowish-brown in colour and lighter in weight, when it has done so. Taste, very astringent, and slightly acid, afterwards sweet; odour, none. Contain 50–70 per cent tannic acid. Chinese and Japanese galls are grotesquely shaped, covered with a thick, grey, velvet down, and are borne by the *Rhus semialata*.

Part Used: The excrescence, commonly known as a gall.

Medicinal Use: Astringent. Have been used in dysentery, diarrhoea, cholera, and passive haemorrhages, etc. As an injection in leucorrhoea, etc., the infusion may be used. Also as a gargle in relaxed throat.

Preparations: Powdered galls: Dose, 10–20 gr; Tinct. Gall.: Dose, ½–2 dr; Liq. extract: Dose, 5–20 min; Ung. Gall. B.P.C.; Ung. Gall. c. Opio B.P.C.

Domestic Use: For generations Galls have been used for tanning owing to the large percentage of Tannic Acid contained in them.

GAMBOGE

Garcinia hanburyi, Hook, f.
Fam. Guttiferae

Synonyms: Camboge, Gutta Cambodia, Gutta Gamba.

Habitat: Siam, Cochin China.

Description: The gum-resin is imported in the form of cylindrical sticks 4–8 in. long and 1–1½ in. in diameter, bearing the striated markings of the interior of bamboo in which it is collected. The transverse fracture, if the Gamboge is of good quality, is clean and smooth, not gritty, deep orange brown, and opaque. Rubbed with water it gives a yellow emulsion. Fracture conchoidal. Taste, very acrid. The powder excites sneezing. Indian Gamboge is derived from *Garcinia morella*, Desr., and has similar properties to those of the Siam variety.

Part Used: Gum-resin.

Medicinal Use: Purgative. Is seldom employed alone, but acts well and safe in combination with cathartics, and is useful wherever such are needed, as it reinforces their action. Dose, ½–2 gr.

It was not introduced into England until the early seventeenth century and was therefore not well known by the early herbalists. Parkinson mentions it, calling it Cambugio quibusdam catharticum aureum, the golden yellow Indian purger.

GARLIC

Allium sativum, Linn.
Fam. Liliaceae

Description: It is a well-known plant in the kitchen garden. The bulb of garlic is compound containing, between membranous scales, a number of smaller bulbs or "cloves." Taste, like onions, but much stronger.

Part Used: Bulb.

Medicinal Use: Antiseptic, diaphoretic, diuretic, expectorant. Garlic juice is made into a syrup with honey or sugar and given with advantage in coughs, colds, and asthma. The oil is also administered in the form of gelatine capsules.

Gerard writes: "With Figge leaves and Cumin it is laid on against the bitings of the Mouse. . . ."

Preparations: Juice: Dose, 10–30 drops; Syrup: Dose, 1 dr; Tincture: Dose, ½–1 dr.

Domestic Use: Garlic is used largely on the Continent for the flavouring of food. The strong and objectionable odour clings to the breath. According to Culpeper this can be removed by chewing a few cummin seeds or a green bean or two.

Biblical References: Numbers XI, 5.

GELSEMIUM

Gelsemium sempervirens, Ait.
Fam. Loganiaceae

Synonyms: *Gelsemium nitidum*, Yellow Jasmine, Wild Woodbine.

Habitat: Southern United States.

Description: A climbing plant producing highly-scented yellow flowers. The root is often mixed with the underground stem, the latter distinguished by its distinct pith, the straight form, and the purplish, longitudinal lines on the bark. The root is usually more or less tortuous, brown and smooth, with a thin bark and woody centre composed of porous woody wedges, and rather broad medullary rays. Fracture, short and woody, showing in the bark a few thin projecting silky fibres. Taste, slightly bitter; odour, faintly aromatic. This plant must not be confused with the yellow flowering Jasmine cultivated in England and elsewhere.

Part Used: Root.

Medicinal Use: Arterial sedative, diaphoretic, febrifuge, antispasmodic. In small doses allays nervous excitement and irritation. Used in inflammation of bowels, diarrhoea, dysentery, but with great success in neuralgia, toothache, insomnia, wherever a sedative is called for. In pelvic disorders of women it is a favourite remedy. In large doses it depresses the nervous system and gives rise to convulsions and toxic symptoms.

Preparations: Fldext. U.S.P.: Dose, 5–10 drops; Solid extract: Dose, 1–2 gr; Tinct. Gelsem. B.P.C.: Dose, 5–15 drops; Gelsemin: Dose, ½–2 gr.

GENTIAN

Gentiana lutea, Linn.
Fam. Gentianaceae

Habitat: Mountainous parts of Europe.

Flowering Time: July.

Description: The root is cylindrical, brown, 1 ft or more in length, or broken up into shorter pieces, usually ½–1 in. thick, the upper portion marked with numerous rings, the lower longitudinally wrinkled, tough and flexible, internally of an orange-brown tint, uniformly spongy. Taste, very bitter; odour, strong and distinctive. When fresh the roots are almost white internally, but develop the brown colour and odour during the drying.

Part Used: Root.

Medicinal Use: Tonic. Deservedly the most popular of tonic medicines. Being a simple bitter it may be given in all cases of weakness of digestive organs, general debility, female weakness, hysteria, etc.

Culpeper writes: "They are under the dominion of Mars, and one of the principal herbs he is ruler of. They resist putrefactions, poison, and a more sure remedy cannot be found to prevent the pestilence than it is. . . ."

Parkinson writes of the esteem in which this plant was held by the Germans who made with it a treacle used as a counter-poison " . . . made of Gentian, Aristolochia, Bayberries and other things. . . ."

Preparations: Powdered root: Dose, 10–30 gr; Ext. Gent. B.P.C.: Dose, 2–8 gr; Inf. Gent. Co. B.P.: Dose, ½–1 fl oz; Inf. Gent. Co. Conc. B.P.: Dose, 30–60 min; Inf. Gent. Co. Rec. B.P.C.: Dose, ½–1 fl oz; Mist. Gent. Acid. B.P.C.: Dose, ½–1 fl oz; Mist. Gent. Acid. c. Nuc. Vom. B.P.C.: Dose, ½–1 fl oz; Mist. Gent. Acid. pro Infant. B.P.C. 1949: Dose, 60–120 min; Mist. Gent. Alk. B.P.C.: Dose, ½ fl oz; Mist. Gent. Alk. c. Nuc. Vom. B.P.C.: Dose, ½–1 fl oz; Mist. Gent. Alk. pro Infant. B.P.C. 1949: Dose, 60–120 min; Mist. Gent. c. Rheo. B.P.C. 1949: Dose, ½–1 fl oz; Mist. Gent. c. Rheo. pro Infant. B.P.C. 1949: Dose, 60–120 min; Tinct. Gent. Co. B.P.: Dose, 30–60 min; Tinct. Gent. Co. U.S.P.: Dose, 1 fl dr.

GENTIAN, ENGLISH

Gentiana campestris, Linn.
Fam. Gentianaceae

Synonym: Field Gentian.

Habitat: Great Britain.

Flowering Time: July.

Description: Herb, 4–6 in. high, branched above, leaves opposite, ovate-lanceolate, or ovate-spatulate below, with entire margins. Flowers bluish purple, tubular, with four segments. Calyx segments five, nearly equal. Taste, bitter; odour, none.

Parts Used: Root and herb.

Medicinal Use: Bitter tonic. Uses as for Gentian.

GERMANDER

Teucrium chamaedrys, Linn.
Fam. Labiatae

Synonyms: Chasse-fièvre (Fr.), Petit Chêne (Fr.).

Habitat: A common European and British wild plant, also cultivated in gardens.

Flowering Time: From end of May to August.

Description: Stem 1–2 ft long. Leaves dark green, shining above, ovate, ½–1¼ in. long and ¼–½ in. broad, with oblong, obtuse teeth and a wedge-shaped, entire base. Floral leaves nearly entire. Flowers purplish-red, upper lip deeply bifid, with projecting stamens. Taste, bitter; odour, none.

Part Used: Herb.

Medicinal Use: Stimulant, tonic, diaphoretic, diuretic. Has been employed in rheumatism, gout, intermittent fevers, scrofula, and skin diseases.

Culpeper places this herb under the dominion of Mercury and states: "It strengthens the brain and apprehension exceedingly and relieves them when drooping."

See also Water Germander.

Preparation: Liquid extract: Dose, ½–1 dr.

GINGER

Zingiber officinale, Rosc.
Fam. Zingiberaceae

Habitat: Although Gerard writes that it grows in Spain, Barbary, the Canary Islands, and the Azores, it is not imported from these parts now. The finest Ginger is cultivated in Jamaica. From China comes Cochin Ginger which as well as being imported dried is also imported in the form of the fresh root preserved in syrup. African Ginger is inferior to the above varieties but is largely used.

Description: The appearance of Ginger is well known. The Jamaican variety has the best aroma. It is freed from the rootlets, peeled and dried in the sun and is known in commerce as unbleached Jamaica Ginger. Bleached Ginger is obtained by treating with lime, making it less susceptible to insect pests. Cochin Ginger is usually thicker than Jamaica and has both pungency and aroma. African Ginger is generally unpeeled giving it a browner colour. Fracture is pale buff, starchy, and fibrous, sometimes horny. Taste, pungent and aromatic; odour, characteristic.

Part Used: Rhizome.

Medicinal Use: Stimulant, carminative, expectorant. Is chiefly used in combination with other remedies, but should be taken alone in cases of colds, spasms, flatulence, etc., in doses of 10–20 gr in warm water sweetened.

Domestic Use: Gerard writes: "Ginger as Dioscorides reporteth is right good with meat in sauces or otherwise in conditures; for it is of an heating and digesting qualitie."

Preparations: Oleores. Zingib. B.P.C.: Dose, ¼–1 gr; Syr. Zingib. B.P.: Dose, ½–2 dr; Tab. Zingib. Co.: Dose, 1–2 tablets; Tinct. Zingib. Fort. B.P.: Dose, 5–10 min; Tinct. Zingib. Mit. B.P.: Dose, ½–1 dr; Powdered root: Dose, 5–15 gr; Fldext. Zingib. U.S.P.: Dose, 10 min.

GINGER, WILD

Asarum canadense, Linn.
Fam. Aristolochiaceae

Synonyms: Indian Ginger, Canadian Snakeroot.

Habitat: North America, Canada.

Description: Rhizome slender, about 4 in. long and ⅛ in. thick, quadrangular or almost two-edged, wrinkled, greyish or purplish brown. Fracture short, whitish rootlets about ½ in. distant on the nodes, scarcely branched. Taste, bitterish and pungent and aromatic; odour, aromatic.

Part Used: Rhizome.

Medicinal Use: Expectorant, carminative, stimulant. As a carminative it is useful in all painful spasms of the bowels and stomach. In colds or in amenorrhoea from cold it is a valuable stimulant. The infusion of ½ oz of the powdered root in 1 pt of boiling water produces copious perspiration, when taken hot. The powder may be taken dry in doses of 20–30 gr.

GINSENG

Panax quinquefolium, Linn.
Fam. Araliaceae

Synonyms: *Aralia quinquefolia*, Panax, Pannag.

Habitat: China.

Description: Root, spindle-shaped, pale brownish yellow, 2–3 in. long, and about ½ in. in diameter, ringed above, divided into two or three equal branches which are wrinkled longitudinally. Fracture short, white, mealy, with a thin bark containing numerous reddish, resin cells; wood wedges narrow, yellowish, medullary rays broad. Taste, sweetish and faintly aromatic; odour, imperceptible.

Part Used: Root.

Medicinal Use: Tonic, stimulant. Useful in loss of appetite, stomach and digestive affections, arising from mental and nervous exhaustion.

Preparation: Powder: 15 gr immediately after meals.

Biblical Reference: Ezekiel, XXVII, 17.

THE Chinese ascribe wonderful medicinal virtues to it. In fact, it was thought to be of such great service in so great a variety of complaints that it was given the botanical name "Panax," which means "all-healing" and is related to the word "Panacea."

GLADWIN

Iris foetidissima, Linn.
Fam. Iridiaceae

Synonyms: Stinking Gladwin, Gladwine, Stinking Gladdon, Spurgewort, Roastbeef Plant. (The word "stinking" is introduced because of the loathsome smell of the plant when bruised.)

Habitat: Woods and shady places, chiefly in Southern England near the sea.

Flowering Time: August. Seeds ripen in September.

Description: Long, narrow leaves similar to the Iris, but smaller. The stalks bear bluish-purple-coloured flowers shaped like the common Iris, but smaller. Seeds are bright orange or scarlet. The rhizome is long and bears many fibres.

Part Used: Rhizome.

Medicinal Use: Antispasmodic, cathartic, anodyne. Occasionally used as a purgative; said to relieve cramps, convulsions and pains, stomachic and rheumatic.

Culpeper writes: "The root is very effectual in all wounds, especially the head; as also to draw forth any splinters, thorns, or broken bones or any other thing sticking in the flesh, without causing pains, being used with a little verdigrease and honey and the great Centaury root."

Preparation: Powdered root: Dose, 5–30 gr.

GOA

Andira araroba, Aguiar
Fam. Leguminosae

Synonyms: Araroba, Bahia Powder, Brazil Powder, Ringworm Powder, Chrysarobin.

Habitat: Brazil.

Description: Goa or Araroba is found in longitudinal fissures in the trunk of the tree. After felling, the tree is split with an axe and yellowish powder scraped out combined with splinters of the wood and vegetable debris. This Goa Powder is purified by sifting and powdering and extracting the residue with benzine and other solvents; this forms purified Chrysarobin. Goa Powder should yield from 50–80 per cent of purified Araroba or Chrysarobin. The powder is very irritating to the nose and eyes and mucous membranes generally.

Medicinal Use: Taenifuge, alterative, detergent. It is used occasionally in the Indies for tapeworm. European medical men use it because of its chrysophanic acid, in skin diseases, such as eczema, psoriasis, acne, etc. The powder is mixed with vinegar, lemon juice, or glycerine to form a paste and applied to the skin. It is also used in form of a paint or ointment.

Preparations: Chrysarobin B.P.C. 1949 is purified Goa Powder. Ung. Chrysarob. B.P.C. 1949.

GOAT'S RUE

Galega officinalis, Linn.
Fam. Leguminosae

Synonym: Galega.

Habitat: It grows wild in moist fields and meadows in England and on the Continent.

Flowering Time: June and July, the seeds ripening in August.

Description: Stem branched. Leaves pinnate, $\frac{3}{4}$–2 in. long, with six to eight pairs of lanceolate leaves and a terminal one, each furnished with a terminal point (mucro). Stipules half-arrow-shaped. Flowers pale purplish or white, in axillary racemes. Legumes almost cylindrical. Taste, bitter and astringent; odour, none.

Part Used: Herb.

Medicinal Use: Galactagogue, diuretic, vermifuge.

Preparation: Powder: Dose, 5–20 gr.

PARKINSON recommends Goat's Rue against the bitings and stings of any venomous creatures. He also writes: "It is no less effectuall for Sheepe, Goates and Cattle, for from the experience of Goat-herds therein, came the name Capraria added unto it; it fatteneth hennes also wonderfully, and causeth them to lay egges the more plentifully."

GOLDEN ROD

Solidago virgaurea, Linn.
Fam. Compositae

Habitat: A common garden plant in England, also growing wild in woods and copses. Gerard writes: "They grow plentifully in Hampstead Wood near the gate that leadeth out of the wood unto the village called Kentish Towne not far from London; in a wood by Rayleigh in Essex, hard by a Gentleman's house called Mr. Leonard, dwelling upon Dawes Heath; in Southfleet in Swainscombe wood also, near to Gravesend."

Flowering Time: July.

Description: Stem somewhat angular. Leaves lanceolate and stalked near the root, narrower on the stem, $2\frac{1}{2}$–$3\frac{1}{2}$ in. long and $\frac{3}{4}$–1 in. broad, sometimes slightly toothed and undulated at the margin, with very short hairs. Flowerheads golden yellow, narrow, about $\frac{1}{4}$–$\frac{1}{3}$ in. long, receptacle honeycombed, pappus hairy, not feathery. Taste, acrid and bitter; odour, when dry, agreeable, slightly aromatic.

Part Used: Leaves.

Medicinal Use: Aromatic, carminative, stimulant. Allays sickness due to weakness of stomach, and also promotes perspiration. The infusion of 1 oz to 1 pt of boiling water is taken in wineglassful doses, repeated frequently.

Preparation: Liquid extract: Dose, ½–1 dr.

GERARD in addition to recommending Golden Rod against stone and pain in the kidneys, states: "It hath in times past beene had in great estimation and regard . . . for in my remembrance I have known the dry herbe which came from beyond the sea sold in Bucklersbury in London for halfe a crowne an ounce. But since it was found in Hampstead Wood . . . no man will give halfe a crowne for an hundredweight of it . . . yet it may be truly said of phantasticall Physitions who when they have found an approved medicine and perfect remedy neere home against any disease, yet not content therewith they will seeke a new farther off and by that means many times hurt more than they helpe. Thus much have I spoken to bring those new fangled fellowes backe againe to esteeme better this admirable plant. . . ."

GOLDEN SEAL

Hydrastis canadensis, Linn.
Fam. Ranunculaceae

Synonyms: Orange Root, Yellow Root.

Habitat: At one time this plant grew wild in the woods of Eastern Northern America. As a wild plant it is rapidly becoming extinct, but it is cultivated.

Description: The whole plant is not seen in this country, the dried rhizome only being imported. This is short, about 1½ in. in length, knotty with the bases of stems, and about ⅛–¼ in. in diameter, often furnished with abundance of rootlets. Fracture greenish yellow, showing a radiate woody centre, with broad medullary rays. Taste, very bitter; odour, strong and disagreeable.

Part Used: Rhizome, gathered in the autumn.

Medicinal Use: Tonic, laxative, alterative, detergent. Since about 1847 Golden Seal has figured conspicuously in the botanic practice. The name was given to this plant by Thomsonians, who employed the root. The demand for "concentrations" was the means of discovering the two alkaloids contained in this drug—Hydrastine, the white, and Berberine, the yellow—besides others of less value. For many years these and the powdered root were the chief forms administered. Latterly, however, the drug in the form of a fluid extract is the most used and popular. It is a very valuable remedy in disordered states of the digestive apparatus. As a general bitter tonic it is applicable to debilitated conditions of mucous tissues. As a remedy for various gastric disorders it takes a leading place, acting very beneficially in acute inflammatory conditions. It will be found of value in all cases of dyspepsia, biliousness, and debility of the system. It is especially indicated in catarrhal states of the mucous membranes, gastric irritability, and passive haemorrhages from the pelvic tissues. Externally it is used as a lotion in treatment of eye affections and as a general cleansing application.

Preparations: Powdered root: Dose, 10 gr; Elix. Viburn. et Hydrast. B.P.C. 1949: Dose, ½–1 dr; Ext. Hydrast. Sicc. B.P.C. 1949 (Hydrastin): Dose, ½–2 gr; Ext. Hydrast. Liq. B.P.C. 1949: Dose, 5–15 min; Tinct. Hydrast. B.P.C. 1949: Dose, ½–1 dr.

GOLD THREAD

Coptis trifolia, Salisb.
Coptis groenlandica
Fam. Ranunculaceae

Synonyms: Mouth Root, Vegetable Gold.

Habitat: The *trifolia* grows in India and the *groenlandica* in Canada and U.S.A.

Flowering Time: From May to July.

Description: Rhizomes thread-like, golden yellow, matted, with very small roots. Leaves stalked, tufted, with slender stalks, evergreen, strongly veined, three parted, with obovate, cuneate segments and crenate, pointed teeth. Taste, very bitter; odour, slight.

Part Used: Rhizome.

Medicinal Use: Bitter tonic. Would be more used than it is, if its good qualities were better known. It may be given alone or in combination with other suitable medicines. It promotes digestion, improves the appetite, and acts as a general stimulant to the system. In convalescence it is highly beneficial.

It has been used in chronic inflammation of the mucous membrane of the stomach.

Preparations: Powdered root: Dose, 10–20 gr; Liquid extract: Dose, ¼–1 dr.

GOUTWORT

Aegopodium podagraria, Linn.
Fam. Umbelliferae

Synonyms: Goutweed, Gout Herb, Ashweed, Ground Ash, Herb Gerarde.

Habitat: A troublesome weed in Europe and Great Britain. Gerard writes of it: "Herb Gerard groweth of it selfe in gardens without setting or sowing and is so fruitful in his increase, that where it hath once taken root, it will hardly be gotten out againe, spoiling and getting every yeere more ground, to the annoying of better herbs."

Flowering Time: From beginning of June to end of July.

Description: Leaves with long stalks, divided once or twice into three-stalked leaflets, which are about 2 in. long and about 1¼ in. broad, have unequal sides, are acutely pointed, and are twice serrate at the margin; the veins are at an acute angle and prominent beneath. Leafstalks channelled above and keeled beneath. Root creeping. Taste, saline; odour, none.

Part Used: Herb.

Medicinal Use: Diuretic, sedative. Recommended internally for aches in joints, gouty and sciatic pains. Also used externally as a fomentation.

Culpeper states: "It is probable it took the name of Gout Herb from its peculiar virtues in healing the cold gout and sciatica as it hath been found by experience to be a most admirable remedy for these disorders. . . . It is even affirmed, that the very carrying of it about in the pocket will defend the bearer from any attack of the aforesaid complaint."

Preparation: Liquid extract: Dose, ½–1 dr.

GRAINS OF PARADISE

Aframomum melegueta, Rosc.
Fam. Zingiberaceae

Synonym: Guinea Grains.

Habitat: Tropical West Africa.

Description: The plant producing the seeds is reed-like growing from 3–5 ft high. The seeds are small, hard, and shining, oyster shape, and red brown in colour. The taste is aromatic and pungent like ginger and cayenne.

Part Used: Seeds.

Medicinal Use: Stimulant. Used principally in veterinary preparations.

Domestic Use: The seeds have been used as a condiment, but are not much used today.

GRAVEL ROOT

Eupatorium purpureum, Linn.
Fam. Compositae

Synonyms: Gravelweed, Queen-of-the-meadow Root.

Habitat: U.S.A.

Description: Rhizome ½–1 in. in diameter, very hard and tough, with a thin, greyish-brown bark and thick, whitish wood, not visibly porous, often hollow in the centre, and with wide medullary rays. The rhizome has short lateral branches all furnished with crowded, tough, woody roots, about

$\frac{1}{12}$ in. in diameter, and several inches long. Taste, bitter, astringent, and slightly acrid.

Part Used: Rhizome.

Medicinal Use: Diuretic, stimulant, tonic. Used principally in the treatment of gravel stone in the bladder and affections of the kidneys and urinary organs. It is also a nervine tonic.

Preparation: Liquid extract: Dose, $\frac{1}{2}$–1 dr.

GRINDELIA

Grindelia camporum, Greene
Fam. Compositae

Synonyms: *Grindelia robusta*, Nutt., Gum Plant, Hardy Grindelia, Scaly Grindelia.

Habitat: California, the United States and South America.

Description: Grindelia in commerce consists of the stems of *G. camporum*, Greene, formerly referred to, *G. robusta*, Nutt., and of *G. squarrosa*, Nutt. The leaves in the former are broad, and in the latter narrowed at the base, leathery, brittle, serrated at the margins, veins at an acute angle, not very prominent below, lanceolate, about 2$\frac{1}{2}$–4 in. long and $\frac{1}{2}$–1 in. broad, not hairy. Flowerheads globular, about $\frac{3}{4}$ in. in diameter, with yellow florets, without hairy pappus, scales of the involucre reflexed, linear, pointed. Taste, aromatic, bitterish; odour, slight.

Part Used: Herb.

Medicinal Use: Anti-asthmatic, diuretic, tonic. Very largely employed in the treatment of asthmatic and bronchial affections, also in whooping cough and kidney diseases. In asthma, etc., it reduces the violence and frequency of the paroxysm. Guy's Hospital uses a mixture of Ext. Grindel. Liq. B.P.C. 1949 $\frac{1}{2}$ dr, Ext. Glycyrrh. Liq. B.P. 1 dr, mucilage to 1 oz.

Preparations: Ext. Grindel. Liq. B.P.C. 1949: Dose, 10–20 min; Solid extract: Dose, 1–15 gr.

GROUND IVY

Glechoma hederacea, Linn.
Fam. Labiatae

Synonyms: Gill-go-over-the-ground, Alehoof, Haymaids, *Nepeta glechoma*, Benth.

Habitat: A common wild plant in Europe and the British Isles.

Flowering Time: Early in the year.

Description: Stem quadrangular, unbranched, 6 or more in. long, with stalked, opposite, somewhat kidney-shaped leaves deeply and obtusely crenate at the margins, paler and gland-dotted beneath, with many-celled hairs. Flowers blue, two-lipped, three or four together in the axils of the upper leaves, which often have a purplish tint. Taste, bitter and acrid; odour, strong, aromatic.

Part Used: Herb.

Medicinal Use: Astringent, diuretic, tonic. Useful in kidney diseases and for indigestion. Also used as an antiscorbutic. Combined with Yarrow or Chamomile Flowers it makes an excellent poultice for abscesses, gatherings, and tumours. The infusion of 1 oz in 1 pt of boiling water is taken in wineglassful doses.

Gerard recommends: "Ground-Ivy, and Daisies, of each a like quantitie, stamped and strained, and a little sugar and rose water put thereto, and dropped with a feather into the eies, taketh away all manner of inflammation, spots, webs, itch, smarting, or any griefe whatsoever. . . ."

PARKINSON says of Ground Ivy: "The country people doe much use it and tunne it up with their drinke, not onely for the especiall good virtues therein, but for that it will helpe also to cleare their drinke. . . ."

GROUND PINE, AMERICAN

Lycopodium complanatum, Linn.
Fam. Lycopodiaceae

Habitat: U.S.A.

Description: Stem long, creeping, yellowish-green, scaly, about $\frac{1}{12}$ in. diameter, giving off at intervals erect, fan-shaped, forked branches, with minute, scale-like leaves, leaving only the sharp tips free, the branches bearing fructification in the form of a stalked tuft of four to five cylindrical spikes consisting of spore cases in the axils of minute bracts. Stem rooting below at long intervals, the roots pale, wiry, and slightly branched. Taste, slightly turpentiney; odour, aromatic. Properties similar to the European variety (*see* below).

GROUND PINE, EUROPEAN

Ajuga chamaepitys, Schreb.
Fam. Labiatae

Habitat: It grows on chalky soil in Great Britain and Europe. According to Gerard it grows plentifully in Kent.

Flowering Time: June and July.

Description: Herb bushy, 3–6 in. high, very hairy, with deeply trifid leaves having linear entire segments, with single flowers in the axils of the leaves. Corolla yellow, with dark spots. Lower leaves lanceolate, scarcely divided. Taste and odour, aromatic and turpentiney.

Part Used: Leaves.

Medicinal Use: Stimulant, diuretic, emmenagogue. Forms a good remedy, combined with other suitable herbs, for gout and rheumatism. Also useful in female disorders. The infusion of 1 oz to 1 pt of boiling water is taken in tablespoonful doses, frequently repeated.

Preparation: Liquid extract: Dose, ½–2 dr.

GROUNDSEL

Senecio vulgaris, Linn.
Fam. Compositae

Synonym: Grounsel

Habitat: A common garden weed in many parts of the world.

Flowering Time: It flowers for the greater part of the year.

Description: Stem angular, branched. Leaves oblong, wider and clasping at the base, with short, lateral, angular-toothed lobes. Flowerheads about ¼ in. long and ⅛ in. broad, cylindrical, with black-tipped linear, involucral scales. Florets all tubular, receptacle dotted, not hairy. Taste, saline; odour, none.

Part Used: Herb.

Medicinal Use: Diuretic, diaphoretic. Relieves bilious pains and in a strong infusion acts as a purgative and an emetic. Dose, ½–1 dr.

Domestic Use: The herb is often fed to canaries.

GUAIACUM

Guaiacum officinale, Linn.
and *Guaiacum sanctum*, Linn.
Fam. Zygophyllaceae

Synonyms: *Lignum vitae, Lignum sanctum.*

Habitat: The *officinale* is native of the West Indies and South America and the *sanctum* of Southern Florida and the Bahamas.

Description: The wood is usually sold in shavings or raspings. The heart wood, of a dark greenish-brown, is heavy and sinks in water; it has an aromatic and irritating taste. Odour, slightly aromatic when rubbed or warmed. The Guaiacum Resin is produced by firing the logs and collecting the melted resin. The yield is about 20 per cent. Generally imported in large blocks, which are covered with a greenish powder.

Parts Used: Wood and resin.

Medicinal Use: Diaphoretic, alterative. Is considered a valuable remedy in gout, chronic rheumatism, impurities of the blood, etc. It is generally used in conjunction with Sarsaparilla and enters into most blood-purifying compounds. The dose of the infusion (of wood) of 1 oz to 1 pt of boiling water is a wineglassful.

Preparations: Liquid extract: Dose, ½–1 dr; Dec. Sars. Co. B.P.C. 1949: Dose, 2–8 fl oz; Dec. Sars. Co. Conc. B.P.C. 1949: Dose, ¼–1 fl oz; Conf. Guaiac. Co. B.P.C. 1949: Dose, 1–2 dr; Mist. Guaiac.: Dose, ½–1 fl oz; Tinct. Guaiac. Ammon. B.P.C. 1949: Dose, ½–1 fl dr; Troch. Guaiac. Resin. B.P.C. 1949; Resin.: Dose, 5–15 g.

Domestic Use: The wood is used to make woods for playing on Bowling Greens.

GUARANA

Paullinia cupana, H., B., & K.
Fam. Sapindaceae

Synonyms: Brazilian Cocoa, Uabano, Uaranazeiro, *Paullinia sorbilis*, Mart.

Habitat: Brazil.

Description: Usually in cylindrical or sausage-shaped rolls, about 1½ in. thick and several inches long, formed of the broken roasted seeds beaten into a paste and dried. Taste, astringent and bitterish, then sweet; odour, recalling that of chocolate. A popular stimulant in Brazil among the natives, who grate a small quantity into the palm of the hand. This is swallowed and washed down with water.

Part Used: The roasted seeds made into a pulp and dried.

Medicinal Use: Nervine tonic, stimulant. This drug owes its properties to the Caffeine it contains, and for this reason will be found serviceable in most cases of headache, particularly those caused by menstrual derangements. Its action is in some cases diuretic, and as such it finds use in rheumatic complaints and lumbago.

Preparations: Powdered Guarana: Dose, 10–60 gr; Elix. Guaran.: Dose, ½–2 dr; Liquid extract: Dose, ½–1 dr; Tinct. Guaran.: Dose, ½–2 dr.

H

HAIR CAP MOSS

Polytrichum juniperum, Willd.
Fam. Polytrichaceae

Synonyms: Bearsbed, Ground Moss, Robinsrye.

Habitat: A common moss growing in woods and hedges of Great Britain and Europe. It is said that this moss is found growing on human skulls.

Description: Stems slender, unbranched, 2–3 in. long, with small, short, awl-shaped, red-tipped leaves, overlapping, and crowded in the upper part of the stem. Fruit stalks when present terminating in a cylindrical, four-angled capsule containing spores.

Part Used: Plant.

Medicinal Use: Diuretic. Possessing but very little smell and taste, it produces no disagreeable sensations. It is a very valuable and important remedy in dropsy, urinary obstruction, and suppression. The infusion is taken in wineglassful doses. Joseph Miller recommends it for stopping bleeding of the nose and other haemorrhages, "being only held in the hand."

HARTSTONGUE

Scolopendrium vulgare, Sym.
Fam. Filices

Synonyms: *Asplenium scolopendrium*, Linn., *Phyllitis scolopendrium*, Greene.

Habitat: It grows in gardens and woodlands in many parts.

Description: Fronds stalked, about $1\frac{1}{2}$–2 ft long and about $1\frac{1}{2}$–2 in. wide, with transverse, simple veins, and linear sori of spore-cases, $\frac{1}{2}$–$\frac{3}{4}$ in. long, in transverse series at the back. Taste, unpleasant; odour, none.

Part Used: Herb.

Medicinal Use: Diuretic, laxative, pectoral. Specially recommended for removing obstructions from the liver and spleen, also for removing gravelly deposits in the bladder. The decoction is made of 2 oz to 1 pt of water. Dose, a wineglassful.

CULPEPER writes: "The distilled water is good for the passions of the heart, and gargled in the mouth will stay the hiccough, help the falling palate and stop the bleeding of the gums. It is a good remedy for the biting of serpents."

HAWTHORN

Crataegus oxycantha, Linn.
Fam. Rosaceae

Synonyms: English Hawthorn, Haw, May Bush.

Habitat: A hedge plant common in the United Kingdom.

Flowering Time: May.

Description: The Hawthorn, being so well known, requires no description. The berries ripen in September.

Part Used: Dried berries.

Medicinal Use: Cardiac, tonic. This drug is claimed to be a curative remedy for organic and functional heart disorders such as dyspnoea, rapid and feeble heart action, hypertrophy, valvular insufficiency, and heart oppression. The dose is from 2–15 gr three to four times a day. Generally prescribed with *Cactus grandiflora.*

Preparation: Liquid extract: Dose, 10–15 drops.

HEARTSEASE

Viola tricolor, Linn.
Fam. Violaceae

Synonyms: Wild Pansy. There are several old English names by which this plant was known such as "Love in Idleness," "Cull me to you," "Three faces in a hood," and "Heart of Trinity." The last name is due to the three colours of its flowers.

Habitat: A common wild plant growing in England and frequently cultivated in gardens.

Flowering Time: Spring and summer.

Part Used: Herb.

Description: Leaves ovate-lanceolate, crenate, with pinnatifid stipules. Flowers violet-like, white, the corolla shorter than the spurred calyx. Fruit of three carpels. Taste, insipid; odour, herbaceous.

Medicinal Use: Diaphoretic, diuretic. Used in blood disorders and in catarrhal affections. Its chief use is for moist cutaneous eruptions in children. Said to prevent convulsions in asthma and epilepsy.

HEDGE-HYSSOP

Gratiola officinalis, Linn.
Fam. Scrophulariaceae

Habitat: A common wild herb in this country growing in damp places. Culpeper writes: ". . . may be found among the bogs on Hampstead Heath."

Flowering Time: June or July.

Description: Stem quadrangular, not hairy. Leaves opposite, not stalked, lanceolate, about 1¼ in. long and ⅛ in. broad, with three to five longitudinal veins, and toothed at the margin above the middle. Flowers irregular, singly in the upper axils, pinkish, with five stamens, of which only two are fertile. Taste, acrid and bitter; odour, none. The rhizome is cylindrical, brownish yellow, about ⅛ in. in diameter, with joints ⅛–½ in. long, having ovate scales on the joints, with slender rootlets below. The transverse section shows a porous white bark and a small, dense, yellowish, woody ring, enclosing a comparatively large pith. Taste, very bitter; odour, none.

Parts Used: Herb, root.

Medicinal Use: Diuretic, cathartic, emetic. In doses of 5–20 gr it has been recommended in chronic affections of the liver, jaundice, and enlargement of spleen. It has also shown itself valuable in dropsical affections in doses of 15–30 gr. Large doses induce vomiting and purging. The infusion of ½ oz of powdered root in 1 pt of boiling water is given in tablespoonful doses.

Many of the ancient herbalists describe the action of this plant as "Churlish" in nature and Culpeper describes it as a herb of Mars "and as choleric and churlish as he is." He states that it is "not safe taken inwardly unless well rectified by the art of the alchymist."

HEDGE MUSTARD

Sisymbrium officinale, Linn.
Fam. Cruciferae

Habitat: A common wild plant in the British Isles and Europe.

Flowering Time: July and August.

Description: Small, yellow petals form a Maltese cross. Grows 1–2 ft high with great number of very thin, spreading flower stems. Seed pods upright, close to the stem, splitting open from the bottom upwards, only adhering at the top.

Part Used: Herb.

Medicinal Use: A remedy for hoarseness and weak lungs. It is said to be a good thing to use in order to recover the voice.

Preparation: Liquid extract: Dose, ½–1 fl dr.

HELLEBORE, AMERICAN

Veratrum viride, Ait.
Fam. Liliaceae

Synonyms: Swamp Hellebore, Green Hellebore, Itchweed, Indian Poke, American Veratrum.

Habitat: North America and Canada.

Description: The rootstock is blackish grey, obconical, 2–3 in. long and ¾–1½ in. in diameter, tufted above with the scaly remains of stem leaves, internally whitish, with darker wavy lines and dots in the central portion, with numerous, yellowish-brown, shrivelled rootlets, about 8 in. long and ⅛ in. thick. The rhizome closely resembles that of White Hellebore (*V. album*) and is considered by many to be of the same species. In commerce Green Hellebore is generally cut longitudinally. White Hellebore is usually entire and sometimes deprived of its roots. Usually employed in certain skin diseases as an external application and for the destruction of Pediculi. White Hellebore grows in the mountains of Central Europe. Taste, bitter and very acrid; odourless, but the powder very irritating to the nostrils.

Part Used: Rhizome.

Medicinal Use: Cardiac depressant. A useful remedy in febrile and inflammatory affections of respiratory organs, and used as a gargle in sore throat. For acute tonsilitis it is an excellent remedy. It relieves irritation of the nervous system, and is of especial value in convulsions, mania, neuralgia, and headache. Owing to its poisonous nature it should be used with caution.

Preparations: Powdered root: Dose, 1–2 gr; Liquid extract: Dose, 1–2 min; Tinct. Verat. (1 in 10): Dose, 5–30 min.

HELLEBORE, BLACK

Helleborus niger, Linn.
Fam. Ranunculaceae

Synonyms: Christmas Rose, Melampodium.

Habitat: A plant found in the sub-alpine woods of Southern and Eastern Europe. It is cultivated as a garden plant in England.

Flowering Time: Mid-winter.

Description: The plant is well known. The rhizome as it appears in commerce is blackish, mostly forming an entangled mass of very short branches, and straight, rather brittle, black rootlets $\frac{1}{10}$ in. in diameter, which exhibit a central, slightly angular cord. Transverse section of the rhizome shows a thick bark and ring of whitish, woody wedges. Taste, bitter and slightly acrid; odour, slight, fatty.

According to Pliny, as reported by Parkinson, the root had a veterinary use: "He saith that a peece of the roote of black Hellebore being drawne through a hole made in the eare of a beast troubled with the cough, or having taken any poisonous thing, cureth it if it be taken out the next day at the same howre."

Part Used: Rhizome.

Medicinal Use: Diuretic, cathartic, emmenagogue. Has been used in dropsy, chlorosis, and amenorrhoea. In nervous disorders, hysteria, and melancholia it is of value. Should be given in minute doses only, as larger ones cause untoward effects.

Preparations: Liquid extract: Dose, 2–10 min; Solid extract: Dose, 1–2 gr.

HELLEBORE, FALSE

Adonis vernalis, Linn.
Fam. Ranunculaceae

Synonyms: Adonis, Pheasant's Eye.

Habitat: N. Europe and Asia.

Description: Stem about 6–9 in. long, alternate, terminated by a single, large, yellow flower about 1½ in. across, followed by an oval head of achenes about 1 in. long. Leaves alternate, finely divided in a pinnate manner into linear segments, sheathing at the base, the whole plant not hairy. Taste, slight; odour, none.

Part Used: Herb.

Medicinal Use: Cardiac, tonic, diuretic. Is not cumulative in its action, but should be used with caution. Highly spoken of in heart diseases and kidney affections. Valuable in cardiac dropsy and heart strain. The dose of an infusion of ¼ oz in 1 pt of boiling water is a tablespoonful every two to three hours.

Preparation: Liquid extract: Dose, 1–2 min; Glucoside, Adonidin: Dose, $\frac{1}{12}$–¼ gr.

HEMLOCK

Conium maculatum, Linn.
Fam. Umbelliferae

Synonyms: Poison Hemlock, Poison Parsley, Conium, Spotted Hemlock.

Habitat: Temperate Europe and Great Britain.

Flowering Time: July and August.

Description: Leaves hairless, repeatedly pinnate, 1 ft long or more, angular in outline, the stem hollow, spotted, as well as the large leafstalks, with purplish spots; the tips of the leaflets end in a white point. Taste, unpleasant; odour, disagreeable, mousey when the leaves are rubbed with Liquor Potassae. The fruits are ovate, plano-convex, indented on the flat surface, with five crenate ridges on the back. Odour, none, unless rubbed with alkali, then mousey like the leaves.

Parts Used: Leaves. Fruits gathered when unripe.

Medicinal Use: Sedative, anodyne. Is of particular service in all spasmodic affections, such as chorea, epilepsy, acute mania, etc. Also used with advantage in whooping cough. Should be administered only under medical supervision, as overdoses produce paralysis.

Preparations: From leaves: Powdered leaves: Dose, 2–8 gr; Ext. Conii B.P.C. 1949: Dose, 2–6 gr; Succ. Conii: Dose, ½–1 dr; Ung. Conii; Liquid extract: Dose, 5–10 min.

From seeds: Liquid extract: Dose, 2–5 min; Tincture: Dose, ½–1 dr.

Biblical References: Hosea x, 4; Amos vi, 12. (These are the only two texts where the word Hemlock is used.)

Deuteronomy xxix, 18, xxxii, 32; Psalm lxix, 21; Jeremiah viii, 14, ix, 15, xxxiii, 15; Samuel iii, 5, 9.

In the above the Hebrew word is rendered as "Gall" and it seems certain that it refers to Hemlock. It is known that Hemlock was used in ancient days to put criminals to death, and others suffered the same fate who would not today be classed as criminals. It will be remembered that Socrates drank a draught of Hemlock juice. The Jews in ancient days used Hemlock to deaden the pains of dying criminals. Such as were being stoned to death were frequently given a cup of wine containing myrrh and Hemlock juice to deaden their death pains. It is thought that as Jesus hung upon the cross he was given vinegar, myrrh, and Hemlock.

HEMP AGRIMONY

Eupatorium cannabinum, Linn.
Fam. Compositae

Synonym: Water Hemp.

Habitat: British Isles and Europe. Gerard says it grows: "On Banks of ditches, running waters, standing pooles and in waterie places everie where."

Flowering Time: July.

Description: Stem angular, striated, rough. Leaves opposite, downy, three to five lobed, the segments elongate-lanceolate, irregularly serrate, the central one longest. Flower heads slender, five to six flowered, florets all tubular, pinkish. Receptacle not hairy, pappus pilose. Taste, sweetish, then bitter; odour, faintly aromatic.

Part Used: Herb.

Medicinal Use: Antiscorbutic, cathartic, diuretic. A good remedy for impurity of the blood. May be used by itself or combined with other herbs. The infusion of 1 oz to 1 pt of water is taken in wineglassful doses four or five times a day.

Preparation: Liquid extract: Dose, ½–1 dr.

HENBANE

Hyoscyamus niger, Linn.
Fam. Solanaceae

Synonym: Hogbean.

Habitat: It grows freely in Europe and Great Britain, especially in hedges and waste places. Culpeper places the herb under the dominion of Saturn because it grows in Saturnine places: "Whole cartloads of it may be found near the places where they empty the common Jakes and scarce a ditch is to be found without growing of it."

Flowering Time: July.

Description: During the first year the plant produces a rosette of large leaves known as First Biennial. The second year the plant grows to a height of 3 ft or more with stout branching stem clusters of yellow flowers veined with purple. This is called Second Biennial. From this the green extract of Henbane and Succus is obtained. The official drug, according to the B.P. 1953, consists of the dried leaves or leaves and flowering tops. Annual Henbane is a smaller plant than the Biennial. The stem does not branch, the flowers are paler and the leaves are smaller and less hairy. The entire plant is generally collected and therefore contains stalk, leaf, and flowers. This forms the bulk of imported Henbane. Taste, slightly acrid; odour, unpleasant, characteristic.

Parts Used: Leaves and flowering tops.

Medicinal Use: Anodyne, narcotic, mydriatic. Principally employed in irritable conditions and nervous affections. Also used in asthma, whooping cough, etc., as a sedative and as a substitute for Opium, where the latter is inadmissible, as in children's complaints. Henbane is poisonous and should never be used except under medical advice.

Gerard writes: "To wash the feet in a decoction of Henbane causeth sleep, or given in a clyster it doth the same, and also the often smelling to the flowers." He states that: "The Seed is used by mountibank tooth-drawers which run about the country, to cause worms to come forth of the teeth by burning it in a chafing dish of coles, the party holding his mouth over the fume thereof; but some crafty companions to gain money convey small lute-strings into the water persuading the patient that these small creepers came out of his mouth or other part which he intended to ease."

Joseph Miller writes: "The roots are frequently hung about children's neck . . . to prevent fits and cause an easy breeding of the teeth."

Preparations: Ext. Hyoscy. Liq. B.P.: Dose, 3–6 min; Ext. Hyoscy. Sicc. B.P.: Dose, ¼–1 gr; Linct. Diamorph. et Hyoscy. B.P.C. 1949: Dose, 30–120 min; Mist. Gelsem. et Hyoscy. Co. B.P.C.: Dose ½–1 fl oz. Mist. Pot. Cit. et Hyoscy B.P.C.: Dose, ½ fl oz; Pil. Coloc. et Hyoscy. B.P. 1948; Pil. Aloin et Podoph. Co. B.P.C. 1949; Pil. Hydrarg. Subchlor. Colocynth. et Hyoscy. B.P.C 1949; Tab. Colocynth. et Jalap Co. B.P.C.; Tinct. Hyoscy. B.P.: Dose, 30–60 min; Tinct. Hyoscy. U.S.P.: Dose, 30 min.

HENNA

Lawsonia alba, Lamk.
Fam. Lythraceae

Synonyms: Henne, Alhenna.

Habitat: Egypt, Arabia, Persia, India.

Description: Leaves opposite, shortly stalked, smooth, lanceolate, mucronate, entire at the revolute margins, about 1 in. long, $1\frac{3}{4}$ in. wide, lateral veins incurved at their apex. Taste, slightly astringent; odour, tea-like. A section of the leaf shows a double row of palisade cells and numerous cluster crystals of Calcium Oxalate. It is often imported in a coarse powder, which is charged with earth and other impurities.

Part Used: Leaves.

Medicinal Use: Astringent. The Indian natives ascribe wonderful properties to this plant, and use it in headache, smallpox, leprosy, etc.

Domestic Use: In the Middle East it is frequently used to dye the nails of the hands and feet. In Europe and other parts of the world it is well known as a dye for the hair.

HOLLY

Ilex aquifolium, Linn.
Fam. Aquifoliaceae

Synonyms: Holm, Hulm, Hulver Bush.

Habitat: A native of Europe. Growing freely in Great Britain.

Flowering Time: May and June.

Description: The leaves are about 2 in. long and $1\frac{1}{4}$ in. broad, oblong-ovate, shiny, leathery, with a spiny margin, but some leaves are almost free from spines. Taste and odour, none.

Parts Used: Leaves, berries.

Medicinal Use: Febrifuge, cathartic. The leaves have been used in fevers and rheumatism, the berries in dropsy.

HOLLYHOCK

Althaea rosea, Linn.
Fam. Malvaceae

Synonyms: Common Hollyhock, Garden Hollyhock.

Habitat: Although not native to this country, it grows very freely in gardens.

Flowering Time: July and August.

Description: The dried flowers are deep purplish black about $2\frac{1}{2}$ in. in diameter, united with the stamens, which form a tube, the one-celled reniform anthers remaining free. The corolla, freed from the calyx, is usually sold.

Part Used: Flowers.

Medicinal Use: Emollient, demulcent, diuretic. Useful in chest complaints; its action is similar to that of Marshmallow.

Joseph Miller writes: "It is mostly used in gargles for the Swelling of the tonsils, and the Relaxation of the Uvula; but it is not often met with in Prescriptions."

Domestic Use: The dark violet-flowered variety is also used for colouring purposes.

HOLY THISTLE

Carbenia benedicta, Berul.
Fam. Compositae

Synonyms: *Cnicus benedictus*, Gaertn.; Blessed Thistle, *Carduus benedictus*, Steud. Melancholy Thistle is *Carduus heterophyllus*.

Habitat: Coastal regions of the Mediterranean and to a lesser extent in the British Isles.

Flowering Time: June.

Description: Leaves greyish green, thin and brittle, with prominent, pale veinlets, clasping the stem, the margins irregularly toothed, each tooth ending in a spine. Flowerheads about 1 in. long and 1¾ in. broad. Fruits cylindrical, ¼ in. long, finely ribbed longitudinally with an outer long and inner short row of stiff bristles within the toothed crown of the fruit. Involucral scales ovate, terminating in a long bristle. Taste, very bitter; odour, none.

Part Used: Herb.

Medicinal Use: Tonic, diaphoretic, emmenagogue. In dyspepsia, intermittent fevers, and loss of appetite it is found very useful. The warm infusion—1 oz to 1 pt of boiling water—in doses of a wineglassful will be found of value in breaking up colds; it acts well also in menstrual derangements due to colds, etc.

Preparation: Liquid extract: Dose, ½–1 dr.

HONEYSUCKLE

Lonicera caprifolium, Linn.
Fam. Caprifoliaceae

Synonyms: Dutch Honeysuckle, Perfoliate Honeysuckle.

Habitat: It grows freely in Europe and the British Isles, and in other parts of the world.

Flowering Time: June.

Description: The dried flowers are yellowish brown, mostly tubular flower-buds mixed with the stalked heads about ¼ in. in diameter of minute young fruits, from which the flowers have fallen. Leaves rather thin, 1½–2 in.

long and 1–1¼ in. broad, oval obtuse, shortly stalked, opposite, smooth, the upper leaves united at the base, and with entire margins paler below. Taste, sweet, mucilaginous; odour, imperceptible.

Parts Used: Dried flowers and leaves.

Medicinal Use: Expectorant, laxative. The flowers, in the form of a syrup, have been used successfully in disorders of the respiratory organs and in asthma. A decoction of the leaves acts as a laxative and has been used with benefit in diseases of liver and spleen.

Joseph Miller states: "The oil made by Infusion of the Flowers, is accounted healing and warming, and good for the Cramp and Convulsions of the Nerves."

HOPS

Humulus lupulus, Linn.
Fam. Moraceae

Habitat: Europe and Great Britain. Introduced into U.S.A., South America, and Australia. English hops are considered superior to all others. The chief county for growing Hops is Kent.

Flowering Time: August.

Description: The leafy female catkin or strobile is about 1–1½ in. long and ¾–1 in. broad, and consists of membranous scales, which are yellowish green, oval, and ⅓ in. long, and reticulate-veined. The scales are of two kinds, the one equal and the other unequal at the base, the latter bearing a small seed-like fruit at the concave base, over which yellowish shining glands are scattered. Taste, bitter, aromatic: odour, aromatic; in old catkins somewhat recalling valerian. The glands when separated by sifting are known as lupuline, employed as a nervine and to produce sleep.

THE chief use of Hops is for the manufacture of beer for which it has been used for generations on the Continent. The use of Hops in beer was not however always popular in this country. In the reign of Henry VI a person was proceeded against for putting into beer "An unwholesome weed called an hopp." Later on it became an indispensable ingredient and Gerard writes: "The manifold vertues of Hops do manifest argue the wholesomenesse of beere . . . for the hops rather make it a physicall drinke to keepe the body in health, than an ordinary drinke for the quenching of our thirst."

Part Used: Flowers (strobiles).

Medicinal Use: Tonic, anodyne, diuretic, and aromatic bitter. Generally used in combination with other remedies in debility, indigestion, worms, nervous conditions, etc. Useful in atonic dyspepsia. A pillow filled with Hops is considered good for sleeplessness and nervous irritation. The infusion of 1 oz in 1 pt of boiling water may be taken in wineglassful doses as a good general tonic and sedative.

Preparations: Ext. Lupul.: Dose, 5–15 gr; Inf. Lupul. Conc.: Dose, 1–2 dr; Tinct. Lupul.: Dose, ½–1 dr; Liquid extract: Dose, ¼–1 dr; Lupulin (the glands of the strobiles separated from Hops): Dose, 2–5 gr.

HOREHOUND

Marrubium vulgare, Linn.
Fam. Labiatae

Synonyms: Hoarhound, White Horehound.

Habitat: Widely distributed in Europe and not very common growing wild in England. It is, however, cultivated.

Flowering Time: June and July, the seeds ripening in August.

Description: Stem and leaves coated with soft woolly hairs. Leaves cordate-ovate, shortly stalked, and crenate at the margins, reticulated on both sides. Flowers small, white, with axillary clusters. Calyx with ten veins and ten teeth ending in rigid hooked points. Taste, bitter, aromatic; odour, characteristic.

Part Used: Herb.

Medicinal Use: Bitter tonic, expectorant, diuretic. Is perhaps the most popular of herbal pectoral remedies. It is exceedingly valuable in coughs, colds, and pulmonary affections. It has a pleasant taste and makes a nice tonic. In many parts it is brewed and sold as Horehound Ale, making an appetizing and healthful beverage. Also a candy is prepared, and if properly made, is no doubt efficacious. An infusion of 1 oz to 1 pt of boiling water is taken in wineglassful doses, frequently.

Culpeper has many other uses for Horehound, such as to repel the afterbirth, as an antidote to poisons and for the bites of venomous serpents. Mattheolus states that this herb is available for those that have hard livers and for such as have itches and running tetters (a term used for various skin ailments).

Preparations: Inf. Marrub. Conc.: Dose, ½–1 dr; Syr. Marrub. B.P.C. 1949: Dose, ½–1 dr; Liquid extract: Dose, ½–1 dr; Solid extract: Dose, 5–15 gr; Powdered Herb: Dose, ¼–½ dr.

HOREHOUND, horseradish, coriander, lettuce, and nettle are the five bitter herbs ordered to be eaten by the Jews at their Passover feast.

HOREHOUND, BLACK

Ballota nigra, Linn.
Fam. Labiatae

Synonym: *Marrubium nigrum*, Crantz.

Habitat: The same as White Horehound.

Flowering Time: July.

Description: Lower leaves cordate, upper leaves ovate, crenate, serrate, hairy. Flowers usually purplish, labiate. Calyx with five spreading, broadly ovate teeth. Taste, unpleasant; odour, disagreeable.

Part Used: Herb.

Medicinal Use: Stimulant, antispasmodic, vermifuge. Recommended in suppressed and excessive menstruation.

This herb is not now much used in medicine although the ancients extolled its worth.

Dioscorides says: "The leaves beaten with salt and applied to the wound cure the bite of mad dogs."

HORSE CHESTNUT

Aesculus hippocastanum, Linn.
Fam. Sapindaceae

Synonym: *Hippocastanum vulgare*, Gaertn.

Habitat: A native of North Asia but now widely cultivated in many countries. Parkinson states that he cultivated it in his orchard.

Flowering Time: May.

Description: The bark occurs in flattened pieces 4–5 in. long, about 11½ in. broad, and about 1–1¼ in. thick, greyish brown externally, with corky warts tangentially elongated; on the inner surface, pinkish brown and finally striated longitudinally. Fracture finely fibrous and laminate towards the inner surface. Taste, bitter and astringent; odour, none. The fruit is a capsule, splitting into three valves, with short splines scattered on the surface, each containing a large, brown, polished seed, about 1 in. broad and ½ in. thick, with a large, dull, rough, and pale-brown scar where it has been attached to the capsule. Seed white, giving a blue fluorescent infusion.

Parts Used: Bark, fruit.

Medicinal Use: Tonic, narcotic, febrifuge, astringent. The bark is used in intermittent fevers infused with boiling water—1 oz to 1 pt—and given in tablespoonful doses three to four times daily; this has also been used as an external application to ulcers. The fruits have been employed with success in treatment of rheumatic and neuralgic disorders; also for rectal complaints, backache, piles, etc. Tincture of seeds 1 in 10 of proof spirit. Used for painful haemorrhoids. Dose, 10 drops night and morning.

The term Horse Chestnut arises from the fact that horses are said to eat the fruit and by it cure coughs. In fact the nuts have been used for feeding horses and cattle and for fattening them.

Preparations: Liquid extract, fruit: Dose, 5–20 drops; Liquid extract, bark: Dose, ½–2 dr.

HORSEMINT

Monarda punctata, Linn.
Fam. Labiatae

Synonym: American Horsemint.

Habitat: U.S.A.

Description: Leaves opposite, stalked, lanceolate, about 2 in. long, toothed, nearly smooth, flowers in axillary tufts, with sessile yellow and purple bracts, and a tubular five-toothed downy calyx. Corolla two-lipped yellow, with purple spots and two stamens. Taste, pungent, bitterish; odour, recalling that of Thyme.

Parts Used: Tops, leaves.

Medicinal Use: Stimulant, carminative, diuretic. Like all the Mint family this drug may be serviceable as a stimulating diaphoretic in flatulence, nausea, and vomiting. The warm infusion is a pleasant diuretic and it has also a reputation as an emmenagogue. The dose is a wineglassful several times daily.

Preparations: Oil (oleum Monardae) U.S.P. 1870: Dose, 2–10 drops.

HORSEMINT, ENGLISH

Mentha sylvestris, Linn.
Fam. Labiatae

Habitat: Europe and Great Britain. Also grows in U.S.A.

Flowering Time: July and August.

Description: Leaves opposite, nearly sessile, ovate lanceolate, serrate, silky beneath, flowers labiate, arranged in axillary clusters crowded into linear spikes, bracts subulate. Taste and odour resembling that of garden mint (*Mentha viridis*, Linn.).

Part Used: Herb.

Medicinal Use: Carminative, stimulant.

HORSENETTLE

Solanum carolinense, Linn.
Fam. Solanaceae

Synonyms: Bullnettle, Sandbrier, Treadsoft, Treadsaf, Apple of Sodom, Poisonous Potato.

Habitat: Eastern U.S.A., growing in sandy soil.

Description: Root cylindrical, smooth, with a few slender rootlets, in pieces of 4–6 in. long, with a thin, pale-brown bark easily abraded, showing white beneath, fracture tough, woody, with a radiate structure, with a few fine, silky fibres projecting from the bark. Taste, bitter, then sweetish; odour, none. Fresh berries are imported in spirit from the U.S.A.

Parts Used: Berries, root.

Medicinal Use: Antispasmodic, sedative. This plant has lately come into prominence as a remedy in infantile and hysterical convulsions, but chiefly in epilepsy and paroxysms connected with menstrual derangements. The dose of the berries has been given as 5–60 gr, and of the root from 10 gr to 2 dr.

HORSERADISH

Cochlearia armoracia, Linn.
Fam. Cruciferae

Habitat: Eastern Europe but cultivated in Great Britain and America.

Flowering Time: It rarely flowers, but when it does it is in July.

Description: Root white, cylindrical, about 1 ft long and about $\frac{3}{4}$ in. in diameter; usually sold fresh. Taste, pungent, mustard-like; odour, when the root is scraped, recalling that of mustard, and irritating to the nostrils.

Part Used: Root.

Medicinal Use: Stimulant, diaphoretic, diuretic. An excellent stimulant to the digestive organs, and useful in the treatment of dropsy. Dr. Coffin recommends for dropsy an infusion prepared by pouring 1 pt of boiling water on 1 oz of Horseradish and $\frac{1}{2}$ oz of Mustard Seed (crushed). The dose is 2–3 tablespoonfuls three times a day.

Preparations: Fluid extract: Dose, $\frac{1}{2}$–1 dr; Comp. Sp. Horseradish: Dose, 1–2 dr.

HORSETAIL

Equisetum arvense, Linn.
Fam. Equisetaceae

Synonyms: Shavegrass, Bottlebrush, Pewterwort.

Habitat: There are eleven species of Horsetail growing in Great Britain. In addition to *Equisetum arvense*, which is abundant in the country, growing on wet ground and waste places, the most common are *E. telmateia* or Great Horsetail, *E. sylvaticum* or Wood Horsetail which is found all over England but which is more common in Scotland, *E. limosum* or Smooth Horsetail, *E. palustre* or Marsh Horsetail, found in boggy land and common in Britain. Most of the other varieties are found in Northern England and Scotland and more rarely in the South.

Flowering Time: The plant does not produce flowers, but spores on the fertile stem. These appear in July and have somewhat the appearance of a catkin.

Description: In the spring the plant shows itself with heads something like asparagus. Afterwards it grows hollow-branched stems which are jointed and about 1 ft high. The plant is leafless but has sheaths at the joints, the teeth of which are long and acute. These plants were represented in the Coal period by trees from 20–30 ft high and 4–6 in. in diameter. Their impression is sometimes found on the surface of a piece of coal.

Part Used: Herb.

Medicinal Use: Culpeper states that this plant belongs to Saturn and recommends it to "staunch bleeding either inward or outward."

Gerard, quoting Dioscorides, says: "Dioscorides saith that Horse-tail, being stamped and laid to, doth perfectly cure wounds; yea, although the sinues be cut asunder, as Galen addeth. It is of so great and singular virtue in healing wounds as that it is thought and reported for truth, to cure wounds of the bladder and other bowles, and helpeth ruptures and burstings."

In modern times, Horsetail has been used as a diuretic and astringent and is said to be of use in dropsy, gravel, and kidney complaints. The ashes of the plant are said to be useful for acidity of the stomach and dyspepsia, taken in doses of 3–10 gr.

Preparation: Liquid extract: Dose, $\frac{1}{4}$–1 dr.

Domestic Use: The variety known as Dutch-rushes was used according to Parkinson by country housewives ". . . to scour both their wooden, pewter, and brass vessels. The young buds are dressed by some like asparagus, or being boiled, are afterwards bestewed with flour and fryed to be eaten."

John Hill, M.D., spoke of this variety being used by artisans for polishing hard wood, brass, ivory, etc.

HOUNDSTONGUE

Cynoglossum officinale, Linn.
Fam. Boraginaceae

Synonym: Dogstongue.

Habitat: Grows commonly in England. As stated by Gerard: "It grows almost anywhere by highwayes and untoiled ground."

Description: Flowers dull red, funnel-shaped, five divisions. Several flowers, each on a small stalk, grow all one side of the flower stalk. Stem 1–2 ft, rough haired. Leaves long, lance shaped, grow alternately, lower leaves stalked, sometimes a foot long.

Part Used: Herb.

Medicinal Use: Anodyne, demulcent, astringent. Has been employed in coughs, colds, catarrhs, diarrhoea, and dysentery. Is very soothing to the digestive organs and relieves piles. Often used externally and internally at the same time.

Gerard writes: "Dioscorides saith that the leaves boiled in wine and drunk doth mollifie the belly, and being stamped with old swines grease are good against the falling away of the haire proceeding of hot humors. Likewise they are a remedy against scaldings or burnings and against biting of dogs."

CULPEPER reports that according to Mizaldus "The leaves laid under the feet will keep dogs from barking at you." He adds: "It is called Houndstongue because it ties the tongues of hounds; whether true or not, I never tried, yet I cured the biting of a mad dog with this medicine only."

HOUSELEEK

Sempervivum tectorum, Linn.
Fam. Crassulaceae

Synonyms: Common Houseleek, Sengreen, Joubarbe des toits (Fr.).
Habitat: A common garden plant in Great Britain and Europe.
Flowering Time: July.
Description: Leaves forming rosettes 2–3 in. in diameter, fleshy, flat, sessile, oblong-obovate, incurved, and pointed, hairy on the margin. Taste, saline, astringent, and acid; odour, none.
Part Used: Fresh leaves.
Medicinal Use: Refrigerant, astringent. The fresh leaves are bruised and applied as a poultice in inflammatory conditions of the skin such as burns, stings, etc. The juice is said to cure warts and corns.

HYDRANGEA

Hydrangea aborescens, Linn.
Fam. Saxifragaceae

Synonyms: Wild Hydrangea, Seven Barks. The synonym, Seven Barks, arises because the bark peels off in separate layers of different colours.
Habitat: U.S.A. Related to the well-known cultivated Hydrangea.
Description: Root pale fawn-coloured, smooth with gradually tapering branches, hard and woody, bark very thin, the wood porous and radiate

in structure; in the larger pieces, of apparently underground branches, there is a distinct white pith. Taste of the bark, slightly sweetish and pungent; odour, none.

Part Used: Root.

Medicinal Use: Cathartic, diuretic, nephritic. A valuable remedy for the removal of stone and gravel in the bladder. Its greatest value is due to its power of preventing any gravelly deposits. The infusion of 1 oz of root in 1 pt of boiling water may be taken in wineglassful doses, hot, if desired.

Preparation: Fluid extract: Dose, ½–2 dr.

HYDROCOTYLE

Hydrocotyle asiatica, Linn.
Fam. Umbelliferae

Synonym: Indian Pennywort.

Habitat: Tropical Asia and Africa.

Description: A small umbelliferous plant with kidney-shaped leaves. The fresh herb is said to be aromatic but the aroma is lost in drying.

Part Used: Leaves.

Medicinal Use: It has been claimed that Hydrocotyle possesses stimulant and diuretic qualities. It has been given in fevers, bowel complaints, and for scrofulous conditions. At one time it was thought to be of use in the treatment of leprosy. It is very little used in medicine today.

HYSSOP

Hyssopus officinalis, Linn.
Fam. Labiatae

Habitat: A common garden plant.

Flowering Time: From June to the end of August.

Description: Stem woody, leaves linear-lanceolate, nearly sessile, about ½ in. long and ⅛ in. broad, hairy on the margin. Flowers in axillary tufts arranged on one side. Calyx of five unequal teeth. Stamens, four. Taste, bitter; odour, aromatic and camphoraceous.

Part Used: Herb.

Medicinal Use: Stimulant, carminative, pectoral. Hyssop forms an agreeable remedy in cases of colds, coughs, and lung complaints. It is generally compounded with other remedies. The dose of the infusion, made from 1 oz of herb in 1 pt of boiling water, is a wineglassful, taken frequently.

Gerard states: "A decoction of Hyssope made with figges, water, honey and rue and drunken, helpeth the old cough."

Preparation: Liquid extract: Dose, ½–1 dr.

Biblical References: Exodus XII, 22; Leviticus XIV, 4, 6, 49, 51, 52; Numbers XIX, 6, 18; I Kings IV. 33; Psalm LI, 7; John XIX, 29, Hebrews IX, 19.

I

ICELAND MOSS

Cetraria islandica, Ach.
Fam. Parmeliaceae

Synonyms: Iceland Lichen, Cetraria.

Habitat: Indigenous to a wide area of the Northern hemisphere. It is imported mainly from Sweden and Central Europe. None is imported from Iceland.

Description: Thallus smooth, grey or light olive brown, foliaceous, branching, about 2–4 in. high, curled, channelled or rolled into tubes, terminating in spreading, flattened lobes with the edges fringed with small papillae. The under-surface is paler with depressed, minute, white spots. Taste, bitter; inodorous, but when wetted its odour recalls that of seaweed.

Iceland Moss contains a large amount of starchy matter known as lichenin which is soluble in boiling water and which gelatinizes on cooling.

Medicinal Use: Demulcent, tonic, nutritive. Ordinary doses improve the appetite and digestion, and do not produce constipation, but excessive doses may induce looseness of bowels.

Highly recommended in chronic catarrh and chronic bronchitis, as it relieves the cough and assists the system by its nutritive properties. The decoction is generally made of the strength of 1 oz to 1 pt, and the moss should be well washed before it is used. This was in the B.P. 1885 and the dose 1–4 oz.

IGNATIUS BEANS

Strychnos Ignatii, Berg.
Fam. Loganaceae

Synonyms: Saint Ignatius Beans, *Ignatia amara*, Linn. F.

Habitat: The Philippines.

Description: Seeds ovoid, irregularly angular, about 1 in. long and 1½ in. in diameter, with a definite hilum at one end. Externally dull grey, granular, with occasionally fragments of brown epidermis still adhering to the surface. Internally hard, horny. Taste, intensely bitter; odour, none.

Part Used: Seeds.

Medicinal Use: Stimulant, tonic. Its properties are similar to those of Nux Vomica, possibly more active, and it is used in functional nervous disorders, neuralgia, debility, etc. It also contains Brucin and Strychnine, poisonous alkaloids, to about the same extent as Nux Vomica. Owing to the highly poisonous nature of this drug it should not be used except under medical advice.

Preparations: Powdered seeds: Dose, ½–2 gr; Tinct. Ignat.: Dose, 5–20 min.

INDIAN HEMP

Cannabis sativa, Linn.
Fam. Cannabinaceae

Synonyms: *Cannabis indica*, Lamk., Guaza, Ganjah, Bhang, Dagga.

Habitat: India, Persia. Cultivated in India.

Description: The herb is usually sold in the form of the dried tops of the female flowering plant, and may be recognized by the presence of hemp seeds, of which there are usually some present in a more or less immature state. The leaves are long-stalked, bearing usually five to seven lanceolate-acuminate leaflets sharply serrate at the margin, arranged in a radiate manner; they are brittle, and usually more or less adherent, owing to the exudation of resin. Taste, very slight; odour, somewhat smoky, but characteristic. The name Haschisch has been given to the plant, and also to an electuary made by digesting the herb in butter, which produces a form of intoxication. The plant is also cultivated in Zanzibar, and also in the United States under Government supervision. They are about half the strength of the Indian Guaza.

Part Used: Tops.

Medicinal Use: Anodyne, hypnotic, antispasmodic. Is principally used to allay spasmodic pains of nervous origin where there is a marked nervous depression. It produces sleep without derangement of the digestive organs, and is therefore more suitable, in many cases, than Opium. Used for smoking by the Arabs and other Eastern tribes.

Indian Hemp is highly poisonous and its use leads to the drug habit. Its sale and use are therefore controlled by the Dangerous Drugs Act.

Preparations: Ext. Cannab. B.P.C. 1949: Dose, ¼–1 gr; Tinct. Cannab. B.P.C. 1949.: Dose, 5–15 min; Liquid extract: Dose, 1–3 min; Tinct. Chorof. et Morph. Co. B.P.C. 1949.: Dose, 5–15 min.

INDIAN PHYSIC

Gillenia trifoliata, Moench
Gillenia stipulacea, Pursh
Fam. Roseaceae

Synonyms: *Spiraea trifoliata*, Linn., *S. stipulata*, Muhl., Indian Hippo, Gillenia.

Habitat: U.S.A.

Description: The roots of both species are collected and sold under the name of Indian Physic. The roots are cylindrical, sometimes undulated, usually fissured transversely, and 6 in. or more long, varying from $\frac{1}{10}$–$\frac{1}{8}$ in. in diameter. They have a blackish hue externally, and the transverse section shows a thick reddish bark, with a short fracture, separating easily from the white woody centre. The bark is pleasantly bitter, the wood tasteless; odour, none.

Part Used: Rootbark.

Medicinal Use: Expectorant, cathartic, emetic. The American Indians use the above-mentioned plants in the same way as Ipecacuanha. They recommend it in dyspepsia, dropsy, habitual constipation, coughs, colds, etc. Being a safe and efficient emetic, it can be used with advantage where such may be indicated. A dose of the powder of 2 gr acts as a stomachic; 5–6 gr produce diaphoresis, and 20–30 gr produce emesis and catharsis. The smaller doses may be repeated every three to four hours.

IPECACUANHA

Cephaelis ipecacuanha (Brot), A. Rich.
Fam. Rubiaceae

Synonyms: *Psychotria ipecacuanha*, Stokes, Ipecac.

Habitat: South America.

Description: Rio Ipecac., or Matto Grosso, is slender, rather tortuous, and is most esteemed. It has the appearance of a number of disks or beads strung together. Johore Ipecac. closely resembles the Matto Grosso variety, but is generally bolder and brighter in colour. Minas Ipecac., grown in the province of Minas Geraes, is a variety of Matto Grosso. The root is often shaped like the sea-horse. Cartagena Ipecac., imported from Columbia, is distinguished from Rio by being larger, and the annulations are narrow, raised ridges. The root appears entire instead of the disk formation of the Rio. Cartagena Ipecac. contains the same amount of total alkaloids, Emetine and Cephaeline, as the other varieties, but in different proportions. Rio contains twice as much Emetine as Cephaeline; Cartagena about twice as much Cephaeline as Emetine.

Part Used: Root.

Medicinal Use: Diaphoretic, emetic, expectorant. Small doses act effectually as an expectorant, and may be given for coughs, colds, dysentery, and to produce perspiration. Full doses produce free emesis. An infusion of 1 oz to 1 pt of boiling water may be taken in teaspoonful to wineglassful doses as above directed. Mostly combined with other remedies.

The Cartagena Root is more emetic and less expectorant than Rio Ipecac. Deprived of its alkaloids, it is used as a remedy for dysentery.

Preparations: Ipecac. Praep. B.P.: Dose, $\frac{1}{2}$–2 gr (Emetic, 15–30 gr); Acet. Ipecac. B.P.C. 1949: Dose, 10–30 min; Ext. Ipecac. Liq. B.P.: Dose, $\frac{1}{2}$–2 min (Emetic, 10–30 min); Fldext. Ipecac. U.S.P.: Dose, 8 min; Mist. Ammon. et Ipecac. Co. B.P.C.: Dose, $\frac{1}{2}$–1 fl oz; Mist. Bellad. et Ipecac.

pro Infant. B.P.C.: Dose, 60–120 min; Mist. Ipecac. Alk. B.P.C.: Dose, $\frac{1}{2}$ fl oz; Mist. Ipecac. pro Infant. B.P.C.: Dose, 60–120 min; Mist. Morph. et Ipecac. B.P.C.: Dose, $\frac{1}{2}$ fl oz; Syr. Ipecac. U.S.P.: Dose, 2 fl dr; Syr. Opii. Camph. B.P.C. 1949; Dose, 30–60 min; Tinct. Ipecac. B.P.: Dose, 10–30 min (Emetic $\frac{1}{2}$–1 fl oz).

From the B.P. Powder (Ipecac. Praep.) are prepared: Pil. Aloin. et Strych. Co. B.P.C. 1949: Dose, 1–2 pills; Pil. Hydrarg. c. Cret. et Opii. B.P.C. 1949: Dose, 1 pill; Pulv. Ipecac. et Opii B.P.: Dose, 5–10 gr; Tab. Acid. Acetylsalicyl. et Opii. Co. B.P.C.: Dose, 1–4 tablets; Tab. Ipecac. et Opii. B.P.; Troch. Ipecac. B.P.C. 1949; Troch. Morph. et Ipecac. B.P. 1949.

IRISH MOSS

Chondrus crispus, Stackh.
Fam. Gigartinaceae

Synonyms: Chondrus, Carragheen, Carrageen, Caragahen.

Habitat: This seaweed (it is not strictly a moss) is found quite commonly on the seashores of Europe and United States, but our supplies come chiefly from Ireland.

Description: This dried seaweed has a flat, forked frond varying in width from $\frac{1}{8}$–$\frac{1}{2}$ in. and about $\frac{1}{16}$–$\frac{1}{12}$ in. thick. It varies in length from $2\frac{1}{2}$–5 in. and has a fan-shaped outline. The fronds of *Gigartina mammillosa*, J. Ag., which have a similar shape, are usually incurved at the margins of the stem, and have papillae on the ultimate segments, but possess similar properties. Taste, mucilaginous and saline; odour, that of seaweed. The seaweed is bleached by exposure to the sun and repeated washing. The cheaper qualities are used for cattle food; also for dressing cotton cloth.

Medicinal Use: Demulcent, pectoral, nutritious. Used in chronic coughs, bronchitis, etc.; also in irritating diseases of the bladder and kidneys, and as a culinary article. A decoction can be made as follows: Steep $\frac{1}{2}$ oz of Irish Moss in cold water for 10 min, then boil in 3 pt of water or milk for $\frac{1}{4}$ hr, strain through linen, and season with liquorice, sugar, lemon juice, cinnamon, nutmeg, or other flavours to taste.

IVY

Hedera helix, Linn.
Fam. Araliaceae

Synonym: Common Ivy.

Habitat: A common European and British plant growing on the ground or climbing trees.

Flowering Time: Late in the year. The berries ripen in January.

Description: Leaves dark green, paler beneath, leathery, shining, long-stalked, about 2–4 in. wide, and long, radiate-veined, with three to four triangular lobes; the upper leaves ovate or oval-lanceolate. The berries are about the size of a pea, purplish black, with a disk at the apex corresponding to the calyx rim. Seeds, two or three ruminated. Taste, bitter and nauseous; odour, when rubbed, aromatic and slightly resinous.

Parts Used: Leaves, berries.

Medicinal Use: Stimulating, diaphoretic, cathartic. Externally the leaves have been employed as poultices or fomentations in glandular enlargements, indolent ulcers, abscesses, etc. The berries are found of use in febrile disorders, and a vinegar of these was extensively used during the London plague.

IVY, AMERICAN

Parthenocissus quinquefolia, Planch., Wild.
Fam. Vitaceae

Synonyms: *Ampelopsis quinquefolia*, Mich., *Cissus hederacea*, Ross, *Cissus quinquefolia*, Desf., Virginian Creeper, *Vitis quinquefolia*, Lam., Woodvine.

Habitat: U.S.A., but cultivated in Europe and Great Britain.

Description: The bark occurs in quilled pieces 2–3 in. long and from $\frac{1}{4}$–$\frac{1}{2}$ in. in diameter, externally brown, with enlarged, transverse scars formed from lenticels. The fracture shows a white bark with coarse, flattened fibres in the inner portion. Taste, insipid; odour, faintly aromatic. The leaves are stalked, digitate, with five oblong, lanceolate leaflets.

Parts Used: Bark, twigs.

Medicinal Use: Tonic, expectorant, astringent. This drug is principally used in scrofulous affections, in the form of a syrup. In dropsy, bronchitis, and in pulmonary complaints it may be recommended. The decoction of 1 oz in 1 pt of boiling water is taken in wineglassful doses.

Preparations: Fluid extract: Dose, $\frac{1}{2}$–1 dr; Ampelopsin: Dose, 2–4 gr.

J

JABORANDI

Pilocarpus microphyllus, Stapf.
Fam. Rutaceae

Habitat: Brazil.

Description: The leaflets are dull green, ½–1½ in. long and ⅓–⅔ in. broad, with entire margins slightly recurved and with unequal bases, except the terminal leaflets which have equal bases. Veins are prominent on the upper surface; furnished with numerous translucent oil cells. These leaves were recognized in the 1949 B.P.C. Originally, the leaves of *Pilocarpus jaborandi*, Holmes, were official. The leaflets of this plant are larger and are rarely imported now.

The leaves of *Pilocarpus pinnatifolius*, Lemaire, which have also appeared in commerce, are about the size of *P. jaborandi*, but they are greyish-green and the veins are not prominent. These leaves are only half as active as those of *P. microphyllus*.

Part Used: Leaves.

Medicinal Use: Stimulant, diaphoretic, expectorant. Specially useful in asthma and diabetes. A teaspoonful of powdered leaves infused in a cupful of boiling water and taken as a dose will cause free perspiration and salivation. Generally the infusion of 1 oz of leaves in 1 pt of boiling water is taken in wineglassful doses or less as required.

It is also used in hair tonics to stimulate growth.

Although Jaborandi is no longer in the B.P. or B.P.C., the active principle Pilocarpine has been retained in the form of the nitrate because of its use in contracting the pupil of the eye. Its action is the opposite to that of Atropine.

Preparations: Ext. Jaborand. Liq. B.P.C. 1949; Tinct. Jaborand. B.P.C. 1949: Dose, 10–30 min; Pilocarpine Hydrochlor.: Dose, $\frac{1}{20}$–$\frac{1}{5}$ gr; Pilocarpine Nitrate B.P. and U.S.P.: Dose, $\frac{1}{20}$–$\frac{1}{5}$ gr; Gutt. Pilocarp. B.P.C.

JACOB'S LADDER

Polemonium coeruleum, Linn.
Fam. Polemoniaceae

Synonyms: Greek Valerian, English Greek Valerian.

Habitat: It occurs in the British Isles, Northern Europe, Asia, and America.

Flowering Time: June, July.

Description: The leaves are 5–6 in. long, imparipinnate, with about 17 lanceolate leaflets about 1 in. long and ⅓ in. broad, which are alternate except towards the apex of the leaf, and entire at the margins; the rachis is channelled above. Flowers rotate, blue, and five-parted. Taste, slightly bitter; odour, none.

Part Used: Plant.

Medicinal Use: Diaphoretic, astringent. Its medicinal uses are similar to those described under Abscess Root, which is another species of Polemonium.

JALAP

Ipomaea purga, Hayne
Fam. Convolvulaceae

Synonyms: *Ipomea jalapa*, Schiede and Deppe, *Convolvulus jalapa*, Linn., *Exogonium purga*, Benth., *Convolvulus purga*, Wend.

Habitat: Mexican Andes.

Description: Root usually ovoid, varying greatly in size, but on the average 2½ in. long by 1½ in. in diameter, dark brown, wrinkled, with paler, small transverse marks, often more numerous at one end. The interior is dirty white, tough, hard, and sometimes horny, with a resinous non-fibrous fracture. Taste, unpleasant, followed by acridity; odour, smoky due to the smoke over which the root has been dried. Good Jalap should contain 10 per cent Resin.

Part Used: Root.

Medicinal Use: Cathartic, purgative. Used in constipation, pain and colic in bowels, and general intestinal torpor. Is combined with other laxatives and with carminatives such as ginger, cloves, etc.

Preparations: Jalap. Praep. B.P.C.: Dose, 5–20 gr; Tinct. Jalap. B.P.C. 1949: Dose, 30–60 min; Jalap. Resin, B.P.C.: Dose, 1–5 gr. From Jalap. Praep. is made: Pulv. Jalap. Co. B.P.C. 1949: Dose, 10–60 gr. From Jalap Resin are made: Pil. Aloin. et Podoph. Co. B.P.C. 1949: Dose, 1–4 pills; Tab. Colocynth. et Jalap. Co. B.P.C.: Dose, 1–3 tablets; Jalapin B.P.C.: Dose, 1–5 gr.

JAMAICA DOGWOOD

Piscidia erythrina, Linn.
Fam. Leguminosae

Synonyms: Fish-poison Tree, Malungu. Called Fish-poison Tree because it is used in Jamaica for poisoning fish.

Habitat: West Indies, South America.

Description: The bark occurs in quilled, curved pieces about 2–6 in. long and ⅛–¼ in. thick, dark grey-brown externally, with thin, longitudinal and transverse ridges, roughish and wrinkled, and somewhat fissured. Fracture tough, fibrous, with blue-green or brownish-green patches. Taste, bitter and somewhat acrid; odour, opium-like.

Part Used: Bark.

Medicinal Use: Anodyne, sedative. Relieves toothache, eases bronchial and consumptive cough. Produces sleep and allays pain and nervous excitement. Unpleasant results have occurred from overdoses. Generally combined with Black Haw and other remedies in female complaints, etc.

Preparations: Ext. Piscid. Liq.: Dose, $\frac{1}{2}$–2 dr; Ext. Piscid.: Dose, 1–5 gr.

JAMBUL

Eugenia jambolana, Lamk.
Fam. Myrtaceae.

Synonyms: Jamboo, Java Plum, Jambol, Jambool, Rose Apple.

Habitat: East India, Australia.

Description: It is a large tree and the seeds as met with in commerce are muller-shaped, blackish brown, about $\frac{1}{4}$ in. long and rather less in diameter, one end truncated with a central depression, hard and tough externally, and internally pinkish brown, with glistening starch grains. Taste, faintly astringent and slightly aromatic; odour, none.

Part Used: Seeds.

Medicinal Use: Astringent, diuretic. This drug has been found very useful in diabetes, as it reduces the amount of sugar present in urine in a very brief space of time. Although not a specific in all cases of diabetes, it promises to be of the greatest value and should be tried whenever an occasion presents itself.

Van Noorden recommends large doses in cases of diabetes mellitus, and says $\frac{1}{2}$ oz of the fluid extract in 8 oz of hot water should be taken one hour before breakfast and last thing at night.

Preparations: Powdered seeds: Dose, 5–30 gr. May be administered in cachets or capsules. Liquid extract: Dose, 1–2 dr.

Domestic Use: Jambul produces an edible fruit which, however, is not seen in this country.

JEQUIRITY

Abrus precatorius, Linn.
Fam. Leguminosae

Synonyms: Indian Liquorice, Wild Liquorice, Prayer Beads, Crab's Eyes.

Habitat: India, Brazil.

Description: Seeds oval, rounded at the ends, about $\frac{1}{8}$ in. in diameter, hard and polished, vermilion red, with the upper third black; very hard and tough.

Part Used: Seeds.

Medicinal Use: Irritant. It may be very cautiously used in eye diseases, and not until other means have been exhausted, as it produces a violent conjunctival inflammation and is likely to destroy the corneal structures.

The seeds are very poisonous and have been used in days gone by for poisoning criminals.

JEWEL WEED

Impatiens aurea, Muhl.
Impatiens biflora, Walt.
Fam. Geraniaceae

Synonyms: *I. aurea*, Muhl. = *I. pallida*, Nutt., Pale Touch-me-not, Balsam Weed. *I. biflora*, Walt. = *I. fulva*, Nutt., Spotten Touch-me-not, Speckled Jewels.

Habitat: East Indies, North America.

Description: Stem jointed, leaves grey-green, thin, ovate-oval, more or less toothed. Flowers axillary, solitary, slipper-shaped, with a long, recurved spur: in *I. pallida*, Nutt., pale yellow, and in *I. fulva*, Nutt., orange-yellow and spotted. Valves of the fruit curling up when dehisced.

Part Used: Herb.

Medicinal Use: Aperient, diuretic. The fresh plants boiled with lard form an excellent application for piles. The juice is reputed to remove warts and corns and to cure ringworm. In jaundice and dropsy the decoction has been found valuable in doses of a wineglassful repeated three to four times a day.

JOHN'S BREAD

Ceratonia siliqua, Linn.
Fam. Leguminosae

Synonyms: St. John's Bread, Locust.

Habitat: Middle East and Italy.

Fruiting Time: Spring, ripening late summer or early autumn.

Description: The pods are 4–8 in. long and about 1 in. broad and $\frac{1}{8}$ or $\frac{1}{8}$ in. thick, compressed, dark brown, glossy, enclosing a light brown, soft, fleshy pulp having a sweet taste. Seeds flattish, ovate, in separate cells, lined with papery endocarp. Odour, slightly valerianic.

Part Used: Pods.

Medicinal Use: Nutritive. Used as a food for man and beast, and by singers to improve the voice.

It is thought probable that St. Luke xv, 16, refers to the husks of this fruit as it was largely used to feed swine.

JUJUBE

Zizyphus vulgaris, Lamk.
Fam. Rhamnaceae

Habitat: Africa, Egypt, Arabia, Syria. Cultivated in Italy and Spain.

Description: Fruits variable in size in different varieties, from $\frac{1}{2}$–1 in. long and $\frac{3}{8}$–$\frac{1}{2}$ in. in diameter, red, smooth, and shiny, but brownish red and wrinkled when dried, fleshy and containing one or two endocarps. Taste, sweet and mucilaginous.

Part Used: Berries.

Medicinal Use: Mucilaginous, pectoral. From these the genuine *Pâte de Jujubes* was formerly prepared for use in the manufacture of pectoral lozenges. The berries were known to the ancient Elizabethan herbalists.

Parkinson writes: ". . . all authors doe agree, that they coole the heate and sharpnesse of the blood, and are therefore good in hot agues, and doe helpe them that have a cough, to expectorate tough flegme."

Joseph Parker gives a similar account of their use and adds: ". . . but they are now quite out of use, and are hardly to be met with in the shops." And so it is today.

JUNIPER

Juniperus communis, Linn.
Fam. Pinaceae

Habitat: Juniper is a widely distributed tree and is found in many parts of the world.

Fruiting Time: The berries (fruit) remain green the first year and ripen during the second autumn.

Description: The tree itself which is well known grows to varying heights, up to 36 ft, in Norway and Sweden. The English plant grows to about 6 ft.

JUNIPER Berries were used by the ancient herbalists of Greece and Arabia and by the Romans. The fifteenth and sixteenth century herbalists praised their use highly, their knowledge of their uses being culled to a large extent from the more ancient writers. The juice from the berries is recommended, as commonly are many herbs, against the bitings of vipers and against the plague and pestilence. Parkinson writes: ". . . to procure safe and easy delivery unto woman with child, Mattheolus adviseth to take seven Juniper and seven Bayberries, half a dramme of Cassia lignea, and a dram of Cinamon, these being grossely bruised put them into the belly of a Turtle Dove to be rosted therewith, let it be basted with the fat of an Hen, whereof they are to eate every other evening. . . ."

Berry (fleshy galbulus) $\frac{3}{10}$–$\frac{4}{10}$ in. in diameter, globular. Purplish black with a blue-grey bloom when recently collected, and a triangular line at the apex, indicating the junction of the three seeds. Taste, aromatic and turpentiney; odour, turpentiney, but characteristic.

Parts Used: Fruit, usually called the berry, and the wood.

Medicinal Use: Diuretic, stimulant, carminative. As a rule these are given in conjunction with other remedies for kidney complaints. The oil distilled from berries and wood is also largely used. The infusion of 1 oz of berries to 1 pt of boiling water is taken in wineglassful doses.

Preparations: Ol. Junip. B.P.C. 1949: Dose, ½–3 min; Sp. Junip. B.P.C. 1949: Dose, 5–20 min; Liquid extract: Dose, ½–1 dr; Ol. Juniper Lig.: Dose, 1–5 min; Solid extract: Dose, 5–15 gr. Juniper Tar Oil (Oil of Cade) B.P.C. and U.S.P. is distilled from *Juniperus oxycedrus* (wood).

Domestic Use: Juniper Berries form an ingredient in Gin.

Biblical References: 1 Kings XIX, 4 and 5; Job XXX, 4; Psalms CXX, 4 and 5.

K

KAMALA

Mallotus philippinensis, Muell., Arg.
Fam. Euphorbiaceae

Synonyms: *Rottlera tinctoria*, Roxb., Kameela, Spoonwood.

Habitat: Abyssinia, Southern Arabia, India.

Description: The red glands covering the fruit, obtained by sifting the fruit, form a red mobile powder which floats on water. The grains after treatment with alcohol or potash solution, to dissolve out the colouring matter, show a radiate structure. The powder often contains a quantity of sand, which can be removed by stirring the Kamala in water, when the latter floats, and can be separated. Tasteless and nearly odourless, but an alcoholic solution poured into water gives off a melon-like odour. The tree produces a three-celled capsular fruit the size of a pea covered with a red powder (Kamala), which is removed by shaking.

Part Used: Capsule hairs and glands.

Medicinal Use: Taenifuge, purgative. Has long been used in India with success. The doses of powder vary from 2–3 dr for adults, repeated if necessary. The worm is usually expelled entire. The fluid extract acts more mildly and with more certainty.

Preparations: Powdered Kamala: Dose, ½–3 dr; Liquid extract: Dose, 2–4 dr.

KAVA KAVA

Piper methysticum, Forst.
Fam. Piperaceae

Synonyms: Ava, Ava Pepper, Kava.

Habitat: South Sea Islands.

Description: Root large, and usually cut into segments 2 in. or more in diameter, externally blackish grey, internally whitish, fracture mealy and somewhat splintery, central portion porous, with irregularly-twisted, thin wood bundles separated by broad medullary rays, so that under the thick bark the wood bundles form distinct meshes. Rootlets, when not removed, often 12 in. long or more, and more or less fibrous. Taste, somewhat pungent and numbing; odour, agreeable, lilac-like. The root contains about 10 per cent of Resin.

Part Used: Root.

Medicinal Use: Tonic, stimulant, diuretic. Has been employed in bronchitis, rheumatism, and gout. Is also a remedy for nocturnal incontinence of urine, due to muscular weakness.
Preparations: Root: Dose, 1 dr; Ext. Kavae Liq.: Dose, ½–1 dr; Solid extract alc.: Dose, 5–15 gr.

THE natives ferment the root to make a liquor which causes a type of intoxication said to be quite distinct from that due to alcohol.

KINO

Pterocarpus marsupium, Roxb.
Fam. Leguminosae

Synonym: Gum Kino.
Habitat: Indian Peninsula, Ceylon.
Description: Formed from the juice of the tree dried in the sun. The tree itself is handsome and grows 40–80 ft high. The gum appears in commerce in small, blackish, shining fragments, or in coarse powder. Taste, very astringent. It adheres to the teeth when chewed. If properly prepared by boiling the juice as collected, it is entirely soluble when the powder is shaken up with cold water; the solution gives a violet colour with a protosalt of iron.
Part Used: Inspissated juice.
Medicinal Use: Astringent. It is considered valuable in diarrhoea and dysentery. Used as an application in leucorrhoea, relaxed throat, etc.
Preparations: Pulv. Kino Co. B.P.C. 1949: Dose, 5–20 gr; Powdered Gum: Dose, 5–20 gr; Tinct. Kino B.P.C. 1949: Dose, ½–1 dr; Tinct. U.S.P. XI (1 in 5): Dose, 30 min.

KNAPWEED

Centaurea nigra, Linn.
Fam. Compositae

Synonyms: Star Thistle, Black Ray Thistle, Hardhack, Ironweed.
Habitat: It grows wild in the fields and hedgerows in Great Britain.
Flowering Time: June and July.
Description: Readily recognized by the globular flowerheads, about 2 in. long and 1¾ in. broad, the outer scales of which have blackish appendages at the apex with comb-like teeth. Florets purplish, tubular. Fruit without

pappus, but surrounded with bristles (paleae). Taste, bitter, slightly saline; odour, none.

Part Used: Herb.

Medicinal Use: Diuretic, diaphoretic, tonic. It is said to equal Gentian as a tonic. Culpeper says: "It is an admirable remedy for a sore throat, swelling of the uvula and jaw, and all green wounds."

KNOTGRASS, RUSSIAN

Polygonum erectum, Linn.
Fam. Polygonaceae

Habitat: Russia.

Description: Stem slender, cylindrical, striated. Leaves narrowly lanceolate, about ½ in. long and $\frac{1}{16}$–⅛ in. broad, sheathing stipules (ochreae) lanceolate. Seed (nut) triangular, striated, with raised points. Taste, astringent; odour, none.

English Knotgrass is *Polygonum aviculare*, Linn., and has similar properties to the Russian variety.

Part Used: Herb.

Medicinal Use: Astringent. The infusion has been found highly beneficial in diarrhoea and children's summer complaints.

KOLA

Cola vera, Schum.
(and other varieties)
Fam. Sterculiaceae

Synonyms: *Sterculia acuminata*, Beauv., Kola Nut, Guru Nut, Cola.

Habitat: Sierra Leone, North Ashanti. Cultivated in other tropical countries.

Description: It is a large and beautiful tree somewhat resembling the Chestnut. The fleshy, dried cotyledons are the form in which the seed is met with in commerce. They are brown, often irregular in shape, usually oblong, convex on one side and flattened on the other, 1½–2 in. long, and about 1 in. in diameter. Taste, astringent, and somewhat earthy; odour, very slight.

Part Used: Seed.

Medicinal Use: Nerve stimulant, diuretic, cardiac tonic. A good general tonic, depending largely for its influence upon the Caffeine it contains. Used by the African natives to enable them to perform arduous tasks without the aid of food. It is an excellent remedy for diarrhoea, and is also prescribed for the alcohol habit.

Preparations: Powdered Kola: Dose, 15–45 gr; Ext. Kolae Liq. B.P.C. 1949: Dose, 10–20 min; Tinct. Kolae: Dose, ½–1 dr.

KOUSSO

Brayera anthelmintica,
Fam. Rosaceae

Synonyms: Kooso, Kusso, Cossoo, Cusso.

Habitat: North-east Africa.

Description: The inflorescence is usually in the form of a cylindrical roll about 12 in. long and 2½ in. in diameter, consisting usually of the female inflorescence. The flowers are nearly ½ in. across, the ten sepals in two rows are veined and leaf-like, and the petals minute and linear. Stamens 11–25, but in the female flower the anthers are sterile.

Part Used: Dried flowers.

Medicinal Use: Purgative, taenifuge, anthelmintic. Used successfully for tapeworms. The infusion of ½ oz in 1 pt of boiling water is taken in teacupful doses, quickly following each other, the powder being consumed with the liquor. Preparation by Castor Oil or other purgative is necessary, the Kousso to be taken on an empty stomach. A gentle cathartic after its operation is also advisable.

Preparation: Liquid extract: Dose, 2–4 dr.

KUMARHOU

Pomaderris elliptica, Linn.
Fam. Rhamnaceae

Habitat: North Island, New Zealand in the dry hills.

Description: It is a branching shrub, 2–10 ft in height, leaves 2–3 in. long, shining above and downy on the under surface. The inflorescence is a many-flowered cyme. The flowers are fragrant with yellowish white calyx and petals.

Part Used: Herb.

Medicinal Use: It is regarded by the Maoris as a general cure-all and particularly for blood impurities. It is also said to give good results in cases of asthma, bronchitis, and rheumatism. Combined with *Vinca rosae* or alone, it is recommended for diabetes.

An infusion of ½ oz of the herb in 1 pt of water should be taken daily for at least six weeks in wineglassful doses; children half the quantity.

L

LABRADOR TEA

Ledum latifolium, Jacq.
Fam. Ericaceae

Synonyms: James's Tea, *L. palustre*, Marsh Tea, Wild Rosemary.

Habitat: North America and Canada.

Description: Leaves linear-lanceolate, alternate, almost sessile, 1–2 in. long and $\frac{1}{4}$ in. broad; the upper surface dark green and smooth, the under surface coated with rusty brown simple hairs, and multi-cellular short-stalked glands; the margin is revolute. Taste, bitter and camphoraceous; odour, aromatic.

Part Used: Leaves.

Medicinal Use: Pectoral, expectorant, diuretic. Is very useful in coughs, colds, bronchial, and pulmonary affections. For internal use the infusion is taken in wineglassful doses. A strong decoction has been recommended for external use as a remedy for itching and exanthematous skin diseases.

LACHNANTHES

Lachnanthes tinctoria, Ell.
Fam. Haemodoraceae

Synonyms: Spiritweed, Red or Paint Root, Wool Flower.

Habitat: West Indies.

Description: Rhizome about 1 in. long, surrounded with long, slender, deep-red roots. Leaves falcate, in a basal rosette $\frac{1}{5}$–$\frac{3}{5}$ in. wide, sheathing at the base and, as well as the stems, reddish brown when dried, and reduced in size on the stem to small bracts. Flowers six, parted, with three stamens in a close, woolly cyme. Taste, somewhat acrid; odour, none.

Parts Used: Root, herb.

Medicinal Use: Stimulating, hypnotic. Has been recommended in cough, pneumonia, etc. Large doses produce unpleasant symptoms.

Preparation: Liquid extract: Dose, 1–5 min.

LADY'S BEDSTRAW

Galium verum, Linn.
Fam. Rubiaceae

Synonyms: Yellow Bedstraw, Maid's Hair, Cheese Rennet, Gailion, Petti-mugget, Wild Rosemary.

Habitat: A common herb growing in meadows and pastures and in hedges.

Description: Stems slender, angular. Leaves linear, with revolute margins, downy beneath, and about eight in a whorl. Flowers in terminal panicles, golden yellow. Taste, astringent, bitterish and slightly acid; odour, none.

Culpeper and other herbalists also describe another variety with white flowers.

Part Used: Herb.

Medicinal Use: Diuretic, alterative. This is a popular remedy in gravel, stone, and urinary diseases, and has been used in hysterical complaints and epilepsy. The infusion is made with 1 oz of herb in 1 pt of boiling water and taken in wineglassful doses several times a day.

Joseph Miller says "Some commend a decoction of it for the gout; and a bath made of it is very refreshing to wash the feet of persons tired with overwalking."

Parkinson writes: ". . . these sorts with white flowers have beene thought unprofitable, and of no use, but Clausius saith, the poore women in Austria, Hungaria and other places in Germany that gather herbes and roots for their uses that neede them, bringing them to the market to sell . . . by their experience found it good for the sinewes, arteries and joints, to bathe them therewith both to take away their wearinesse and weakenesse in them, and to comfort and strengthen them also after travaile, cold or paines."

Domestic Use: In the North at one time they used the yellow flowers for making cheeses instead of using Rennet.

LADY'S MANTLE

Alchemilla vulgaris, Linn.
Fam. Rosaceae

Synonym: Lion's Foot.

Habitat: A British wild plant.

Flowering Time: May and June.

Description: Leaves rounded, about 2 in. in diameter, having nine obtuse, serrate lobes, and slender stalks about 4 in. long, the whole plant furnished with soft silk hairs. Flowers green, in small clusters, borne on a forked stem which has small three-lobed leaves and broad stipules at the base of each fork. The flowers have no petals and only one to four stamens. Taste, slightly astringent; inodorous.

Part Used: Herb.

Medicinal Use: Astringent, styptic. Used as a cure for excessive menstruation and flooding. Taken internally as an infusion of 1 oz to 1 pt of boiling water in teacupful doses as required. Also employed as an injection.

Culpeper refers to it as a wound herb "and therefore highly praised by the Germans who use it in all wounds inward and outward, to drink a decoction thereof, and wash the wounds therewith, or dips tents therein and put them into the wounds which wonderfully dries up all humidity of the sores, and abates inflammations therein."

Preparation: Liquid extract: Dose, ½–1 dr.

LADY'S SLIPPER

Cypripedium pubescens, Willd.
Fam. Orchidaceae

Synonyms: *Cypripedium hirsutum*, Mill., American Valerian, Nerveroot, Noah's Ark, Yellow Lady's Slipper.

Habitat: Varieties of this plant grow in many parts of Europe and U.S.A.

Description: Rhizome 2–4 in. long, and ⅛–¼ in. thick, with numerous cup-shaped scars on the upper surface, and many unbranched, wavy, densely-matted roots below. Fracture, short, white. Odour, slightly valerianic; taste, sweetish, acrid, bitter, and aromatic. The drug of commerce is derived from both *Cypripedium pubescens*, Willd., and *C. parviflorum*, Salisb.

Part Used: Rhizome.

Medicinal Use: Antispasmodic, nervine, tonic. It allays pain, gives sleep, and is useful in headache, neuralgia, and female weaknesses. For this reason it is given in hysteria and most nervous disorders. Prescribed with tonic medicines its power is increased. The powder may be taken in sweetened water.

Preparations: Powdered root: Dose, 1 dr; Liquid extract: Dose, ½–1 dr; Cypripedin: Dose, 1–3 gr; Solid extract, alc.; Dose, 5–10 gr.

LARCH

Larix europaea, D.C.
Fam. Pinaceae

Synonyms: *Pinus larix*, Linn., European Larch.

Habitat: Europe. The British Isles.

Description: The inner bark of the tree, deprived of its grey, inert, outer portion, is preferred for medicinal use. It occurs in flattish pieces, externally red-brown, with a rosy tint internally, the inner surface smooth, and pinkish brown or yellowish. Fracture short, slightly fibrous. Odour, terebinthinous; taste, astringent, turpentiney, somewhat bitter.

Part Used: Bark.

Medicinal Use: Astringent, balsamic, diuretic. A strong tincture has been used in chronic urinary inflammations, also in bronchitis to check secretions.

Preparation: Venice Turpentine is made by boring the stems and collecting the oleo-resin.

LARKSPUR

Delphinium consolida, Linn.
Fam. Ranunculaceae

Synonyms: Lark's Claw, Lark's Heel, Knight's Spur.
Habitat: A common European and British plant.
Flowering Time: The summer months.
Description: Seeds black, tetrahedral, flattened, $\frac{1}{24}$–$\frac{1}{16}$ in. in diameter, with acute edges and pitted surface. Albumen oily. Taste, bitter and acrid; inodorous.
Part Used: Seeds.
Medicinal Use: A tincture of the seeds acts as a parasiticide and insecticide, and is used to destroy lice and nits in the hair. Used also in spasmodic asthma and dropsy; the tincture (1 oz to 1 pt dilute alcohol) is given in 10 drop doses, gradually increased.

LAUREL

Laurus nobilis, Linn.
Fam. Lauraceae

Synonyms: Bay, Sweet Bay, Noble Laurel, Roman Laurel.
Habitat: Europe and Great Britain.
Description: The leaves are leathery, dark green, rather paler beneath, about 3 in. long and 1 in. broad, elliptic-lanceolate, slightly broader above the middle, entire, but wavy at the margins, the small whitish veins forming a network of nearly square, minute meshes. Taste, aromatic; odour, aromatic, when bruised.

Bay Rum is distilled from the leaves of *Pimenta acris* (West Indies).

This plant must not be confused with the Cherry-Laurel (q.v.).

Parts Used: Leaves, fruit and essential oil.
Medicinal Use: Stomachic. The ancients valued Laurel greatly, but nowadays hardly any other preparation is used in medicine but the oil, as an application in rheumatism, etc.

LAVENDER

Lavandula officinalis, Chaix
Fam. Labiatae

Synonym: *Lavandula vera*, D.C.
Habitat: Mediterranean countries. Cultivated in England and other parts.

Flowering Time: July.

Description: The flowers are usually met with in commerce separated from the flower spikes. The calyx is tubular, purplish grey, and five-toothed, with 13 veins, one tooth being larger than the others. The tubular corolla is two-lipped, the upper lip with two and the lower with three lobes. The whole of the flowers have a dense covering of stellate hairs, with minute, shining oil glands, visible under a lens. Taste, pleasant; odour, fragrant and characteristic. Spike Lavender Oil is distilled from *Lavandula latifolia*, Vill., and other species growing in France and Spain. This is largely used for preventing insect bites.

Parts Used: Flowers and essential oil.

Medicinal Use: Stimulant, carminative. Seldom used in medicine. The infusion is made from 1 dr of flowers to 1 pt of boiling water.

Preparations: Ol. Lavand. B.P. and U.S.P.: Dose, 1–3 min; Sp. Lavand. U.S.P.; Tinct. Lavand. Co. B.P.C. 1949: Dose, 30–60 min; Tinct. Lavand. Co. U.S.P.

Domestic Use: Lavender Oil is used to make Lavender Water and also enters into the composition of other perfumes. Lavender sachets have also been made for generations to hang with clothes to keep away moths. In 1387 cushions stuffed with Lavender were made for King Charles VI of France.

LAVENDER COTTON

Santolina chamaecyparissias, Linn.
Fam. Compositae

Habitat: Italy and the Mediterranean countries. Cultivated in England.

Flowering Time: July and August.

Description: Stem white, with cottony hairs. Leaves linear, about 1–2 in. long and $\frac{1}{4}$ in. wide, with short, linear-oblong, obtuse teeth arranged in four rows. The flowerheads are sub-globular, borne on long, leafless flowerstalks, yellow, with the outer bracts lanceolate and pointed, and the inner, obtuse and membranous at the tips. The fruits have no pappus. The taste is bitter; odour, strong and aromatic, recalling that of chamomile.

Part Used: Herb.

Medicinal Use: Used as an emmenagogue and a remedy for worms in children.

Joseph Miller states: "The leaves and sometimes the flowers are used, and are reputed to have great success in destroying worms. . . . The ancients commend it as good against all sorts of poisons and bites and stings of venomous creatures as likewise against obstructions of the Liver, the Jaundice. . . ."

Preparation: Infusion (1 oz to 1 pt): Dose, a wineglassful frequently.

LEMON

Citrus limonia, Osbeck.
Fam. Rutaceae

Synonym: Limon.

Habitat: Probably a native of India but cultivated on a large scale in Mediterranean countries, particularly in Italy, Sicily.

Description: This well-known fruit occurs in several varieties, which differ in thickness of rind, and consequent percentage of juice. Those with moderately thin peel, and of medium size, about 2½–3 in. long and 2 in. in diameter, are the best, and the Messina lemons have the finest flavour. Coarser lemons from Malaga arrive in September and October. These have thick skins and numerous seeds and less juice. A medium-sized lemon yields about 2 oz of juice containing 40–46 gr of citric acid per oz., or about 9½ per cent.

Parts Used: Fruit, rind, juice, oil.

Medicinal Use: Tonic, refrigerant, antiscorbutic. The juice may be freely used as such, or in syrup form as a refreshing drink in all febrile diseases. It is a popular remedy in coughs and colds. The rind is mostly employed for flavouring purposes both in household preparations and in medicine. The juice of a lemon served with hot water and sugar is a well-known French and English remedy for colds.

Preparations: From dried peel: Inf. Aurant. Co. Conc. B.P.C.: Dose, 30–60 min; Inf. Aurant. Co. Rec. B.P.C. 1949: Dose, ½–1 fl oz; Inf. Gent. Co. Rec. B.P.C. 1949: Dose, ½–1 fl oz.

From fresh peel: Syr. Limon. B.P.: Dose, 30–120 min; Tinct. Limon. B.P.: Dose, 30–60 min; Tinct. Limon. U.S.P.; Tinct. Limon. Conc. B.P.C. 1949: Dose, 8–15 min.

From the oil: Sp. Aurant. Co. B.P.C.; Sp. Colon. B.P.C. 1949 (Eau-de-Cologne).

LETTUCE, WILD

Lactuca virosa, Linn.
Fam. Compositae

Synonym: Lettuce-opium.

Habitat: Central and Southern Europe.

Description: The Lettuce plant is well known and requires no description. Lactucarium is obtained by cutting the stem in sections and collecting the latex. Lettuce-opium, or Lactucarium, is usually in angular fragments or quarters, curved on one side, indicating removal from a cup or saucer in which the milky juice has been collected and dried. Externally it is dark reddish brown, internally opaque and wax-like. Odour, resembling opium; taste, very bitter.

Parts Used: Dried juice (Lactucarium), leaves.

Medicinal Use: Anodyne, sedative, expectorant. Is frequently used in the form of a syrup to allay irritable coughs when a soothing agent is wanted. Also used as an anodyne and hypnotic when opium cannot be given.

Preparations: Lactucarium: Dose, 5–15 gr; Liquid extract, leaves: Dose, $\frac{1}{6}$–1 dr; Syrup: Dose, 2 dr; Tincture: Dose, 30 drops; Ext. Lactuc: Dose, 5–15 gr.

LIFE EVERLASTING

Antennaria dioica, Gaertn.
Fam. Compositae

Synonyms: Catsfoot, *Gnaphalium dioicum*, Linn., Cat's-ear.

Habitat: Northern Europe, Asia, and America. It also grows in many parts of the United Kingdom.

Flowering Time: Early summer.

Description: The herb is 4–8 in. high with obovate-spatulate root-leaves, which are smooth above but cottony beneath. Stems cottony. Flowerheads hemispherical, shortstalked, terminal, in clusters of four or five together almost hidden by the long hairy pappus; the male with white, the female with rose-coloured, membranous scales (phyllaries). Taste, astringent; odour, pleasant, stronger in the female heads. The flowerheads, with about 1 in. of the flowerstalk, are usually sold under the name of Catsfoot.

Part Used: Herb.

Medicinal Use: Astringent. Used as a gargle or injection; internally as a styptic in looseness of bowels, etc.

LIFE ROOT

Senecio aureus, Linn.
Fam. Compositae

Synonyms: Squaw Weed, Golden Senecio.

Habitat: Europe, Great Britain, and America.

Flowering Time: Spring and summer.

Description: Stems slender, fluted 1–2 ft high, cottony, unbranched. Rhizome, 1–2 in. long, resembling arnica in size, but with more numerous roots, the bark of the roots hard and blackish surrounding a ring of short, white wood bundles, which enclose a large dark-coloured pith. Root-leaves up to 6 in. long, with long leafstalks ovate, reniform. Stem-leaves decreasing in size upwards, incised and pinnatifid, and the upper ones sessile. Flowerheads few, in a loose corymb, $\frac{2}{3}$ in. to nearly 1 in. broad, and about half as long. Florets of the ray golden yellow, slightly reflexed, pistillate; the central tubular florets hermaphrodite. Pappus pilose. Taste, bitter, astringent, slightly acrid; odour, feeble.

Parts Used: Rhizome, herb.

Medicinal Use: Emmenagogue, diuretic, pectoral, astringent, tonic. A most useful plant, deserving of careful attention. For suppressed menstruation it is considered by many as a specific, and given in conjunction with other remedies there is no doubt it has a certain and effectual action. It is also valuable in gravel, stone, diarrhoea, etc. In suppression of menstruation, ½ oz of powder or fluid extract in 1 pt of water is taken in wineglassful doses four times a day until the desired effect is produced. In pulmonary complaints, 1 teaspoonful of the fluid extract should be taken in sweetened water or combined with other pectorals.

Preparations: Powdered root: Dose, ½–1 dr; Solid extract: Dose, 5–10 gr; Liquid extract: Dose, ½–1 dr; Senecin: Dose, 1–3 gr.

LILY-OF-THE-VALLEY

Convallaria majalis, Linn.
Fam. Liliaceae

Synonyms: Convallaria, May Lily, Conval Lily, Lily Confancy.

Habitat: A common garden flower growing freely in Great Britain. Culpeper says: "They grow plentifully upon Hampstead Heath and many other places in this nation."

Flowering Time: May with seeds ripening in September.

Description: Leaves broadly lanceolate, 4–6 in. long by 1½–2½ in. wide, parallel-veined, and entire at margins. Flowering stem distinct, bearing eight to twelve stalked, small, bell-shaped, white flowers, with six stamens and a superior ovary, sweet scented when fresh. Rhizome slender, the internodes about 2 in. long and 1/12–1/8 in. thick, cylindrical, pale brown, bearing at each joint eight or ten slender, branched, long rootlets. Taste, gummy, sweetish and bitterish, then acrid; odour, pleasant.

Parts Used: Flowers, leaves, whole plant.

Medicinal Use: Cardiac tonic, diuretic. Its action closely resembles that of Foxglove, without causing unpleasant disturbances. In larger doses it causes emesis and purgation. Has been used in dropsy and cardiac debility. Is strongly recommended in valvular heart disease. The infusion of ½ oz of herb to 1 pt of boiling water is taken in tablespoonful doses.

CULPEPER writes of Lily-of-the-valley: "The herb is under the dominion of the moon and therefore cools and moistens like the former . . . the syrup helps much to procure rest and to settle the brain of frantic persons, by cooling the hot temperature of the head. . . . The distilled water of the flowers is very effectual . . . and is recommended to take freckles, spots, sunburn and morphew from the face and other parts of the body."

Preparation: The flowers appear in the B.P.C. 1949.

From flowers: Ext. Convallar. Liq.: Dose, 5–10 min; Tinct. Convallar.: Dose, 5–20 min.

From whole plant: Liquid extract: Dose, 10–30 min.

From leaves: Liquid extract: Dose, 10–30 min.

LIME FLOWERS

Tilia europoea, Linn.
Fam. Tiliaceae

Synonyms: Lindenflowers, Linnflowers, *T. platyphylla*, Scop., *T. cordata*, Mill., *T. vulgaris*, Heyne.

Habitat: Europe and Great Britain.

Flowering Time: July.

Description: These flowers are really derived in commerce from more than one species of *Tilia*, the European species of which are closely allied. *Tilia platyphylla*, Scop., has cordate leaves, hairy beneath, and doubly serrate, and an oblong, obtuse bract attached to the lower third of the flowerstalk. The flowerstalk bears about three to six yellowish-white, five-parted flowers, with numerous stamens at the apex, of which the two anther cells are separated on short divergent stalks.

In Southern Europe the flowers of *T. argentea*, Desf., are used. They differ in that their petals bear staminodes on their inner surface, and in the jonquil-like odour of the flowers.

Part Used: Flowers, with or without the bract.

Medicinal Use: Nervine, stimulant, tonic. This is a common domestic remedy for nervous and catarrhal disorders following upon colds. It is also of service in restlessness, headaches, indigestion, and hysteria. The hot infusion of 1 dr in 1 pt of boiling water is useful in checking diarrhoea from cold. Sometimes a bath is prepared in similar strength and the patient immersed therein to produce sleep.

At one time Lime Flowers had a great reputation for the cure of Epilepsy and it was even stated that persons sitting under the shade of the tree were cured.

LIME FRUIT

Citrus medica, var. *Acida*, Brandis.
Citrus limetta, Risso.
Fam. Rutaceae

Synonym: *Citrus acris*, Mill.

Habitat: West Indies, Italy. Cultivated in many warm countries.

Description: The lime fruit exists in several varieties. The limes usually imported into this country resemble the lemon in colour and appearance, but are nearly globular instead of oval, and average only about 1½ in. in diameter. The flavour of the rind is slightly different from that of the lemon, but the juice is equally acid.

Parts Used: Fruit, juice.

Medicinal Use: Refrigerant, antiscorbutic. The juice is popularly used as a beverage, by itself, sweetened as a syrup, or in conjunction with alcoholic beverages.

LINSEED

Linum usitatissimum, Linn.
Fam. Linaceae

Synonym: Flax Seed.

Habitat: All temperate and tropical countries.

Flowering Time: June.

Description: The seed varies much in size and in tint, a yellowish variety occurring in India. The English and Dutch varieties are usually imported, as being more free from weed seeds and dirt. If containing more than 4 per cent of weed seeds, linseed may be considered to be adulterated. Of English and Dutch seeds, about twelve weigh one grain, but with some of the Indian and Mediterranean varieties, which are nearly twice as large, about six weigh one grain. The seed is brown, oval, pointed at one end, polished, and $\frac{1}{6}$–$\frac{1}{4}$ in. long. The taste is mucilaginous and slightly unpleasant. Inodorous, except when powdered. The seeds yield about 6 per cent of mucilage, which is contained in the seed coat. The seed itself contains from 30–40 per cent of Linseed Oil. The meal of the seeds is sold in two forms, viz. crushed linseed, and linseed meal made by powdering linseed cakes from which the oil has been expressed. The former is preferable for poultices.

Parts Used: Seed and the oil expressed from the seed.

THE fibre of Linseed is used for the manufacture of textiles and it has been so used as far back as the twenty-third century B.C. The roasted seeds form a food eaten by the Abyssinians.

Medicinal Use: Pectoral, demulcent, emollient. Is largely used as an addition to cough medicines, etc. The infusion of 1 oz of seed to 1 pt of boiling water, and sweetened, may be taken in wineglassful doses. The crushed seeds make a valuable poultice in bronchitis, alone or with mustard. The addition of a little powdered Lobelia Seed makes it of value in ulcers, boils, etc. The oil is used externally as an application for burns, scalds, etc., and occasionally internally as a laxative.

Preparations: Inf. Lini.: Dose, 1–4 fl oz; Linum Contus. B.P.C. (containing the oil) distinct from Linseed Meal from which the oil is extracted; Ol. Lini. B.P. from which is prepared Lot. Calc. Hydrox. Oleos. B.P.C. 1949.

LIPPIA

Lippia dulcis, Trev.
Fam. Verbenaceae

Synonyms: Yerba dulce, Mexican Lippia.

Habitat: Mexico.

Description: The leaves are 1½–2 in. long, ovate, narrowed into the petiole, pointed, serrate above, with prominent veins, and are glandular hairy. The odour and taste are agreeably aromatic.

Part Used: Leaves.

Medicinal Use: Demulcent, expectorant. It is an excellent remedy in coughs, colds, whooping cough, and bronchial affections in general. It also seems to act upon the mucous membrane as an alterative.

Dose, 20–60 gr.

LIPPIA CITRIODORA

Aloysia citriodora, Ort.
Fam. Verbenaceae

Synonyms: Lemon-scented Verbena, Herb Louisa, *Verbena triphylla*, L'Hérit., *Lippia triphylla*, L'Hérit.

Habitat: U.S.A., also warm regions of Asia and Africa. It is found cultivated in English gardens.

Description: The leaves are opposite on the stem, often three in a whorl, or even four, elongate-lanceolate, attenuated at both ends, about 3–4 in. long, 1¾ in. wide in the middle, with the lateral veins almost at a right angle to the midrib. When rubbed they give off a lemon odour. The taste resembles that of the lemon.

Part Used: Dried leaves.

Medicinal Use: Febrifuge and sedative. Decoction, 1 oz to 1 pt. Wineglassful three times a day. Not often used in medicine.

Domestic Use: The dried leaves are very fragrant and are used in sachets. The oil distilled from the plant is used in perfumery.

LIQUORICE *Glycyrrhiza glabra*, Linn.
Fam. Leguminosae

Synonym: Licorice.

Habitat: The plant is a native of the warmer parts of Europe and Asia. It is cultivated in the British Isles and other parts of the world.

Flowering Time: August.

Description: The root varies in size and character. The English-grown root is usually sold fresh. It is greyish brown externally, with transverse scars, and internally yellowish and fibrous. The transverse section shows a radiate structure. The taste is sweetish, and the odour, when chewed, pea-like, but characteristic. The root of commerce often contains, especially the Spanish and Russian sorts, a large proportion of underground stem, which is less sweet and can be recognized by the absence of transverse scars, and the presence of a central pith. The Russian and Persian Liquorice are often in large pieces, ¾–1 in. or more in diameter, and has a red-brown scaly surface, and a slight bitterness and acridity. They are derived from *G. glabra*, var. *glandulifera*, W. and K. The Russian sort is also sold in a decorticated state. The peeled and unpeeled roots are both official in the B.P.

Part Used: Root.

Medicinal Use: Demulcent, pectoral, emollient. One of the most popular and well-known remedies for coughs and chest complaints. Beach mentions the following recipe as being used by the late Dr. Malone, of London, and speaks most highly of its efficacy—

Take a large teaspoonful of Linseed, 1 oz of Liquorice Root, and ¼ lb of best raisins. Put them into 2 qt of soft water and simmer down to 1 qt. Then add to it ¼ lb of brown sugar candy and a tablespoonful of white wine vinegar or lemon juice. Drink ½ pt when going to bed and take a little whenever the cough is troublesome. N.B. It is best to add the vinegar to that quantity which is required for immediate use.

Liquorice is one of the best covers for bitter vegetable medicines such as Cascara, etc. Liquorice was known to the ancients as far back as the third century B.C. for its efficacy in the case of dry coughs.

Preparations: Ext. Glycyrrh. B.P.C.: Dose, 10–30 gr; Ext. Glycrrh. Liq. B.P.: Dose, ½–1 dr; Pulv. Glycyrrh. Co. B.P.: Dose, 1–2 dr; Troch. Glycyrrh. B.P.C.

LITMUS *Roccella tinctoria*, *R. montagnei*, D.C.
(and other species)
Fam. Roccellaceae

Synonyms: Lacmus, Persio.

Habitat: The mosses from which it is made come from Cape Verde, Madagascar, and other parts. It is prepared largely in Holland.

Use: Pigment. Obtained from various lichens. Used as an analytical indicator. The prepared Litmus is made into various forms, such as papers or tinctures, and as such used in chemistry for testing purposes. The blue colour, which is natural, has the property of turning to red whenever substances of an acid character are brought into contact with it. This acquired red colour will again return to blue in contact with alkalies. This colouring matter is of a pure, deep-blue colour, and is usually sold in the form of granules, or in a prepared solution, or impregnated paper.

Cudbear (Synonym, Persio) is a purplish-red powder prepared from lichens of the same botanical origin. Archil or Orchilla is another colouring matter obtained from the same source and appears in three forms, liquid, crystal, and powder.

LIVERWORT, AMERICAN

Anemone hepatica, Linn.
Fam. Ranunculaceae

Synonyms: Kidneywort, Liverleaf, *Hepatica triloba*, Choisy.

Habitat: U.S.A. Cultivated in English gardens.

Description: The leaves are long-stalked, leathery, smooth, dark green above, rounded, about 2 in. in diameter, with three broad, angular lobes. Flowers solitary. Fruit of several achenes. Taste, slightly astringent and bitterish; inodorous.

Part Used: Herb.

Medicinal Use: Tonic, astringent, pectoral. A mild remedy in disorders of the liver, indigestion, etc. Possessing pectoral properties, it may be used in coughs, bleeding of the lungs, and chest diseases. The infusion of 1 oz to 1 pt of boiling water is taken in doses of ½ teacupful frequently.

Preparation: Liquid extract: Dose, ½–2 dr.

LIVERWORT, ENGLISH

Peltigera canina, Hoffm.
Fam. Hepaticeae

Synonyms: Liverwort, Ground Liverwort, Lichen Caninus.

Habitat: It grows in moist, shady places in Great Britain and Europe.

Description: This plant has rounded lobes, an unequal surface, and greyish colour, and is downy above, but beneath is whitish, with pale nerves and white rootlets. The fruit, when present, forms blackish oblong spots on the tips of the upper surface.

Part Used: Plant.

Medicinal Use: Deobstruent, slightly purgative. Held in esteem as a remedy for liver complaints, but is generally combined with other remedies. Was believed to be a specific against rabies, but has fallen into disuse. The infusion of 1 oz to 1 pt of boiling water is taken in wineglassful doses, repeated frequently.

Preparation: Liquid extract: Dose, ½–2 dr.

LOBELIA

Lobelia inflata, Linn.
Fam. Campanulaceae

Synonyms: Indian Tobacco, Pukeweed.

Habitat: Eastern United States of America.

Description: Stem slightly hairy, angular. Leaves alternate, 1–3 in. long, sessile, ovate-lanceolate, obscurely toothed, with small, whitish glands on the edge. The fruit consists of a flat, oval capsule containing a number of minute ovate-oblong, brown seeds, about ⅛ in. long, with a reticulated, pitted surface. Taste, burning acrid, like that of tobacco; odour, slight.

Part Used: Herb.

Medicinal Use: Expectorant, emetic, diaphoretic, anti-asthmatic, stimulant. This plant is extensively employed and is regarded as one of the most valuable remedies ever discovered. It is chiefly used as an emetic, and may be prescribed wherever one is indicated. In bronchial troubles and pulmonary complaints its action is speedily and wonderfully beneficial. All accumulation of mucus is instantly removed after a full dose of the infusion and many lives have been saved by its timely use. In croup, whooping cough, and asthma it is specially valuable, and it may be regarded as certain to give relief in the distressing paroxysms which characterize the last-named disease; in fact it may be used wherever there is bronchial spasm. In cases of infantile cough and bronchitis, when the child seems likely to be suffocated by phlegm, a dose will remove obstruction. Dr. Thomson recommends Lobelia in nearly every complaint, and there is no doubt of its general applicability in some way to most diseases. In liver or stomach troubles an emetic of Lobelia will remove all immediate obstructions, and pave the way for the use of other remedial medicines. Mixed with powdered Slippery Elm it forms a stimulating poultice for inflammations, ulcers, swellings, etc. The infusion of 1 oz of powdered herb in 1 pt of boiling water may be taken in doses of ½–1 wineglassful.

Preparations: Powdered Herb: Dose, 3–10 gr; Liquid extract: Dose, 10–30 min; Solid extract: Dose, 2–4 gr; Mist. Lobel. et Stramon. Co. B.P.C.: Dose, ½ fl oz; Pulv. Stramon. Co. B.P.C. 1949; Tinct. Lobel. Aether B.P.C.: Dose, 5–15 min; Tinct. Lobel. Simp. B.P.C. 1949: Dose, 10–30 min; Lobelin Hydrochlor. (salt of alkaloid) from which is prepared: Inj. Lobelin Hydrochlor. B.P.C.

LOGWOOD

Haematoxylon campechianum, Linn.
Fam. Leguminosae

Synonyms: Haematoxylon, Peachwood.

Habitat: Honduras and other parts of Central America. Naturalized in Jamaica.

Description: Logwood is usually sold in the form of chips for dyeing purposes, and has a dark, purplish-brown colour and a greenish iridescence, which indicates that it has been submitted to fermentation. For medicinal purposes the unfermented chips, which have a bright, reddish-brown tint, are preferable. It can also be obtained in the form of extract, which is used as a dye and in the manufacture of ink.

Sappan (*Caesalpina Sappan*) from India, Fustic (*Chlorophora tinctoria*) from S. America, Brazil Wood (*Caesalpina brasiliensis*) from Brazil, are used as dyes and consist of the heart-wood of trees.

Part Used: Wood.

Medicinal Use: Astringent. Being less constipating than other astringents, this drug may be used in cases of diarrhoea, dysentery, haemorrhage from lungs, uterus, and bowels, infantile diarrhoea, etc. The decoction may be freely given in doses of a wineglassful when required, or the solid extract in the form of pills.

Preparations: Dec. Haematox.: Dose, ½–2 fl oz; Ext. Haematox. Liq.: Dose, ½–2 dr; Ext. Haematox.: Dose, 10–30 gr.

LOOSESTRIFE

Lysimachia vulgaris, Linn.
Fam. Primulaceae

Synonyms: Yellow Loosestrife, Yellow Willow-herb.

Habitat: By watery places and river-sides in England.

Flowering Time: June and July.

Description: The herb is 2–3 ft high, bearing opposite leaves, or sometimes three together, elongate-lanceolate, nearly stalkless, 3–6 in. long by 1¼ in. broad, with short, spreading, soft hairs, especially on the stem and veins beneath the leaf. Flowers yellow, about ¾ in. in diameter, in axillary and terminal panicles. Taste, astringent, slightly acid; odour, none.

Part Used: Herb.

DIOSCORIDES according to Gerard, describes a special virtue to Loosestrife: "In appeasing the strife and unrulinesse which falleth out among oxen at the plough if it be put about their yokes"; also: "The smoke of the burned herb driveth away serpents and killeth flies and gnats in a house. It dieth the hair yellow."

Medicinal Use: Astringent, expectorant. Useful in bleeding of mouth, nose, and wounds. It restrains profuse menstruation. As a gargle it finds use in relaxed throat, etc.

Joseph Miller states that "the ancients commend this plant for a great astringent and good for all kinds of fluxes from any part of the body; as also to consolidate the lips of fresh wounds, prevent their bleeding and heal them in a short time. It is not often used."

LOVAGE

Levisticum officinale, Koch
Fam. Umbelliferae

Synonyms: *Ligusticum levisticum*, Linn., Chinese Tang Kui, Man-mu.

Habitat: A herb cultivated in English gardens.

Flowering Time: End of July.

Description: The rootstock or upper portion, usually about 1½ in. long and 2¾ in. thick, sometimes shows leaf-scales at the apex, with annular rings below it, and lateral branches 2–4 in. long and ¼–½ in. in diameter. The external surface is greyish brown and in the rootlets is furrowed longitudinally, The bark of the root is thick, spongy, and whitish, occupying nearly half the diameter, and is separated by a darker line from the woody centre, which is radiate and yellowish, and glistening oil cells are visible in the transverse section. In the outer part of the root bark there are often small cavities. It has a sweet, slightly bitter taste, and a flavour like that of Foenugreek.

This must not be confused with the Scotch Lovage (*Ligusticum scoticum*), which is hot and disagreeable and is sometimes chewed by the Highlanders as tobacco.

Part Used: Root.

Medicinal Use: Diuretic, carminative. Used in febrile affections and in stomach disorders; also for dysmenorrhoea.

Gerard writes: "The roots are very good for all inward diseases, driving away ventosities or windinesse especially of the stomacke. The seed thereof warmeth the stomacke, helpeth digestion; wherefore The people of Gennes in times past did use it in their meates as wee do pepper. . . . The distilled water of Lovage cleareth the sight and putteth away all spots, lentils, freckles and rednesse of the face, if they be often washed therewith."

Preparation: Liquid extract: Dose, 5–30 min.

LUCERNE *Medicago sativa*, Linn.
Fam. Papilionaceae

Synonyms: Alfalfa, Purple Medick.

Habitat: Europe and Great Britain.

Description: Herb about 1½ ft high. Leaves trifoliate. Leaflets obovate, emarginate, mucronate, dentate above, about ¾ in. long and ¼ in. broad, with veins at an acute angle and appressed hairs. Flowers, when present, usually blue, in a many-flowered raceme. Pods loosely spiral with two to three turns, with appressed hairs.

Part Used: Whole herb.

Medicinal Use: Lucerne is given to cattle for fattening purposes. In medicine the infusion of 1 oz to 1 pt of milk or water in cupful doses is prescribed for increasing the weight and to put on flesh.

LUNGWORT *Sticta pulmonaria*, Linn.
Fam. Pulmonaceae

Synonyms: Oak Lungs, Lungmoss.

Habitat: Europe and Great Britain.

Description: This lichen is flat, greyish, or greenish brown, leathery, branched in a forked manner, the lobes about ½ in. broad, decreasing to ¼ in. towards the circumference. The inner surface is reticulated with small concavities, which on the lower surface are evident as corresponding whitish convexities. Taste, mucilaginous, bitter, and a little acrid; odour, characteristic. The plant Lungwort (*Pulmonaria officinalis*) has similar properties. It is easily recognized by its spotted leaf and violet-blue flowers.

Part Used: Lichen.

Medicinal Use: Astringent, mucilaginous, pectoral, healing. Especially valuable in the treatment of coughs, lung complaints, asthma, etc. It heals the parts affected and takes away inflammation. The infusion of 1 oz in 1 pt of boiling water is taken in frequent doses of a wineglassful.

Preparation: Liquid extract: Dose, ½–1 dr.

M

MACE

Myristica fragrans, Houtt.
Fam. Myristicaceae

Synonym: *Arillus myristicae.*

Habitat: Molucca Islands, New Guinea. Introduced into the West Indies and Ceylon.

Description: The arillus known as Mace is a growth outside the shell of the nutmeg seeds. It is about $1\frac{3}{4}$ in. long and $\frac{1}{20}-\frac{1}{10}$ in. thick, irregularly branched, when dry of an orange-brown colour, has a horny, translucent appearance, but is brittle, and exudes oil when pressed by the nails. Taste, strongly aromatic, pungent; odour, characteristic.

Two other varieties of Mace occasionally appear in commerce, viz. Bombay Mace (*Myristica malabarica*, Lam.), which is nearly tasteless and of a redder colour; and Macassar Mace (*Myristica argentea*, Warb.), which is very acrid, and unfit for medicinal use.

Part Used: The arillus, the fleshy, net-like covering of the nutmeg.

Medicinal Use: Stimulating, carminative. The powdered Mace may be used in doses from 5–20 gr.

Domestic Use: Mace is used as a flavouring agent in cookery.

MADDER

Rubia tinctorum, Linn.
Fam. Rubiaceae

Synonyms: Dyer's Madder, Garance (Fr.)

Habitat: Southern Europe, Caucasus.

Description: The root, as met with in commerce, consists of short cylindrical pieces about $\frac{1}{8}-\frac{1}{6}$ in. in diameter, with a thin, easily-detached, corky layer, leaving a red-brown, longitudinally-furrowed inner bark. The transverse section shows a pale-red column, marked with concentric striae. Taste, sweetish, then acrid; odour, slight.

Part Used: Root.

Medicinal Use: Although not used generally in medicine, this has at various times been reputed effectual for promoting menstrual and urinary discharges. Madder has been used as a remedy in liver diseases, jaundice, gall, and spleen complaints. Root, leaves, and seeds are all reputed as medicinally active.

Dose, 10–30 gr.

Domestic Use: It is used in the dyeing industry as Turkey Red.

MAGNOLIA *Magnolia virginiana*, Linn.
Fam. Magnoliaceae

Synonyms: *Magnolia glauca*, Linn., *M. acuminata*, and *M. tripetata.*

Habitat: U.S.A. Cultivated in Great Britain.

Description: The bark occurs in long, fibrous strips, 6–12 in. long, and $\frac{3}{4}$–1 in. broad, with the corky part removed, the outer surface rough, and almost granular, and coarsely pitted, the inner surface striated, but nearly smooth. Fracture, shortly fibrous, except the inner portion, which is formed of tough, fibrous layers. Taste, slightly astringent and irritating; odour, none.

Part Used: Bark. At one time official in the *United States Pharmacopoeia.*

Medicinal Use: Stimulant, tonic, aromatic, diaphoretic. A one-time popular remedy for rheumatism. Used also in malaria. It is not very often used in medicine today.

Preparations: Powder in warm infusion: Dose, $\frac{1}{2}$–1 dr; Liquid extract: Dose, $\frac{1}{2}$–1 dr.

MAIDENHAIR *Adiantum capillus-veneris*, Linn.
Fam. Filices

Synonyms: Venus Hair, Rock Fern.

Habitat: Southern Europe, and found wild occasionally in the British Isles, mainly in the North. There are some eighty varieties of the plant, some of which grow abundantly in Canada.

Description: Stem slender, black, shining. Frond repeatedly forked, bearing short, wedge-shaped leaflets with forked veins, and membranous indusia covering the spore-cases at the outer edge of the under-surface of the incised leaflets. Taste, sweetish and a little astringent; odour, weak.

Part Used: Herb.

Medicinal Use: Mucilaginous, pectoral, expectorant. Is used as a popular cough medicine throughout most parts of Europe. In France large quantities are employed in the preparation of the well-known *Sirop de capillare.* It may be used in all coughs, throat affections, and bronchial disorders. The infusion of 1 oz to 1 pt of boiling water may be taken frequently in wineglassful doses. To improve taste add sugar and orange-flower water. It has also been used as a hair tonic.

MALABAR-NUT *Adhatoda vasica*, Nees.
Fam. Acanthaceae

Synonyms: Adatodai, Arusa, Adulsa, Bákas, *Justicia adhatoda*, Linn.

Habitat: India.

Description: The leaves are opposite, short-stalked, lanceolate, entire, taper-pointed, 5–6 in. long and 1½ in. broad, smooth on both sides. Taste, bitter; odour, tea-like.

Part Used: Leaves.

Medicinal Use: Antispasmodic, expectorant, febrifuge. In India this drug is highly esteemed as a remedy in all bronchial, asthmatic, and pulmonary diseases. It is mostly administered in the form of an infusion, although in asthma the leaves are sometimes smoked. European practitioners have used it with success in intermittent and typhus fevers, and also in diphtheria.

Preparations: Liquid extract: Dose, 20–60 min; Tincture: Dose, ½–1 dr; Powdered drug: Dose, 15–30 gr.

MALE FERN

Dryopteris filix-mas, Linn.
Fam. Polypodiaceae

Synonyms: *Aspidium filix-mas*, Sw., Male Shield Fern.

Habitat: A native of many parts of Europe, and some parts of Asia. It grows in Great Britain but most of the root used for medicinal purposes comes from Italy and Hungary.

Description: The dried rootstock averages about 1½–2½ in. in diameter and about 3 in. long, and consists, as met with in commerce, of the scaly leaf-bases attached to the rhizome, and trimmed free of rootlets. The transverse section shows ten large wood bundles in a ring, and some scattered smaller ones, but the leaf base shows only eight, forming an irregular circle. In appearance it is reddish brown externally, and somewhat greenish internally. Taste, bitterish, sweet, acrid, and astringent; flavour and odour, unpleasant.

Part Used: Root, and the oleoresin extracted from it.

Medicinal Use: Taenifuge, vermifuge, anthelmintic. Mostly used for expulsion of tapeworm. The powder or the fluid extract may be taken, but the ethereal extract or oleoresin, if given in pill or capsule form, is the more pleasant way of taking it. The last dose should be followed by a purgative of castor oil.

The use of the root as a vermifuge was known to the ancients and the Elizabethan Apothecaries. The oleoresin was first used in Great Britain about 1851.

Preparations: Powdered root: Dose, 1–3 dr; Ext. Filic. B.P.: Dose, 45–90 min; Oleores Aspid. U.S.P.: Dose, 60 gr; Caps. Ext. Filic. B.P.C. 1949; Haust. Ext. Filic. B.P.C.: Dose, 1½ fl oz.

MANACA

Brunfelsia hopeana, Hook.
Fam. Solanaceae

Synonyms: *Franciscea uniflora*, Pohl, Vegetable Mercury.

Habitat: Brazil, West Indies.

Description: A slender shrub with lanceolate-oblong, dark-green leaves. It bears small, violet flowers. The root occurs in pieces about 4–6 in. in length, with a pale-brown, papery epidermis. The transverse section shows a thin, dark-brown bark about $\frac{1}{16}$ in. thick, and several concentric rings of wood traversed by slender medullary rays. Taste, sweetish and faintly aromatic.

Part Used: Root.

Medicinal Use: Alterative, diuretic, antirheumatic. Used as a rheumatic remedy in South America. Is considered a most valuable alterative in rheumatic arthritis. A decoction of 1 oz in 1 pt of water is taken in tablespoonful to wineglassful doses.

Preparation: Liquid extract: Dose, 10–60 drops.

MANDRAKE, AMERICAN

Podophyllum peltatum, Linn.
Fam. Berberidaceae

Synonyms: May Apple, Racoonberry, Wild Lemon.

Habitat: North America.

Description: A perennial herb growing to about 1 ft high producing a large white flower and later a yellow fruit which is sometimes eaten. The rhizome is of a reddish-brown colour, and occurs in pieces of 3 in. or more long, usually smooth, with knotty joints at intervals of about $1\frac{1}{2}$–2 in., having a depressed stem-scar above, and a few brittle roots beneath it. Fracture mealy, whitish, showing 20–40 yellow wood bundles enclosing a central pith. This drug must be carefully distinguished from English Mandrake (*see Bryonia dioica*).

Part Used: Rhizome and the resin extracted from it.

Medicinal Use: Antibilious, cathartic, hydragogue, purgative. Mandrake is a powerful medicine, exercising an influence on every part of the system, stimulating the glands to a healthy action. Its most beneficial action is obtained by the use of small doses frequently given, as large ones cause violent evacuations and debility. In all chronic scrofulous, and dyspeptic complaints it is highly valuable; also in dropsy, biliousness, and liver disorders. Preparations of the root are to be preferred to those of the resin. This is one of the many illustrations of the fact that isolated principles do not act so well as in their natural position where they are associated with other remedial factors.

Preparations: Powdered root: Dose, 2–10 gr; Liquid extract: Dose, 5–10 min; Solid extract: Dose, $\frac{1}{2}$–2 gr; Podoph. Resin B.P.: Dose, $\frac{1}{4}$–$\frac{1}{2}$ gr, from which are prepared: Pig. Podoph. 1949; Pil. Aloin. et Podoph. Co. B.P.C. 1949: Dose, 1–4 pills; Tab. Casc. Sagr. Co. B.P.C.: Dose, 1 or 2 tablets; Tab. Colocynth. et Jalap Co. B.P.C.: Dose, 1–3 tablets; Tinct. Podoph. B.P.C. 1949: Dose, 5–15 min.

Indian Podophyllum, derived from *Podophyllum emodi*, Wall., is used for the production of Podophyllin (resin) Emodi, which has similar uses to those described under *Podophyllum peltatum*.

MANNA

Fraxinus ornus, Linn.
Fam. Oleaceae

Synonym: Flake Manna.
Habitat: Southern Europe specially in Sicily.
Description: A saccharine exudation from the incised bark of the tree. In pale yellowish or whitish pieces, irregular on one side and smoother and curved on the other, rarely more than 1 in. broad and 2–3 in. or more long. Taste, sweet, honey-like, without bitterness; odour, slight.
Part Used: Concrete exudation.
Medicinal Use: Nutritive, laxative. A useful laxative for children and infants, and for females during pregnancy. May be used alone in doses of a teaspoonful up to 1 or 2 oz, or combined with other laxatives and carminatives.

JOSEPH MILLER writes: ". . . the common Manna of the shops is the concreted Sacharine Exudation of a species of Ash in Calabria, a Province in the Kingdom of Naples; it having been proved beyond contradiction, that it is not an Honey-Dew, which falls from the Heavens, but what comes from the tree itself. . . . It is gathered every year, a little before the Dog-days and the August rains come in."

MAPLE, RED

Acer rubrum, Linn.
Fam. Sapindaceae

Synonym: Swamp Maple.
Habitat: America.
Description: In long, quilled pieces 6–12 in. or more long and $\frac{1}{4}$–$\frac{3}{4}$ in. wide, externally blackish brown, slightly polished, with innumerable fine transverse lines, and scattered, brownish, small warts. Inner bark, in very tough

and fibrous layers, pale reddish brown or buff. Taste, astringent and faintly bitter.

Part Used: Bark.

Medicinal Use: Rarely used in this country. The American Indians use it as an application to sore eyes, owing to its astringent nature.

MARIGOLD

Calendula officinalis, Linn.
Fam. Compositae

Synonyms: *Caltha officinalis*, Marygold, Garden Marigold, Calendula.

Habitat: A common garden plant.

Flowering Time: Most of the summer and frequently into the autumn.

Description: Stem angular, and, as well as the leaves, pubescent. Lower leaves spatulate with a large stalk, the upper sessile amplexicaul terminated by a small, obtuse point. The flowerheads yellow, with the tubular florets sterile. Fruit semi-circular, rough, angular, without pappus. Taste, bitter; odour, strong and unpleasant.

Parts Used: Petals, herb.

Medicinal Use: Stimulant, diaphoretic. Chiefly used as a local remedy. Given internally it assists the local action and prevents suppuration. Useful in chronic ulcers, varicose veins, etc. The infusion of 1 oz to 1 pt of boiling water may be taken in doses of a tablespoonful or wineglassful, and used as an application for external purposes.

Preparations: Liquid extract: Dose, ¼–1 dr; Tinct. Calend.

GERARD writes: "Fuchius writeth that if the mouth be washed with the juice it helpeth the tooth-ache." He also states: "The leaves of the floures are dried and kept throughout Dutchland against winter to put in broths, in Physicall potions, and for divers other purposes, in such quantity that in some grocers or spice sellers houses are to be found barrels filled with them and retailed by the penny more or less, insomuch that no broths are well made without dried Marigolds."

MARJORAM, SWEET

Origanum majorana, Linn.
Fam. Labiatae

Synonyms: *Majorana hortensis*, Moench.

Habitat: Europe and Great Britain. It is a common sweet herb grown in gardens.

Flowering Time: July and August.

Description: The herb is about 10 in. high, branched above, with opposite, whitish, small, oval-obtuse leaves, about ½ in. long and ⅓ in. broad, and small flowers almost hidden by green bracts arranged in small, hop-like, rounded spikes or heads forming a terminal panicled cyme. Flowers white or pink, with the calyx open like one of the bracts. Taste, aromatic, agreeable.

Parts Used: Herb, leaves.

Medicinal Use: Tonic, emmenagogue, stimulant. Hardly ever used for medicinal purposes. The volatile oil, Oleum majoranae, is an excellent external application for sprains, bruises, etc.

Domestic Use: It is used as a seasoning in cookery.

MARJORAM, WILD

Origanum vulgare, Linn.
Fam. Labiatae

Habitat: Europe and the British Isles.

Description: Herb, with opposite-stalked, usually entire leaves which are ovate, hairy, but not whitish. The purplish flowers are arranged in oval or oblong heads with usually pink bracts, and the calyx is tubular and five-toothed. Taste and odour, thyme-like. The oil sold under the name is distilled from *Thymus vulgaris*, Linn., in France; that of the Wild Marjoram, *Origanum vulgare*, is not an article of commerce.

Part Used: Herb.

Medicinal Use: Emmenagogue, stimulant. The whole herb is medicinal and contains a volatile oil, which can be separated by distillation. Perspiration may be produced by a warm infusion, and this is also taken to promote the menstrual flow, when suppressed by cold. The oil distilled from *Thymus vulgaris* is stimulant and rubefacient, and often used as a liniment. Barton and Castle describe the plant as having tonic, stimulant, and carminative properties and therefore of use in asthma, coughs, and various spasmodic affections.

MARSHMALLOW

Althaea officinalis, Linn.
Fam. Malvaceae

Synonyms: Mallards, Guimauve, Schloss Tea.

Habitat: Europe and Great Britain.

Flowering Time: August and September.

Description: The root is greyish white externally, with transverse scars, internally white and fibrous. It is generally sold in the decorticated state, when the outer surface is fibrous and white. It has deep, longitudinal furrows due to drying, and tapers gradually below. Taste, mucilaginous, mawkish; odour, slight. It should be kept dry or it will give a yellowish decoction of unpleasant odour. The leaves are greyish green and velvety, due to a dense covering of stellate hairs, cordate-ovate, pointed, irregularly serrate at the margins, about 2½ in. long and 1¼ in. broad, brittle when dry. Flowers pink, with the stamens united into a tube, and the anthers kidney-shaped and one-celled. The calyx has eight linear bracts attached to its outer surface.

Parts Used: Leaves, root.

Medicinal Use: Demulcent, emollient. This plant constitutes a popular remedy for coughs, bronchitis, etc., generally in combination with other remedies. In painful complaints of the urinary organs and cystitis it exerts a relaxing effect upon the passages as well as acting as a curative. The powdered or crushed fresh roots make a good poultice, which may be relied upon to remove the most obstinate inflammation and prevent mortification. Its powers in this direction are so great that it has been termed Mortification Root. The addition of Slippery Elm is an advantage, and it should be applied to the part as hot as can be borne, renewing the poultice when dry. An infusion of 1 oz of leaves to 1 pt of boiling water is taken frequently in wineglassful doses.

Preparations: Liquid extract, leaves: Dose, ½–2 dr; Syr. Alth, B.P.C. 1949 (root): Dose, ½–2 dr.

MASTERWORT

Imperatoria ostruthium, Linn.
Fam. Umbelliferae

Habitat: A native of Australia and the Alpine countries and cultivated in the British Isles.

Flowering Time: July.

Description: Rhizome cylindrical, compressed, knotty at intervals of about ½ in., 2–4 in. long and ½–¾ in. in thickness, with few scattered roots and scattered, rounded warts, sometimes in shorter, conical, compressed pieces, some pieces terminating in nearly smooth, underground suckers about ¼ in. in diameter. Fracture short, hard, and tough, showing a central pith, surrounded by a circle of oil cells, another circle of similar cells occurring in the bark. Taste and odour, ivy-like but pungent.

Part Used: Rhizome.

Medicinal Use: Stimulant, antispasmodic, carminative. Recommended in asthma, apoplexy, and menstrual complaints. Has also been of use in flatulence and dyspepsia. A decoction of 1 oz to 1 pt of water is taken in wineglassful doses.

Culpeper writes: "The juice thereof dropped, or tents dipped therein, and applied either to green wounds or filthy rotton ulcers, and those that come by envenomed weapons, doth soon cleanse and heal them. The same is also very good to help the gout coming of a cold cause."

Preparation: Liquid extract: Dose, 1–2 dr.

MASTIC

Pistacia lentiscus, Linn.
Fam. Anacardiaceae

Synonyms: Mastich, Lentisk.

Habitat: Grecian Archipelago, Cyprus.

Description: The resin occurs in small, rounded, or pear-shaped, transparent tears which, when masticated, forms a dough-like mass, unlike gum-sandarac, which is in cylindrical tears and goes to powder when chewed. Taste, cedar-like; odour, slight.

Part Used: Resin.

Medicinal Use: The resin by itself or in a spirituous solution is used in dentistry as a filling for carious teeth.

Joseph Miller says: "The wood is drying and binding. . . . A tooth-pick made of it is accounted a Preserver of the Teeth."

MATICO

Piper angustifolium, R. and P.
(and other varieties)
Fam. Piperaceae

Synonyms: Matica, *Artanthe elongata*, Miq.

Habitat: The leaves which were described in the B.P. 1885 come from the North of South America.

Description: The leaves as they arrive in this country may be described as usually more or less broken, but easily recognized by their surface being reticulated on both sides, convexly on the upper surface due to the deeply-sunk veinlets, and the under surface being similarly tessellated with corresponding minute depressions clothed with shaggy hairs. The stems are slender, and, as well as the hairs, have knotted joints. Taste, aromatic and bitterish; odour, herbaceous.

Part Used: Leaves.

Medicinal Use: Astringent, stimulant, diuretic, and styptic. Has been recommended and used in leucorrhoea, piles, and chronic mucous discharges. Also in bleeding from the lungs, dysentery, and other haemorrhages. Its action is very similar to that of cubebs. The infusion of 1 oz to 1 pt of boiling water is taken in wineglassful doses. The powdered leaves are said to stop the bleeding of wounds.

Preparations: Powdered leaves: Dose, $\frac{1}{2}$–2 dr; Liquid extract: Dose, $\frac{1}{2}$–1 dr.

MAYWEED

Anthemis cotula, Linn.
Fam. Compositae

Synonyms: *Maruta cotula*, D.C., *Maruta foetida*, Cass., Wild Chamomile, Dog Chamomile, Dog Fennel, Cotula, Stinking Mayweed.

Habitat: Europe and Great Britain frequently amongst corn.

Flowering Time: May and June.

Description: The herb resembles Chamomile in appearance, but the white flowers have no membranous scales at their base. When the florets are pulled off there remain only a few bristly paleae on the top of the conical receptacle. The outer florets have usually no styles. Taste, disagreeable and acrid. *Anthemis arvensis*, Linn., a common cornfield weed, has lanceolate paleae, and the white florets of the ray have always styles.

Part Used: Herb.

Medicinal Use: Tonic, antispasmodic, emmenagogue, emetic. Has been used with success in sick headache, in convalescence from fevers, and in amenorrhoea. The warm infusion of 1 oz in 1 pt of boiling water is taken in wineglassful doses when required.

Joseph Miller states: "This is a Plant, but rarely used, though some Authors commend it as good against Vapours and Hysteric Fits. Mr. Ray says it is sometimes made use of in scrofulous cases: and Tournefort, That about Paris they use it in Fomentations for pains and swellings of the Haemorrhoides."

MEADOW FERN

Comptonia asplenifolia, Gaertn.
Fam. Myricaceae

Synonyms: *Comptonia peregrina*, *Myrica asplenfolia*, Sweet Fern, Ferngale, Spleenwort.

Habitat: Nova Scotia to Michigan.

Description: A shrubby plant with a resinous, spicy odour.

Part Used: Burrs.

Medicinal Use: Tonic and astringent. Decoction of 1 oz to 1 pt of water taken in wineglassful doses is said to be useful for diarrhoea.

MEADOW LILY

Lilium candidum, Linn.
Fam. Liliaceae

Synonyms: White Lily, Madonna Lily.

Habitat: A native of Southern Europe and now cultivated in gardens in the British Isles and America.

Description: The bulb consists of free, fleshy scales, lanceolate and curved, about 1½ in. long, and rather less than ½ in. broad in the centre. Taste, mucilaginous, bitter, and unpleasant.

Part Used: Bulb.

Medicinal Use: Mucilaginous, demulcent, astringent. Combined with Life Root it is of value in treating leucorrhoea, prolapse of the womb, and female complaints generally. The fresh bulb has been used with success in dropsy. A decoction of the bulb in water or milk is taken internally in wineglassful doses. Externally the latter forms a useful cataplasm for tumours, ulcers, and external inflammations.

CULPEPER writes of Meadow Lily: "The root roasted, and mixed with a little Hog's grease, makes a gallant poultice to ripen and break plague-sores. The ointment is excellently good for swellings and will cure burnings and scaldings without a scar, and trimly deck a blank space with hair."

MEADOWSWEET

Spiraea ulmaria, Linn.
Fam. Rosaceae

Synonyms: Queen-of-the-meadow Herb, Bridewort, Lady-of-the-meadow, Dolloff.

Habitat: A common wild plant in the British Isles growing in meadows and woods.

Flowering Time: June, July, and August.

Description: The leaves are interruptedly pinnate, having a few large, serrate leaflets and very small intermediate ones, dark green above and whitish and downy beneath, the terminal lobes larger and three- to five-lobed. Flowers small, yellowish white, in large, irregularly-branched, dense cymes. Taste, astringent and slightly aromatic.

Part Used: Herb.

Medicinal Use: Aromatic, astringent, diuretic. Has a pleasant taste and is incorporated in many herb beers. A good remedy in strangury, dropsy, etc., and in children's diarrhoea, for which alone it may be deemed a specific. The infusion of 1 oz to 1 pt of water is taken in wineglassful doses.

Preparation: Liquid extract: Dose, ½–1 dr.

PARKINSON writes: ". . . many doe much delight therein to have it layd in their Chambers, Parlars etc., and Queene Elizabeth of famous memory, did more desire it than any other sweet herbe to strew her Chambers withall. . . ."

MELILOT

Melilotus officinalis, Willd.
Melilotus arvensis, Lamk.
Fam. Leguminosae

Synonyms: King's Claver, King's Chafer.

Habitat: It grows freely in all parts of the British Isles.

Flowering Time: June and July.

Description: Two species are sold under this name. Both have trifoliate leaves and yellow flowers, but *M. arvensis*, Lamk., has small, glabrous, one- to two-seeded pods, and *M. officinalis*, Willd., has hairy pods. The leaves are obcordate, serrate in the former, and ovate-truncate in the latter. Taste and odour, like hay.

Part Used: Herb.

Medicinal Use: Aromatic, emollient, carminative. Relieves flatulence and is taken internally for this purpose. Externally it is applied as a fomentation or poultice for pains and aches.

Culpeper states: "The head often washed with the distilled water of the herb and flowers or a lye made therewith, is effectual for those that have suddenly lost their senses, as also to strengthen the memory, comfort the head and brain, and to preserve them from pains and apoplexy."

MESCAL BUTTONS

Lopophora lewinii, Henn.
Fam. Cactaceae

Synonyms: Muscal Buttons, Pellote, *Anhalonium lewinii*, Henn.

Habitat: North Mexico and Texas.

Description: The dried tops of this cactus are about $1\frac{1}{4}$–$1\frac{1}{2}$ in. in diameter and about $\frac{1}{3}$ in. thick, the centre covered with white silky tufts of hairs, with a few solitary tufts scattered over the surface. It is from these tufts that the small, vase-shaped, pink flowers arise, but the flowers and fruits are not often seen in the drug. Fracture short and horny, pale brown. Taste, gritty, mucilaginous, slightly acrid, pungent, and bitterish.

Part Used: Fruit.

Medicinal Use: Cardiac tonic, emetic, narcotic. This drug has been reputed as a remedy in all paroxysmal complaints, dyspnoea, angina pectoris, etc. It should be used with caution, as it causes emises even when taken in small doses.

The Aztecs called it "Sacred Mushroom" and believed it to have divine properties. They are said to have used it in certain religious rites.

MEZEREON

Daphne mezereum, Linn.
(and other species)
Fam. Thylmelaeceae

Synonyms: Spurge Olive, Spurge Laurel, Wild Pepper.

Habitat: A native of the hilly parts of Europe and cultivated in the United Kingdom.

Flowering Time: In the British Isles, June or July.

Description: The root of *Daphne mezereum* is brownish, very tough, in branched pieces about 1–1½ ft long, the epidermis peeling off when bent and the inner bark consisting of very fine strong fibres. The bark of *D. gnidium*, Linn., which is used in France under the name of *Garou*, occurs in commerce in this country, and is usually sold in the form of bark only. It has a purplish brown tint, and the stem-bark is slightly hairy. The brown stem-bark of *D. laureola*, Linn., which is also sold as Mezereon Bark, has the leaf scars crowded at well-defined intervals. Taste, very acrid and caustic; odour, unpleasant in the fresh state.

Parts Used: Bark, root, root-bark.

Medicinal Use: Stimulant, alterative, diuretic. Acts favourably in scrofula, and rheumatism. The decoction of ½ oz in 1 pt of water is taken in wine-glassful doses. Externally it is used as a lotion to blistered surfaces, indolent ulcers, etc.

Preparations: Powdered bark: Dose, 10 gr; Liquid extract: Dose, 2–10 drops.

MISTLETOE

Viscum album, Linn.
Fam. Loranthaceae

Synonyms: European Mistletoe, Birdlime Mistletoe. Culpeper spells it Misselto.

Habitat: The plant is a parasite, growing principally on fruit trees, and more rarely on the oak or chestnut.

Flowering Time: It flowers in the spring and the berries ripen in October, remaining on the branches most of the winter unless eaten by the birds.

Description: It has a woody stem growing out of the tree which branches freely and has a greyish-green bark. The leaves are opposite, leathery, oblanceolate, and about 2 in. long, entire at the margins. The small yellow flowers grow at the joints of the branches producing later small, round, white, translucent berries. Mistletoe of the United States is another plant (*Phoradendron flavescens*). It has shorter leaves, somewhat hairy.

Part Used: Leaves.

Medicinal Use: Culpeper places this plant under the dominion of the Sun and because it also grows upon oaks, apples and pears it participates something of the nature of Jupiter. He quarrels with the assertion made by some ancient herbalists that Mistletoe grown on the oak has greater virtues than other varieties.

Many superstitions have surrounded this plant. Clusius for example states that after gathering, the plant should not be allowed to touch the ground or it loses some of its efficacy. He also believed, with others, that being hung round the neck it repelled witchcraft.

Today the principal use for Mistletoe is as a nervine, although it is also recognized as antispasmodic, tonic, and narcotic.

Preparations: Powdered leaves: Dose, $\frac{1}{2}$–2 dr; Liquid extract: Dose, $\frac{1}{4}$–1 dr.

Domestic Use: The Mistletoe and other plants produce a substance known as Bird-lime which is excessively sticky and is used on fly papers. It was formerly employed to catch small birds, rats, mice, etc.

The Saxons regarded the Mistletoe growing on the oak as a gift of the gods. It was gathered by the Druidical priest clothed in a white robe and armed with a golden sickle. This ceremony was performed annually and was accompanied by the sacrifice of two white bulls. Hymns were sung in honour of the divinity and prayers offered for a blessing in their solemnities. At the commencement of the new year the plant was distributed among the people as a sacred relic and was deemed a panacea against every disease and a remedy for poisons.

MONSONIA

Monsonia ovata, Cav.
Fam. Geraniaceae

Habitat: South Africa.

Description: Stems $1\frac{1}{2}$ ft high, branched, with slender spreading hairs. Leaves opposite, stalked, ovate, serrate, about $\frac{1}{4}$ in. long and $\frac{1}{2}$ in. broad, with filiform stipules. Flowers, when present, geranium-like, white, axillary, stalked, solitary or two borne on one peduncle. Taste, astringent, slightly aromatic, and faintly acrid.

Part Used: Whole plant.

Medicinal Use: A South African remedy for acute and chronic dysentery. It is particularly recommended in ulcerated conditions of the lower bowels.

Preparation: Tincture: Dose, 1–4 dr every three or four hours.

MOTHERWORT

Leonurus cardiaca, Linn.
Fam. Labiatae

Synonyms: Lion's Ear, Lion's Tail.

Habitat: Grows commonly in English gardens, and wild in some places.

Flowering Time: June.

Description: Stem square. Leaves stalked, palmately five-lobed, the lobes trifid at apex, coarsely serrate, reticulate veined, the veinlets prominent beneath, with slender, curved hairs; the upper leaves trifid, entire, and wedge-shaped below. Flowers pinkish, in thick whorls in the axils of the upper leaves; calyx teeth rigid and sharp. Taste, very bitter; odour, none.

Part Used: Herb.

Medicinal Use: In modern times, Motherwort is known as antispasmodic, tonic, nervine, emmenagogue. Is especially valuable in female weakness and hysteria, acting as a tonic to the generative organs and allaying nervous irritability. It promotes the flow of the menses, and generally braces up the uterine membranes. It will be found useful as a simple tonic in heart diseases or weakness and in recovery from fevers when other tonics are inadmissible. The infusion of 1 oz of herb to 1 pt of boiling water is taken in wineglassful doses.

Culpeper writes: "There is no better herb to take melancholy vapours from the heart, to strengthen it, and make merry, cheerful, blithe soul than this herb."

Preparations: Powdered herb: Dose, ½–1 dr; Solid extract: Dose, 5–15 gr; Liquid extracts: Dose, ½–1 dr.

TO many, Motherwort is known as a herb of life. There is an old saying, "Drink Motherwort and live to be a source of continuous astonishment and grief to waiting heirs."

MOUNTAIN ASH

Pyrus aucuparia, Gaertn.
Fam. Rosaceae

Synonyms: *Sorbus aucuparia*, Linn., *Mespilus aucuparia*, Web., Rowan Tree, Witchen.

Habitat: Europe and British Isles, especially at high altitudes.

Description: The fruit is red and globose, with calyx teeth at the apex, and two- to three-seeded cells. The bark has a soft, spongy, yellowish-grey outer layer, and an inner thicker portion, with many layers of a light-brown colour. The transverse section shows that the layers have abundant stone cells but are without visible radiate structure. Fracture rough, short, and coarsely granular with few fibres. Taste, bitterish; odour, none. American Mountain Ash Bark is derived from *Pyrus americanus*, D.C.

The Rowan Tree was supposed to be efficacious against witchcraft.

Parts Used: Fruit, bark.

Medicinal Use: Astringent. The ripe berries furnish an acidulous and astringent gargle in sore throat and inflamed tonsils. A decoction of the bark is given in diarrhoea, and used as a vaginal injection in leucorrhoea, etc.

MOUNTAIN FLAX

Linum catharticum, Linn.
Fam. Liliaceae

Synonym: Purging Flax.

Habitat: A common plant in meadows in Europe and Great Britain.

Flowering Time: Most of the summer.

Description: Stem simple, 2–6 in. high. Leaves opposite, small, the lower obovate, the upper lanceolate entire. Flowers small, white, five-parted with serrate sepals, and pointed petals arranged in a forked, loose panicle. Taste, bitter and acrid; odour, none.

Part Used: Herb.

Medicinal Use: Laxative, cathartic. Is preferred to Senna, though the action is very similar. Used in cases of constipation, gravel, dropsy, etc., generally combined with other herbs. Also recommended in muscular rheumatism and catarrhal affections. The infusion of 1 oz in 1 pt of boiling water is taken in wineglassful doses.

Preparation: Liquid extract: Dose, ½–1 dr.

MOUNTAIN GRAPE

Berberis aquifolium, Pursh
Fam. Berberidaceae

Synonyms: Oregon Grape, Holly-leaved Berberry.

Habitat: California and British Columbia.

Flowering Time: Early spring.

Description: The plant grows to about 6 ft in height producing bright-green, coriaceous leaves and small, yellowish flowers. The root occurs in pieces averaging about ¾–1 in. in diameter, with a thin, greyish-yellowish-brown bark, internally greenish yellow, and a hard, yellowish wood with numerous medullary rays and very short, broken, white, waved lines between them. The rhizomatous part has a small pith. Taste, bitter; odour, none.

Part Used: Root.

Medicinal Use: Alterative, tonic. Has been justly extolled as an alterative and tonic, as it improves digestion and absorption, and is useful in most diseases arising from impurity of blood. In scrofulous conditions and skin diseases of a scaly character it may be used with advantage. In chronic constipation it is generally used in conjunction with Cascara Sagrada.

Preparation: Liquid extract: Dose, 10–30 drops.

MOUNTAIN LAUREL

Kalmia latifolia, Linn.
Fam. Ericaceae

Synonyms: Sheep Laurel, Lambkill, Spoonwood, Kalmia, American Laurel, Broad-leaved Laurel, Calico-bush.

Habitat: U.S.A.

Description: An evergreen shrub. Leaves broadly lanceolate, about 2½ in. long and 1¼ in. broad, leathery, but brittle when dry, with narrowly-reflexed entire margins, the midrib prominent on both sides, but the lateral veins obscure. Taste, astringent and tea-like, slightly bitter; odour, none.

Part Used: Leaves.

Medicinal Use: Cardiac sedative, astringent, alterative. Large doses produce symptoms of narcotic poisoning, but moderate doses—10–30 gr—are valuable in all febrile complaints and inflammatory diseases. It is regarded as a most efficient remedy in blood disorders, and useful in overcoming obstinate chronic irritation of the mucous membrane. It is also employed with benefit in active haemorrhage, diarrhoea, and dysentery. The decoction of 1 oz in 1 qt of water boiled down to 1 pt, is taken in tablespoonful doses.

Serious and sometimes fatal cases of Sheep poisoning have occurred as a result of eating this plant. It is said however that goats and deer can eat it without harmful effect.

MOUSE-EAR

Hieracium pilosella, Linn.
Fam. Compositae

Synonym: Pilosella.

Habitat: It is a common herb growing on dry banks and in ditches. It grows best in sandy soil. It is found in many places in the British Isles and Europe.

Flowering Time: It flowers in June and July. The leaves remain green throughout the winter.

Description: It is a small herb and creeps along the ground sending out runners in a similar manner to the Strawberry. The leaves form small rosettes on the creeping stems, elongate-lanceolate, about $1\frac{1}{4}$ in. long and $\frac{1}{4}$–$\frac{1}{3}$ in. broad, greyish above, with long, slender, scattered, composite and serrate hairs, and covered on the under surface with a dense white coat of stellately-branched hairs. The small flowers are pale yellow. Taste is bitter and aromatic.

Part Used: Herb.

Medicinal Use: Astringent, tonic, expectorant. A good remedy for whooping cough and affections of the lungs. An infusion of 1 oz in 1 pt of boiling water is taken in wineglassful doses.

Culpeper says: "The moon owns this herb also; and though authors cry out upon Alchymists for attempting to fix quicksilver by this herb and moonwort, a Roman would not have judged a thing by the success; if it be fixed at all, it is by lunar influence."

Preparation: Liquid extract: Dose, $\frac{1}{2}$–1 dr.

GERARD in his "General History of Plants" states that a decoction of the juice of Mouse-ear is of such excellency that "if steel-edged tools red hot be drenched and cooled therein, oftentimes it makes them so hard that they will cut stone or iron be they never so hard without turning the edge or waxing dull."

MUGWORT

Artemisia vulgaris, Linn.
Fam. Compositae

Synonym: Felon Herb.

Habitat: It grows wild in this country in hedges and waste places.

Flowering Time: June.

Description: Stem angular, furrowed longitudinally. Leaves dark green above, alternate, pinnatisect, with five to seven lobes, which are semi-erect, decurrent, deeply incised, with sharply-serrate teeth, nearly smooth above, but silvery white, with appressed, bifid, cottony hairs beneath. Taste, bitterish and aromatic; odour, aromatic.

Part Used: Leaves.

Medicinal Use: Emmenagogue, diuretic, diaphoretic. Chiefly used in female medicines and for obstruction of menstruation, usually in combination with Pennyroyal and Southernwood. The infusion of 1 oz to 1 pt of boiling water is taken in wineglassful doses.

Culpeper states: "Being made up with hog's grease into an ointment, it takes away wens and hard knots and kernels that grow about the neck and throat . . . and eases the pains . . . if some Field Daisies be put with it." Also: "Three drams of the powder of the dried leaves taken in wine, is a speedy and the best certain help for the sciatica."

Preparation: Liquid extract: Dose, ½–1 dr.

MUIRA-PUAMA

Liriosma ovata, Miers
Fam. Oleaceae

Habitat: Brazil.

Description: The root as met with in commerce occurs in light-brown, woody splinters 2–3 in. long and ¼ in. in diameter, without any root bark. These splinters are hard, very tough, and coarsely fibrous. The transverse section shows few porous vessels, and crowded, slender medullary rays. Taste, slightly astringent; odour, none.

Part Used: Root.

Medicinal Use: Aphrodisiac, nerve stimulant. Is reputed in Brazil to be one of the most powerful aphrodisiacs.

Preparation: Liquid extract: Dose, 10–60 drops.

MULBERRY

Morus nigra, Linn.
Fam. Moraceae

Synonym: Black Mulberry, Purple Mulberry.

Habitat: Asia Minor, Persia, Italy. Cultivated in Europe and the British Isles.

Fruiting Time: July and August.

Description: The fruit of the Black Mulberry only is obtainable in this country. The fruit differs from the blackberry in that it is the product of an agglomeration of flowers, and on each little portion of the fruit the four fleshy lobes of the calyx forming part of it can be detected.

Part Used: Fruit.

Medicinal Use: Nutritive, refrigerant, laxative. The fruit juice forms a grateful drink for convalescents from febrile diseases, as it checks the thirst and cools the blood. It was official in B.P. 1885 in the form of syrup. The bark of the tree is purgative and vermifuge.

Preparation: Syr. Mori.: Dose, ½–1 dr.

Domestic Use: Silk worms feed upon the leaves of the Mulberry.

Biblical References: 2 Samuel v, 23, 24; 1 Maccabees vi, 34; 1 Chronicles xiv, 14; Luke xvii, 6. The reference in Luke is to the Sycamine tree, which is the Purple Mulberry.

MULLEIN

Verbascum thapsus, Linn.
Fam. Scrophulariaceae

Synonyms: Blanket Herb, Lady's Foxglove, Cow's Lungwort.

Flowering Time: Late summer.

Description: The basal leaves are lanceolate oblong, the upper more ovate and decurrent. The stem leaves are about 6–8 in. long and 2–2½ in. broad, densely coated with woolly hairs which are stellately branched. The corolla, which is usually the part used in medicine, is yellow, cup-shaped, about 1 in. across with five unequal, rounded lobes to the base of which two nearly smooth and three hairy stamens are attached. The dried corollas turn brownish unless carefully dried.

Parts Used: Leaves, flowers.

Medicinal Use: Demulcent, astringent, pectoral. Both leaves and flowers are used in cases of pulmonary complaints in an infusion of 1 oz to 1 pt of boiling water taken in wineglassful doses.

Gerard states: "The leaves are worn under the feet in a manner of a shoe sole or sock and assist to bring down in young maidens their desired sickness being so kept under their feet that they do not fall away." And also: "The later physicians commend the yellow flowers being steeped in oil and set in warm dung until they be washed into the oil and consumed away, to be a remedy for piles."

Culpeper found many other uses for this plant which he described as being under the dominion of Saturn. He writes: "A decoction of the leaves thereof and of Sage, Marjoram and Camomile Flowers and the places bathed therewith, that have the sinews stiff with cold or cramp doth bring them much ease and comfort. . . ." "The juice of the leaves and flowers being laid upon rought warts, and also the powder of the dried roots rubbed on, doth easily take them away, but doth no good to smooth warts. . . . The powder of the dried flowers is an especial remedy for those that are troubled with the belly-ache or the pains of colic."

Preparation: Liquid extract: Dose, ½–1 dr.

MUSKSEED

Hibiscus abelmoschus, Linn.
Fam. Malvaceae

Synonym: *Abelmoschus moschatus*, Medik.

Habitat: A native of India but growing also in other tropical countries.

Description: The seeds are reniform compressed, about ⅛ in. in diameter, greyish brown, with numerous brown striae which are concentric round the hilum. Taste, oily and musky; odour, musky when rubbed.

Part Used: Seeds.

Medicinal Use: Aromatic, insecticide. It is known as an insecticide, being dusted over woollens to protect them from moths, etc. For medicinal purposes the seeds are made into a paste with milk and employed as a remedy for itch.

MUSTARD

Brassica nigra, Koch
(Black Mustard)
Brassica alba, Linn.
(White Mustard)
Fam. Cruciferae

Synonyms: Black: *Sinapis nigra*, Linn., *Brassica sinapioides*, Roth. White: *Sinapis alba*, Linn.

Habitat: Both widely distributed in Europe, Asia and Great Britain.

Description: Both varieties are well known by their bright yellow flowers with cruciform calyx and corolla. The white variety closely resembles the black, but is a somewhat smaller plant. The pods of the black mustard are smooth, whereas those of the white are bristly.

Black mustard seeds are between oval and spherical, dark reddish brown, about $\frac{1}{25}$ in. in diameter and $\frac{1}{50}$ gr in weight, more or less covered with a white pellicle. Triturated with water they form a yellowish emulsion, emitting the acrid vapour of mustard and irritating the eyes and nose. Taste, at first bitterish, but quickly pungent. The powdered seeds are inodorous until moisture is absorbed, but the powder loses its power of producing pungency if long exposed to the air.

White mustard seeds are globular, yellowish, about $\frac{1}{12}$ in. in diameter and $\frac{1}{10}$ gr in weight. The inner seed coat contains a quantity of mucilage, and hence the seeds are used to absorb the last traces of moisture in bottles which are not chemically dry, by shaking the seeds up in them. The cotyledons of the seeds contain oil and give a pungent, but inodorous, emulsion when rubbed with water. Taste, pungent; odour, none.

Part Used: Seeds.

Medicinal Use: Both varieties are irritant, stimulant, diuretic, emetic. Used chiefly as a poultice in acute local pains, pneumonia, bronchitis and other diseases of the respiratory organs. The volatile oil is a powerful irritant, rubefacient and vesicant, and combined with other remedies is an excellent application in rheumatic pains, colic, etc.

Preparations: Ol. Sinap. Vol. B.P.C. 1949 and Ol. Sinap. Express. B.P.C. are made from Black Mustard. Mustard Leaves, Mustard Plasters. Rape Oil (Ol. Rap. B.P.C.), commonly known as Colza Oil, is expressed from a variety of Mustard seed, *Brassica napus*.

Domestic Use: Both Black and White Mustards have been used as condiments since about A.D. 301.

Biblical References: Matthew XIII, 3, XVII, 20; Mark IV, 31; Luke XIII, 19, XVII, 6.

MYROBALANS

Terminalia chebula, Retz.
Fam. Combretaceae

Synonym: Black Chebulic.

Habitat: India.

Description: The immature fruits of a large tree, roundish or ovate in shape, and about the size of a hazel nut. If gathered later they are about the size of a walnut and brown in colour, pointed at the ends.

Part Used: Fruit.

Medicinal Use: Astringent; and like Rhubarb, has both cathartic and astringent properties. It has been used in the treatment of diarrhoea and dysentery. Not often used today.

Domestic Use: The large fruits, known as Chebulic Myrobalans are used for tanning.

MYRRH

Commiphora molmol, Eng.
(and other species)
Fam. Burseraceae

Synonyms: *Balsamodendron myrrha*, Nees, *Commiphora myrrha*, var. *molmol*, Eng.

Habitat: North-east Africa and Arabia.

Description: The plant is a shrub or small tree. The bark being cut allows the oleo-gum-resin to exude as a yellowish-white fluid which dries into the form in which it is found commercially. This oleo-gum-resin occurs in various qualities and varies in size from $\frac{3}{4}$–2 in. or more in diameter, some pieces containing gum in white streaks, and others hardly any, and some pieces more oil than others. The best for making emulsions or for use in pills are the pieces with white streaks. The oily pieces, with few streaks, are more useful for tincture. The gum left when the tincture is made with rectified spirit is closely allied to Acacia, possesses adhesive properties, and forms an excellent mucilage for sticking purposes.

Part Used: Oleo-gum-resin.

Medicinal Use: Stimulant, tonic, healing antiseptic. A valuable and deservedly popular medicine. The tincture is used in inflammatory sore throat, ulcers, bad legs, thrush, and other complaints. Makes an excellent wash for ulcerated mouth, tongue, etc.

Preparations: Dec. Aloes Co. B.P.C. 1949: Dose, $\frac{1}{2}$–2 fl oz; Dec. Aloes Co. Conc. B.P.C. 1949: Dose, 60–240 min; Pil. Rhei. Co. B.P.C.: Dose, 1 or 2 pills; Pil. Aloes et Myrrh B.P.C. 1949: Dose, 1 or 2 pills; Pil. Aloin Co. B.P.C. 1949: Dose, 1 pill; Tab. Rhei. Co. B.P.C.: Dose, 1 or 2 tablets; Tinct. Myrrh B.P.C.: Dose, 30–60 min; Tinct. Myrrh U.S.P.: Dose, 30 min; Tinct. Myrrh et Borac. B.P.C. 1949.

Biblical References: Genesis XXXVII, 25, XLIII, 11; Exodus XXX, 23; Esther II, 12; Psalm XLV, 8; Song of Solomon I, 13, III, 6, IV, 6, 14; Ecclesiasticus XXIV, 15; Matthew II, 11; Mark XV, 23; John XIX, 39.

MYRTLE

Myrtus communis, Linn.
Fam. Myrtaceae

Habitat: Southern Europe, but cultivated in Great Britain.

Description: An evergreen shrub. Leaves ovate, smooth, glossy, contain a volatile oil and Tannin.

Part Used: Leaves.

Medicinal Use: An infusion or tincture of the leaves has given excellent results as an injection for prolapsus and leucorrhoea. 10–30 gr of the powdered leaves is said to check night sweats of phthisis and to be of use in all pulmonary disorders.

Domestic Use: The leaves have been used to make a tea.

Biblical References: Nehemiah VIII, 15; Isaiah XLI, 19, LV, 13; Zechariah I, 8, 10, 11.

N

NETTLE

Urtica dioica, Linn.
Fam. Urticaceae

Synonym: Stinging Nettle.

Habitat: Nettles grow in waste places everywhere.

Description:

"Tender-handed, grasp the nettle
And it stings you for your pains.
Grasp it like a man of mettle
And it soft as silk remains."

Stem 2–3 ft high, quadrangular, with opposite, stalked, heart-shaped or lanceolate-oval leaves, serrated at the margin. The flowers are small, green, and four-parted, the male flowers arranged in erect, and the female in reflexed, panicles longer than the leaf-stalks. Fruit one-seeded. When growing it is easily recognized by its yellow creeping root, that of *Urtica urens*, which is only a foot high and is usually a garden weed, being white and not creeping, and the inflorescence being not so long as the leaf-stalks.

Chlorophyll is generally obtained from nettles; many tons are gathered yearly for that purpose.

Parts Used: Flowers, leaves, seeds.

Medicinal Use: Diuretic, astringent, tonic. The herb makes a nice botanic beer, and is also used as a medicine in nettle rash. The seeds are used in coughs and shortness of breath. The infusion of either herb or seed of 1 oz to 1 pt of boiling water is taken in wineglassful doses.

Preparations: Liquid extract, herb: Dose, $\frac{1}{2}$–1 dr.

Biblical References: Job xxx, 7; Proverbs xxiv, 31; Isaiah xxxiv, 13; Zephaniah ii, 9.

Domestic Use: In Judea the salt decoction of the herb was used to curdle milk and it is said to do this without communicating any bad taste to the milk.

It is said that the Roman Nettle which thrives in England was originally planted there by Caesar's soldiers, who not having breeches thick enough to enable them to withstand the climate suffered much in the cold, raw fogs; so when their legs were numb they plucked nettles and gave those members such a scouring that they burned and smarted gloriously for the rest of the day.

NIGHT-BLOOMING CEREUS

Cereus grandiflorus, Mill.
Fam. Cactaceae

Synonyms: Sweet-scented Cactus, *Cactus grandiflorus*, Mill.
Habitat: Jamaica.
Description: The stem and flowers are usually sold crushed and preserved in spirit. The stems are, when fresh, fleshy, five- to seven-angled and $\frac{1}{2}$–$\frac{3}{4}$ in. in diameter, and the flowers 4–5 in. across. The calyx consists of numerous linear, hairy, orange, segments, and the petals are oblong-lanceolate, white; the stamens are numerous and the stigma has many rays.

The small, dried flowers of *Opuntia decumana*, Haw., which are of little or no use and are only about 1$\frac{1}{2}$ in. in diameter, and other species of Opuntia, are sometimes sold as *Cereus grandiflorus*. A figure of the flower was published in the *Pharm. J.*, August, 1897, p. 165.
Part Used: Fresh plant.
Medicinal Use: Cardiac stimulant and tonic, diuretic. It gives prompt relief in most cardiac diseases, such as palpitation, angina pectoris, cardiac neuralgia, etc. Also useful in prostatic diseases, irritable bladder, and congested kidneys. It has been used in tropical America for dropsy. Prof. Locke recommends it for nervous menstrual headache.
Preparations: Ext. Cerei Liq.: Dose, 1–10 min; Tinct. Cerei: Dose, 2–30 min.

NIKKAR NUTS

Guilandia bondue, G. Bonducella
Fam. Leguminosae

Synonym: Nichol Seeds.
Habitat: The Savannas.
Description: The pods are covered with straight prickles and contain the hard, polished, yellow seeds about the size of an acorn. The trees grow in the Savannas everywhere.
Part Used: Seeds.
Medicinal Use: The seeds contain a bitter principle—a little alkaloid, but nothing very definite. They appear to be largely used in India as an anti-periodic and tonic. Employed with success in intermittent fevers. In Jamaica the seeds are roasted, which removes in part the bitterness, and made into Coffee. This is taken twice daily in cases of diabetes. Some patients have derived benefit, but further investigation is required.

It is said that in India these seeds, combined with Chiretta, have been used with success for treating malaria.

NUTMEG

Myristica fragrans, Houtt.
Fam. Myristicaceae

Synonyms: *Myristica officinalis*, Linn., Nux Moschata.

Habitat: Molucca Islands. Introduced into Penang, Malacca, Java, West Indies, and Ceylon.

Description: Nutmegs vary in size and in shape, as well as in quality, and are sold according to size. The average size runs 60–100 to the lb and are about 1¼ in. long and 1¾ in. in diameter. They should be variegated with brown and white internally, and cut with an oily surface. The outside shows, under a powerful lens, minute oblong or rounded black specks. The fragrant odour is characteristic. Long nutmegs about 1½ in. long of the genuine kind are occasionally met with, and these can be distinguished from the Papua nutmegs (*Myristica argentea*, Warb.), which are similar in size and shape, by the absence of black specks externally, and the acrid taste of the latter, which otherwise resemble true nutmegs. Bombay long nutmegs also occur in commerce, but these lack fragrance and are usually 2 in. long by rather more than ¾ in. broad.

Parts Used: Seeds, oil.

Medicinal Use: Carminative, stomachic. Useful in flatulency, nausea, and vomiting.

Joseph Mill states: "They are heating, drying, and carminative, strengthen the stomach and bowels, stop vomiting, help digestion, comfort the head and nerves, cure the palpitation of the heart and prevent swooning, and are of service against vapors."

Preparations: Powdered Nutmegs: Dose, 5–10 gr; Ol. Myrist. B.P. and U.S.P.: Dose, 1–3 min; Sp. Myrist. B.P.C. 1949: Dose, 5–20 min; Pulv. Cret. Aromat.: Dose, 10–60 gr; Pulv. Cret. Aromat. c. Opio.: Dose, 10–60 gr.

NUX VOMICA

Strychnos nux vomica, Linn.
Fam. Loganiaceae

Synonyms: Quaker Buttons, Poison Nut.

Habitat: Indigenous to India but growing in Burma, China, and Australia.

Description: The seeds are of a light greenish-grey colour, with a satiny surface due to the closely-appressed hairs. They are circular, usually rather less than 1 in. in diameter and about ¼ in. in thickness, depressed on one side and convex on the other, and often with a keeled or sharp margin. On the convex side there is usually a raised line (raphe) proceeding from a central scar (hilum) to a small protuberance at the edge (micropyle). Internally it is very hard and horny, but when split open shows a small embryo with heart-shaped, three-veined, white cotyledons, and a straight radicle. Taste, extremely bitter; inodorous.

Nux Vomica seeds are poisonous, but vary in the amount of Strychnine they contain, the large seeds from Ceylon being the richest.

Part Used: Seeds.

Medicinal Use: Tonic, bitter, stimulant. Used as a general tonic, mostly in combination with other remedies, for neuralgia, dyspepsia, debility, impotence, and in chronic constipation, as it increases peristalsis. Should be given with great care owing to its poisonous nature.

The ancient herbalists did not use Nux Vomica medicinally. Parkinson and later Joseph Miller both mention its use in poisoning dogs, cats, crows, and ravens.

Preparations: Nux Vom. Praep. B.P.: Dose, 1–4 gr; Ext. Nuc. Vom. Liq. B.P.: Dose, 1–3 min; Ext. Nuc. Vom. Sicc. B.P.: Dose, ¼–1 gr; Mist. Gent. Acid. c. Nuc. Vom. B.P.C.: Dose, ½–1 fl oz; Mist. Gent. Alk. c. Nuc. Vom. B.P.C.: Dose, ½–1 fl oz; Mist. Nuc. Vom. Acid. B.P.C.: Dose, ½–1 fl oz; Mist. Nuc. Vom. Alk. B.P.C.: Dose, ½–1 fl oz; Mist. Pot. Brom. et Nuc. Vom. B.P.C.: Dose, ½–1 fl oz; Pil. Aloes et Nuc. Vom. B.P.C.: Dose, 1 pill; Pil. Aloin. Co. B.P.C. 1949: Dose, 1 pill; Pil. Aloin. et Podoph. Co. B.P.C. 1949: Dose, 1–4 pills; Pil. Casc. Bellad. et Nuc. Vom. B.P.C. 1949: Dose, 1–3 pills; Tab. Aloes et Nuc. Vom. B.P.C.: Dose, 1 or 2 tablets; Tab. Aloin. Co. B.P.C.: Dose, 1 or 2 tablets; Tab. Casc. Sagr. Co. B.P.C.: Dose, 1 or 2 tablets; Tinct. Nuc. Vom. B.P.: Dose, 10–30 min.

O

OAK

Quercus robur, Linn.
Quercus sessiliflora, Salisb.
Fam. Fagaceae

Synonym: Tanner's Bark.

Description: The bark and branches of the young tree are greyish, and more or less polished externally and brownish internally. The fracture is fibrous, nd the inner surface rough, with projecting medullary rays. Taste, astringent; odour, slightly aromatic.

Part Used: Bark.

Medicinal Use: Slightly tonic, strongly astringent, antiseptic. Useful in chronic diarrhoea and dysentery, either alone or in conjunction with aromatics. A decoction is made from 1 oz of bark in 1 qt of water, boiled down to 1 pt, and taken in wineglassful doses. Externally an excellent gargle for sore and relaxed throat and a good injection for leucorrhoea.

Preparations: Liquid extract: Dose, ½–1 dr; Dec. Querc.

Domestic Use: Oak bark is used in tanning.

Biblical References: Genesis xxxv, 4, 8; Joshua xxiv, 26; Judges vi, 11, 19; 2 Samuel xviii, 9, 10, 14; I Kings xiii, 14; 1 Chronicles x, 12; Isaiah i, 29, 30, ii, 13, vi, 13, xliv, 14; Ezekiel vi, 13, xxvii, 6; Hosea iv, 13; Amos ii, 9; Zechariah xi, 2; 2 Esdras xiv, 1.

OATS

Avena sativa, Linn.
Fam. Graminaceae

Synonym: Groats.

Habitat: Widely distributed over Europe, Great Britain, the U.S.A., and other countries.

Description: The seeds with the husk removed are sold in two or more forms. Crushed or in coarse powder they are known as groats, and in fine or coarse powder as oatmeal. Like all other cornmeal it should be kept dry, or it undergoes alteration and acquires a bitter taste. The starch of the oat is quite characteristic, consisting of simple and compound grains, the former always containing some spindle- or lemon-shaped grains, which rice starch never does.

Part Used: Seeds.

Medicinal Use: Nerve tonic, stimulant, antispasmodic. Avena forms an important restorative in nervous prostration and exhaustion after all febrile diseases, and as a tonic in spermatorrhoea, insomnia, etc. It seems to exert a very beneficial action upon the heart muscles and on the urinary organs, speedily relieving spasmodic conditions of bladder and ureter. It is mostly used in the form of a liquid extract.

Preparation: Liquid extract: Dose, 10–30 drops.

Domestic Use: A well-known food in many forms.

OLIVE

Olea europaea, Linn.
Fam. Oleaceae

Habitat: Mediterranean countries.

Description: An Evergreen tree from the fruit of which is expressed the oil.

Olive Oil is much adulterated. The purest or virgin oil, known as Provence or Virgin Oil, has usually a faint greenish tinge, and is more expensive. Ordinary Olive Oil often contains purified Cotton Seed Oil. The latter is a drying oil to a certain degree, and Olive Oil containing it usually forms a thin skin on the glass over which it has run. The taste of the oil is a good guide to purity. Anyone who compares it with the taste of a preserved olive will recognize it at once.

Olive Oil enters into the composition of many soaps. Sapo Durus B.P.C., known as Castile Soap or Hard Soap, is made from Olive Oil and Sodium Hydroxide. Sapo Mollis B.P., Soft Soap, is prepared from Olive Oil and Potassium Hydroxide. The former is used medicinally in pills and plasters, whereas the latter enters into the composition of liniments, cleansing solutions, and rectal injections.

Part Used: Oil.

Medicinal Use: Emollient, nutritive, aperient. Olive Oil (or Lucca Oil, Sweet Oil, Salad Oil, Provence Oil, Virgin Oil), apart from its use in the household, is a valuable remedy in bowel diseases generally. Being pleasant to the taste, it is often substituted for Castor Oil as a children's laxative, and as remedy in habitual constipation and lead colic. It removes intestinal worms and in large doses dispels biliary concretions. Externally it forms part of a large number of embrocations, ointments, liniments, etc., used in bruises, burns, scalds, rheumatic and cutaneous affections. As an inunction in teething children it is invaluable, keeping the bowels regular and acting as a tonic by absorption. The dose of the oil varies from 1 teaspoonful to 2 tablespoonfuls.

Preparations: Emuls. Ol. Oliv.: Dose, ¼–1 fl oz; Ext. Malt c. Ol. Oliv.: Dose, 1–2 dr; Lin. Calc. Hydrox.; Ung. Hydrarg. Co. B.P.C.; Ung. Hydrarg. Nit. fort. B.P.

Domestic Use: Olives are used as a food, more especially in the countries where the tree grows. The oil is used for culinary purposes and also in the manufacture of cosmetics.

Biblical References: Genesis VIII, 11; Exodus XXIII, 11, XXVII, 20; Deuteronomy VI, 11, VIII, 8, XXIV, 20, XXVIII, 40; Joshua XXIV, 13; Judges IX, 8, 9, XV, 5; 1 Samuel VIII, 14; 1 Kings VI, 23, 31, 32, 33; 2 Kings V, 26, XVII, 32; 1 Chronicles XXVII, 28; Nehemiah V, 11, VIII, 15, IX, 25; Job XV, 33; Psalm LII, 8, CXXVIII, 3; Isaiah XVII, 6, XLI, 19; Jeremiah XI, 16; Hosea XIV, 6; Amos IV, 9; Micah VI, 15; Habakkuk III, 17; Haggai II, 19; Zechariah IV, 11, 12, XIV, 4; Judith XV, 13; Matthew XXI, 1, XXVI, 30; Mark XI, 1, XIV, 26; Luke XIX, 29, XXII, 39; Romans XI, 17, 21, 23; James III, 12; Revelation XI, 4.

OLIVER BARK

Cinnamomum Oliveri, Baill.
Fam. Lauraceae

Synonyms: Black Sassafras, Australian Cinnamon.

Habitat: New South Wales, Queensland.

Description: Flat strips, coarsely granular outer surface brown with white cork patches. Odour of sassafras and cinnamon.

Part Used: Bark.

Medicinal Use: Stimulant and corrective. Dose, 10–30 gr.

Preparations: Tincture: Dose, 30–60 drops.

ONION

Allium cepa, Linn.
Fam. Liliaceae

Habitat: Widely distributed in Europe, Africa, Asia, and America.

Description: The onion is a well-known plant growing in the kitchen garden and not requiring description.

Part Used: Bulb.

Medicinal Use: Diuretic, expectorant. Besides being used for culinary purposes, Onions often form an ingredient in domestic medication. Who has not heard of roasted Onion as a poultice for suppurating tumours or earache? The juice, made into a syrup, is beneficial as a cough medicine. Onions are macerated in Hollands gin, and the resulting tincture is serviceable in gravel and dropsical affections. The large or Portugal Onion when boiled forms a useful remedy for a cold. In the spring the head of the Onion is apt to decay and should be removed.

Domestic Use: Onions form a well-known food.

Biblical Reference: Numbers XI, 5.

ORANGE, BITTER

Citrus aurantium, Linn.
Subsp. *amara*, Eng.
Fam. Rutaceae

Synonyms: Seville Orange, Bigarade or Bigaradier Orange, *Citrus bigaradria*, Loisel, Naranja.

Habitat: Originated in Northern India but now cultivated in Mediterranean countries.

Description: The new rind is best purchased in March or April, since the new crop of fruit is imported in February. English dried peel is of better quality than the imported dried peel. A fine-cut peel with very little of the white spongy parts is known as Maltese Orange Peel.

Orange Water is made from the flowers by distillation, and Oil of Neroli is also produced in the South of France by distilling the flowers with water.

Parts Used: Fruit rind, oil, flowers.

Medicinal Use: Tonic, stomachic, carminative. Orange peel is mostly used as an agreeable flavour for bitter medicinal compounds and to allay a tendency to nausea. It can be used with most forms of medications, especially in infusions, decoctions, tinctures, and syrups.

Preparations: From fresh peel: Ol. Aurant. B.P.C. (Bitter); Elix. Simp. B.P.C. 1949: Dose, 60–120 min; Syr. Aurant. B.P.: Dose, 30–120 min; Tinct. Aurant. B.P.: Dose, 30–60 min; Tinct. Aurant. Amar. U.S.P.; Tinct. Aurant. Conc. B.P.C. 1949: Dose, 8–15 min.

From dry peel: Ext. Aurant. Liq. B.P.C. 1949: Dose, 10–20 min; Inf. Aurant. Conc. B.P.C.: Dose, 30–60 min; Inf. Aurant. Co. Rec. B.P.C. 1949: Dose, ½–1 fl oz; Inf. Aurant. Rec. B.P.C. 1949: Dose, ½–1 fl oz; Syr. Aromat. B.P.C. 1949: Dose, 30–60 min.

From flowers: Ol. Neroli, from which is prepared—Aq. Aurant. flor. conc. B.P.C. 1949; Sp. Colon (Eau de Cologne); Syr. Aurant. flor. B.P.C. 1949: Dose, 30–60 min; Aq. Aurant. flor. U.S.P. (distilled from flowers), from which is made Syr. Aurant flor. U.S.P.

ORANGE, SWEET

Citrus sinensis, Linn.
Fam. Rutaceae

Synonyms: Portugal Orange, China Orange, *Citrus dulcis*, Pers.

Habitat: Sicily, West Indies, Africa.

Description: The Sweet Orange Peel has less bitterness than that of the Seville Orange. The flowers of the orange are white, oblong, five-parted, with a cup-shaped calyx, and fleshy, oblong petals and numerous stamens united at the base. The unopened flowers are usually sold. They are about $\frac{3}{4}$ in. long and $\frac{1}{4}$ in. broad.

Parts Used: Peel, flowers.

Medicinal Use: Aromatic, carminative. Possesses the same properties as Bitter Orange and is used for similar purposes.

Preparations: Ol. Aurant. B.P.C. (sweet); Ol. Aurant. U.S.P.; Sp. Aurant. Co. B.P.C. and U.S.P.; Elix. Aromat. B.P.C. 1949: Dose, 30–120 min; Tinct. Aurant. dulc. U.S.P.; Syr. Aurant. U.S.P.

ORRIS

Iris florentina, Linn.
(and other species)
Fam. Iridaceae

Synonyms: Florentine Orris, Orris Root.

Habitat: Italy, Morocco. Cultivated in other countries including Great Britain.

Flowering Time: June.

Description: The rhizome is sold in several forms. Florentine is white, irregular in shape, bearing small marks where the rootlets have been removed. The Verona root is usually somewhat compressed, and less suddenly tapering than the Florentine root: that from Morocco has the cortical portion not removed, and is of a dirty white colour. The Verona root is also sold trimmed for infants' use when teething. The rhizome has a violet odour.

Part Used: Rhizome.

Medicinal Use: It is used principally in dusting powders, toilet powders, dentifrices, cachous. Joseph Miller states it is "Good for disorders of the lungs caused by sharp humors . . . it helps coughs, hoarseness and soreness at stomach. It is likewise commended against the gripes in children. . . ."

OSIER, RED, AMERICAN

Cornus sericea, Linn.
Fam. Cornaceae

Synonyms: Rose Willow, Red Willow, Silky Cornel.

Habitat: U.S.A.

Description: Bark in thin, irregular pieces or short quills, purplish externally, somewhat warty, inner surface cinnamon brown, even, and finely striated. Fracture even, scarcely fibrous. Taste, astringent, bitter; odour, slight. The English Red Osier (*Salix rubra*) is very seldom used in medicine.

Parts Used: Bark, root-bark.

Medicinal Use: Astringent, bitter, tonic. Has been found of service in diarrhoea, dyspepsia, and in fevers. Is also recommended in dropsy. The infusion is useful in checking vomiting due to pregnancy or disease of the womb.

OX-EYE DAISY

Chrysanthemum leucanthemum, Linn.
Fam. Compositae

Synonyms: White Daisy, Field Daisy, Moon Daisy, Maudlin Daisy, Great Ox-eye, White Weed, Goldens, Horsegowan, Marguerite, *Leucanthemum vulgare*, Lam.

Habitat: Europe, Great Britain, Russian Asia.

Flowering Time: It starts in the spring and continues for most of the summer.

Description: The leaf stem is angular, 1–2 ft long, bearing stalked, serrate, spatulate leaves in the lower half, with a serrate, clasping base, and serrate upper leaves, which are oblong and sessile. The yellow-centred, white flowerheads have an involucre of green bracts with thin, black, membranous edges. The receptacle is hemispherical and without paleae. The fruit has no pappus. Taste, bitter and tingling; odour, faintly valerianic.

Part Used: Herb.

Medicinal Use: Antispasmodic, diuretic, tonic. Ox-eye Daisy has been employed successfully in whooping cough, asthma, and nervous excitability. As a tonic it acts similarly to Chamomile, and has been recommended in nightsweats. The decoction—of usual strength—is taken in wineglassful to teacupful doses three to four times a day. Externally it is serviceable as an injection in leucorrhoea, and as a lotion for ulcers, wounds, etc. Large doses produce emesis.

P

PAPAW

Carica papaya, Linn.
Fam. Papayaceae

Synonyms: Melon Tree, Mamaeiro, *Papaya vulgaris*, D.C., Fruta de Bomba.

Habitat: Cultivated in most tropical countries.

Description: The Papaw is a handsome tropical tree with a large crown of spreading palmate leaves, at the base of which the fruits are produced on the female tree. The fruit is the size of a small melon, and when ripe is of a greenish-yellow or even orange colour. The flesh consists of a yellow, sweet pulp with numerous black seeds. The most remarkable characteristic of the Papaw is the presence of an active enzyme called Papain, which occurs in the fruit seeds and leaves. Five grains are said to digest a pint of milk in thirty minutes.

"Papain" is a white powder soluble in glycerine, and is prepared from the juice of the Papaw tree. Another preparation of a brownish-white tint, and granular in character consists of the dried juice of the fruit.

Part Used: Papain, prepared from the juice of the unripe fruit.

Medicinal Use: Digestive. "Papain," a white powder, is administered generally in all digestive disorders where albuminoid substances pass away undigested. It is generally used in combination with an alkali, such as bicarbonate of soda, and acts best in an alkaline medium. A solution of the ferment is reputed to dissolve the false membranes in diphtheria and croup, when applied frequently.

Preparations: Papain: Dose, 2–10 gr; Elix. Papain B.P.C. 1949: Dose, ½–1 dr; Glyc. Papain: Dose, ¼–1 dr; Liq. Papain et Iridin: Dose, ¼–1 dr.

PARAGUAY TEA

Ilex paraguensis, Hook.
(and other varieties)
Fam. Aquifoliaceae.

Synonyms: Maté, Yerba maté, Jesuit's Brazil Tea.

Habitat: Brazil, Paraguay and other parts of S. America.

Description: The leaves are sold in two forms. The Brazilian is sold in the form of roughly powdered leaves and stalks. The Paraguay kind, which is considered the best, consists of broken leaves only. The leaves are coriaceous in texture, but are rarely perfect enough to show their form. The characteristic features under the microscope are the thick striated cuticle, the straight-walled polygonal cells of the epidermis, and the stomata overhung by three or four contiguous cells. Taste, bitterish; flavour, recalling those of tea, lime flowers, and orange.

Part Used: Leaves.

Medicinal Use: Stimulant, diuretic. The peculiar properties it possesses are chiefly due to Caffeine. Its action resembles such stimulants as Tea, Coffee, and Coca, although different from either. If taken in large doses it acts as a purgative and anti-scorbutic. Recommended for rheumatism and gout.

Preparation: Liquid extract: Dose, $\frac{1}{2}$–1 dr.

Domestic Use: Fifty million people in South America use Paraguay Tea in place of ordinary tea.

PAREIRA

Chondodendron tomentosum, R. & P.
Fam. Menispermaceae

Synonym: Pareira brava.

Habitat: Peru and Brazil.

Description: The root occurs in tortuous woody pieces of varying length, and about 1–2 in. in diameter, black externally, longitudinally furrowed, with transverse ridges and some constrictions, and internally greyish yellow or brownish. The transverse section shows three or four concentric rings, usually about $\frac{1}{4}$ in. in diameter and each separated from the contiguous one by a wavy line of softer tissue. The medullary rays are broad, sometimes broader than the woody wedges. The taste is bitter and slightly sweet but the root is inodorous. The stem, which often forms more than one-third of the imported drug, is similar in structure, but differs in the outer surface, being grey, with numerous round, warty lenticels. Substitutes often appear in the market, but all of them have narrower rings and thinner medullary rays, and in some kinds no bitterness is present, and in all except the African false Pareira the outer surface is not black. The African kind is recognizable by the narrow rings and thinner medullary.

Part Used: Root.

Medicinal Use: Tonic, diuretic, aperient. Used as a stimulant to kidneys, relieving urinary irritation, and in chronic inflammation of bladder and various urinary diseases. The infusion of 1 oz to 1 pt of boiling water is taken in wineglassful doses as required.

Preparation: Liquid extract: Dose, $\frac{1}{4}$–2 dr.

PARSLEY

Carum petroselinum, Benth. & Hook.
Fam. Umbelliferae

Synonyms: *Apium petroselinum*, Linn., *Petroselinum sativum*, Hoffm.

Habitat: Eastern Mediterranean countries. Now well established in many countries, including Great Britain.

Description: Parsley is a well-known plant easily distinguished by its dissected leaves and characteristic taste.

Parts Used: Root, seeds, leaves.

Medicinal Use: Aperient, diuretic, emmenagogue. Is chiefly used on account of its diuretic properties. In gravel, stone, congestion of kidneys, and in dropsy, it will be found of great service. The seeds contain Apiol, which is considered a safe and efficient emmenagogue, and is used in amenorrhoea and dysmenorrhoea.

Parkinson writes: "Tragus setteth downe an excellent medicine to help the jaundies and falling sicknesse, the Dropsie and stone in Reynes or Kidneyes in this manner; take saith he of the seeds of Parsley, Fennell, Anise and Carawayes, of each an ounce, of the roots of Parsley, Burnet, Saxifrage and Carawayes of each one ounce and a halfe; let the seedes be bruised and the rootes washed and cut small; let them all lye in steepe in a pottle of white wine, and in the morning boyled in a close earthen vessell until a third part or more be wasted, which being strained and cleared, take foure ounces thereof at a time, morning and evening first and last, abstaining from drinke for three houres after. . . ."

Preparations: Liquid extract, root: Dose, ½–1 dr; Liquid extract, seeds: Dose, ½–1 dr; Apiol: Dose, 3–10 min; Oil: Dose, 3–5 min.

Domestic Use: Parsley leaves are used in sauces and generally as an adjunct to food.

PARSLEY PIERT

Alchemilla arvensis, Scop.
Fam. Rosaceae

Synonym: Parsley Breakstone. Gerard says: "Our herbe women in Cheapside know it by the name of Parsley Breakstone."

Habitat: Widely distributed in Europe and the British Isles.

Flowering Time: May.

Description: This small herb varies from 3–5 in. in height, has small, palmate leaves below, about ½ in. in diameter, the upper leaves being trifid and wedge-shaped at the base. The greenish flowers in axillary tufts are very small. The whole plant is hairy, with slender, scattered hairs. Taste, astringent; odour, none.

Part Used: Herb.

Medicinal Use: Demulcent, diuretic. Used in cases of gravel, kidney, and bladder complaints. It acts directly on the parts affected, and will be found exceedingly valuable even in seemingly incurable cases. Several London doctors prescribe this remedy regularly. The infusion is taken in teacupful doses three times daily.

Preparation: Liquid extract: Dose, 1 dr.

Domestic Use: Culpeper recommends it as a good salad herb.

GERARD says Parsley Piert is found "upon dry and barren grounds, as in Hyde Park, Tuthill fields etc.," and Culpeper states that it grows plentifully about Hampstead.

Although Joseph Miller does not highly commend this herb, saying ". . . the vulgar have a great opinion of it" and "It is seldom prescribed by Physicians" yet it was a herb known to the ancients and spoken of highly by Gerard and Culpeper. Culpeper writes: "It were good the gentry would pickle it up as they pickle up Samphire for their use all the Winter . . . and it is a very wholesome herb."

PASSION FLOWER

Passiflora incarnata, Linn.
Fam. Passifloraceae

Synonym: Maypops.

Habitat: Most tropical countries. It is grown in hot-houses in England and occasionally will grow outdoors in the south in well-protected positions.

Description: A climbing plant, leaves cordate-ovate and palmately three-lobed. The plant bears solitary, large, and very beautiful flowers, white with a purple centre. The fruit is a large berry.

Parts Used: Plant and leaves.

Medicinal Use: Antispasmodic, sedative, narcotic. Used as a rest-producing remedy in nervous, irritative, and neuralgic pains with debility, and also in nervous headache, hysteria, spasms, and convulsions.

Preparation: Liquid extract: Dose, 10–20 drops.

Domestic Use: The fruit is edible.

PATCHOULI

Pogostemon patchouli, Pell.
Fam. Labiatae

Habitat: Malay Peninsula.

Description: Patchouli leaves, as imported, are usually of dark-brown colour, crumpled, and often mixed with other leaves. The genuine leaves, when soaked out in water, are seen to be ovate in form; they attain to 4 in. long and $5\frac{1}{2}$ in. broad, but younger leaves are only half that size; the margin is lobed, with irregular, crenate-serrate teeth, the lobes being obtuse, and the base of the leaf not toothed. The hairs are simple and usually four-celled. Taste, aromatic; odour, strong and persistent.

Part Used: Leaves.

Medicinal Use: None.

Domestic Use: The leaves are used in sweet-smelling sachets. There is also an oil distilled from the leaves which is used in perfumery.

PAWPAW, AMERICAN

Asimina triloba, Dur.
Fam. Anonaceae

Synonym: Custard Apple.

Habitat: U.S.A.

Description: A small tree bearing an edible fruit. Seeds flat, oblong-oval, with the greyish hilum at one end, brown and slightly polished, with darker brown pinnate lines on the surface, about 1 in. long and $\frac{5}{8}$–$\frac{3}{4}$ in. broad and $\frac{1}{6}$ in. thick. The seed has ruminated, horny albumen, and exudes oil when pressed by the nail. Taste and odour, resinous.

Part Used: Seeds.

Medicinal Use: The seeds contain an emetic alkaloid. They are rarely used medicinally.

Domestic Use: The fruit is edible and is said to have a high nutritive value.

PEACH

Prunus persica, Stokes
Fam. Rosaceae

Synonyms: *Amygdalus persica*, Linn., *Persica vulgaris*, Nutt.

Habitat: Peaches grow in many tropical and semi-tropical parts of the world and are also cultivated in temperate climates usually under glass.

Description: Leaves elliptical, about 4 in. long and $1\frac{1}{2}$ in. broad, tapering to a sharp point above, with a short leafstalk about $\frac{1}{2}$ in. long, the margins minutely serrate with a gland at the base on each side, replacing the lowest teeth of the leaf, under surface pale green. Bark in small, thin, pale-brown fragments, rarely exceeding $1\frac{1}{2}$ in. in length and $\frac{1}{4}$ in. in thickness, having a smooth, dark-brown epidermis, which readily exfoliates, and an inner surface with a faint network of fibres. Fracture short, but fibrous. Taste, bitter and very astringent; flavour, slight.

Parts Used: Bark, leaves, oil expressed from the seeds.

Medicinal Use: Sedative, diuretic, expectorant. For irritation and congestion of the gastric surfaces this has been found almost a specific. It is also used in coughs, whooping cough, and chronic bronchitis. An infusion of $\frac{1}{2}$ oz of bark or 1 oz of leaves to 1 pt of boiling water is taken in doses from a teaspoonful to a wineglassful as required.

Persic Oil is expressed from the seeds of the *P. persica* and *P. armeniaca* (Apricot). It is largely used in the manufacture of toilet preparations and as a substitute for almond oil.

PELLITORY

Anacyclus pyrethrum, D.C.
Fam. Compositae

Synonyms: Pellitory Root, Spanish Pellitory, Spanish Chamomile, *Anthemis pyrethrum*, Linn., *Matricaria pyrethrum*, Baill.

Habitat: Spain and the Mediterranean countries.

Flowering Time: June and July.

Description: In dark-brown, cylindrical pieces, about 2–3 in. long and $\frac{1}{2}$ in. broad, tapering slightly to either end and often having at the crown a tuft of soft, woolly hairs furrowed longitudinally, with a short fracture and a radiate structure, with dark resin cells in the bark. Taste, slowly pungent and acrid, causing a flow of saliva; odour, characteristic.

Part Used: Root.

Medicinal Use: Local irritant, rubefacient. Used externally it is an excellent remedy for toothache.

Preparation: Tincture.

PELLITORY-OF-THE-WALL

Parietaria officinalis, Linn.
Fam. Urticaceae

Synonym: Paritary (O.E.).

Habitat: A common wild plant in Europe and the British Isles.

Flowering Time: June and July.

Description: Herb about 1–2 ft high, with brittle, reddish stems and stalked, lanceolate leaves 1–2 in. long and $\frac{1}{2}$–1 in. broad, with slender stalks about $\frac{3}{4}$ in. long. Flowers small, green, sessile, axillary. The stems and veins of the under surface of the leaves are furnished with short soft hairs; the upper surface of the leaves is nearly smooth, with sunken veins. Taste, insipid; odour, none.

Part Used: Herb.

Medicinal Use: Laxative, diuretic. A most efficacious remedy in stone, gravel, dropsy, and suppression of urine. Usually combined with Wild Carrot and Parsley Piert. The infusion of 1 oz to 1 pt of boiling water is taken in wineglassful doses.

Parkinson recommends it as follows: "The dried herbe made up with Hony, is a singular remedy for any old continuall or dry cough, the shortnesse of breath and wheezings in the throate. . . ."

Preparation: Liquid extract: Dose, 1 dr.

PENNYROYAL

Mentha pulegium, Linn.
Fam. Labiatae

Synonym: European Pennyroyal.

Habitat: A common garden plant in Europe and Great Britain. It also grows wild in moist places. Culpeper speaks of it being found wild "by the highways from London to Colchester."

Flowering Time: August.

Description: Herb 8–12 in. high. Stems bluntly quadrangular. Leaves opposite, shortly stalked, oblong-oval, obtuse, about 1–1½ in. long, and ½ in. broad, faintly serrate, nearly smooth, or hairy. Taste and odour, mint-like, but characteristic.

American or Mock Pennyroyal consists of the dried leaves and flowering tops of *Hedeoma pulegioides*, a plant with similar properties to the above but quite distinct in appearance.

Parts Used: Herb, oil.

Medicinal Use: Carminative, diaphoretic, stimulant, emmenagogue. It is principally used as a remedy in obstructed menstruation for which it forms a reliable cure, especially where sudden chill or cold is the cause. It may also be employed with advantage in cases of spasms, hysteria, flatulence, and sickness, as it is very warming and grateful to the stomach. The infusion of 1 oz of herb to 1 pt of boiling water is taken warm in teacupful doses, frequently repeated. The oil is an excellent preventive application against mosquito and gnat bites.

The herb was at one time thought to be of use in whooping cough. John Hill writes: "Mr. Boyle has left an account of its virtues against chincough; this is worth trying. The method of giving it is in the expressed juice, sweetened with sugar-candy, a spoonful for dose."

Gerard writes: "A garland of Pennie-Royal made and worne about the head is of great force against the swimming of head and the pains and giddeness thereof."

Domestic Use: Pennyroyal leaves, dried and rubbed are used as a culinary flavouring.

Preparations: Oil: Dose, 1–3 min; Liquid extract: Dose, ¼–1 dr; Sp. Puleg: Dose, 10–20 min.

PEONY

Paeonia officinalis, Linn.
Fam. Ranunculaceae

Synonyms: Paeonia, Common Peony, Piney.
Habitat: A common English garden flower.
Flowering Time: May.
Description: The plant is well known and does not require description. The root appears in commerce in scraped, spindle-shaped pieces, averaging 3 in. long and $\frac{1}{2}$–$\frac{3}{4}$ in. in diameter, pinkish grey or dirty white, strongly furrowed, and shrunken longitudinally. The transverse section is starchy, radiate, with the medullary rays more or less tinged with purple. Taste, sweet then bitter; inodorous.
Part Used: Root.
Medicinal Use: Antispasmodic, tonic. Successfully employed in convulsive and spasmodic nervous affections such as chorea, epilepsy, spasms, etc. The infusion of 1 oz powdered root in 1 pt of boiling water is taken in wineglassful to teacupful doses three to four times daily.

Culpeper describes it as a herb of the Sun and under the lion. He recommends it for the falling sickness (Epilepsy) and states "but the surest way is (besides hanging it about the neck, by which children have been cured) to take the root of the male peony washed clean and stamped small and infuse it in sack for twenty-four hours at least; afterwards strain it, and take, morning and evening, a good draught for sundry days together before and after a full moon. . . ."

PEPPER

Piper nigrum, Linn.
Fam. Piperaceae

Synonym: Black Pepper.
Habitat: Travancore and Malabar. Introduced into Sumatra, Java, Borneo, the Malay Peninsula, Siam, the Philippines, and the West Indies.
Description: Black pepper is the dried, unripe fruit, externally black and wrinkled, $\frac{1}{5}$ in. in diameter, spherical, containing only one seed, which is horny and grey and starchy internally. Taste, very pungent; odour, characteristic.

White Pepper: The berries are collected when nearly ripe; the outer pericarp is removed by soaking in water and rubbing.

Long Pepper is the dried unripe fruit of *Piper chaba.*, exported from Java.
Part Used: Unripe berries.
Medicinal Use: Carminative, stimulant. Besides its use as a condiment, Pepper is a valuable gastro-intestinal stimulant, of great service in flatulence, congestive chills, and indigestion. It has been recommended in

intermittent fevers, and forms an ingredient in "Asiatic Pills." The powdered Peppercorns may be taken in doses of 3–15 gr.

Preparations: Conf. Piper. B.P.C. 1949: Dose, 1–2 dr; Oleoresin: Dose, ½ gr.

PEPPERMINT

Mentha piperita, Linn.
Fam. Labiatae

Synonyms: Brandy Mint, Curled Mint, Balm Mint.

Habitat: It grows over a wide area of Europe and North America.

Flowering Time: August.

Description: Stem usually purplish, 2–4 ft high, quadrangular, leaves stalked, 2–3 in. long and ¾–1½ in. broad, serrate, slightly but not visibly hairy. Taste and odour, characteristic.

Hairy Mint: downy leaves (*Mentha aquatica*).

Corn Mint: rings of flowers around stem with pair of leaves below each ring (*Mentha arvensis*).

Menthol is obtained mainly from *M. arvensis*, var. *piperaseus*, in Japan and China, being separated from the oil by freezing. The dementholized Japanese oil is then sold as a cheap grade of oil very largely used for flavouring.

Parts Used: Herb, distilled oil.

Medicinal Use: Stimulant, stomachic, carminative. Used for allaying nausea, flatulence, sickness, vomiting and as an infants' cordial. Generally combined with other medicines when its stomachic effects are required. The infusion of 1 oz to 1 pt of boiling water is taken in wineglassful doses.

Preparations: Powdered herb: Dose, 30–60 gr; Ol. Menth. Pip. B.P. and U.S.P., from which is made: Aq. Menth. Pip. U.S.P., Aq. Menth. Pip. Conc. B.P.: Dose, 5–15 min.

Aq. Menth. Pip. Dest. B.P.C. 1949: Dose, ½–1 fl oz; Emuls. Anis. et Menth. Pip. B.P.C. 1949: Dose, 5–30 min; Sp. Menth. Pip. B.P.: Dose, 5–30 min; Sp. Menth. Pip. U.S.P., Tab. Sod. Bicarb. Co. B.P.: Dose, 2–6 tablets; Liquid extract: Dose, ½–1 dr.

PERIWINKLE

Vinca major, Linn.
Fam. Apocynaceae

Synonym: Greater Periwinkle.

Habitat: Southern Europe. Grown in many other parts of the world as an ornamental plant.

Flowering Time: Spring.

Description: Stems cylindrical smooth, leaves opposite, shining, at intervals of 2–3 in., stalked, ovate, entire at the margins, 1½–3 in. long and 1–2 in. broad, the lower leaves largest. Flowers blue, rotate, and as large as a florin. Taste, bitterish, slightly acrid; odour, none.

Part Used: Herb.

Medicinal Use: Astringent, tonic. It is reputed to be useful in menorrhagia and haemorrhages generally.

Joseph Miller describes it as "a good vulnerary plant, and of frequent use in wound-drinks. . . ."

VINCA rosea, a fairly common, pinkish-white-flowered plant growing in South Africa, has been used by the natives for many years as a cure for diabetes. It is said to be more efficacious than Insulin. A registration officer in Durban was declared cured after two months' treatment, and considerable notice appeared in the South African and London Press as to its virtues.

PERUVIAN BALSAM

Myroxylon pereirae, Klotsch
Fam. Leguminosae

Synonyms: Balsam of Peru, *Toluifera pereirae*, Baill.

Habitat: Central America.

Description: The tree from which the balsam is obtained grows to about 50 ft in height and produces loose racemes of strong-smelling flowers. The balsam is a black, oily fluid of sp. gr. 1·15–1·16, and a sweet, balsamic odour. It is liable to adulteration, but tests to ascertain its purity are given in the B.P.C.

The balsam exudes from the tree after the bark has been beaten and scorched. This is soaked off by rags and boiled in water.

Part Used: Balsam.

Medicinal Use: Stimulating, expectorant. Useful in all chronic mucous affections, catarrh, leucorrhoea, diarrhoea, dysentery. Externally used in ulcers, wounds, ringworm, eczema, and other cutaneous affections. Dose, 5–15 min.

Joseph Miller describes it as of a "warming, strengthning nature, comforting the brain . . . and useful in Asthmas, the Collick and pains in the stomach and bowels. Outwardly used it strengthens the Nerves, helps the Cramp and all kinds of Convulsions and Contractions of the Sinews, old Aches and Pains, and is very serviceable in Cuts and green Wounds."

PICHI

Fabiana imbricata, R. & P.
Fam. Solanaceae

Habitat: Bolivia, Peru, Chile, and Argentine.

Description: The drug consists of stems irregularly branched with erect twigs covered with closely-imbricated, heath-like leaves, which are fleshy, obtuse, and keeled with a prominent midrib beneath. The stem bears short, glandular hairs and is marked with spirally-arranged, paler scars where the twigs have fallen. Flowers, when present, white, tubular, constricted at the throat. Taste, bitterish; odour, faint but agreeable.

Parts Used: Leaves, twigs.

Medicinal Use: Diuretic, tonic, hepatic, stimulant. It favourably influences digestion in dyspepsia and jaundice, acting upon the stomach and liver. As a diuretic it is of value in catarrhal and functional diseases of the kidneys. The infusion of 1 oz in 1 pt of boiling water is taken in wineglassful doses every four hours.

Preparation: Liquid extract: Dose, ½–1 dr.

PILEWORT

Ranunculus ficaria, Linn.
Fam. Ranunculaceae

Synonyms: Small Celandine, Lesser Celandine.

Habitat: Europe and Western Asia. Grows commonly in Great Britain.

Flowering Time: Early spring.

Description: Leaves mostly radical, with stalks 4–5 in. long, the blade 1–1½ in. long and 1½–2 in. broad, broadly cordate-angular, one to three only on a stem. Flowers solitary, stalked, buttercup-like, about 1 in. in diameter, petals yellow, usually eight, sepals three. Root of several fleshy knobs, oblong-rounded or club-shaped, ¼–1 in. long, ⅛ in. broad. Taste, acrid; odour, none.

Part Used: Herb.

Medicinal Use: Astringent. As its name denotes, it is chiefly used for piles, for which it is almost a specific. Internally the infusion of 1 oz in 1 pt of boiling water is taken in wineglassful doses. Generally this is sufficient to cure most cases. Sir James Sawyer, M.D., used the entire herb, macerated in boiling lard for 24 hr at a temperature of 100°F, as an ointment for piles with good results. Applied locally twice daily. The B.P.C. 1932 also contained a formula for Pilewort Ointment.

PIMPERNEL, SCARLET

Anagallis arvensis, Linn.
Fam. Primulaceae

Synonyms: Red Pimpernel, Shepherd's Barometer, Poor Man's Weatherglass. Gerard explains how the two last names arise when he says: "They floure in Summer and especially in the moneth of August, at what time the husbandmen having occasion to go unto their harvest worke will first behold the floures of Pimpernell, whereby they know the weather that shall follow the next day after; as for example, if the floures be shut close up, it betokeneth raine and foule weather; contrariwise, if they be spread abroad, faire weather."

Habitat: Europe, Asiatic Russia, Great Britain.

Flowering Time: All the summer.

Description: Stem weak, procumbent or ascending, leaves opposite, about ½ in. long and ⅜ in. broad, ovate, sessile, with entire margins, and black dots on the under surface. Flowers scarlet, corolla rotate. Fruit one-celled and globular, splitting open horizontally. Taste, acrid, mucilaginous. Said to be poisonous.

Part Used: Leaves.

Medicinal Use: Diuretic, diaphoretic, expectorant. This plant possesses very active properties, although its virtues are not fully known. For this reason caution should be exercised in its use for dropsy, rheumatic affections, hepatic and renal complaints. The fresh leaves are made into a tincture—10 oz to 1 pt of diluted alcohol—the dose of which is from 1–5 drops. The powder of the dry leaves is given in 15–60 gr doses.

PINE OILS

Siberian Pine Oil, Ol. Abietis B.P.C., distilled from *Abies sibirica.* Fam. Pinaceae.

Pumilio Pine Oil, Ol. Pini Pumilionis B.P.C., distilled from *Pinus mugo.* Fam. Pinaceae.

Sylvestris Pine Oil, Ol. Pini Sylvestris, distilled from various conifers.

Medicinal Use: All the above oils are used largely as inhalations for bronchitis and laryngitis. Externally they may all be used as rubefacients. The Siberian Pine Oil is preferred because of its more pleasant aroma.

Preparations: All made with Pumilio Oil: Elix. Diamorph. et Pini Co. B.P.C. 1949: Dose, ½–1 dr; Pastill. Diamorph et Pini Co. B.P.C. 1932; Syr. Pini B.P.C. 1949: Dose, ½–1 dr.

PINE, WHITE

Pinus strobus, Linn.
Fam. Pinaceae

Synonym: Deal Pine.

Habitat: Widely distributed in the Northern hemisphere, especially in North America.

Description: The inner bark, which is the part used, occurs in pieces about $\frac{1}{12}$ in. thick, 2 in. or more in width, and 5–6 in. long, of a bright buff colour on the inner surface, smooth and finely striated, having on the outer surface numerous scattered, small, round oil receptacles. Fracture pale buff, tough, with short, fibrous layers. Taste, mucilaginous, astringent; odour, slight.

Part Used: Bark.

Medicinal Use: Expectorant, diuretic, demulcent. Owing to its balsamic properties it is used for the relief of coughs, colds, and chest diseases generally. It seems also to exert a favourable influence upon the urinary apparatus. The compound syrup is the most popular form of administration and it is made from Wild Cherry, Bloodroot, Balm of Gilead, etc.

Preparations: Ext. Pini Alb. Liq.: Dose, $\frac{1}{4}$–1 dr; Syr. Pini Alb. Co.: Dose, 1–2 dr.

PINKROOT

Spigelia marilandica, Linn.
Fam. Loganiaceae

Synonyms: Wormgrass, Carolina Pink, Maryland Pink, Indian Pink.

Habitat: U.S.A.

Flowering Time: May to July.

Description: It is a perennial herb growing to about 1½ ft and bearing bright red flowers. The whole herb is usually sold in the country under the name of Indian Pinkroot and is preferable, because it is easier to distinguish the root with the herb attached than the root alone, which is sometimes adulterated. The rhizome somewhat resembles that of Serpentary, but is darker in colour and is not aromatic. It is about $\frac{2}{10}$ in. in diameter, with cup-shaped scars on the upper surface and numerous rootlets below. The large cells of the middle bark of the roots show fine, spiral markings.

Parts Used: Whole plant, root.

Medicinal Use: In general use in U.S.A. as a vermifuge for children and adults, and considered a certain and powerful remedy. For children an infusion (1 oz to 1 pt) is given, sweetened, in tablespoonful doses morning and evening. The dose should be increased according to age, that for an adult being a teacupful. Its effects are more certain if a purgative, such as Senna, is added.

Preparations: Powdered plant or root: For children, four years old, 10–20 gr; adults, 1–2 dr, repeated for a few days morning and evening; Liquid extract $\frac{1}{4}$–1 dr.

PINUS BARK

Tsuga canadensis, Carr.
Fam. Pinaceae

Synonyms: Hemlock Spruce, Hemlock Bark, *Pinus canadensis*, Linn., *Abies canadensis*, Michx.

Habitat: North America and Canada.

Description: The bark occurs in small pieces 1 in. or more long and ½–1 in. broad and ¼ in. thick, with a madder-red outer corky layer, and an inner fibrous layer. Fracture rough, shortly fibrous, showing groups of whitish stone cells. Taste, astringent, slightly turpentiney; odour, slightly terebinthinate. Canada Balsam is obtained by incision from the Balsam Fir and Hemlock Spruce.

Part Used: Bark.

Medicinal Use: Astringent, tonic. Used as an astringent injection in female complaints, such as leucorrhoea, falling of the womb, etc., in the shape of an infusion of 2 oz of crushed bark to 1 pt of water, or the fluid extract may be diluted with four times its weight of water and so used. The bark forms an ingredient in Composition Powder.

Preparation: Ext. Pini Canad. Liq.: Dose, ¼–1 dr.

Domestic Use: Pinus Bark is used in tanning.

PIPSISSIWA

Chimaphila umbellata, Nutt.
Fam. Ericaceae

Synonyms: Prince's Pine, Ground Holly.

Habitat: Found in most northern latitudes.

Description: Leaves leathery, oblanceolate, with a rounded apex, about 1¼ in. long and ⅜ in. broad, distantly serrate, except towards the base, upper surface minutely wrinkled, paler beneath, usually mixed with slender, reddish-brown, woody stems.

Part Used: Leaves.

Medicinal Use: Astringent, alterative, diuretic, tonic. Its alterative properties make it very useful in long-standing rheumatic and kidney affections. It is especially valuable in scrofulous debility. The infusion of 1 oz in 1 pt of boiling water is taken in doses of a wineglassful to a teacupful as required.

Preparations: Liquid extract: Dose, ½–1 dr; Chimaphilin: Dose, 1–3 gr.

PITCHER PLANT

Sarracenia purpurea, Linn.
Fam. Sarraceniaceae

Synonyms: Fly Trap, Water Cup, Saddleplant.

Habitat: North America.

Description: A carnivorous plant with pitchers 6–8 in. or more long, formed from the leafstalks and stipules, the latter forming a sharp wing on the inner side, the leaf-blade forming a roundish, heart-shaped hood. The taste is bitter and somewhat astringent; odour, none.

Parts Used: Root, leaves.

Medicinal Use: Stomachic, diuretic, laxative. Useful in derangements of stomach, liver, and kidneys, such as constipation, dyspepsia, menstrual complaints, etc. An infusion of 1 oz to 1 pt of water is taken in doses of a tablespoonful to a wineglassful as may be required. At one time achieved a great reputation as a prophylactic against smallpox.

Preparations: Powdered root: Dose, 10–30 gr; Liquid extract: Dose, ½–1 dr.

PLANTAIN

Plantago major, Linn.
Fam. Plantaginaceae

Synonyms: Ripple Grass, Waybread.

Habitat: A common weed all over Europe, Great Britain, and other parts of the world.

Flowering Time: June and July.

Description: Leaves ovate, blunt, abruptly contracted at the base, with a long, broad-channelled petiole. The blade is 4–8 in. long and 3–6 in. broad, with five to eleven strong fibrous ribs: the margin is sometimes entire and sometimes coarsely and unequally dentate-serrate. The inflorescence is a dense spike of four-parted flowers, with purple anthers and about two to four seeds in each cell of the fruit. Taste, astringent; odour, none.

Part Used: Leaves.

Medicinal Use: Cooling, alterative, diuretic. The fresh leaves rubbed on parts of the body stung by insects, nettles, etc., will afford relief and will stay bleeding of minor wounds. Useful in diarrhoea, piles, etc. The infusion of 1 oz to 1 pt of boiling water is taken in wineglassful doses.

The ancient writers such as Dioscorides and Pliny give the plant a long list of uses including inflammation, pustules, bleedings, bites from mad dogs, tumours, ulcers, asthma, and intermittent fevers.

Preparation: Liquid extract: Dose, ½–1 dr.

PLEURISY ROOT

Asclepias tuberosa, Linn.
Fam. Asclepiadaceae

Synonyms: Butterfly Weed, Swallowwort, Wind Root, Tuber Root.

Habitat: U.S.A.

Description: Rootstock with a knotty crown, slightly annulate. Root longitudinally wrinkled, buff brown externally, whitish internally. Fracture uneven, tough, that of the bark short, brittle. Taste, bitterish, somewhat acrid.

Part Used: Root.

Medicinal Use: Antispasmodic, diaphoretic, expectorant, tonic. Is also mildly cathartic and carminative. As its name implies, it is of great use in pleurisy, in which disease it mitigates the pain and relieves the difficulty of breathing. It is valuable in all chest complaints and possesses a specific action on the lungs, assisting expectoration, subduing inflammation, and exerting a generally mild tonic effect on the system. Recommended especially in pulmonic catarrh. A very useful medicine may be made as follows: Essence of Composition, 1 oz, Fluid extract Pleurisy Root, 1 oz; mix and take a teaspoonful three or four times daily in warm, sweetened water.

Preparations: Liquid extract: Dose, $\frac{1}{2}$–1 dr; Asclepin: Dose, 1–4 gr.

The diaphoretic action may be obtained by taking a teacupful of warm infusion (1 in 30) every hour.

POISON OAK

Rhus toxicodendron, Linn.
Fam. Anacardiaceae

Synonyms: Poison Ivy, Poison Vine.

Habitat: U.S.A.

Description: Leaves trifoliate, the terminal leaflet with a longer stalk, the lateral nearly sessile, about 4 in. long, obliquely ovate, entire or sometimes notched, downy beneath, papery and brittle when dry, sometimes with black spots of exuded juice, turned black on drying. Taste, acrid, somewhat astringent; odour, none.

The plant is poisonous on contact, causing a kind of dermatitis.

Part Used: Leaves.

Medicinal Use: Stimulant, narcotic, irritant. Has been used with success in treatment of obstinate skin diseases, and is, in small doses, an excellent sedative to the nervous system. Valuable in acute rheumatism, articular stiffness, etc. It has been used in the form of a homoeopathic tincture.

Preparation: Liquid extract: Dose, 5–30 drops.

POKE ROOT

Phytolacca decandra, Linn.
Fam. Phytolaccaceae

Synonyms: Pigeon Berry, Garget.

Habitat: North America.

Description: The root is usually sold in transverse slices, or in pieces split longitudinally, but in either case the characteristic concentric rings are easily seen. The outer surface is brownish grey and wrinkled, the inner whitish and hard, but not woody. Fracture fibrous. Taste, sweetish and acrid; inodorous. The berries are depressed-globular, purplish black and fleshy, about $\frac{1}{3}$ in. in diameter and composed of 10 carpels, each containing one lens-shaped seed. Taste, sweetish.

Parts Used: Root, berries.

Medicinal Use: Emetic, cathartic, alterative. Poke Root is considered a valuable remedy in dyspepsia, but is mostly used in chronic rheumatism. It also finds use in the treatment of ulcers, ringworm, scabies, granular conjunctivitis, and dysmenorrhoea. The berries are milder in action.

Preparations: Liquid extract, berries: Dose, $\frac{1}{2}$–1 dr; Liquid extract, root: Dose, $\frac{1}{4}$–$\frac{1}{2}$ dr; Phytolaccin: Dose, 1–3 gr; Powdered root: Dose, 1–5 gr.

POLYPODY ROOT

Polypodium vulgare, Linn.
Fam. Filices

Synonyms: Rock Polypody, Brake Root, Rockbrake, Polypodi of the Oak.

Habitat: Grows in Europe and Great Britain on old walls, trunks of trees, etc. Also grows in America.

Description: The slender rhizome, about $\frac{1}{8}$ in. in diameter and striated longitudinally, knotty, with cup-shaped leaf bases on the upper side at intervals of about $\frac{1}{4}$ in., the rootlets of the under surface being usually removed. Transverse section horny, greenish, or brown if old, with an irregular circle of minute, woody plates near the circumference. Taste, very sweet, faintly acrid; odour, none. Probably contains Glycyrrhizin, the sweet principle of Liquorice.

Parts Used: Rhizome, leaves.

Medicinal Use: Alterative, tonic pectoral, expectorant. It is much used in coughs, consumption, and chest diseases, for which complaints it is considered highly valuable. As a tonic in dyspepsia and loss of appetite, and as an alterative in skin diseases it will be found certain and safe. Its action is peculiar in that it occasionally produces a rash of red spots, but this disappears in a short time and causes no inconvenience. The infusion of $\frac{1}{2}$ oz of crushed root to 1 pt of boiling water and sweetened is taken in teacupful doses frequently.

Salmon writes: ". . . it prevails against Frensies, and radically cures the most profound madness whether it be raging or otherwise. . . ."

Preparation: Liquid extract, root: Dose, 1 dr.

POMEGRANATE *Punica granatum*, Linn.
Fam. Pumicaceae

Habitat: It is indigenous to N.W. India and countries S. and S.W. of the Caspian to the Persian Gulf and Palestine. It is cultivated in the Mediterranean regions.

Flowering Time: June. Fruit ripening in September.

Description: It is a beautiful green tree, with its spiry shape, and thick-tufted foliage of vigorous green, each growing shoot shaded into tenderer verdure and bordered with crimson and adorned with lovely scarlet flowers. It is thought by some to be the tree of life which flourished in Eden. For medicinal purposes the following is a description of its appearance in commerce—

The bark is chiefly that of the stem. It occurs in pieces 3–4 in. long, flat, or slightly quilled. In the root the outer surface is yellowish grey, often furrowed, with bands of cork sometimes united to form broad, flat scales. The inner surface is smooth or finely striated, greyish yellow, and has often strips of the tough, whitish wood attached to it. The stem bark is usually less corky, and has traces of lichens upon it. Fracture short and granular. Taste, astringent; odour, none.

The rind of the fruit is usually in irregular concave fragments, $\frac{1}{20}-\frac{1}{10}$ in. thick, brownish red externally, and dull yellowish on the inner surface, with depressions left by the seeds. The toothed tubular calyx is present on some pieces. Taste, astringent; odour, none.

Parts Used: Root-bark, stem bark, fruit rind.

Medicinal Use: Taenifuge. This is one of the oldest of drugs, and is considered a specific for removal of tapeworm. It is mostly administered in a decoction preparation as follows: 8 oz of coarse bark of the root is put into a vessel and 3 pt of cold water poured upon it. Boil for 1 hr, strain, and boil down until it measures 1 pt. After preparing the patient, give the decoction in doses of 4 oz (teacupful), followed by a purgative. If necessary, repeat every four hours.

Joseph Miller states that Pomegranate is useful to strengthen the gums, fasten loose teeth, help the falling down of the uvula and ulcers in the mouth and throat. There is a custom in Turkey for the bride to throw a

THE rinds of the fruit have been used for the tanning of leather. The Moors introduced the art into Spain and large quantities of fine leather were thus prepared at Cordova, which became known as Cordovan leather. (Hence the old English word Cordwainer.) The art of making wine from Pomegranates of which Solomon speaks is still practised in Persia.

Pomegranate to the ground, the seeds that fall out indicating the number of children she will bear.

Preparations: Pomegranate fruitbark: Dose, 1–2 dr; Fluid extract root-bark: Dose, ¼–2 dr; Alkaloid Pelletierine: Dose, 5–20 gr; Decoction: Dose, ½–2 oz.

Biblical References: There are many: Exodus xxviii, 33, 34, xxxix, 24; Numbers xiii, 23, xx, 5; Deuteronomy viii, 8; 1 Samuel xiv, 2; 1 Kings vii, 17, 20, 42; 2 Kings v, 18, xxv, 17; 2 Chronicles iii, 16, iv, 13; Nehemiah xi, 29; Song of Solomon iv, 3, 13, vi, 7, vii, 12, viii, 2; Jeremiah lii, 22, 23; Joel i, 12; Haggai ii, 19; Zechariah xiv, 10; Ecclesiasticus xlv, 9.

POPLAR

Populus tremuloides, Michx.
Fam. Salicaceae

Synonyms: Quaking Aspen, White Poplar.

Habitat: A common tree in England.

Description: The bark, which is used medicinally, appears in curved or flattened pieces about 1½ in. or more in width and about ¼ in. in thickness, with the greyish epidermis removed, leaving a dull-brown surface, or, where it has been cut more deeply, alternate layers of buff and white tissue. The inner surface is smooth and brownish white. The transverse fracture is whitish and granular, with two or three layers of pale-brownish stone cells, the inner portion showing fibrous laminae. Taste, bitter; odour, none. The *Populus alba* is used in Italy.

Part Used: Bark.

Medicinal Use: Tonic, diuretic, stimulant. This remedy deservedly holds a high position as a universal tonic. It takes the place of Peruvian Bark and Quinine and has none of the drawbacks which interfere with the continued administration of the last-named drug. For all cases of debility, indigestion, faintness, hysteria, etc., it may be freely given. It is also used in urinary complaints. The powdered bark is generally given in combination with other remedies.

Gerard translates a Latin verse by Serenus Sammonicus as follows—

"An hidden disease doth oft rage and raine
The hip overcome and vex with the paine
It makes with vile aking one tread slow and shrinke
The bark of White Poplar is helpe had in drinke."

He also says that Dioscorides "writeth, the barke to the weight of an ounce (or as others say, and that more truly a little more than a dram) is a good remedy for the sciatica or ache in the huckle bone."

Preparations: Liquid extract: Dose, 1 dr; Populin: Dose, 1–4 gr.

Biblical References: Genesis xxx, 37; Hosea iv, 13.

POPPY

Papaver somniferum, Linn.
Fam. Papaveraceae

Synonym: Mawseed.

Habitat: Native of Asia but now also grown in Europe and Great Britain.

Flowering Time: July.

Description: The capsules of the opium poppy are usually hemispherical, but depressed at the top, where the many-rayed stigma occupies the centre, and have a swollen ring below, where it joins the stalk. The small kidney-shaped seeds are attached to lateral projections (placentae) from the inner walls of the capsule. Ovoid capsules are sometimes met with. The broken capsules and the broken fruits are sold at a cheaper price for making fomentations. The grey seeds are sold for birds' food under the name of "maw" seed. The flowers vary in colour from pure white to reddish purple. In the wild plant they are pale lilac with a purple basal spot.

Part Used: Capsules.

Medicinal Use: Anodyne, narcotic. The crushed capsules are used generally as a poultice in combination with Chamomile flowers. Syrups are prepared from the flowers or capsules, which are prescribed as ingredients in cough medicines. Opium is extracted from Poppies grown in the East, but those of European growth yield but little of the drug.

Preparations: Dec. Papav. et Anthem. Fort. Ext. Papav. Liq. B.P.C. 1949: Dose, 10–30 min; Syr. Papav. B.P.C. 1949: Dose, ½–1 dr.

POPPY, RED

Papaver rhoeas, Linn.
Fam. Papaveraceae

Synonyms: Corn Poppy, Corn Rose, Flores Rhoeados.

Habitat: Europe and the British Isles. Commonly seen growing in fields of corn.

Flowering Time: June to August.

Description: There are several varieties of the Red Poppy, differing in the character of the fruit, which may be nearly cylindrical or globular, smooth or furnished with stiff hairs, and in the size of lobes of the leaves. The Red Poppy, with petals having a dark spot at the base (probably a hybrid with *Papaver umbrosum*), makes the deepest-coloured syrup.

Part Used: Flowers.

Medicinal Use: Anodyne, expectorant. The fresh petals were used in B.P. 1885 for preparing a syrup (Syr. Rhoeados).

Gerard states: "Most men being led rather by false experiments than reason, commend the floures against the Pleurisie, giving to drinke as soon as the pain comes, either the distilled water, or syrup made by infusing the leaves. And yet many times it happens, that the paine ceaseth by that meanes, though hardly sometimes."

Preparation: Syr. Rhoead. B.P.C. 1949: Dose, ½–1 dr.

PRICKLY ASH

Zanthoxylum americanum, Mill.
Zanthoxylum clava-nerculis, Linn.
Fam. Rutaceae

Synonyms: *Fagara calva-herculis*, Toothache Tree, Yellow Wood, Suterberry, *Xanthoxylum fraxineum*, Willd., *X. carolinianum*, Lamb.

Habitat: Canada and U.S.A.

Description: The Northern bark is in curved or quilled fragments about $\frac{1}{24}$ in. thick, externally brownish grey, with whitish patches, faintly furrowed, with some linear-based two-edged spines about $\frac{1}{4}$ in. long. Fracture short, green in the outer, and yellow in the inner part. Taste, bitterish and very pungent, causing salivation. The Southern bark, which is usually sold, is $\frac{1}{12}$ in. thick and has conical, corky spines sometimes $\frac{4}{5}$ in. in height.

Parts Used: Bark, berries.

Medicinal Use: Stimulant, alterative, tonic, diaphoretic. The berries are considered the more active, and are also carminative and antispasmodic. May be used wherever a general stimulant is required, and will be found of especial service in the treatment of rheumatism and skin diseases.

Preparations: Liquid extract, bark: Dose, $\frac{1}{2}$–1 dr; Solid extract: Dose, 2–4 gr; Liquid extract, berries: Dose, 10–30 min; Xanthoxylin: Dose, 1–2 gr.

PRIMROSE

Primula vulgaris, Huds.
Fam. Primulaceae

Habitat: A well-known wild flower in English woods.

Flowering Time: March and April.

Description: The leaves are about 5 in. long and 1$\frac{1}{4}$ in. broad, tapering, oblanceolate, rounded above, and tapering below into a winged stalk, reticulated and smooth above, the veins and veinlets prominent beneath and hairy, the margin irregularly and shortly dentate. Taste, insipid; odour, none. Rootstock knotty, with successive bases of fallen leaves with cylindrical branched rootlets on all sides. Transverse section reddish, with a central pith.

Parts Used: Root, herb.

Medicinal Use: Astringent, antispasmodic, vermifuge. In the early days of medicine this plant constituted an important remedy in muscular rheumatism, paralysis, and gout. In America, Prof. Scudder used a tincture of the fresh plant in bloom, in a strength of 10 oz to 1 pt of alcohol, in doses of 1–10 drops, in extreme sensitiveness, restlessness, and insomnia. The infusion of root is taken in tablespoonful doses.

Gerard writes: "A practitioner of London who was famous for curing the phrensie, after he had performed his cure by the due observation of physick, accustomed every yeare in the moneth of May to dyet his Patients after this manner; Take the leaves and floures of the Primrose, boile them a little in fountaine water and in some Rose and Betony waters, adding thereto sugar, pepper, salt and butter, which being strained he gave them to drinke thereof first and last."

ALTHOUGH Primrose is seldom used now in this country, the old herbalists extolled its merits. Culpeper states: "Of the leaves of Primroses is made as fine a salve to heal wounds as any that I know . . . do not see your poor neighbours go with wounded limbs when an halfpenny cost will heal them."

PRUNE

Prunus domestica, Linn.
var. *Juliana*, D.C.
Fam. Rosaceae

Synonyms: Plum Tree, Prune Tree.

Habitat: Probably a native of Greece and Persia but now cultivated in many countries.

Description: The prune, or dried plum, is well known and does not require description.

Part Used: Fruit.

Medicinal Use: Laxative, refrigerant. Prunes are often added to cathartic decoctions, improving their flavour and promoting their effect. In leucorrhoea, irregular menstruation, and in debility following miscarriage, the following has been used: Small Raisins or Currants, 2 oz; Aniseed, Mace, and Cinnamon, of each ½ oz, and 1 Nutmeg powdered; Prune brandy, 1 qt. Powder the drugs and macerate in brandy for 2 weeks. One tablespoonful of the clear tincture is the dose, repeated thrice daily.

Preparation: Confection of Senna B.P.C. Dose, 60–120 gr.

PSYLLIUM

Plantago ovata, Forsk.
Plantago psyllium, Linn.
Plantago arenaria, W. & K.
Fam. Plantaginaceae

Synonyms: Flea Seed, Fleawort Spogel, Ispaghula.

Habitat: *Ovata:* India. Official in B.P.C. under the name *Ispaghula*.
Psyllium: Barbary and Southern Europe. In B.P.C. under *Psyllium*.
Arenaria: Southern Europe and North Africa. In B.P.C. under *Psyllium*.

Description: The *Plantago ovata* or light Indian Psyllium seeds are greyish brown in colour and boat-shaped, one end being more pointed than the other. On the convex surface there is a small brown spot. Soaked in water they become surrounded with a transparent mucilage.

The *Plantago psyllium* or dark Psyllium seeds are the most popular for use in medicine. They do not however contain so much mucilage as the former.

The *Plantago arenaria*, or golden Psyllium seeds contain little mucilage and are used principally for feeding birds.

Part Used: Seeds.

Medicinal Use: These seeds when moistened swell into a gelatinous mass, which lubricates the intestine, at the same time stimulating its normal activity. They are tasteless and odourless, the action being gentle and certain. No griping is experienced and the dose may be repeated. Psyllium is used successfully in dysentery in the tropics.

Dose: Adults, two to four teaspoonfuls after each meal; children, one teaspoonful after each meal. Place the Psyllium in a cup or tumbler, adding a wineglassful or more of warm water; stir until the mixture thickens and drink the contents. It may be flavoured with a trace of lemon or orange juice, or eaten with stewed fruit.

PUFF BALL

Lycoperdon bovista, Linn.
Fam. Fungi

Synonyms: *Lycoperdon giganteum*, Huss.

Habitat: Europe and Great Britain.

Description: This fungus forms a globose or depressed ball, varying from 4 in. to 1 ft or more in diameter, sometimes furrowed at the base, whitish when young, the internal mass white, consisting of spores and fine thread-like fibres (capillitium), which, from yellow, change to brownish olive or blackish, and are discharged by the bursting of the skin.

Part Used: Lower, spongy portion.

Medicinal Use: Haemostatic.

Domestic Use: The smoke produced by burning it is used for stupefying bees.

PULSATILLA

Anemone pulsatilla, Linn.
Fam. Ranunculaceae

Synonyms: Pasque Flower, Passe Flower, Wind Flower, Meadow Anemone, Easter Flower.

Habitat: Europe and Russian Asia. It also grows in the southern part of England.

Flowering Time: Spring.

Description: Leaves hairy, 3–5 in. long or more, and 2–3 in. broad, bipinnate, the leaflets opposite, stalked below, the segments trifid and linear, with acute points. Leafstalks round, with a narrow channel on the upper surface and purplish at the base. Flowers large, with purple sepals, hairy outside, and hairy-tailed carpels. Taste, when fresh, acrid and burning; odour, none. In the *Anemone pratensis*, Linn., the flowers are smaller, blackish purple, with the tips of the segments bent backwards. This species is used in homoeopathic medicine.

Part Used: Herb.

Medicinal Use: Nervine, antispasmodic, alterative. Much esteemed as a remedy for nerve exhaustion in women, especially when due to menstrual troubles. Its stimulating action on all mucous surfaces makes it valuable in catarrh, amenorrhoea, etc.

Preparations: Elix. Euonym. et Pulsat.: Dose, 1–4 dr; Ext. Pulsat. Liq.: Dose, 2–5 min; Liq. Cauloph. et Pulsat.: Dose, 1–2 dr; Liq. Cauloph. et Pulsat. Co.: Dose, 1–2 dr; Tinct. Pulsat.: Dose, 5–30 min.

PUMPKIN

Cucurbita maxima, Duchesne
Fam. Cucurbitaceae

Synonym: Pumpkin seed.

Habitat: Tropical countries, but cultivated in Great Britain.

Description: The seeds are broadly ovate, nearly 1 in. long, whitish, with a shallow groove and flat ridge round the margin. The hilum is near the pointed end. Cotyledons flat, white, oily, with a short, conical radicle. Taste, nutty; inodorous.

Part Used: Seeds.

Medicinal Use: Taenicide, diuretic, demulcent. It has long been a popular worm remedy. Lately it has also been used for tapeworm. The patient fasts for a day, and takes a saline cathartic. Then a mixture—made as follows: 2 oz of seeds are beaten up with as much sugar and milk or water added to make 1 pt—is given in three doses every two hours, and a few hours after the last dose, a dose of Castor Oil is given. The ordinary infusion—1 oz to 1 pt—has also been used in urinary complaints and scalding of urine.

PYRETHRUM, DALMATIAN

Chrysanthemum cinerariaefolium, Vis.
Fam. Compositae

Synonym: Insect flowers.

Habitat: The Dalmatian coast and Japan.

Description: The closed flowers are preferred as being more active. The phyllaries or bracts outside the flowers are lanceolate, acute, and hairy.

The receptacle has no paleae and is nearly flat; the marginal florets are whitish, and the fruit calyx has five slender rib-like wings, and five teeth, but no pappus. Taste, slightly acrid; odour, none.

Varieties: Persian Insect Flowers derived from *Ch. marschallii* and *Ch. roseum* from the Caucasus are both met with on the market and have similar properties to the Dalmatian Flower.

Part Used: Closed flowers.

Use: Insecticide, vermin killer. Insect powder is harmless to human beings, and is used in powder, lotions, and in fumigations to destroy insects, etc. The activity of the powder ground from insect flowers depends upon the content of Pyretherin, and should not contain less than 0·4 per cent.

Q

QUASSIA *Picraena excelsa*, Lindl.
Fam. Simarubaceae

Synonyms: Bitter Wood, Bitter Ash, *Quassia amara*, Linn.
Habitat: Jamaica, Antigua, and St. Vincent.
Description: The tree from which this wood is obtained is 50–60 ft in height and resembles the Ash in appearance. The wood is usually sold in yellowish-white chips about 1 in. wide, 1–4 in. long, and $\frac{1}{8}$–$\frac{1}{12}$ in. thick, but sometimes much smaller. Taste, very bitter; odour, none. Some samples of a yellowish colour contain starch, and the infusion made with boiling water would then not keep well. These are possibly derived from *Quassia amara* or Surinam Quassia, which differs in containing no raphides, and in the medullary rays being only two cells broad, whilst there are usually three in the genuine or Jamaica Quassia. Exhausted Quassia having hardly any bitterness is sometimes met with in commerce, and also Quassia with greyish markings due to fungus, and therefore not fit for infusion.
Part Used: Wood.
Medicinal Use: Tonic, bitter, anthelmintic. The wood is generally sold in small chips but cups turned out of the log may be obtained. They are sold as Bitter Cups, and water standing in them for a short time acquires the bitterness of the wood. It is especially useful in the treatment of dyspepsia and debility of the digestive apparatus. For worms it is also a valuable remedy. The infusion of 1 oz of chips in 1 pt of cold water is taken in wineglassful doses.
Preparations: Powdered bark: Dose, 2–8 gr; Ext. Quass. B.P.C. 1949: Dose, 3–5 gr; Inf. Quass. Conc. B.P.: Dose, $\frac{1}{2}$–1 dr; Inf. Quass. Rec. B.P.: Dose, $\frac{1}{2}$–1 fl oz; Tinct. Quass. B.P. 1948: Dose, $\frac{1}{2}$–1 dr.
Horticultural Use: Quassia is used extensively in horticultural insecticides in the form of sprays. It is poisonous to flies and sometimes is injurious to other higher animals.

QUEBRACHO *Aspidosperma quebracho*, Schlecht.
Fam. Apocynaceae

Synonym: White Quebracho.
Habitat: Argentine.
Description: The bark occurs in curved or flattish pieces $\frac{1}{2}$–1 in. thick, greyish and deeply fissured externally. The inner surface is yellowish

brown, often with a reddish tint and striated. The transverse fracture shows a coarsely granular, yellowish-brown, outer layer, and a shortly fibrous or splintery, darker, inner layer. Taste, bitter; odour, none.

Part Used: Bark.

Medicinal Use: Antiperiodic, tonic, anti-asthmatic. Very useful in the suffocating symptoms of bronchitis, asthma, etc. Also recommended in pulmonary complaints.

Preparations: Liquid extract: Dose, $\frac{1}{4}$–$\frac{1}{2}$ dr; Aspidospermin (Alkaloid).

Domestic Use: An extract made from the dark hardwood is imported from the Argentine and used in the tanning industry.

QUEEN'S DELIGHT

Stillingia sylvatica, Linn.
Fam. Euphorbiaceae

Synonyms: Queen's Root, Yaw Root.

Habitat: U.S.A.

Description: In pieces several inches in length and from $\frac{3}{4}$–2 in. thick, tapering, greyish brown, wrinkled longitudinally. Bark thick and, as well as the central wood, pinkish white, with numerous, minute resin cells, tough and finely fibrous, and often starchy. Taste, bitter and acrid, and pungent; odour, characteristic and unpleasant.

Part Used: Root.

Medicinal Use: Alterative, laxative, tonic, diuretic. This is principally used in cases of scrofula and impure conditions of the blood, for which it forms a certain and valuable remedy. It is generally given in combination with other medicines.

Preparations: Powdered root: Dose, $\frac{1}{4}$–$\frac{1}{2}$ dr; Solid extract: Dose, 2–5 gr; Liquid extract: Dose, 10–30 drops; Tincture: Dose, $\frac{1}{2}$–2 dr; Stillingin: Dose, 1–3 gr.

QUINCE

Cydonia oblongata, Mill.
Fam. Rosaceae

Synonyms: Quince Seed, *Cydonia vulgaris*, Pers.

Habitat: A tree grown in England for its fruit. It is not a native of this country but of Persia.

Description: The small tree which bears a fruit somewhat the shape of a pear is well known. The seeds or pips are usually glued together in a double row of three to fourteen by the dried mucilage, contained in the outer seed coats. In appearance, size, and taste they resemble apple pips, but have become angular by mutual pressure.

Part Used: Seeds.

Medicinal Use: Mucilaginous, demulcent. It is of use in dysentery and diarrhoea; externally also, in eye diseases, as a soothing lotion.

Domestic Use: Quinces are edible and enter into the composition of some jams.

CULPEPER recommends the fruit juice as a preservative against the force of deadly poisons. . . . "For it hath been found most true that the very smell of a quince hath taken away all the strength of the poison of white hellebore."

R

RAGWORT

Senecio jacobaea, Linn.
Fam. Compositae

Synonyms: Stinking Nanny, St. James's Wort, Staggerwort, Ragweed, Dog Standard, Fireweed.

Habitat: A widely distributed wild plant in Europe and Great Britain. It has been introduced into New Zealand where it also grows wild.

Flowering Time: July and August.

Description: Stem striate, 1½–2 or 3 ft high, leaves alternate, lower lyrate-pinnatifid, stalked, upper sessile bi-pinnatifid, with oblong segments deeply and irregularly toothed. Flowerheads yellow. Florets of the ray smooth, with deciduous pappus. Florets of the disk hairy.

Part Used: Herb.

Medicinal Use: Diaphoretic, detergent. Useful in coughs, colds, influenza, and catarrh of mucous membranes generally. It gives relief to sciatica and rheumatic or gouty pains in limbs. The decoction of 1 oz in 1 pt of water is taken in wineglassful doses as required. Externally this is used as an application to ulcers, wounds, etc., and as a gargle in relaxed throat. A poultice may be made from the herb and applied to gouty swellings of joints. Ragwort Ointment prepared from the fresh plant is excellent for inflammation of the eyes.

Gerard writes: "The leaves stamped very small, and boyled with some hogs grease unto the consumption of the juyce, adding thereto in the end of the boyling a little Masticke and Olibanum, and then strained, taketh away the old ache in the huckle bones called Sciatica."

Preparation: Liquid extract: Dose, ½–1 dr.

RASPBERRY

Rubus idaeus, Linn.
Fam. Rosaceae

Synonyms: *Rubus strigosus*, Michx., American Raspberry.

Habitat: Cultivated in most temperate countries.

Flowering Time: May. Fruits ripen in June.

Description: Leaves stalked, pinnate, with two pairs of ovate leaflets, and a larger terminal one, the leaflets doubly serrate at the margins, rounded at the base, and abruptly pointed at the apex, and greyish white beneath, with appressed, felted hairs, 2½–3½ in. long and 2–3 in. broad. Taste, astringent; odour, none.

Parts Used: Leaves, fruit.

Medicinal Use: Astringent, stimulant. The infusion of 1 oz in 1 pt of boiling water is used as a general gargle in sore mouths, canker of the throat, etc., and as a wash for ulcers and wounds. Combined with Slippery Elm the leaves form a good poultice for removing proud flesh and cleansing wounds. It will be found very valuable for the stomach complaints of children.

Preparation: Liquid extract (leaves): Dose, 1–2 dr.

DR. THOMPSON and Dr. Coffin recommend the drinking of the Raspberry Leaf tea by pregnant females for giving strength and rendering parturition easy and speedy. It should be taken freely before and during the confinement. The addition of Composition Essence will form a valuable adjunct at such times. This should always be taken warm.

RED CLOVER

Trifolium pratense, Linn.
Fam. Leguminosae

Synonyms: Trefoil, Purple Clover.

Habitat: Widely distributed in Europe, the British Isles, and many other countries.

Flowering Time: May to the end of summer.

Description: Flowerheads ovate, sessile, usually with a stalked, trifoliate leaf and two purplish-veined, ovate stipules beneath the head, purplish pink, about 1 in. long and $1\frac{3}{4}$ in. broad. Flowers slender, $\frac{1}{2}$ in. long, small, papilionaceous. Taste and odour, agreeable.

Part Used: Flowers.

Medicinal Use: Alterative, sedative. Is an excellent remedy in spasmodic and bronchial coughs, whooping coughs, etc. The infusion of 1 oz to 1 pt of boiling water may be used freely. Generally combined with other drugs of an alterative character, as Stillingia, Lappa, Xanthoxylum, etc. Externally Red Clover is often used as a plaster.

Gerard reports: "Pliny writeth and setteth downe for certaine, that the leaves hereof do tremble and stand right up against the coming of a storme or tempest."

Preparations: Liquid extract: Dose, $\frac{1}{2}$–2 dr; Solid extract (for use as a plaster).

RED ROOT

Ceanothus americanus, Linn.
Fam. Celastraceae

Synonym: Jersey Tea Root.

Habitat: U.S.A.

Description: Root tough, woody, usually in pieces about ¾ in. thick and several inches in length, dark brown, striated, or finely wrinkled longitudinally. Fracture hard, tough, and splintery. Bark thin, deep brown, and brittle. Wood dense, reddish, concentric rings obscure, porous vessels arranged in single concentric and radiate lines. Taste, astringent; inodorous.

Part Used: Root.

Medicinal Use: Astringent, expectorant, antispasmodic. Used internally for asthma, bronchitis, and pulmonary complaints. For sores in the mouth it makes an excellent wash.

Preparation: Liquid extract: Dose 1–30 drops.

RED SAGE

Salvia officinalis, Linn.
Fam. Labiatae

Synonym: Garden Sage.

Habitat: This plant is a native of the Mediterranean countries, but it is quite commonly found in Great Britain and America in the kitchen garden.

Flowering Time: June, July, and August.

Description: Stem and leaves reddish. The leaves stalked, 1½–2 in. long and ¾–1 in. broad, oblong-lanceolate rounded at the ends, crenulate at the margins, the surface strongly reticulated on both sides. Taste, pungently aromatic, astringent.

Part Used: Leaves.

Medicinal Use: Aromatic, astringent. Makes an excellent gargle for relaxed throat, quinsy, laryngitis, and tonsils: also for ulceration of mouth and throat. To make the gargle, pour ½ pt of hot malt vinegar upon 1 oz of leaves and add ½ pt cold water. Dose, a wineglassful frequently, as well as a gargle.

Preparation: Liquid extract: Dose, ¼–1 dr.

Domestic Use: Both red- and green-leafed Sage are largely used for culinary purposes.

REST HARROW

Ononis spinosa, Linn.
Fam. Leguminosae

Synonym: Cammock.

Habitat: It grows commonly on arable and waste land.

Flowering Time: July.

Description: The plant grows to about 1½ ft in height. The leaves are roundish and dark green in colour, without thorns when young, but later growing short, sharp prickles. The flowers, somewhat like broom blossoms are of a faint purplish colour and occur at the tops of the branches.

The root is more or less flattened, twisted, and branched, deeply wrinkled and brown in colour. The taste is mucilaginous, at first sweet and then bitter and disagreeable; odour, resembles liquorice.

Part Used: Root.

Medicinal Use: Diuretic. A popular remedy in France for dropsy. Externally it is used as a wash for ulcers, hydrocele, and enlarged glands. Internally, it is administered for jaundice, gout, and rheumatism. Decoction, 1–2 oz to 1 pt of boiling water: Dose, a wineglassful four times a day.

Parkinson writes: "Four pounds of the rootes first sliced small and afterwards steeped in a gallon of Canary Wine . . . and put into a stone pot close stopped . . . and so set to boyle in a Balneo Marie for 24 hours is as daintie a medicine for tender stomachs as any the daintiest Lady in the land can desire to take. . . ."

"It is recorded that in former times the young shoots and tender stalkes before they become prickly were picled up to bee eaten as a meate or sauce, wonderfully commended against a stinking breath, and to take away the smell of wine in them that had drunke too much."—Parkinson on Rest Harrow.

RHATANY

Krameria triandra, R. & P.
Fam. Krameriaceae

Synonym: Rhatanhia.

Habitat: Peru and Bolivia.

Description: Root woody, cylindrical, branched, deep reddish brown and rough externally, with a coarsely fibrous bark, and hard, tough, woody centre. The root of Para Rhatany, derived from *K. argentea*, Mart., has transverse cracks and a short, not fibrous, fractuıe. Taste, very astringent; odour, none. Varying in diameter from ¼–¾ in.

Part Used: Root.

Medicinal Use: Astringent, tonic. Used internally to advantage in passive haemorrhages, mucous discharges and in menstrual disorders. Also in diarrhoea and incontinence of urine. Is useful as an application to spongy and bleeding gums.

Preparations: Ext. Kramer. Sicc. B.P.C.: Dose, 5–15 gr; Inf. Kramer. Conc. B.P.C. 1949: Dose, ½–1 dr; Inf. Kramer. Rec.: Dose, ½–1 fl oz; Tinct Kramer. B.P.C. 1949: Dose, ½–1 dr; Tinct. Myrrh et Borac. B.P.C. 1949; Troch. Kramer. B.P.C. 1949; Troch. Kramer. et Cocain. B.P.C.

RHUBARB, EAST INDIAN, CHINA, OR TURKEY

Rheum palmatum, Linn.
(and other species)
Fam. Polygonaceae

Habitat: Central and Western China. It was called East Indian or Turkey Rhubarb because it was brought to ports in these countries for export to Europe.

Description: Shensi Rhubarb is the most expensive and undoubtedly the best. The rhizome is heavy and smooth, having been peeled and dressed, and is distinguished by the presence of dark-brown spots or warts, with network of white lines. Canton Rhubarb is more fibrous and not so bright, without the warty appearance, and network of white lines less marked. High-dried or stove-dried is very hard, shrunken, and waxy. Rough Rounds, the poorest quality of Chinese Rhubarb, are partially trimmed, showing dark patches on the outer surface. The rhizome is generally perforated with a hole through which a piece of cord is strung for drying. The principal forms are known as rounds and flats; the quality is judged by the fracture, which ranges from a bright to a dull brown.

Part Used: Rhizome.

Medicinal Use: Astringent, tonic, stomachic, aperient. In small doses the powder will cure diarrhoea; in large doses it acts as a simple and safe purgative, and is justly esteemed one of the most valuable remedies we possess. The tincture is chiefly used, but the powder is perhaps as effective and reliable.

Preparations: Conf. Guaiac. Co. B.P.C. 1949: Dose, 60–120 gr; Ext. Rhei Liq. B.P.C. 1949: Dose, 10–30 min; Ext. Rhei Sicc. B.P.C.: Dose, 30–60 min; Inf. Rhei Recens B.P.C. 1949: Dose, ½–1 fl oz; Inf. Rhei Conc. B.P.C.: Dose, 30–60 min; Mixt. Gent. c. Rheo. B.P.C. 1949: Dose, ½–1 fl oz; Mixt. Gent. c. Rheo. pro infant B.P.C. 1949: Dose, 60–120 min; Mist. Rhei Ammon. c. Sod. B.P.C.: Dose, ½–1 fl oz; Mist. Rhei Co. B.P.C.: Dose, ½–1 fl oz; Mist. Rhei Co. pro infant. B.P.C.: Dose, 60–120 min; Pil Rhei Co. B.P.C.; Pil. Hydrarg. c. Rheo B.P.C. 1949: Dose, 1 pill; Pulv. Rhei Co. B.P.: Dose, 10–60 gr; Syr. Fic. Co. B.P.C.: Dose,

30–120 min; Syr. Rhei B.P.C. 1949: Dose, 30–120 min; Syr. Rhei Aromat. U.S.P.: Dose, $2\frac{1}{2}$ fl dr; Tab. Casc. Sagr. Co. B.P.C.: Dose, 1 or 2 tablets; Tab. Rhei Co. B.P.C.: Dose, 1 or 2 tablets; Tab. Rhei et Sod. Bicarb. B.P.C.: Dose, 1 or 2 tablets; Tinct. Rhei Co. B.P.: Dose, 30–60 min; Tinct. Rhei Aromat. U.S.P.; Pulv. Rhei: Dose, 3–15 gr.

RHUBARB, ENGLISH

Rheum officinale, Baill.
Rheum rhaponticum, Willd.
Fam. Polygonaceae

Description: English Rhubarb, derived from *Rheum rhaponticum*, Willd., or from *Rheum officinale*, Baill., presents a shrunken surface, and the transverse section shows that the bark has not been removed as in the Chinese drug. When holes are present, they are round and clean, evidently made with a rat's-tail file. The English Rhubarb from *Rheum rhaponticum* shows red veins, and that from *R. officinale* blackish veins; the latter is usually in large pieces. Chinese *rhaponticum* closely resembles the English, but is generally heavier and dark rather than pink fracture.

Parts Used: Rhizome and root.

Medicinal Use: Stomachic, aperient. Similar in action to Turkey Rhubarb, though milder. Is especially useful in infantile stomach troubles and looseness of bowels. In fairly large doses it acts as a laxative.

Preparation: Powdered root: Dose, 5–60 gr.

Domestic Use: The stems of the English Rhubarb are used for food.

RICE

Oryza sativa, Linn.
Fam. Gramineae

Habitat: South-east Asia.

Description: Rice is a well-known product which does not require description.

Part Used: Seeds.

Medicinal Use: Nutritive, demulcent. Boiled rice is very useful in disorganized digestion, in bowel derangements, and in diarrhoea. Rice-water, made in a similar manner to Barley-water, is used as a soothing, nourishing drink in febrile diseases and inflammatory states of intestines.

Domestic Use: Rice forms a well-known food. A very fine-grained starch is also made from it.

ROSE, PALE

Rosa centifolia, Linn.
Fam. Rosaceae

Synonyms: Cabbage Rose, Hundred-leaved Rose.

Habitat: Southern Europe, but cultivated in gardens in many countries.

Flowering Time: May to August and later in mild climates.

Description: The petals are pink, whitish towards the base, and are usually supplied free from the calyx. The odour is that of the Cabbage Rose. Taste, slightly astringent and sweet.

Part Used: Petals.

Medicinal Use: Aperient. Seldom, if ever, used internally. On account of its fragrancy it is used in France for distillation of Rosewater.

Biblical References: Song of Solomon II, 1; Isaiah XXXV, 1; 2 Esdras II, 19; Wisdom II, 8; Ecclesiasticus XXIV, 14, XXXIX, 13.

ROSE, RED

Rosa gallica, Linn.
Fam. Rosaceae

Synonyms: Rose Flowers, Provence Rose.

Habitat: Native of Southern Europe but cultivated as a garden plant in many countries.

Flowering Time: The chief flowering time is from May to August but in some mild districts Roses have been known to bloom up to Christmas.

Description: The Red Rose flowers consist of the unopened flowerbuds with the calyx removed. They are of deep, dark-rose colour, slightly paler at the base. Taste, astringent and sweetish; odour, that of the damask rose.

Triple Rose Water and Oil of Rose are prepared from the flowers of *Rosa damascena*, Linn., cultivated in Bulgaria.

Part Used: Petals.

Medicinal Use: Tonic, astringent. Seldom used internally. The infusion is used as a flavouring for other medicines or as a lotion in ophthalmia, etc. The confection is mostly used in pill-making.

Preparations: Inf. Ros. Acid. Conc. B.P.C. 1949: Dose, ½–1 fl dr; Inf. Ros. Acid. Rec. B.P.C. 1949: Dose, ½–1 fl oz.

From *Rosa damascena* and other varieties is distilled: Ol. Ros. B.P.C. 1949 and U.S.P. from which are made: Aq. Ros. Conc. B.P.C. 1949; Aq. Ros. U.S.P.; Aq. Ros. Fort. U.S.P.; Ung. Aq. Ros. B.P.C. 1949.

From the fruits (hips) of the *Rosa canina* and other varieties is made a Syrup rich in ascorbic acid which is prescribed for children to make up the deficiency of Vitamin C. *See also* Dog Rose.

Domestic Use: The oil, or otto, of Roses is used in perfumery.

ROSEMARY

Rosmarinus officinalis, Linn.
Fam. Laciatae

Synonyms: Romero. Rosemary is not a rose and is not dedicated to Mary. It takes its name from the Latin *Ros marinus* or sea-dew, for it is fond of water.

Habitat: It grows on the dry, rocky hills of the Mediterranean region from the Spanish peninsula to Greece and Asia Minor. It prefers the neighbourhood of the sea but also grows inland and is to be found in the Sahara. It is a common garden plant in England, having been cultivated prior to the Noıman Conquest. It is mentioned in the Old Anglo-Saxon herbals of the eleventh century.

Flowering Time: April and May and sometimes again in August.

Description: Stem somewhat woody, square. Leaves linear obtuse, dark green above, white below, with branched, stellate hairs, the margins strongly revolute. Flowers, when present, bluish lilac, two-lipped, with two stamens only. Taste, aromatic; odour, characteristic.

Part Used: Herb.

Medicinal Use: Tonic, astringent, diaphoretic. Also an excellent stomachic and nervine. Cures many cases of headache. Used externally, an infusion combined with Borax makes a good hair wash and will prevent premature baldness.

Preparation: Ol. Rosemarin. B.P. and U.S.P.; Lin. Sapon. B.P.; Sp. Colon B.P.C. 1949; Sp. Rosemarin. B.P.C. 1949.

Domestic Use: John Philip de Liguamine in the fifteenth century describes Rosemary as the usual condiment of salted meals.

THERE is an old belief that: "If a maid is curious as to her future she may obtain information by dipping a spray of Rosemary into a mixture of wine, rum, gin, vinegar and water in a vessel of ground glass. She is to observe this rite on the Eve of St. Magdalen in an upper room in company with two other maids, and each must be less than 21 years old. Having fastened the sprigs to their bosoms and taken three sips of the tonic—sips are quite enough—all three go to rest in the same bed without speaking. The dreams that follow will be prophetic."

ROSINWEED

Silphium laciniatum, Linn.
Fam. Compositae

Synonyms: Compass Plant, Compass Weed, Polar Plant.

Habitat: Northern Europe.

Description: The article in commerce consists of broken-up leaves. The rachis of the leaves is plano-convex, with the marks of decurrent leaflets.

The fragments of leaves are stiff, papery, but brittle, and without hairs, with the surface faintly reticulated. Main root 1–2 in. long, and 1 in. in diameter, ending abruptly below, and laterally branched at the base, the roots enlarging downwards, from $\frac{1}{2}$–$\frac{1}{3}$ in. in diameter, dark greyish brown, striated longitudinally; transverse section showing concentric lines and radiate structure, variegated with dark grey and white, and a small central pith. Fracture rough and fibrous. Taste, bitter and then acrid; odour, none.

Parts Used: Herb, root.

Medicinal Use: Antispasmodic, diuretic, expectorant, emetic. It is reputed to have effected cures of dry, obstinate coughs of asthma and pulmonary catarrhal diseases. It is also beneficial in intermittent fevers.

Preparation: Liquid extract: Dose, $\frac{1}{2}$–1 dr.

RUE

Ruta graveolens, Linn.
Fam. Rutaceae

Synonyms: Garden Rue, Herb of Grace, Herbygrass, Ave-grace.

Habitat: It is a native of Southern Europe, but has been cultivated in Great Britain for a great number of years.

Flowering Time: June to September.

Description: Stem cylindrical, branched, smooth. Leaves alternate, bipinnate with oblanceolate segments, wedge-shaped below, with numerous immersed, translucent, small, round oil glands. Flowers yellow with five wavy petals incurved at the tips and a gland-dotted ovary, situated on the disk. Barton and Castle write: "The stamens exhibit a curious and remarkable phenomenon. They are all fixed in nearly a horizontal position at first, viz. reclining upon the petals, but one by one they successively rise and discharge the pollen upon the stigma and then return to their original position."

Part Used: Herb.

Medicinal Use: Stimulant, antispasmodic, emmenagogue. It is chiefly used in suppression of the menses, but should not be taken in large doses as it is liable to produce inflammations and nerve derangements. For hysteria, amenorrhoea, etc., it is of great use. The infusion of 1 oz to 1 pt of water is taken in doses of a teacupful. Dioscorides writes that "a twelve pennyweight of the seed drunk in wine is a counterpoison of serpents, the stinging of Scorpions, Bees, Hornets and Wasps; and it is reported that if a man be anointed with the juice of the Rue, these will not hurt him; and that the serpent is driven away at the smell thereof when it is burned; insomuch that when the weesle is to fight with the serpent she armeth herself by eating Rue, against the might of the Serpent."

Preparations: Powdered herb: Dose, 15–30 gr; Liquid extract: Dose, ½–1 dr; Oil: Dose, 2–5 min.

Biblical Reference: Rue is mentioned once in the Scriptures, in St. Luke XI, 42: "But woe unto you Pharisees! for ye tithe Mint and Rue and all manner of herbs, and pass over judgment and love of God."

RUE was believed to possess the merits of dispelling infection and to this day the old custom of strewing the courts with herbs (of which Rue is an ingredient) is maintained. It was also used in the exorcisms ordained by the Roman Catholic Church, hence the synonym Ave-grace.

RUPTUREWORT

Herniaria glabra, Linn.
Fam. Caryophyllaceae

Synonyms: Herniary, Breastwort.

Habitat: It grows commonly in England in dry places. Gerard says he found it in Kent "not farre from Chistle-hurst."

Flowering Time: May, June, July, and August.

Description: Stem slender, herbaceous, clothed with minute, decurved hairs. Leaves opposite, oval-oblong, about $\frac{1}{16}$ in. long, at intervals of about ½ in. Flowers minute, greenish, sessile in the axils, approximated in the lateral branches into a slightly leafy spike. Taste, insipid; odour, none.

Part Used: Herb.

Medicinal Use: Astringent, diuretic. Used in catarrhal affections of the bladder. Generally taken in the form of infusion, 1 oz to 1 pt of hot water, and drunk freely.

Gerard writes: "It is reported that being drunke it is singular good for Ruptures and that very many that have been bursten were restored to health by the use of this herbe also the powder hereof taken with wine . . . wasteth away the stone in the kidneys and expelleth them."

S

SABADILLA *Schoenocaulon officinale*, A. Gray.
Fam. Liliaceae

Synonyms: Cevadilla, *Veratrum officinale*, Schlecht., *Asagroea officinalis*, Lindl., Caustic Barley.
Habitat: Mexico, Guatemala, Venezuela.
Description: The seeds are usually met with freed from the capsules, and are linear, pointed, shining, wrinkled, and angular, or concave by mutual pressure, and contain oily albumen. The capsules are more rarely met with. They consist of thin, oblong, pointed, light-brown, papery carpels about ½ in. long, and united at their base, each containing two seeds. Taste, bitter, acrid; odour, none.
Part Used: Seeds.
Medicinal Use: Vermin destroying.
Preparations: Acetum (1 in 10); Ointment (1 in 4).

SAFFLOWER *Carthamus tinctorius*, Linn.
Fam. Compositae

Synonyms: American Saffron, False Saffron, Bastard Saffron, Flores Carthami, Dyer's Saffron.
Habitat: India.
Description: The commercial article consists of the florets separated from the flowerheads, either loose or compressed into small circular cakes. The florets are cylindrical, slender, orange, nearly ½ in. long, with five linear teeth. The taste is feebly bitter, and the odour not unpleasant when recent, but faintly valerianic on keeping.

These flowers have been used to adulterate genuine saffron but can easily be recognized by their tubular shape and yellow style.
Part Used: Flowers.
Medicinal Use: Laxative, diaphoretic. In domestic practice these flowers are used for similar purposes as Saffron proper, as in children's and infants' complaints and diseases, measles, fevers, and eruptive skin complaints. The infusion made of ½ oz to 1 pt of boiling water, if taken warm, is said to restore the menstrual discharge, and will produce diaphoresis.

SAFFRON

Crocus sativus, Linn.
Fam. Iridaceae

Synonyms: Crocus, Alicante Saffron, Valencia Saffron, Gatinais Saffron, Hay Saffron.

Habitat: Of Greek and Roman origin, but for generations cultivated in Spain from which the bulk of supplies are obtained. It was at one time grown commercially at Saffron Walden in Essex and in Cambridgeshire. In fact Joseph Miller writes: "The best Saffron in the world is grown in England being cultivated in Essex, Suffolk and Cambridgeshire."

Description: Saffron of commerce is only part of the flower and consists of the three filiform, deep orange-red stigmas attached to the upper part of the style, the whole about 1–1½ in. long. The stigmas are tubular and slit open at the end, and toothed at the apex. Taste, aromatic, but characteristic. Odour, pleasant, and also characteristic. Saffron, if pure, should not contain anything different in form from the above description, should not throw down a deposit when placed in water, and should not fizz or decrepitate when burnt. Alicante Saffron is frequently adulterated. Cake Saffron is generally a mixture of Saffron and Safflower made into cakes with honey.

Part Used: Flower pistils gathered in the autumn.

Medicinal Use: Carminative, diaphoretic, emmenagogue. It has been used with benefit in amenhorroea, dysmenorrhoea, hysteria, etc. It arrests chronic discharges of blood from the uterus. Used as a diaphoretic, especially for children. The infusion of 1 dr in 1 pt of boiling water is given in wineglassful to teacupful doses.

Culpeper describes Saffron as a herb of the Sun and under the Lion: "let not above 10 grains be given at one time for the Sun which is the fountain of light may dazzle the eyes and make them blind."

Preparations: Glycer. Croc.; Syr. Croc.; Tinct. Croc. (1 in 5): Dose, 5–15 min; Powdered Saffron: Dose, 12–40 gr.

Domestic Use: Saffron is used as a dye and is also an ingredient of Saffron cakes made in Cornwall.

SAFFRON is mentioned once in the Bible in the Song of Solomon IV, 14, where Solomon places it in his garden of sweets thus: "Spikenard and saffron; calamus and cinnamon, with all trees of frankincense."

SAGO *Metroxylon rumphii*, Mart.
Fam. Palmaceae

Synonyms: Pearl Sago, Sago Meal, Sago Flour, *Sagus rumphii*, Willd., *Sagus genuina.*

Habitat: Malayan Archipelago.

Description: Sago occurs in various forms and sizes in commerce. Genuine Sago is rarely quite white. The ordinary Sago of commerce is often made from potato starch. The starch grains of the two plants are quite different in shape and size, those of the potato being larger with a round hilum at the smaller end, and those of Sago smaller, more or less muller-shaped, with one truncate end, and a linear hilum at the larger, rounded end. The heat employed in making Sago is apt to break most of the granules, but in Sago Meal or Flour they are easily distinguished.

Part Used: Prepared pith-starch.

Medicinal Use: Nutritive, demulcent. Mostly used in the household and for convalescents as food or demulcent.

SALEP *Orchis mascula*, Linn.
Orchis maculata, Linn.
Orchis latifolia, Linn.
Fam. Orchidaceae

Synonyms: Salep Root.

Habitat: Central and Southern Europe and Great Britain.

Description: Salep is the dried roots of many species of Orchis, the principal varieties of which are those listed above. The dried root is imported into this country from Europe. Tubers whitish or pale brownish yellow, about 1–1½ in. long and ⅓–½ in. in diameter, oblong-oval or elliptical, somewhat cylindrical compressed, usually with a stem-scar at one end, and tapering to a point at the other. Some varieties are compressed palmate, with three to five pointed lobes, also with a stem scar at the crown, sometimes wrinkled or shrivelled, but always horny and tough, and not easily fractured. Taste, mucilaginous; odour, none.

Part Used: Root.

Medicinal Use: Demulcent, highly nutritious. Used similarly to Arrowroot.

SAMPHIRE *Crithmum maritimum*, Linn.
Fam. Umbelliferae

Synonyms: Rock Fennel, Rock Sampire.

Habitat: It grows upon rocks near the sea-coast in many parts of England, especially on the saltings in Essex.

Description: Samphire grows to a height of about 10 in. It is well distinguished by its glaucous, twice-ternate leaves, the divisions of which are very succulent, and taper towards either extremity.

Part Used: Herb.

Medicinal Use: An infusion of 1 oz of the herb in 1 pt of boiling water is taken freely in wineglassful doses. It is reputed to be an excellent treatment for obesity. It is also recommended as a diuretic and as an acid to the kidneys.

Domestic Use: The fleshy leaves are used in pickles.

SANDALWOOD

Santalum album, Linn.
Fam. Santalaceae

Synonym: Santalwood.

Habitat: India, Malay Archipelago.

Description: This wood is usually sold in the form of fine raspings, yellowish, and of fragrant odour.

Varieties: Oil of Australian Sandalwood is distilled from the wood of *Eucarya spicata*, sometimes known as *Santalum spicatum*, growing in West Australia. This oil is also in the B.P.C. 1949 and has similar uses to Ol. Santal. Album. Oil of West Indian Sandal, known also as Oil of Amyris, is obtained from the *Schimmelia oleifera*, Holmes (*Amyris balsamifera*, Linn.). This oil has from time to time been used to adulterate Ol. Santal. B.P.C. 1949. It has a lower specific gravity and is much less soluble in 70 per cent spirit than the official oil.

Part Used: Wood oil.

Medicinal Use: Diuretic, antiseptic. Is chiefly employed in treatment of chronic mucous affections such as inflammation of bladder, and other diseases. The fluid extract of the wood is often better tolerated than the oil.

Preparations: Ol. Santal. B.P.C. 1949: Dose, 5–15 min; Liquid extract: Dose, 1–2 dr; Liq. Copaib., Buchu et Cubeb c. Ol. Santal.: Dose, 1–2 dr; Liq. Copaib et Ol. Santal.: Dose, 1–2 dr; Liq. Santal. Co.: Dose, 1–2 dr.

Domestic Use: Sandalwood Oil is used in perfumery, and the fine wood raspings frequently form a component part of potpourri mixtures.

SANDERSWOOD, RED

Pterocarpus santalinus, Linn.
Fam. Leguminosae

Synonyms: Rubywood, Red Sandalwood, *Santalum rubrum*, *Lignum rubrum*.

Habitat: Southern India, Philippine Islands.

Description: Imported in billets, but usually met with in commerce in the form of raspings of a deep purplish-red tint, which do not colour water when soaked in it. Nearly tasteless; odour, none.

Part Used: Wood.

Medicinal Use: Tonic, astringent. Hardly ever used for its medicinal properties. As a colouring agent it forms part of Comp. Tincture of Lavender.

SANICLE

Sanicula europaea, Linn.
Fam. Umbelliferae

Synonyms: Pool Root, Butterwort.

Habitat: Growing in woods and shady places in England.

Flowering Time: May and June.

Description: The herb has a nearly simple stem, reddish and furrowed, the long-stalked leaves are firm, shining green above, rather paler below, about 2–3 in. across, rounded in outline, and divided deeply into five irregularly trifid and serrate lobes which are broadly wedge-shaped below. Taste, bitter, astringent, subsequently acrid; odour, none.

Part Used: Herb.

Medicinal Use: Astringent, alterative. Generally given in combination with other herbs in the treatment of blood disorders, for which it is highly esteemed. It is useful also in leucorrhoea, dysentery, diarrhoea, etc. The infusion of 1 oz to 1 pt of boiling water is taken in wineglassful doses.

Culpeper describes this plant as one of the herbs of Venus which will therefore cure "The wounds and mischiefs Mars inflicts upon the body of man." Joseph Miller also describes it as one of the primary vulnerary plants. Parkinson writes: "The country people who live where it groweth, doe use it to annoint their hands when they are chapt by the winde. . . ."

Preparation: Liquid extract: Dose, ½–1 dr.

SARSAPARILLA, AMERICAN

Smilax aristolochiaefolia, Mill.
Fam. Liliaceae

Synonym: Bamboo Brier.

Habitat: South America.

Description: Rhizome about ¾ in. thick, with cup-shaped disks at alternate intervals of about ½ in., with a greyish, scaly epidermis, easily removed from the whitish bark, which itself does not adhere to the wood when dry; the woody centre is finely porous and encloses a small pith. Taste, slightly aromatic and bitterish; odour, none. Described by Maisch as 12 in. or more long, 1¼ in. thick, annulate above, with cup-shaped scars. Bark light grey, brown, exfoliating, internally whitish, with yellowish wood and spongy pith. Fracture short. Taste, mawkish and slightly aromatic.

Part Used: Rhizome.

Medicinal Use: Alterative, pectoral, diaphoretic, sudorific. Though quite distinct from Jamaica Sarsaparilla, it will be found a very efficient substitute and by many is regarded as superior in alterative properties. It may be used in all cases of skin diseases, and rheumatism, and is best given in the form of a decoction, made from 1 oz of root boiled in 1 pt of water for half an hour, in wineglassful doses frequently. For coughs, colds, etc., it should be used as a syrup.

Gerard speaks about "Zarzaparilla of Peru" sent over from "Countries of the new world called America," but not much was known at that time concerning its use. He recommends it for "continuall paine in the joynts and head and against cold diseases."

Preparations: Fldext. Sarsap. U.S.P.; Syr. Sarsap. Co. U.S.P.

SARSAPARILLA, INDIAN

Hemidesmus indicus, Brown
Fam. Asclepiadaceae

Synonyms: Hemidesmus, Country Sarsaparilla.

Habitat: India and Ceylon.

Description: In cylindrical, transversely-cracked pieces, 6 in. or more in length and about ½ in. thick, with a corky layer often loosely attached, violet brown, or of a reddish tint. The section shows a white, mealy, corky layer, somewhat violet tinted, and a yellowish, woody centre. Taste, pleasant, sweetish, slightly acrid; odour, recalling heliotrope.

Part Used: Root.

Medicinal Use: Diuretic, alterative. Used in constitutional debility, chronic rheumatism, and ulcerations. Much thought of by the Indian natives, who ascribe to it several medicinal virtues besides those mentioned.

Preparation: Syrup: Dose, ½–1 dr.

SARSAPARILLA, JAMAICA

Smilax ornata, Hook, f.
(and other species)
Fam. Liliaceae

Synonyms: *Smilax medica*, Schlecht and Cham., *Smilax officinalis*, H., B., & K.

Habitat: In spite of its name, Jamaica Sarsaparilla is a native of Central America, but was exported via Jamaica.

Description: Root rusty brown, cylindrical, about ¼–½ in. in diameter, with numerous slender rootlets, deeply furrowed longitudinally, the transverse section showing a brown, hard, non-mealy bark, and a porous central wood portion. Taste, slightly acrid; odour, none. The orange-brown Jamaica native Sarsaparilla with a starchy rind is sometimes preferred. The so-called "Brown" Jamaica Sarsaparilla comes from Costa Rica. Honduras Sarsaparilla is generally imported in long, thin bundles with few rootlets attached. Bales often consist of a cow's hide. Vera Cruz or Mexican Sarsaparilla is free from beard (roots), and is usually attached to the root-stock.

Part Used: Root.

Medicinal Use: Alterative. This is the root introduced by the Spaniards in 1563 as a sure cure for syphilis. It has been thoroughly tested since then, and experience has demonstrated the fact that it is not an absolute specific. However, it contains active alterative principles which cause it still to be held in high opinion as a general purifier of the blood. It is chiefly given in conjunction with other remedies, such as Sassafras, Burdock, etc. It forms the chief ingredient in the Concentrated Compound decoction of Sarsaparilla of the B.P.C. 1949.

Preparations: Powdered root: Dose, $\frac{1}{4}$–1 dr; Liquid extract: B.P. 1898: Dose, 2–4 fl dr; Solid extract: Dose, 10–20 gr; Dec. Sars. Co. B.P.C. 1949: Dose, 2–8 fl oz; Dec. Sars. Co. Conc. B.P.C. 1949: Dose, $\frac{1}{4}$–1 fl oz.

SASSAFRAS

Sassafras variifolium, (Salisb.) Kuntze
Fam. Lauraceae

Synonyms: *Sassafras officinale*, Nees & Eberm.

Habitat: Eastern United States and Canada.

Description: The root-bark is of a bright, rust-brown colour, in irregular pieces, soft and brittle. The transverse fracture is short and corky, in definite layers, and shows numerous oil cells. Taste, sweetish aromatic, slightly astringent; odour, agreeable aromatic.

The woody root is usually sold in the form of chips of a brownish-white tint, which show distinct concentric rings marked off by two or three rows of porous vessels, and slender medullary rays. The wood tastes distinctly of Sassafras, but that of the stem, which is often mixed with it, does not, and is further indicated by the grey surface of the bark.

Parts Used: Root and bark of the root.

Medicinal Use: Stimulant, diaphoretic, diuretic. Used with success in eruptions of the skin, rheumatism, gout, etc. A decoction is beneficial as a wash for the eyes in ophthalmia, inflammation, etc. An infusion of 1 oz of crushed bark in 1 pt of boiling water is taken in doses of a wineglassful, repeated frequently. Is generally given in combination with other remedies.

Preparations: Liquid extract: Dose, $\frac{1}{2}$–1 dr; Oil: Dose, $\frac{1}{2}$–5 drops.

A volatile Oil of Sassafras is official in U.S.P., being distilled from the rootbark.

SASSY BARK

Erythrophloeum guineense, G. Don
Fam. Leguminosae

Synonyms: Mancona Bark, Casca Bark, Doom Bark.

Habitat: West Coast of Africa, Sudan, Nyasaland.

Description: In flat or slightly curved pieces about 2 in. broad and $\frac{1}{4}$ in. thick, but varying in length, externally warty, and sometimes with a grey epidermis furrowed longitudinally, internally red-brown, hard; the inner surface nearly smooth, sometimes with black stains. Fracture coarsely granular, with numerous pale groups of stone cells. Taste, astringent, bitter and acrid; inodorous. Very poisonous. Should not be used except under medical direction.

Part Used: Bark.

Medicinal Use: Narcotic, astringent, laxative. Has been found efficient in diarrhoea, dysentery, passive haemorrhages, etc. The infusion is made from $\frac{1}{2}$ oz of bark in 1 pt of boiling water and taken in doses of a tablespoonful as required. Used by the natives of West Africa as an ordeal in witchcraft, etc. As it possesses toxic properties it should be used with caution. The bark is seldom imported into England now.

SAVIN

Juniperus sabina, Linn.
Fam. Pinaceae

Synonym: Savin Tops.

Habitat: Alpine regions of Switzerland, Italy and Austria, and in other parts of the world, such as Newfoundland.

Description: The herb as imported from Italy consists of small, broken, nearly cylindrical, or scale-like leaves about $\frac{1}{12}$ in. long and lanceolate, rhombic in shape, with an oblong gland sessile in the back of the midrib. Taste, disagreeable, resinous, and bitter; odour, recalling turpentine, but quite characteristic. The fresh plant as sold in England consists of tufts of the terminal branches about 6 in. long with the leaves longer, acute, and spreading, especially below, but the taste is the same. The twigs of *Juniperus virginiana*, Linn., and *J. phoenicea*, Linn., are different in taste, and the latter has the leaves arranged in three, not four, rows.

Part Used: Tops of herb.

Medicinal Use: Emmenagogue, diuretic, anthelmintic. Is sometimes combined with Tansy, Pennyroyal, and Hemlock. Although uncertain in its action, it has been used for worms in conjunction with Spigelia and Senna. It is now rarely administered internally because of its possible poisonous effects. Externally it may be used as an ointment as a dressing for blisters. Culpeper says: ". . . it may be safely used outwardly but inwardly it cannot be taken without manifest danger."

Preparations: Powdered Savin: Dose, 5–10 gr; Liquid extract: Dose, 5–15 min; Tincture (1 in 8): Dose, 20–60 min; Oil: Dose, 1–4 min.

SAVORY, SUMMER

Satureia hortensis, Linn.
Fam. Labiatae

Synonym: Garden Savory.

Habitat: A well-known kitchen-garden plant which grows in most parts of the world.

Description: Stem woody and oppositely branched, about 10 in. high, with linear, entire leaves about ½ in. long. Flowers small, pinkish, in axillary cymes, calyx teeth five, nearly equal, linear, tapering upwards, and ciliate, at the margins. Hairs, on the stem short, rather rigid, decurved. Taste, aromatic, recalling thyme and marjoram, but distinct.

Part Used: Herb.

Medicinal Use: Aromatic, carminative. May be added to medicines for its aromatic and warming qualities.

CULPEPER says of Summer Savory: "The juice heated with a little oil of roses, and dropped into the ears, easeth them of the noises and singing in them, and of deafness also. Outwardly applied with flour, in manner of a poultice, it giveth ease to the sciatica. . . ."

SAW PALMETTO

Serenoa serrulata, Hook, f.
Fam. Palmae

Synonym: Sabal.

Habitat: Eastern North America.

Description: The fruits are oval or globular, from ¾–1 in. long, ⅝–1⅛ in. broad, externally black, with a thin, hard, but fragile pericarp covering a shrunken, pale-brown, spongy pulp, which contains oils, and a thin, papery endocarp. The seed is pale brown, globular or oval, with the hilum near the base. Taste of the pulp, soapy; odour, of a nutty vanilla type.

Part Used: Berry.

Medicinal Use: Nutritive tonic, diuretic, sedative. Is highly recommended in all wasting diseases, as it has a marked effect upon all the glandular tissues, increasing flesh rapidly and building up the strength. Should be used in atrophy of testes, mammae, etc.

Preparations: Ext. Sabal. Liq.: Dose, 10–25 min; Solid extract (alc.): Dose, 5–15 gr; Powdered Berries: Dose, 15 gr.

SCAMMONY ROOT, MEXICAN

Ipomoea orizabensis (Pellet) Ledanois
Fam. Convolvulaceae

Synonyms: Ipomoea, Orizaba Jalap.
Habitat: Mexico.
Flowering Time: September and November.
Description: The plant is a climbing herb producing lilac-purple flowers. The root occurs in large, transverse slices. It is wrinkled and has coarse, woody strands in irregular circles. Very little odour, and acrid resinous taste. The root contains up to 20 per cent of resin. The resin obtained from this root is in brownish, brittle lumps or pale-brown powder. A white Scammony Resin Powder is also prepared by a special process of bleaching during the operation of extraction.

Varieties: Scammonium, or Virgin Scammony is a gum resin obtained by cutting and draining the living roots of *Convolvulus scammonia*, Linn. (Fam. Convolvulaceae). The milky sap is allowed to dry in shells. This is generally imported from Smyrna in flat cakes 1 or 2 in. in diameter. This product contains from 70–80 per cent of Scammony Resin and the remainder is mostly gum. Dose, 5–10 gr.

Part Used: Resin extracted from the root.
Medicinal Use: Drastic purgative. The root is seldom used, although the dose is stated in some books of reference as 5–20 gr. The resin extracted from the root is used and is frequently combined with other ingredients to diminish its action.
Preparations: Ipom. Res. B.P.C.: Dose, $\frac{1}{2}$–3 gr; Pulv. Scammon. Co.: Dose, 10–30 gr; Pil. Scammon. Co.: Dose, 1–2 pills.

SCOPOLIA

Scopola carniolica, Jacq.
Fam. Solanaceae

Synonym: *Scopola atropoides*, Linn.
Habitat: Hungary.
Description: Rhizome knotty, about $\frac{1}{2}$–$\frac{3}{4}$ in. in diameter, with closely-approximated, large, cup-shaped remains of annual stems; sometimes ending in a piece of tapering, cylindrical root, but usually consisting of the rhizome only. Fracture short.
Part Used: Rhizome.
Medicinal Use: Narcotic, mydriatic. Used for similar purposes to Belladonna or Henbane, both of which it resembles very much in action. It is said to be richer in alkaloids than either of the above, and for this reason is preferred by makers of alkaloids and plasters.

It is a powerful poison which should be used only under medical direction.

Preparations: Liquid extract: Dose, 1–5 drops; Powdered extract: Dose, 1–5 gr.

SCULLCAP

Scutellaria laterifolia, Linn.
Fam. Labiatae

Synonyms: Skullcap, Madweed, Quaker Bonnet.

Habitat: U.S.A.

Description: Herb with square stems, opposite, cordate-lanceolate, shortly-stalked leaves with a tapering apex. Flowers blue, with a helmet-shaped upper lip, in axillary racemes. Taste, bitterish; odour, slight. Other species, with the flowers in one-sided terminal racemes, are sometimes substituted for it.

Part Used: Herb.

Medicinal Use: Tonic, nervine, antispasmodic, slightly astringent. Is one of the finest nervines ever discovered, and may be prescribed wherever disorders of the nervous system exist. In hysteria, convulsions, hydrophobia, St. Vitus dance, rickets, etc., its action is invaluable. Many cases of hydrophobia are known to have been cured by this remedy alone, while it may be regarded as a specific in St. Vitus dance. The dose of an infusion of 1 oz to 1 pt of boiling water is half a teacupful frequently.

Preparations: Powdered herb: Dose, $\frac{1}{4}$–$\frac{1}{2}$ dr; Liquid extract: Dose, $\frac{1}{2}$–1 dr; Solid extract: Dose, 5–10 gr; Scutellarin: Dose, 1–2 gr.

Scutellaria integrifolia, Linn. (Western Scullcap) and *S. galericulata*, Linn. (European Scullcap) possess similar properties and are often used.

SCURVY-GRASS

Cochlearia officinalis, Linn.
Fam. Cruciferae

Synonym: Spoonwort.

Habitat: It grows wild in many parts of England and is also cultivated in gardens. Culpeper writes that it is found along the Thames-side on the Essex and Kentish shores from Woolwich and round about the sea-coasts to Dover, Portsmouth, and even Bristol.

Flowering Time: April and May: the seeds ripen quickly afterwards.

Description: The root-leaves are long-stalked, roundish, kidney-shaped, and nearly entire, the stem-leaves ovate, with a few angular teeth, becoming sessile upwards. Flowers white and cruciform, in terminal racemes. Fruit globular-ovate, two-celled, containing four red-brown seeds in each of the two cells. Taste, pungent, cress-like, bitterish, but becoming much less pungent when dry.

Part Used: Herb.

Medicinal Use: Antiscorbutic, diuretic. This is a strong antiscorbutic, and may be given in all cases where such a remedy is required. The infusion of 2 oz to 1 pt of boiling water is taken in wineglassful doses frequently repeated.

Gerard states: "The herb stamped and laid upon spots and blemishes of the face will take them away within six hours, but the place must be washed after with water wherein bran hath been sodden."

Culpeper describes it as a herb of Jupiter and goes on to say: "The juice also helps all foul ulcers and sores in the mouth gargled therewith. . . ."

SEA LAVENDER

Limonium carolinianum, Walt.
Fam. Plumbaginaceae

Synonyms: Marsh Rosemary, Inkroot.

Habitat: U.S.A.

Description: Root large, spindle-shaped, or branched, compact, rough, of a purplish-brown colour. Taste, bitter and astringent; odour, none. The English Sea Lavender (*Statice limonium*) has similar properties.

Part Used: Root.

Medicinal Use: Astringent. This will be found very efficient wherever an astringent tonic is needed, as in bronchial haemorrhage, sore throat, ulcerated mouth, and catarrhal disorders. Externally it is recommended for piles and as a lotion in leucorrhoea and urinary complaints. The decoction of the powdered root, 1 oz to 1 pt, is given in doses of a wineglassful.

SELF-HEAL

Prunella vulgaris, Linn.
Fam. Labiatae

Synonyms: Heal-all, Hook-heal, Siclewort.

Habitat: A wild plant growing commonly in woods and fields.

Flowering Time: April and May.

Description: A small low-creeping herb, 4–8 in. long, branched, with square stems, oblong-ovate, obtuse leaves, about 1 in. long and ½ in. broad, usually entire, with scattered, appressed hairs. Flowers purplish blue, in a dense terminal spike, with two broad, kidney-shaped, acute bracts under each whorl. Upper lip of calyx with short, truncate mucronate teeth. Taste, saline, faintly bitter; odour, none.

Part Used: Herb.

Medicinal Use: Astringent. Is useful in sore and relaxed throat; also in internal bleeding. leucorrhoea, etc. The infusion of 1 oz to 1 pt of boiling water is taken internally in doses of a wineglassful. Externally it is used as a gargle and injection.

Culpeper writes: "Here is another herb of Venus, Self-heal whereby when you are hurt you may heal yourself; it is a special herb for inward and outward wounds. Take it inwardly in syrups for inward wounds; outwardly in unguents and plaisters for outward. . . . The juice thereof used with oil of roses to annoint the temples and forehead is very effectual to remove headache."

There is an old German saying that "He needs neither physician nor surgeon that hath Self-heal and to help himself."

SENEGA

Polygala senega, Linn.
Fam. Polygalaceae

Synonyms: Seneka, Senega Snakeroot.

Habitat: Widely distributed in America.

Description: Root usually having a knotty crown, from which the slender stems arise, having the remains of rudimentary leaves at their base. The root is of a light yellowish-grey colour, $\frac{1}{5}$–$\frac{1}{3}$ in. thick, usually sparingly branched, and having a keel-shaped ridge running along the main root on the concave side. Fracture short and brittle, showing a cleft central column. Taste, acrid and slightly acid, and recalling that of Gaultheria, with a characteristic, somewhat rancid odour.

Part Used: Root.

Medicinal Use: Diaphoretic, diuretic, expectorant, emetic. Very useful in chronic catarrh, chronic bronchitis, asthma, and croup. Recommended as local stimulant in sore throat. The infusion of 1 oz to 1 pt of boiling water is taken in tablespoonful to wineglassful doses.

It was first introduced into England about 1735 by the Scottish physician Tennant who noticed its use as a remedy for the bite of the rattlesnake and afterwards proved its use in pleurisy and pneumonia. It was then known as Seneca Rattlesnake Root.

Preparations: Ext. Seneg. Liq. B.P.C.: Dose, 5–15 min; Inf. Seneg. Conc. B.P.C.: Dose, 30–60 min; Inf. Seneg. Rec. B.P.C. 1949: Dose, $\frac{1}{2}$–1 fl oz; Syr. Cocillan. Co. B.P.C. 1949: Dose, 30–60 min; Tinct. Seneg. B.P.C.: Dose, 30–60 min; Powdered root: Dose, 6–12 gr.

SENNA

Cassia angustifolia, Vahl
Cassia acutifolia, Del.
Fam. Leguminosae

Synonyms: *Angustifolia*: Tinnevelly Senna, East Indian Senna; *Acutifolia*: Alexandrian Senna.

Habitat: *Angustifolia*: Indigenous to Southern Arabia but cultivated in

Southern and Eastern India. *Acutifolia*: Upper and Middle Nile in Egypt and the Sudan. They are called Alexandrian because Alexandria was used as the port from which exports were made. They are now exported from Port Sudan.

Description: Senna leaves, or more properly leaflets, are greyish green, lanceolate, unequal at the base, varying from ½–1½ in. long, and ¼–⅓ in. broad. Those of *Cassia angustifolia* (Tinnevelly Senna) are broader near the middle, and longer in proportion than those of *Cassia acutifolia* (Alexandrian Senna) which are broadest below the midrib. The Mecca Senna of commerce, which seems to contain a mixture of both species and is often full of leafstalks and discoloured leaflets, is an inferior quality. The pods are also used. Alexandrian Senna Pods are green, 1½–2½ in. long and ¾–1 in. broad. Indian Senna Pods are darker, narrower, only ¾ in. broad, and have the base of the style prominent on the upper edge. Taste, sweetish, but sickly; odour, somewhat tea-like, but characteristic.

Parts Used: Leaves, pods.

Medicinal Use: Laxative, cathartic. Is generally combined with aromatics and stimulants to modify its griping effects. The following may be regarded as a good formula for making an infusion: Senna leaves 2 oz; ginger 1 dr; boiling water 1 pt. Let it stand for one hour, strain through muslin and take in wineglassful doses. Alexandrian Senna leaves and pods are considered to have a milder and yet as certain an action as the East Indian variety, to which they are generally preferred.

Preparations: From leaves: Conf. Senn. B.P.C.: Dose, 60–120 gr; Conf. Senn. et Sulphur. B.P.C. 1949: Dose, 60–120 gr; Fldext. Senn. U.S.P.: Dose, 30 min; Pulv. Glycyrrh. Co. B.P.: Dose, 60–120 gr; Syr. Senn. U.S.P.: Dose, 2 fl dr; Tinct. Senn. Co. B.P.C. 1949: Dose, 30–60 min; Powdered leaves: Dose, 10–30 gr.

From pods: Elix. Senn. B.P.C. 1949: Dose, 30–60 min; Ext. Senn. Liq. B.P.: Dose, 10–30 min; Inf. Senn. Conc. B.P.C.: Dose, 30–120 min; Inf. Senn. Rec. B.P.C. 1949: Dose, ½–2 fl oz; Mist. Senn. Co. B.P.C.: Dose, 1–2 fl oz; Syr. Fic. Co. B.P.C.: Dose, 30–120 min; Syr. Senn. B.P.: Dose, 30–120 min.

SHALLOT

Allium ascalonicum, Linn.
Fam. Liliaceae

Synonym: Eschallot.

Habitat: Widely distributed in temperate countries.

Description: The bulbs are compound like those of garlic, but are much smaller and milder. The bulblets are termed cloves.

Medicinal Use: Rarely used in medicine.

Part Used: Bulb.

Domestic Use: Used chiefly as an ingredient in the preparation of sauces.

SHEEP-SORREL

Rumex acetosella, Linn.
Fam. Polygonaceae

Synonym: Field-sorrel.

Habitat: A common wild plant in Europe and Great Britain.

Flowering Time: June, July.

Description: Leaves oblong, arrow-shaped below, rather firm, with a broad-toothed, membranous, stipular sheath round the stem at its base. Taste, acid and astringent; odour, none.

Part Used: Herb.

Medicinal Use: Diuretic. The fresh plant juice is refrigerant and diaphoretic, and is of use in urinary and renal diseases. Dose, $\frac{1}{2}$–1 dr.

SHEPHERD'S PURSE

Capsella bursa-pastoris, Medik.
Fam. Cruciferae

Synonyms: Shepherd's Sprout, Mother's Heart, Permacety, Toywort, Pickpurse, Casewort.

Habitat: A common wild plant.

Flowering Time: All the Summer. Some plants flower twice a year.

Description: A common weed, with leaves irregular in character, somewhat lanceolate, and either entire or much toothed, but always recognizable by its triangular seed pods. The flowers are small and white. Taste, pungent; odour, cress-like.

Part Used: Herb.

Medicinal Use: Antiscorbutic, stimulant, diuretic. Chiefly used in kidney complaints and dropsy, etc. Also useful in chronic diarrhoea. The infusion of 1 oz to 1 pt of boiling water is taken in wineglassful doses.

Culpeper writes: "The juice being dropped into the ears, heals the pains, noise and mutterings thereof. A good ointment may be made of it for all wounds, especially wounds in the head." Parkinson states: "Some doe hold that the greene herbe bruised and bound to the wrists of the hands, and soles of the feete will helpe the yellow jaundice. . . ."

Preparation: Liquid extract: Dose, $\frac{1}{4}$–1 dr.

SIEGESBECKIA

Siegesbeckia orientalis, Linn.
Fam. Compositae

Habitat: Mauritius.

Description: Stem usually about 2 ft high, branched. Leaves opposite, broadly triangular, coarsely toothed. Flowerheads small, leafy, panicled.

Outer row of phyllaries spatulate and twice as long as the inner, and covered with glandular pubescence. Taste and odour, slight, but characteristic.

Part Used: Whole plant.

Medicinal Use: Alterative. Has been used in leprous, and other skin diseases, and contains a white crystalline body resembling salicylic acid.

Preparation: Liquid extract: Dose, 10–30 min.

SILVERWEED

Potentilla anserina, Linn.
Fam. Rosaceae

Synonym: Wild Tansy.

Habitat: A common weed in Europe and the British Isles.

Flowering Time: June and July.

Description: Leaves silvery below, often on the upper surface also, interruptedly pinnate, with 12–15 pairs of oval, toothed segments, with minute leaflets between each pair. Flowers yellow, buttercup-like borne singly on the slender runners. Taste, astringent: odour, none.

Part Used: Herb.

Medicinal Use: Astringent. Tonic.

Culpeper, no doubt owing to its astringent action, recommends Silverweed, which ". . . boiled in vinegar with honey and alum, and gargled in the mouth, easeth the pains of the tooth-ache, fasteneth loose teeth, helpeth the gums that are sore, and settleth the palate of the mouth in its place when it is fallen down."

Gerard writes: "The distilled water takes away freckles, spots, pimples in the face, and sun-burning, but the herb, laid to infuse or steep in white wine is far better: but the best of all is to steepe it in strong white wine vinegar, the face being often bathed or washed therewith."

SIMARUBA

Simaruba amara, Aubl.
Fam. Simarubaceae

Synonym: Mountain Damson.

Habitat: Guiana, Brazil, Florida, West Indian Islands.

Description: The bark occurs in flat, yellowish, or greyish-yellow, tough, fibrous pieces, impossible to break, and usually folded, about ⅛ in. thick and 2–2½ in. wide. Taste, very bitter; inodorous.

Part Used: Bark.

Medicinal Use: Tonic. Is very useful in weakened digestion, loss of appetite, and in convalescence from fevers, etc. The infusion of ½ oz to 1 pt of boiling water is taken in tablespoonful to wineglassful doses as required.

At one time it was used for dysentery, but is very little used in medicine today.

Preparation: Liquid extract: Dose, $\frac{1}{2}$–1 dr.

SKUNK CABBAGE

Symplocarpus foetidus, Nutt.
Fam. Araceae

Synonyms: Skunkweed, Meadow Cabbage, Polecatweed, *Dracontium foetidum*, Linn.

Habitat: U.S.A.

Description: Root obconical, truncate at both ends, 3–4 in. long and about 2 in. in diameter, with numerous long, shrivelled roots. Often sold in transverse slices about $\frac{1}{4}$ in. thick, with a grey-brown irregular margin, and the tiansverse section whitish and starchy, with scattered, yellowish wood bundles showing near the circumference sections of the rootlets at their origin. Taste, acrid, biting; odour, disagreeable.

Part Used: Root.

Medicinal Use: Antispasmodic, diaphoretic, expectorant. Enters into several of the Compound Herbal Powders for fever. In small doses the powder may be mixed with honey—$\frac{1}{2}$ oz to 4 oz honey—and forms an efficacious remedy for asthmatic and bronchial affections, in doses of $\frac{1}{2}$–1 teaspoonful.

Preparation: Liquid extract: Dose, $\frac{1}{2}$–1 dr.

SLIPPERY ELM

Ulmus fulva, Mich.
Fam. Ulmaceae

Synonyms: Red Elm, Moose Elm. The Red Indians who use it as a demulcent and sometimes as a food call it "Oohooska" meaning "It slips."

Habitat: Central and Northern United States of America.

Description: The bark occurs in flat pieces, about 2 in. wide and 2 ft or more long, usually folded, about $\frac{1}{24}$ in. thick. It has a pinkish or faintly rusty tint, a tough, fibrous texture, and mealy fracture, and is slightly striated longitudinally. Taste, very mucilaginous; resembling lovage or foenugreek in odour.

Part Used: The inner bark.

Medicinal Use: Diuretic, emollient, demulcent, pectoral; one of the most valuable articles in the botanic practice, and one which should be in every household. The finely powdered bark makes an excellent gruel or food, and may be used as such in all cases of weakness, inflammation of the stomach, bronchitis, etc. It has a wonderfully soothing and healing action on all the parts it comes in contact with, and in addition possesses as much nutrition as is contained in oatmeal. The food or gruel should be made as follows: Take a teaspoonful of the powder, mix well with the same quantity of powdered sugar and add 1 pt of boiling water slowly, mixing as it is poured on. This may be flavoured with cinnamon or nutmeg to suit the taste, and makes a very wholesome and sustaining food for infants. The coarse powder forms the finest poultice to be obtained for all inflamed surfaces, ulcers, wounds, burns, boils, skin diseases, purulent ophthalmia, chilblains etc. It soothes the part, disperses the inflammation, draws out impurities, and heals speedily. We cannot speak too highly of this remedy, and are confident there is nothing to equal it in the world for its above-mentioned uses. Inflammation in the bowels of infants and adults has been cured, when all other remedies have failed, by an injection into the bowels of an infusion of 1 oz of powdered bark to 1 pt of boiling water, used while warm. Slippery Elm is also used in lozenges to relieve irritation of the pharynx.

Preparation: Mucilage: made by digesting 6 g (93 gr) of bruised Slippery Elm in 100 cc (3 fl oz, 183 min) of water. Should be placed in a closed vessel and heated on a waterbath for one hour and then strained.

SMARTWEED

Polygonum hydropiper, Linn.
Fam. Polygonaceae

Synonyms: Water Pepper, Arsesmart, Biting Persicaria, Pepperwort, Culrage.

Habitat: A common English plant growing in dry places.

Flowering Time: June, and the seeds ripening in August.

Description: Stem 1–2 ft high. Leaves, lanceolate, alternate, entire. Inflorescence a drooping slender, interrupted raceme of small, greenish flowers. Leaves with a pungent biting taste; odour, none.

Parts Used: Herb, leaves.

Medicinal Use: Stimulant, diuretic, emmenagogue. Used principally for obstructions of the menses, amenorrhoea, etc. The infusion, made by pouring 1 pt of cold water upon 1 oz of leaves, is taken in wineglassful doses.

Joseph Miller writes: "This has been accounted an extraordinary plant against the stone, Mr. Boyle having in his book of the usefulness of experimental philosophy given the distilled water of this plant a mighty character for its virtues against that distemper. It is commended also as very cleansing and good for stubborn ulcers." Culpeper states that:

"The juice destroys worms in the ears, being dropped into them"; also: "If Arsesmart be strewed in a chamber, it will soon kill all the fleas."

Preparations: Liquid extract: Dose, 1–2 dr; Tincture: Dose 2–4 dr.

SNAKE ROOT

Aristolochia reticulata, Nutt.
Fam. Aristolochiaceae

Synonyms: Red River or Texan Snake Root, Serpentary.

Habitat: U.S.A.

Description: Rhizome about 1 in. long and $\frac{1}{8}$ in. thick, with numerous filiform, branching roots below, 2 in. long or more and furrowed longitudinally and on the upper side the short bases of stems of the previous years. Taste, aromatic camphoraceous, bitterish; odour, aromatic.

Snake Root is frequently referred to as Virginian Snake Root, although strictly speaking this name applies only to *A. serpentaeria*, Linn., which is regarded as a substitute for Texan Snake Root. It is very similar in appearance to the Texan root, with the difference that the thin rootlets are matted.

Part Used: Rhizome.

Medicinal Use: Stimulant, diaphoretic, anodyne, antispasmodic, tonic, nervine. Is a valuable remedy in all cases of fever, especially in typhoid, and will be found to agree with the digestive organs when Peruvian Bark cannot be taken. It may be employed with advantage whenever it is desirable to promote perspiration and in bilious complaints. The infusion of $\frac{1}{2}$ oz to 1 pt of boiling water is taken in 1–2 tablespoonful doses.

Preparations: Inf. Serpent. Conc.: Dose, $\frac{1}{2}$–1 dr; Tinct. Serpent.: Dose, $\frac{1}{2}$–1 dr; Powdered root: Dose, $\frac{3}{4}$–1$\frac{1}{2}$ gr; Liquid extract: Dose, $\frac{1}{2}$–1 dr; Tinct. Cinchon. Co. B.P.C. 1949: Dose, 30–60 min.

SOAP TREE

Quillaja saponaria, Mol.
Fam. Rosaceae

Synonyms: Quillaia, Soap Bark, Panama Bark, Cullay (native).

Habitat: Chile, Peru.

Description: Imported in large, flat pieces 1–2 ft long or more, 4–6 in. broad and $\frac{1}{8}$–$\frac{1}{4}$ in. thick. The outer surface is pale yellowish white with irregular patches of imperfectly-removed, reddish outer bark. The inner surface is smooth. The fracture splintery in layers. Under a lens, glittering solitary prismatic crystals of calcium oxalate are visible. The powder, when the bark is broken, causes violent sneezing. Taste, acrid; odour, none.

A variety of the bark, apparently from a different species of the same genus, has the brown patches covering most of the bark, and marked with oblique lines. This kind is much less active, containing only half as much saponin as the genuine.

Part Used: Bark.

Medicinal Use: Expectorant, diuretic, detergent, sternutatory. Used to loosen cough in chronic bronchitis and pulmonary complaints. The infusion of ½ oz of bark in 1 pt of boiling water is taken in tablespoonful doses or more as required. Used externally as a cleansing application to cutaneous ulcers and eruptions.

Preparations: Ext. Quill. Liq. B.P. (used in the preparation of certain B.P. emulsions); Tinct. Quill. B.P.C.: Dose, 30–60 min; Powdered Bark: Dose, 1–3 gr.

Domestic Use: A heading for beers is made from Quillaia.

SOAPWORT

Saponaria officinalis, Linn.
Fam. Caryophyllaceae

Synonyms: Soaproot, Bouncing Bet, Fuller's Herb.

Habitat: It is a garden plant and also grows wild in many parts of Great Britain and Europe.

Flowering Time: June and July.

Description: The leaves are opposite, entire, and smooth, elliptical-lanceolate, about 2 in. long and ¾ in. broad, the longitudinal nerves curved towards the apex of the leaf, greyish green when dried. Flowers pinkish. Taste, bitter and acrid; odour, none.

Parts Used: Leaves, root.

Medicinal Use: Alterative, detergent. Used as a remedy for scrofula, and skin diseases generally. Is said to be superior to Sarsaparilla. A decoction of 2 oz boiled in 1 pt of water is taken in doses of 1–2 tablespoonfuls three to four times a day.

Preparation: Liquid extract: Dose, ¼–1 dr.

Domestic Use: The root is used for producing a head on beers.

Gerard states: "It is commonly called Saponaria, of the great scouring qualitie of the leaves have; for they yield out of themselves a certaine juice when they are bruised, which scoureth almost as well as Sope. . . ."

SOLOMON'S SEAL

Polygonatum multiflorum, Allem.
Fam. Liliaceae

Habitat: It is largely a cultivated plant in this country, growing in gardens. It may also be found growing wild in many places. Culpeper writes:

". . . as, namely in a wood two miles from Canterbury, by Fish-Pond Hill, as also in Bushy Close belonging to the parsonage of Alderbury, near Clarendon, two miles from Salisbury; in Chaffon wood, on Chesson Hill, between Newington and Sittingbourne in Kent, and divers other places in Essex."

Flowering Time: May.

Description: The plant is well known, and is about 1½ ft high, with a round stalk containing alternate, pinnate leaves, terminating in a sharp point. The white, hollow, pendulous flowers occur at the foot of each leaf almost from the bottom to the top of each stalk. The rhizome, which is the part used, may be described as cylindrical, somewhat flattened above, with circular stem scars at intervals, about ½ in. in diameter and 2–3 in. or more long, with transverse ridges. Fracture short, waxy, yellowish. Taste, mucilaginous, sweetish, then bitter and acrid; odour, none.

Part Used: Rhizome.

Medicinal Use: Astringent, demulcent, tonic. Useful in female weakness, fluor albus, etc. Combined with other remedies, it may be given in pulmonary complaints and bleeding of lungs. The powdered root also makes an excellent poultice for bruises, piles, inflammations, and tumours. The infusion of 1 oz to 1 pt of boiling water is taken in wineglassful doses. Also used externally as an injection.

Gerard writes: "Galen saith that neither herbe nor root thereof is to be given inwardly; but not what experience hath found out specially among the vulgar sort of people in Hampshire which Galen, Dioscorides or any other that have written about plants have not so much as dreamed of; which is that if any of what age or sex soever chance to have any bones broken in what part of their bodies soever their refuge is to stampe the root hereof and give it unto the patient in ale to drinke, which sodereth and glues together the bones in very short space and very strongly, yea though the bones be but slenderly and unhandsomely placed and wrapped up. . . ." and also "Matthiolas teacheth that the water is drawn out of the roots wherewith the women of Italy use to scoure their faces from sunne-browning, freckles, morphew or any such deformities of the skinne."

SORREL

Rumex acetosa, Linn.
Fam. Polygonaceae

Habitat: Moist meadows in Europe and Great Britain.

Flowering Time: June and July.

Description: Leaves oblong, arrow-shaped below, rather firm, with a broad-toothed, membranous, stipular sheath round the stem at its base. Taste, acid and astringent; odour, none.

Part Used: Leaves.

Medicinal Use: Refrigerant, diuretic. May be used as a cooling drink in all febrile diseases. In cutaneous tumours the following preparation has been used: Burnt Alum 1 dr; Citric Acid 2 dr; inspissated juice of Sorrel 1 oz; water to 10 oz; applied as a paint.

Gerard writes: "The leaves of Sorrel taken in good quantitie, stamped and strained into some ale, and a posset made thereof, coole the sicke body, quench thirst, and allay the heate of such as are troubled with a pestilent fever, hot ague, or any great inflammation within."

Domestic Use: The leaves are occasionally eaten as a salad or boiled as spinach.

SOUTHERNWOOD

Artemisia abrotanum, Linn.
Fam. Compositae

Synonyms: Old Man, Lad's Love.

Habitat: A common plant in Great Britain and Europe.

Flowering Time: July and August.

Description: Leaves greyish green, stalked, twice pinnate, with very slender, linear, pointed segments, covered with minute white pubescence. Taste, bitterish, aromatic; odour, sweet, characteristic.

Part Used: Herb.

Medicinal Use: Stimulant, emmenagogue, antiseptic, detergent. This well-known garden plant is used to promote the flow of the menses. For worms in children it is given in teaspoonful doses of the powder in treacle morning and evening. The infusion of 1 oz of herb to 1 pt of boiling water is taken in wineglassful doses.

Culpeper calls the plant "a gallant mercurial plant worthy of more esteem than it hath." It is recommended by the old herbalists as an antidote to poisons and it was said that the burnt herb would drive away serpents.

Preparation: Liquid extract: Dose, $\frac{1}{2}$–1 dr.

CULPEPER states "The ashes thereof dries up and heals old ulcers that are without inflammation . . . the ashes mixed with old salad oil helps those that have hair fallen and are bald, causing the hair to grow again either on the head or beard."

SOYA BEANS

Glycine max, Linn.
Fam. Leguminosae

Synonyms: Soy Beans, Soja.

Habitat: China.

Description: The seeds are produced from hairy legumes containing two to five. The seeds themselves vary in colour from pale yellow to black. The cotyledons are surrounded by a leathery skin. Odour, slight; taste, oily.

Parts Used: Oil, flour.

Medicinal Use: The beans are chiefly used to produce an oil which is edible. The flour which is left after the oil has been expressed contains proteins and carbohydrates but no starch. The flour has, therefore, been used to manufacture food products, more especially for those suffering from diabetes. In America it has been recommended as a children's food in summer diarrhoea and similar complaints.

Domestic Use: The oil has been used in the manufacture of soap.

SPEARMINT

Mentha viridis, Linn.
Fam. Labiatae

Synonyms: Mackerel Mint, *Mentha spicata*, *Mentha crispa*, Peamint, Yerba buena, Mint.

Habitat: Europe, Asia, North Africa, Great Britain.

Flowering Time: July.

Description: The true Spearmint has sessile, elliptic-oblong sharply-serrate leaves, smooth and strong ribbed below. Taste and odour, characteristic. Flowers in axillary whorls approximately so as to form a tapering spike. In *Mentha cardiaca*, J. G. Baker, which is sometimes sold as Spearmint, the leaves are smaller, and the whorls of flowers are distant and leafy.

Parts Used: Herb, essential oil.

Medicinal Use: Stimulant, carminative, antispasmodic. This herb is added to many compounds on account of its carminative properties and its pleasant taste. The infusion of 1 oz in 1 pt of boiling water is taken in doses of a wineglassful or less as may be required. For infantile troubles generally the sweetened infusion is an excellent remedy.

Parkinson commends a decoction of Mint to wash the hands of children when suffering from scabs and blotches.

Preparations: Liquid extract: Dose, ¼–1 fl dr; Ol. Menth. Vir. U.S.P.; Aq. Menth. Vir. Conc.: Dose, 5–15 min; Aq. Menth. Vir. Dest.: Dose, ¼–1 fl oz; Aq. Menth. Vir. U.S.P.; Sp. Menth. Vir. U.S.P.: Dose, 15 min.

Biblical References: Matthew xxiii, 23; Luke xi, 42.

SPEEDWELL

Veronica officinalis, Linn.
Fam. Scrophulariaceae

Synonyms: Bird's-eye, Cat's-eye.

Habitat: A common wild plant in Europe and Great Britain.

Flowering Time: June and July.

Description: Stems slender and shortly hairy. Leaves opposite, oval, obtuse, serrate, shortly stalked, $\frac{1}{2}$–$\frac{3}{4}$ in. long, and $\frac{1}{4}$–$\frac{3}{8}$ in. broad. Flowers small, blue, in axillary spikes. Taste, bitter and astringent; odour, slightly tea-like when dry.

Speedwell is also referred to by some Welsh authors as Fluelin.

Part Used: Herb.

Medicinal Use: Alterative, expectorant, diuretic. Useful in coughs, catarrhs, etc. It promotes menstruation and is a simple and effective remedy in skin diseases.

SPEEDWELL was formerly used as a substitute for Tea, was believed to strengthen the frame, and was called by the French Thé de l'Europe.

SPIKENARD, AMERICAN

Aralia racemosa, Linn.
Fam. Araliaceae

Synonyms: Spignet, Pettymorrel, Indian Spikenard.

Habitat: North America.

Description: Rhizome oblique, 4–6 in. long, with prominent concave scars, about 1 in. broad in diameter. Roots about 1 in. thick at the base, pale-brown, wrinkled. Fracture short and whitish. Taste, aromatic; odour, similar.

Part Used: Rhizome.

Medicinal Use: Alterative, diaphoretic. Used in rheumatic, pulmonary, and cutaneous disorders. The infusion of $\frac{1}{2}$ oz in 1 pt of boiling water is taken in wineglassful doses.

Preparation: Liquid extract: Dose, $\frac{1}{2}$–1 dr.

SQUAW-VINE

Mitchella repens, Linn.
Fam. Rubiaceae

Synonyms: Partridgeberry, Checkerberry, Winter Clover, Deerberry.

Habitat: North America.

Description: Stem slender, with a deep furrow on one side, creeping. Leaves opposite, evergreen, nearly sessile, $\frac{3}{8}$ in. long and $\frac{1}{2}$ in. broad, roundish, broadly ovate and smooth. Flowers in pairs, corolla four-lobed, bearded inside, pinkish. Fruit baccate, red, four-seeded. Taste, astringent, bitter; odour, none.

Part Used: Herb.

Medicinal Use: Parturient, diuretic, astringent. Used in dropsy, diarrhoea, and suppression of urine. Has been found highly beneficial in uterine derangements, such as amenorrhoea, dysmenorrhoea, menorrhagia, etc. The decoction of 2 oz in 1 pt of water is taken in wineglassful doses.

Preparation: Liquid extract: Dose, $\frac{1}{2}$–1 dr.

SQUILL

Urginea maritima, Baker
Fam. Liliaceae

Synonym: *Scilla maritima*, Linn.

Habitat: Mediterranean countries.

Description: The large, bulbous root is usually cut up, and the dried curved segments, met with in commerce, are about $1\frac{1}{2}$–2 in. long and $\frac{1}{8}$–$\frac{1}{4}$ in. wide, yellowish white, tough, and often flexible. Fracture short. Taste, bitterish and acrid. The powder rapidly attracts moisture, and forms a solid mass unless air is excluded. Two varieties are used—White bulbs collected in Malta and Sicily and Red Squills collected in Algeria, which are generally used in France. The latter is also used as a rat poison.

Urginea, obtained from *Urginea indica*, or *U. maritima*, a smaller bulb than the European, is used in India and the East in place of European Squills and has the same properties.

Indian Squills are cut into slices and dried. The plant occurs in curved or sickle-shaped pieces generally connected, several together.

Part Used: Bulb.

Medicinal Use: Diuretic, expectorant, cathartic, emetic. Is useful in small doses to relieve irritation of mucous surfaces and check excessive secretions. Used extensively in dropsy not due to organic changes. Also as an expectorant in catarrh, asthma, pneumonia, cough, and chronic bronchial affections.

This is a very ancient medicine. Pliny was conversant with it and knew the two varieties. Dioscorides described the method of making vinegar of squills which is today a preparation in the B.P.C.

Preparations: Acet. Scill. B.P.C.: Dose, 10–30 min; Ext. Scill. Liq. B.P.C.: Dose, 1–3 min; Linct. Scill. B.P.C. 1949: Dose, 30–60 min; Linct. Scill. Opiate B.P.C.: Dose, 30–60 min; Linct. Scill. Opiat. pro infant. B.P.C.: Dose, 30–60 min; Oxymel Scill. B.P.C.: Dose, 30–60 min; Pil. Digit. Co. B.P.C.: Dose, 1 or 2 pills; Pil. Scill. Co. B.P.C. 1949: Dose, 1 or 2 pills; Syr. Opii Camph. B.P.C. 1949: Dose, 30–60 min; Syr. Scill. B.P.C.: Dose, 30–60 min; Powdered bulb: Dose, 1–3 gr; Tab. Digit. Co. B.P.C.: Dose, 1 or 2 tablets; Tinct. Scill. B.P.C.: Dose, 5–30 min.

ST. JOHN'S WORT

Hypericum perforatum, Linn.
Fam. Hypericaceae

Habitat: In woods and copses and open spaces in England.

Flowering Time: June and July, the seed ripening the end of July or beginning of August.

Description: Stem angular, 1–1½ ft high. Leaves opposite, sessile, oval, and oblong, with small black dots on the edges, and numerous transparent, round oil glands immersed in the surface. The name *perforatum* is due to the number of small hole-like dots in the leaf. Flowers yellow, with numerous stamens arranged in three bundles, and the ovary has three dark red styles. Taste, aromatic, bitter, and astringent.

Part Used: Herb.

Medicinal Use: Slightly astringent, expectorant, diuretic. Useful in coughs, colds, and all lung diseases generally. It is highly esteemed in affections of the urinary passages. The infusion of 1 oz to 1 pt of boiling water is taken in wineglassful doses. The fresh flowers infused in Olive Oil make the Oil of St. John's Wort, a healing application to wounds, sores, ulcers, and swellings.

Preparation: Liquid extract: Dose, ½–1 dr.

This herb is supposed to show its red spots on 29th August, the day on which St. John the Baptist was beheaded—hence its name. Also it was thought by some that, if hung in windows on the anniversary of St. John's birth, 24th June, it would keep away "ghosts, devils, imps, and thunderbolts."

STAR-ANISE

Illicium verum, Hook, f.
Fam. Magnoliaceae

Synonyms: Chinese Anise, Badiana, *Anisa stellata.*

Habitat: China.

Description: Fruits about 1 in. in diameter, formed of eight boat-shaped carpels, open when ripe, each containing one smooth, oval, polished brown seed. Pericarp brown, wrinkled below, and beaked at the apex. Taste, sweet, aromatic, fennel or anise-like; the odour is similar.

A spurious kind, the fruit *Illicium religiosum*, Sieb. and Zucc., with similar shape but rather shorter, with a turpentiney taste, imported from Japan, is sometimes met with. It possesses poisonous properties. The oil resembles Oil of Aniseed, and can only be distinguished by chemical tests.

Parts Used: Seeds, oil distilled from the seeds.

Medicinal Use: Stimulant, carminative, diuretic. For uses see Anise, which it resembles very much in properties and action.

Preparations: Powdered seeds: Dose, 10–20 gr; Ol. Anis. B.P.: Dose, 1–3 min, from which is made: Aq. Anis. Conc. B.P.C.: Dose, 5–15 min; Emuls. Anis. B.P.C.: Dose, 5–30 min; Emuls. Anis. et Menth. pip. B.P.C. 1949: Dose, 5–30 min; Sp. Anis. B.P.C. 1949: Dose, 5–20 min.

STAVESACRE

Delphinium staphisagria, Linn.
Fam. Ranunculaceae

Synonyms: Starvesacre, Staphisagris.

Habitat: Italy, Greece, Asia Minor.

Description: A herb growing to 3 or 4 ft in height. The seeds are greyish black, wrinkled and pitted, more or less triangular, or four-sided, with the back convex, about $\frac{3}{4}$ in. long and rather less in width, ten weighing about 6 gr. Albumen oily. Taste, bitter and tingling; odour, none.

Part Used: Seeds.

Medicinal Use: Vermifuge and vermin destroying. Used as lotion, wash or ointment in destroying lice in hair, etc.

Preparations: Lot. Staphisag.; Ung. Staphisag.

STOCKHOLM TAR

Pinus sylvestris, Linn.
(and other species)
Fam. Pinaceae

Synonyms: *Pix liquida*, Tar.

Description: Stockholm Tar is obtained by the destructive distillation of various species of Pinus stems and roots. It is a viscous liquid, dark brown or black in colour with a characteristic odour and acid taste.

Medicinal Use: Antiseptic, expectorant. Administered in cases of obstinate bronchial coughs and consumption. It is also used externally in the form of ointment for eczema and other skin diseases. Dose, 2–10 gr.

Preparations: Syr. Pic. Liq. B.P.C. 1949: Dose, 60–120 min; Ung. Pic. Liq. B.P.C.; Ung. Pic. Pin. U.S.P.

STONECROP, VIRGINIA

Penthorum sedoides, Linn.
Fam. Crassulaceae

Synonyms: Ditch Stonecrop, Penthorum.

Habitat: North America and the mountains of some parts of South America.

Description: Stem about 1 ft long. Leaves alternate, short-stalked, 2–3 in. long and one-third as broad, lanceolate, acute, serrate, smooth, and thin. Flowers small, greenish, in rows along the upper sides of the branches of the terminal cyme, five-parted, with 10 stamens. Taste, slightly astringent; odour, characteristic.

Part Used: Herb.

Medicinal Use: Astringent, laxative, demulcent. Has been employed successfully in the treatment of diarrhoea, haemorrhoids, cholera infantum, etc. It is of value in catarrhal gastric disorders in general. This drug is of undoubted power, and deserves a careful study.

Preparations: Fluid extract: Dose, $\frac{1}{2}$–1 dr.

STONE ROOT

Collinsonia canadensis, Linn.
Fam. Labiatae

Synonyms: Rich Weed, Rich Leaf, Knob Root, Knob Weed, Horsebalm, Horseweed.

Habitat: Canada.

Description: Rhizome brown-grey, about 4 in. long, with knotty, short, irregular branches, and numerous shallow stem-scars, very hard, with a thin bark, irregular woody wedges, and numerous brittle rootlets. Taste, bitterish, disagreeable; odour, none.

Part Used: Rhizome.

Medicinal Use: Stomachic, diuretic, tonic. Is regarded by many as a certain remedy in cases of gravel, stone in the bladder, piles, etc. As a general diuretic it is undoubtedly of great value. It is largely used among American veterinary surgeons as a diuretic. As a gargle use one part of fluid extract to three of water.

Preparations: Liquid extract: Dose, 15–60 drops; Collinsonin: Dose, 2–4 gr; Tinct. Collinson.: Dose, $\frac{1}{2}$–2 dr.

STORAX

Liquidambar orientalis, Mill.
Fam. Hamamelidaceae

Synonyms: Styrax, Prepared Storax, Liquid Storax, *Balsam Styracis*, Sweet Gum.

Habitat: South-west Asia Minor.

Description: A viscid, treacly liquid, greyish brown, opaque, heavier than water. In the early summer the tree is beaten, causing a flow of balsam. This is soaked up by the bark, which is boiled in water and pressed. This forms the Storax of commerce, which always contains water and pieces of vegetable fibre. This when warmed and strained forms Styrax (water strained) or, dissolved in alcohol, filtered and evaporated, Styrax Preparatus of the *British Pharmacopoeia.* The bruised bark when coarsely ground and mixed with Balsam of Storax is known as Styrax Calamitus. Taste, sharply pungent, burning, and aromatic; odour, recalling that of hyacinth.

Part Used: Balsam obtained by making incisions in the bark.

Medicinal Use: Expectorant, stimulant. Like most balsams it acts very beneficially upon the mucous membranes, and has been used internally in asthma, bronchitis, catarrh, cough, and pulmonary affections; externally in gleet, and leucorrhoea. The ointment forms a valuable application in a number of cutaneous disorders such as scabies, ringworm, etc. The dose is from 10–30 min.

STRAMONIUM

Datura stramonium, Linn.
Fam. Solanaceae

Synonyms: Thorn Apple, Jamestown Weed, Jimson Weed, Stinkweed.

Habitat: It grows commonly in the British Isles in waste places and it is also cultivated here and on the Continent for medicinal use.

Flowering Time: July.

Description: Stem widely forked or ternate. Leaves long-stalked, unequal at the base, somewhat fleshy, ovate, sinuate-dentate, with large, irregular, pointed teeth, glabrous when mature. Flowers white, tubular, with five teeth, funnel-shaped when open, falling off with the upper part of calyx. Capsule spiny. Taste, bitter and saline; odour, when fresh, rank and disagreeable, but tea-like when dried. The under surface of the leaf, when dry, is minutely wrinkled. Seeds, black, kidney-shaped, and flat, about $\frac{1}{6}$ in. long and $\frac{1}{24}$ in. thick, reticulated and finely pitted, the embryo coiled in white, oily albumen, parallel to the face of the seed.

Datura tatula is a variety of *Datura stramonium*, with violet corolla and purple veins. The plant is extensively cultivated in Hungary, and is generally greener and brighter than *Datura stramonium.*

Datura fastuosa, or Metel, and *Datura innoxia* are grown in India, where they have acquired a bad reputation as a secret poison used by criminals. The leaves contain from 0·2 to 0·5 per cent of alkaloids, chiefly scopolamine (hyoscine) and atropine, which varies according to the climatic conditions. Crops grown in England during a dry summer have exceeded the average alkaloidal strength of Italian or Hungarian plants, but generally the warmer climates produce the best results.

Parts Used: Leaves, seeds.

Medicinal Use: Antispasmodic, anodyne, narcotic. It acts similarly to Belladonna, and does not constipate. The inhalation of the smoke from the burning leaves is recommended for relieving attacks of asthma. It is a better cough remedy than opium, and it does not arrest secretions.

The old herbalists recommended the leaves for burns and scalds and inflammations used externally. Gerard instances the following: "The juice of the Thorn-apple boiled with Hog's grease to the form of an unguent or salve cures all inflammations whatsoever, all manner of burnings or scaldings as well as of fire, water, boiling lead, gunpowder as that which comes by lightning and that in a very short time as my selfe have found by my daily practice to my great credit and profit. The first experience came from Colchester where Mistress Lobel, a merchant's wife, there being most grievously burned by lightning and not finding ease or cure in any other thing, by this found helpe and was perfectly cured when all hope was past, by the report of Mr. William Ram, publique Notarie of the said towne."

Preparations: Ext. Stramon. Liq. B.P.: Dose, 1–3 min; Ext. Stramon. U.S.P.: Dose, $\frac{1}{3}$ gr; Ext. Stramon. Sicc. B.P.: Dose, $\frac{1}{4}$–1 gr; Mist. Lobel. et Stramon. Co. B.P.C.: Dose, $\frac{1}{2}$ fl oz; Mist. Stramon. et Ephed. pro Infant. B.P.C.: Dose, 60–120 min; Mist. Stramon. et Pot. Iod. B.P.C.: Dose, $\frac{1}{2}$ fl oz; Mist. Stramon. et Pot. Iod. pro Infant. B.P.C.: Dose, 60–120 min; Pulv. Lobel. Co. B.P.C. 1949; Pulv. Stramon. Co. B.P.C. 1949; Tab. Stramon. B.P.C.; Tinct. Stramon. B.P.: Dose, 10–30 min; Tinct. Stramon. U.S.P.: Dose, 12 min.

STRAWBERRY

Fragaria vesca, Linn.
Fam. Rosaceae

Habitat: Most parts of Europe and Great Britain.

Flowering Time: May and June.

Description: Leaves long-stalked, trifoliate, leaflets obovate, shortly stalked, paler beneath, 2–3 in. long, and 2–$2\frac{1}{2}$ in. broad, with large, serrate teeth, feather-veined, the veins erect, each ending in a tooth. Taste, astringent; odour, feeble.

Part Used: Leaves.

Medicinal Use: Mildly astringent, diuretic. Used in children's diarrhoea and affections of the urinary organs. The infusion of 1 oz to 1 pt of boiling water is taken in doses from a teaspoonful to a wineglassful.

Gerard writes: "The leaves boyled and applied in the manner of a pultis taketh away the burning heate of wounds: the decoction thereof strengthneth the gummes, and fastneth the teeth."

Domestic Use: The fruit is a delicious food and is used also in making jams.

STROPHANTHUS

Strophanthus kombe, Oliver
Fam. Apocynaceae

Habitat: Eastern Tropical Africa.

Description: A climbing plant producing greenish-brown seeds, ½ in. long and ⅛ in. broad, with appressed hairs, elliptical, furnished with a long awn. A section of the seed gives a deep-green colour with a mixture of strong sulphuric acid 8 parts, and water 2 parts, recently made. The seeds of *S. hispidus*, D.C., are smaller and brown, but give the same reaction.

Part Used: Seeds.

Medicinal Use: Cardiac tonic. Used in muscular debility of the heart and cardiac pains with dyspnoea. This drug should be used very cautiously owing to its great variation in strength. Used in Africa as an arrow poison.

Owing to the very poisonous nature of these seeds they should never be used except under medical direction.

Preparations: Strophanthin-K: Tinct. Strophanth. B.P.C. 1949: Dose, 2–5 min.

SUMACH, SMOOTH

Rhus glabra, Linn.
Fam. Anacardiaceae

Synonyms: Upland Sumach, Pennsylvania Sumach.

Habitat: Canada and U.S.A.

Description: The root-bark occurs in quilled pieces about 2 in. long and ⅛–¼ in. in diameter, dull reddish brown, with scattered transversely-oval lenticels. Fracture whitish or brown, with transverse rows of minute, blackish, linear oil cells. Taste, gummy, astringent; odour, none.

The berries are a deep crimson, ovoid or reniform, and covered with a short, velvety covering. They are odourless and have an acid taste.

Parts Used: Root-bark, berries.

Medicinal Use: Astringent, tonic. Berries: refrigerant, diuretic. The bark is useful in diarrhoea, dysentery, and leucorrhoea. The decoction of 1 oz to 1 pt of water is used in doses of a wineglassful or more internally, externally as an application or lotion. The berries are used in bowel complaints, febrile diseases, etc. An infusion of 1 oz of berries in 1 pt of boiling water is taken in wineglassful doses.

Preparations: Liquid extract; bark: Dose, 1–2 dr; Liquid extract, berries: Dose, 1–2 dr; Rhusin: Dose, 1–2 gr; Powdered berries: Dose, 10–30 gr.

SUMACH, SWEET

Rhus aromatica, Ait.
Fam. Anacardiaceae

Synonym: Fragrant Sumach.

Habitat: Canada and U.S.A.

Description: The root-bark occurs in small, quilled pieces about ¼ in. in diameter and 2 in. or more long, of a dirty-brown colour externally, with scattered, transversely oval, red-brown lenticels. Transverse fracture short, with radiate rows of minute, dark, flattened oil cells. Taste, mucilaginous; odour, none.

Part Used: Root-bark.

Medicinal Use: Astringent, diuretic. Largely used in diabetes and in the treatment of excessive discharges from kidneys and bladder. Valuable in treatment of incontinence of urine in children and aged persons. Also in leucorrhoea, diarrhoea, and dysentery. The infusion of 1 oz to 1 pt of boiling water is taken in wineglassful doses. Externally may also be used as an injection.

Preparation: Liquid extract: Dose, ½–1 dr.

SUMBUL

Ferula sumbul, Hook.
Fam. Umbelliferae

Synonym: Musk Root, because it was introduced into Russia about 1835 as a substitute for Musk. Afterwards cultivated in Russia.

Habitat: A Far Eastern plant.

Description: The root occurs in commerce in transverse slices, about 1–2 in., rarely up to 5 in., in diameter, and 1 in. or more thick; the bristling crown of the root and the tapering lower parts of the root also occur, externally covered with a thin, papery, dark-brown bark. The transverse section is dirty brown and resinous, marbled with white. The white part is seen to consist of a spongy, fibrous, mealy tissue. Taste, bitter and aromatic; odour, musky. The root is represented in commerce, at present, by that of *Ferula suaveolens*.

Part Used: Root.

Medicinal Use: Nerve stimulant, antispasmodic, tonic. Has been found very useful in nervous diseases, in low typhus fevers, asthma, bronchitis, etc. Also employed in amenorrhoea, hysteria, and other allied female disorders.

Preparations: Liquid extract: Dose, 10–60 drops; Solid extract: Dose, 4 gr; Tinct. Sumbul.: Dose, ½–1 dr.

SUNDEW

Drosera rotundifolia, Linn.
Fam. Droseraceae

Synonyms: Roundleaved Sundew, Dewplant, Red Rot, Youthwort, Rosa Solis. The name Sundew arises because of the numerous red hairs on the leaves upon which the moisture settles and does not disperse even on the hottest day. The sun shining on these hairs produces a dew-like effect.

Habitat: A plant growing in England and in Europe generally, usually in bogs and wet places or in moist woods.

Flowering Time: June, when the leaves are in the best condition for picking.

Description: Leaves all radical, six to ten in number, reddish, orbicular, fleshy, covered with stalked sticky glands. Flowering stem leafless, about 4 in. high, bearing small white flowers. An allied species, *D. longifolia*, Linn., has larger, linear-oblong leaves.

Part Used: Herb.

Medicinal Use: Pectoral, expectorant, demulcent, anti-asthmatic. Exerts a peculiar effect upon the respiratory organs. In small doses it is almost a specific in dry, spasmodic, and tickling coughs, also in whooping cough, for which it is considered a good prophylactic. An infusion of ½ oz in 1 pt of boiling water may be taken in tablespoonful doses as required. The fresh juice has been used as an application to warts and corns.

Culpeper says that "the leaves outwardly applied to the skin will raise blisters; but there are other things which will also draw blisters, yet nothing dangerous to be taken inwardly. There is a usual drink made thereof with aqua vitae and spices frequently and without any offence or danger but to good purpose used in qualms and passions of the heart."

Preparations: Liquid extract: Dose, 10–20 drops; Solid extract (alc.): Dose, 2–5 gr.

SUNFLOWER

Helianthus annuus, Linn.
Fam. Compositae

Synonym: Helianthus.

Habitat: Widely distributed in America, Europe, and the British Isles.

Flowering Time: July and August.

Description: Seeds, or more correctly fruits, opaque, white in colour, obovate or shortly wedge-shaped, broader and truncate at the apex, but convex, compressed on two sides which meet and form two sharp margins. The black variety has a black, glossy surface and is rather larger and thinner as a rule, but otherwise does not differ from the white variety, which sometimes has black, longitudinal stripes. Seed white, oily. Taste, nutty; odour, none.

As a matter of interest it is worthy of mention that the plant known as the Jerusalem Artichoke producing potato-like tubers for human food, is a variety of Helianthus (*Helianthus tuberosus*).

Part Used: Seeds (fruit).

Medicinal Use: Diuretic, expectorant. This drug has been successfully used in bronchial, laryngeal, and pulmonary affections, coughs, and colds. The following preparation has been found efficacious: Sunflower seeds, 2 oz, 1 qt of water; boil down to 12 oz and strain, add 6 oz of Hollands gin and 6 oz of sugar. The dose is 1–2 teaspoonfuls three to four times a day. An oil contained in the seeds has also been found to possess similar properties, and may be given in doses of 10–15 drops, or more, two to three times a day.

Sunflower leaves have also been used for the treatment of Malaria.

Domestic Use: The stems yield a fibre used in the textile industry.

SWAMP MILKWEED

Asclepias incarnata, Linn.
Fam. Asclepiadaceae

Synonyms: Swamp Silkweed, Rose-coloured Silkweed.

Habitat: U.S.A.

Description: Rhizome about 1 in. in diameter, irregularly globular or oblong, yellowish brown, hard, knotty, with a thin bark, tough, whitish wood, and rather thick central pith. Rootlets about 4 in. long, light brown. Taste, sweetish, acrid, and bitter; inodorous.

Parts Used: Root and rhizome.

Medicinal Use: Emetic, cathartic. Has been recommended in rheumatic, asthmatic, and catarrhal affection, and as a vermifuge. It acts as a good stomachic and a quick diuretic, and is taken as an infusion, hot or cold, made of ½ oz of root in powder to 1 pt of boiling water. The dose of the powder is from 15–60 gr.

T

TAG ALDER

Alnus serrulata, Willd.
Fam. Betulaceae

Synonyms: Common Alder, Smooth Alder, Red Alder, *Alnus rubra*, Desf.

Habitat: A well-known tree growing commonly in Europe, Great Britain, and America.

Flowering Time: April and May.

Description: Bark blackish grey, with small, corky warts, inner surface orange-brown, striated. Fracture uneven, but not fibrous. Taste, astringent and somewhat bitter; almost odourless.

Part Used: Bark.

Medicinal Use: Tonic, alterative, astringent, emetic. Used in scrofulous conditions. Also of importance in indigestion and dyspepsia caused by debility of stomach. Where diarrhoea is caused by the same complaints it will be found of great utility. The infusion of 1 oz of bark in 1 pt of boiling water is taken in wineglassful doses.

TAMARAC

Larix americana, Michx.
Fam. Coniferae

Synonyms: American Larch, Black Larch, Hackmetack, *Pinus pendula*, Salisb.

Habitat: U.S.A.

Description: In dull, purplish-brown fragments, about 1–2 in. broad and long, with irregular depressions on the outer surface, and smooth, finely striated on the inner. Fracture shortly fibrous and laminate. Taste, mucilaginous, astringent, and faintly terebinthenous; odour, none.

Part Used: Bark.

Medicinal Use: Alterative, diuretic, laxative. Recommended in jaundice, obstructions of liver, rheumatism, and cutaneous disorders. The decoction of the bark, combined with Spearmint, Juniper, Horseradish, etc., taken in wineglassful doses, has proved valuable in dropsy. Externally it has been used in piles, menorrhagia, dysmenorrhoea, etc.

TAMARINDS

Tamarindus indica, Linn.
Fam. Leguminosae

Synonyms: Tamarind fruit, Tamarind pulp, *Tamarindus officinalis*, Hook.

Habitat: A native of central Africa. Cultivated in India, the West Indies, and East Indies.

Description: West Indian Tamarinds consist of the fruits, after removal of the pericarp, preserved in syrup, and are the kind chiefly used in medicine. East Indian Tamarinds arrive without being preserved in syrup, but with the pericarp removed. Egyptian Tamarinds arrive pressed into bun-shaped cakes.

Parts Used: Fruit, pulp.

Medicinal Use: Nutritive, refrigerant, laxative. These form a part of confection of Senna, but they may be used equally well by themselves in doses of 2–4 dr. In smaller quantities and diluted with water they form an agreeable refrigerating drink in febrile diseases. One ounce of the pulp boiled in 1 pt of milk and strained forms Tamarind Whey.

Joseph Miller writes: "They are accounted Specific for all disorders of the Spleen, as being believed to lessen it much; nay they used to drink out of cups made of this wood to cure those illnesses."

TANSY

Tanacetum vulgare, Linn.
Fam. Compositae

Habitat: Europe and Great Britain.

Flowering Time: July.

Description: Stem with alternate, oblong leaves, about 6–8 in. long, and about 4 in. wide, deeply cut in a pinnate manner, dark green, with about twelve pointed, serrate segments on either side, and a terminal one, attached to a toothed midrib or rachis. Flowers yellow. Taste, bitter and aromatic; odour, strong and characteristic, disagreeable.

Parkinson writes of Tansy: "It is much used both in Lent and in the beginning of Spring while the Hearbe is young and tender, to make cures thereof with egges fried, which are called Tansies and are very profitable for those stomackes, that are troubled with bad humours cleaving thereunto. . . ."

Part Used: Herb.

Medicinal Use: Anthelmintic, tonic, emmenagogue. Largely used for expelling worms in children. Also valuable in female disorders, such as hysteria, nausea, etc., and in kidney weakness. The infusion of 1 oz to 1 pt of boiling water should be taken in teacupful doses night and morning, fasting for worms. In other complaints, a wineglassful repeated frequently.

Preparations: Liquid extract: Dose, ½–2 dr; Solid extract: Dose, 5–10 gr.

TAPIOCA

Jatropha manihot, Linn.
Fam. Euphorbiaceae

Synonyms: Manihot, Mandioc, Tapioca Meal, Brazilian Arrowroot, Cassava Starch, *Manihot utilissima*, Pohl, *Janipha manihot*, Kunth.

Habitat: Brazil.

Description: Tapioca, like sago, is often prepared from potato starch. Under the microscope, the genuine is easily distinguished, especially in the form of meal, by the truncate, muller-shaped starch grains, with a central hilum.

Tapioca is prepared from the root of the plant which itself is poisonous. The poisonous ingredient, however, is volatile and is driven off in the process of manufacture.

Part Used: Root-starch.

Medicinal Use: Nutritive, demulcent. It makes an excellent article of diet for infants and invalids, and may be sweetened or used in combination with fruits, preserves, wines, or spices.

TEA

Camellia sinensis, Linn.
Fam. Theaceae

Synonyms: *Thea chinensis*, Sims, *Camellia theifera*, Griff.

Habitat: Ceylon, Assam, Java, China.

Medicinal Use: An evergreen shrub grown in the hills. The leafbuds, together with two or three youngest leaves, are collected, and allowed to wither. They are then rolled and fermented, when the colour changes from green to black; part of the tannin is oxidized, and traces of volatile oil are produced. Green Tea is obtained by drying over a fire, in which case the tannin is not oxidized and the leaves retain their green colour. The principal constituents are Caffein and Tannin.

Part Used: Leaves.

Medicinal Use: Stimulant, astringent. Its general effect is stimulating, and it also acts as a nerve sedative and frequently relieves headache. Occasionally it causes unpleasant nervous and digestive disturbances.

Domestic Use: Tea is perhaps one of the most important articles in the domestic economy, where freshly-made infusions form the beverage at one or more meals during the day. It was rarely used in Elizabethan days.

THUJA

Thuja occidentalis, Linn.
Fam. Coniferae

Synonyms: Arbor Vitae, Yellow Cedar, Tree of Life, False White Cedar.

Habitat: Canada and U.S.A. It is sometimes cultivated in English and European gardens but does not grow to any height.

Description: The spreading, flat, fan-shaped, pinnate branches are furnished with scale-like leaves so closely imbricated and appressed that they are easily overlooked. They are opposite, broadly awl-shaped, the points projecting more on the stems than on the branchlets. Taste, bitter and camphoraceous; odour, recalling strawberries and juniper, characteristic, not agreeable.

Parts Used: Leaves and tops.

Medicinal Use: Anthelmintic, irritant, expectorant, emmenagogue. Recommended in chronic coughs, fevers, gout, amenorrhoea, etc. It is also used as an outward application for the removal of warts and fungoid growths. The infusion of 1 oz in 1 pt of boiling water is taken internally in tablespoonful to wineglassful doses; also used externally as a lotion or injection.

Parkinson writes: "Although we have no forraigne experience to report to you, yet upon tryall of the leaves by some in our owne land, we have found that they that were long time troubled with a purulentous cough, and shortnesse of breath, have been much releived and holpen thereof by use of the leaves taken fasting with some bread and butter . . . for some dayes together. . . ."

Preparation: Liquid extract: Dose, $\frac{1}{3}$–1 dr.

THYME

Thymus vulgaris, Linn.
Fam. Labiatae

Synonyms: Garden or Common Thyme, Tomillo.

Habitat: Native to the southern parts of Europe but cultivated in kitchen gardens in Great Britain and America.

Flowering Time: July.

Description: Stems 4–8 in. high, with opposite, small, elliptical, greenish-grey, shortly-stalked leaves, about $\frac{1}{3}$ in. long and $\frac{1}{16}$ in. broad, reflexed at the margin. Taste and odour aromatic.

The garden variety known as Lemon Thyme has a lemon flavour as well as that of Thyme proper, and differs in the rather broader leaves not recurved at the margin, and is referred by botanists to the next species as var. *citriodorus*.

Part Used: Herb.

Medicinal Use: Tonic, antiseptic, antispasmodic. Generally used in combination with other remedies. The infusion of 1 oz in 1 pt of boiling water is taken in doses of a wineglassful repeated frequently.

Culpeper describes it as "a noble strengthener of the lungs, as notable a one as grows; neither is there scarce a better remedy growing for that disease in children which they commonly call Chin-cough than it is."

Preparations: Elix. Thym. B.P.C. 1949: Dose, 1–2 dr; Ext. Thym. Liq. B.P.C. 1949: Dose, 10–60 min; Linct. Diamorph. et Thym.: Dose, ½–1 dr; Oil: Dose, 1–5 min.

THYME, WILD

Thymus serpyllum, Linn.
Fam. Labiatae

Synonyms: Mother of Thyme, Serpyllum.

Habitat: A common wild plant in Europe and Great Britain.

Flowering Time: July.

Description: Plant resembling the last, but the leaves are ⅛ in. broad, tapering below, green, ciliate at the base, not recurved at the margins, and have the veins prominent on the under surface. The odour is weaker than that of *Thymus vulgaris*.

Part Used: Herb

Medicinal Use: Antispasmodic, carminative, tonic. Favourable results have been obtained in convulsive coughs, whooping cough, catarrh, and sore throat from the use of this herb. The infusion should be given. It is prepared with 1 oz of herb to 1 pt of boiling water, sweetened with sugar or honey and made demulcent by Linseed or Acacia. This is given in doses of one or more tablespoonfuls several times daily.

Culpeper states: "It is under the dominion of Venus and under the sign of Aries and therefore chiefly appropriated to the head. . . . If you make a vinegar of the herb and anoint the head with it, it presently stops the pains thereof. It is excellently good to be given either in phrenzy or lethargy, although they are two contrary diseases."

TOADFLAX, YELLOW

Linaria vulgaris, Mill.
Fam. Scrophulariaceae

Synonyms: Flaxweed, Pennywort, Butter and Eggs.

Habitat: Europe and Great Britain, usually on dry banks and in corn fields.

Flowering Time: July to September.

Description: Pale yellow flowers, mouth closed by deep-orange lower lip, grow in numbers crowded together at end of stem. It derives its name from the fancied resemblance of the flowers to a toad. Stem upright, 1–2 ft high, branches but slightly. Leaves many, grass-like, narrow, taper to a point, smooth, pale-bluish tint.

In some books this is called Fluellin.

Part Used: Herb.

Medicinal Use: Astringent, hepatic, detergent. Is recommended as an alterative in jaundice, liver, skin diseases, and scrofula. An ointment made from the fresh plant forms a good application for piles. An infusion of 1 oz to 1 pt of water is taken in the usual way.

The old writers considered it a powerful diuretic, cathartic, and deobstruent. It was therefore recommended by Tragus to carry off the water of dropsies and to remove obstructions of the liver, etc.

TOBACCO

Nicotiana tabacum, Linn.
(and other species)
Fam. Solanaceae

Synonyms: Leaf Tobacco, Tobacco Leaf, Tobacca.

Habitat: A native of America but now cultivated in many sub-tropical countries. The plant is cultivated in a small way in England.

Description: Tobacco is so well known that a description is needless. Several species are employed to yield tobacco. *N. tabacum* yields Virginian; *N. acuminata*, R. Grah., Latakia; *N. rustica*, Linn., a good deal of Persian tobacco; but there are many varieties of *N. tabacum* itself. Some of these can be distinguished under the microscope.

Part Used: Leaves.

Medicinal Use: Narcotic, sedative, emetic. In the employment of Tobacco as a medicinal agent much care should be exercised, as it produces great depression, emesis, and convulsions, sometimes by very moderate doses. Internally it is for this reason seldom used. As an ointment, made by simmering the leaves in lard, it has been employed in curing old ulcers and painful tumours. The leaves were official in B.P. 1885.

TOLU BALSAM

Myroxylon balsamum, Harms.
Fam. Leguminosae

Synonyms: Balsam Tolu, *Toluifera balsamum*, Baill.

Habitat: Columbia.

Description: A light-brown, fragrant, balsamic, resin, softening in the warm hand, but on keeping becomes brittle in winter. In a thin, even layer between two warmed pieces of glass it is seen to be transparent and to contain numerous crystals of cinnamic acid. Taste, sweetly aromatic and faintly acid; odour, recalling vanilla, but different. Obtained by tapping and collecting the balsam in gourds.

Part Used: Balsam.

Medicinal Use: Stimulant, tonic, expectorant. Used in chronic catarrhs, pulmonary and bronchial affections, coughs, etc.

Preparations: Dose of Balsam: 5–15 gr; Linct. Codein B.P.C.: Dose, 30–60 min; Linct. Diamorph. et Hyoscy. B.P.C. 1949: Dose, 30–120 min; Linct. Tolu Co. pro infant. B.P.C.: Dose, 30–60 min; Liq. Tolu B.P.C.; Syr. Tolu B.P.: Dose, 30–120 min; Syr. Tolu U.S.P.; Tinct. Tolu B.P.C.: Dose, 30–60 min; Tinct. Tolu U.S.P.: Dose, 30 min.

TONKA BEANS

Dipteryx odorata, Willd.
Dipteryx oppositifolia, Willd.
Fam. Leguminosae

Synonyms: *Coumarouna odorata*, Aubl., Tonguin Beans, Tonco Beans.

Habitat: *Odorata,* a native of Guiana; *Oppositifolia,* a native of Brazil.

Description: The beans are about 1–2 in. long, black, wrinkled, nearly ½ in. in diameter, flattened, with one edge sharp. They vary in size and appearance. The Surinam beans are often greyish, and the largest, Angustura beans, are more slender, long, and shining; the Para shorter and smaller. Some varieties are covered with a greyish efflorescence of crystals of coumarin. These have been steeped in rum, which removes a good deal of the coumarin. The odour resembles that of new-mown hay.

Part Used: Seeds.

Medicinal Use: Aromatic, narcotic, cardiac tonic. Although this drug has been used in whooping cough, it seems to have fallen into disuse, probably owing to its heart-paralysing effects in large doses. It contains an odorous principle, Coumarin.

Domestic Use: Owing to their aromatic nature the seeds are used in perfumery and in the making of essences.

TORMENTILLA

Potentilla tormentilla, Neck.
Fam. Rosaceae

Synonym: Septfoil.

Habitat: Europe and Great Britain.

Flowering Time: June and July.

Description: The plant produces long, slender stalks. Leaves are long and narrow, serrated at the ends. Flowers of four petals are small, and yellow in colour. The root appears in dull, brown, hard, cylindrical, shortly-tapering pieces, rough on the surface, with irregularly-rounded elevations, and pits or depressed stem scars, and minute scars of filiform rootlets. Fracture short, light brownish red, showing small, distant wood bundles in one or two distant circles, and a large pith.

Parts Used: Usually the root, but occasionally the herb.

Medicinal Use: Tonic, astringent. The root being the stronger is mostly used and may be given in all cases of relaxed bowels, diarrhoea, cholera, etc. The infusion of 1 oz of herb to 1 pt of boiling water is taken in wine-glassful doses as required. As a lotion it is applied to ulcers and old sores as a wash. The fluid extract acts as a styptic to cuts, wounds, etc. This root may be regarded as one of the safest and most powerful of astringents.

Preparation: Liquid extract, root: Dose, ½–1 dr.

TORMENTILLA was regarded as a counter-poison of great value by the Elizabethan apothecaries and Parkinson writes: ". . . and so doth also the distilled water of the herbe and roote, rightly made and prepared, which is to steepe them in wine for a night and then distilled in Balneo marie; this water in this manner prepared taken with some Venice Treakle, and thereupon being presently laid to sweate, will certainly by God's helpe, expell any venome or poyson, or the plague, or any fever or horror, or the shaking fit that happeneth. . . ."

TRAGACANTH

Astragalus gummifer, Labill.
(and other species)
Fam. Leguminosae

Synonyms: Gum Tragacanth, Syrian Tragacanth, Green Dragon. The plant from which the gum is derived was known as Goat's Thorn.

Habitat: Persia, Asiatic Turkey, and some parts of Southern and Eastern Europe.

Description: The plant is a thorny shrub. The stem is incised, the gum exudes and dries in ribbon-shaped pieces or flakes. The first tapping is white, then lemon-coloured, and finally yellow. An inferior quality known as Hog or Caramaria Gum consists of dark tears and irregular masses mixed with fragments of bark. Indian Tragacanth or Karaya Gum, from *Sterculia urens*, occurs in pale-yellow pieces, often vermiform, with fragments of bark attached. This is often used to adulterate Tragacanth Powder. Tragacanth loses on drying about 14 per cent of water. It swells up in water and forms a mucilage with even 50 parts of water, but only a portion of it soluble. It dissolves in alkali, but gives a yellow solution. It yields only 4 per cent of ash.

Part Used: Gummy exudation.

Medicinal Use: Mucilaginous, demulcent. Occasionally it is used as a remedy in cough or diarrhoea where demulcents are desirable, but mostly in the shape of a mucilage for the purpose of suspending heavy, water-insoluble powders, such as bismuth or zinc preparations. The powder forms an ingredient in most lozenges and in many emulsions.

Preparations: Glycer. Trag. B.P.C. 1949; Mucil. Trag. B.P. and U.S.P.; Past. Trag. Co. B.P.C.; Pulv. Acac. et Trag. B.P.C. 1949; Pulv. Trag. Co. B.P.: Dose, 10–60 gr.

TREE OF HEAVEN

Ailanthus glandulosa, Desf.
Fam. Rutaceae

Synonyms: Ailanto, Chinese Sumach, Tree of the Gods.

Habitat: Europe.

Description: Bark brownish grey, with numerous warts, and on some pieces large, triangular scars of leaf base; the inner surface is striated longitudinally. Fracture short, in the outer, pale buff-coloured and fibrous in the inner part, the fibres forming a porous layer. Taste, bitter and slightly acrid; odour, scarcely any.

Parts Used: Bark, root-bark.

Medicinal Use: Antispasmodic, cardiac depressant, astringent. The bark has been used with success in dysentery, diarrhoea, leucorrhoea and also for tape-worm; but its nauseating effects upon human beings render it undesirable. The root-bark is employed in heart complaints, asthma, and epilepsy. The doses should not exceed 20 gr of the powder. The leaves of this tree have been used in France for adulterating mint and when rubbed and mixed they are only identifiable by means of a microscope.

TURKEY CORN

Dicentra canadensis, Walt.
Dicentra cucullaria, Bernh.
Fam. Papaveraceae

Synonyms: Turkey Pea, Squirrel Corn, Staggerweed, Corydalis, *Corydalis canadensis*, Goldb.

Habitat: Canada and U.S.A.

Description: Tubers tawny yellow, about ¼ in. in diameter, globose-depressed, with a scar on both the depressed sides, internally horny, or somewhat mealy as well. Taste, bitter; inodorous.

Part Used: Root.

Medicinal Use: Tonic, diuretic, alterative. It is generally combined with other remedies and acts especially well in conjunction with Queen's Delight, Burdock, or Prickly Ash. It is also recommended in menstrual complaints. The infusion of ½ oz to 1 pt of boiling water is taken in wineglassful doses.

Preparations: Liquid extract: Dose, ½–1 dr; Corydalin: Dose, 2 gr.

TURMERIC

Curcuma longa, Linn.
Fam. Zingiberaceae

Synonyms: Curcuma, *Curcuma rotunda*, Linn., *Amomum curcuma*, Jacq.

Habitat: Southern Asia.

Description: Turmeric occurs in commerce in several varieties. The Madras kind is sold in both round and long pieces. The round pieces, or bulbs, are the large central rhizome, about the size of the pigeon's egg, and are more or less pyriform, and marked with transverse ridges or leaf scars, and the long are the lateral rhizomes. Both are yellowish brown internally, with a short fracture. The Madras kind is preferred for flavouring purposes. The Bengal kind occurs in smaller, cylindrical pieces, greyish externally, and about ½ in. in diameter, and dark brownish yellow internally, with a resinous fracture. It is preferred for dyeing purposes. Taste, aromatic; odour, characteristic. The roots are boiled when collected, which gelatinizes the starch, giving them a horny consistence and diffusing the colour throughout the drug.

Part Used: Rhizome.

Medicinal Use: Carminative, stimulating but seldom used in medicine.

Domestic Use: As an ingredient in curry powders; also in cattle condiments. It is sometimes used as a colouring agent.

TURPENTINE

Oil distilled from: *Pinus palustris*, Mill.
Pinus maritima, Lam.
(and other species)
Fam. Pinaceae

Medicinal Use: Rubefacient, irritant, diuretic. Administered internally, it acts upon the urinary apparatus, and is valued as a remedy in chronic affections of the kidneys and bladder, gleet, and diseases of the mucous membranes of the respiratory organs. Externally, it is used most frequently in liniments and embrocations as an application for rheumatism and chest complaints. Terebene, which is prepared from Turpentine, is valued as an inhalation in cases of colds and bronchitis, either by itself or mixed with other oils.

Preparations: Ol. Terebinth. B.P.: Dose, 3–10 min; Lin. Alb. B.P.C.; Lin. Terebinth. B.P.; Lin. Terebinth. Acet. B.P.C.; Terebene B.P.C.; Pix. Liquida B.P. and Pine Tar U.S.P. are made from the same trees and form ingredients in Syr. Pic. Liq. B.P.C. 1949: Dose, 60–120 min; Ung. Pic. Liq. B.P.C.; Ung. Pic. Liq. U.S.P.

TURPETH

Ipomoea turpethum, R. Br.
Fam. Convolvulaceae

Synonym: Turpeth Root.

Habitat: India, Ceylon, Malay Archipelago, N. Australia.

Description: The root appears in commerce in varying lengths and thicknesses. It is deeply wrinkled and a dull grey or brown colour. Odour faint; taste, nauseous. It contains 5–10 per cent of a purgative resin.

Part Used: Root.

Medicinal Use: Cathartic, purgative. Used in India for similar purposes as Jalap, which it resembles closely in its action. Dose, 5–20 gr.

U

UNICORN ROOT, FALSE

Chamaelirium luteum, A. Gray
Fam. Liliaceae

Synonyms: Starwort, Helonias, *Helonias dioica*, Pursh, *Helonias lutea*, Ker-Gawl., *Chamaelirium carolinianum*, Willd.

Habitat: U.S.A.

Description: Rhizome about 1 in. long and ¼ in. thick, nearly cylindrical, ringed transversely, greyish brown, with a few stem scars on the upper, and wiry rootlets on the lower, side. Fracture horny, wood bundles numerous in the centre. Taste, bitter; inodorous.

Part Used: Rhizome.

Medicinal Use: Tonic, diuretic. Acts as a general tonic in dyspepsia and in weakness of the reproductive organs. Also given in spermatorrhoea.

Preparations: Liquid extract: Dose, ½–1 dr; Helonin: Dose, 2–4 gr.

UNICORN ROOT, TRUE

Aletris farinosa, Linn.
Fam. Liliaceae

Synonyms: Blazing Star, Star Grass, Colic Root.

Habitat: U.S.A.

Description: Rhizome brownish grey, flattened, and tufted at the upper side with leaf bases, convex, with numerous wiry rootlets, on the lower side, about 1¼ in. long and ⅛ in. thick, indistinctly jointed. Fracture mealy, white, somewhat fibrous. Taste, bitter; inodorous.

Part Used: Rhizome.

Medicinal Use: Tonic and stomachic. As a female tonic it has but few equals and may be given in all cases of debility. Small doses only should be given, as large ones produce nausea and giddiness.

Preparations: Elix. Aletr.: Dose, ½–1 dr; Ext. Aletr. Liq.: Dose, 5–15 min; Powdered root: Dose, 5–10 gr; Aletrin: Dose, ½–2 gr.

UVA-URSI

Arctostaphylos uva-ursi, Spreng.
Fam. Ericaceae

Synonyms: Bearberry, Rockberry, Mountain Box.

Habitat: Central and Northern Europe, North America, Great Britain.

Flowering Time: May.

Description: An evergreen shrub. Leaves leathery, obovate or oblanceolate, rounded at the apex, dark green and shining above, and tesselated by sunken veinlets, paler beneath and reticulated, with dark veinlets; margin entire and reflexed, about $\frac{3}{4}$–1 in. long and $\frac{1}{4}$–$\frac{3}{8}$ in. broad. Taste, astringent; odour, faintly tea-like.

Part Used: Leaves.

Medicinal Use: Mucilaginous, astringent, diuretic. Has a specific action on the urinary organs and is especially useful in cases of gravel, ulceration of kidneys or bladder, catarrh, gleet, leucorrhoea, and menorrhagia. The infusion of 1 oz to 1 pt of boiling water is taken in wineglassful doses three to four times a day.

Preparations: Liquid extract: Dose, $\frac{1}{2}$–1 dr; Inf. Uvae Ursi Conc.: Dose, $\frac{1}{2}$–1 dr; Inf. Uvae Ursi Rec.: Dose, $\frac{1}{2}$–1 fl oz.

V

VALERIAN *Valeriana officinalis*, Linn.
Fam. Valerianaceae

Synonyms: Great Wild Valerian, Setwall.

Habitat: Watery places in the British Isles. Some of the best specimens are to be seen in Derbyshire. Also imported from European sources.

Flowering Time: May.

Description: The root is at once distinguished by its strong and disagreeable odour. It consists of a short root-stock, about ¾ in. long and ½ in. in diameter, with numerous short lateral branches, and rootlets 3 or 4 in. long, the crown often showing the lead scales of the stem base. The transverse section is horny with a very narrow woody ring, and is of a pale, grey-brown colour. Old roots are often hollow. Taste, sweetish, bitter; odour, characteristic.

Part Used: Rhizome.

Medicinal Use: Anodyne, antispasmodic, nervine. May be given in all cases of nervous debility and irritation; also in hysterical affections. It allays pain and promotes sleep. Is strongly nervine without any narcotic effects, and enters into various herbal nervine and antispasmodic compounds. The infusion of 1 oz to 1 pt of boiling water is taken in wineglassful doses. Indian Valerian, derived from *Valeriana wallichii*, D.C., grows in the Himalayas, and is practically identical in action to the European variety. The ammoniated tincture of this root may be used in the same doses as the B.P.C. ammoniated tincture.

According to Gerard: "Dioscorides teacheth that the dry root is put into counterpoysons and medicines preservative against the pestilence, as are treacles, mithridates and such like; whereupon it hath been (and is to this day among the poore people of our Northern parts) in such veneration amongst them that no broths, pottage or physicall meats are worth anything if Setwall were not at an end: whereupon some woman poet or other hath made these verses.

They that will have their heale
Must put Setwall in their Keale."

Preparations: Elix. Valerian. et Chloral. Co. B.P.C. 1949: Dose, ½–1 fl oz; Ext. Valerian. B.P.C.: Dose, 1–5 gr; Ext. Valerian. Liq. B.P.C.: Dose, 5–15 min; Inf. Valerian. Conc. B.P.C.: Dose, 30–60 min; Inf. Valerian. Rec. B.P.C. 1949: Dose, ½–1 fl oz; Mist. Pot. Brom. et Valerian. B.P.C.: Dose, ½–1 fl oz; Tinct. Valerian. Ammon. B.P.C.: Dose, 30–60 min; Tinct. Valerian. Simp. B.P.C. 1949: Dose, 60–120 min.

VERNAL GRASS, SWEET

Anthoxanthum odoratum, Linn.
Fam. Graminaceae

Habitat: Europe and temperate Asia. Common in Great Britain.

Flowering Time: Spring and early Summer. Sometimes it flowers again in Autumn.

Description: Flowers in dense spikes, tapering at both ends, about 1½ in. long and ⅓ in. wide. It is distinguished from the allied genera by having only two stamens in the flowers, and by its aromatic, hay-like taste.

Part Used: Flowers.

Medicinal Use: It has been used in hay fever, internally in the form of a tincture and externally as a snuff.

Preparation: Tincture of fresh plant 1 in 10 of 40 O.P. Spirit: Dose, 2–6 min internally for hay fever. The Tincture may be diluted and used as a nasal lotion.

VERVAIN

Verbena officinalis, Linn.
Fam. Verbenaceae

Synonym: Verbena hastata, Linn.

Habitat: As Culpeper states, "It grows generally throughout this land in divers places of the hedges and waysides and other waste grounds."

Flowering Time: July, the seed ripening soon after.

Description: Stem 1–2 ft high, quadrangular. Leaves distant and opposite, pinnately-lobed, serrate, rough. Flowers small, pinkish blue, two-lipped, with didynamous stamens and an entire, four-seeded ovary. Taste, very bitter; odour, when rubbed, slightly aromatic.

Part Used: Herb.

Medicinal Use: Nervine, tonic, emetic, sudorific. May be employed with advantage in the early stages of fevers, colds, etc., and in the treatment of fits, convulsions, and nervous disorders. The sweetened infusion of 1 oz to 1 pt of boiling water is a good remedy for coughs, colds, etc., when taken frequently in wineglassful doses.

Pliny is reported to have said that "If the dining roome be sprinkled with

GERARD writes: "It is reported to be of singular force against Tertian and Quartaine Fevers but you must observe Mother Bombie's rules to take just so many knots or sprigs and no more, lest it fall out so that you do no good, if you catch no harme by it. Many odde old wives fables are written of Vervaine tending to witchcraft and sorcery."

water in which the herbe hath been steeped the guests will be the merrier."

Dioscorides also mentions this.

Joseph Miller states: "The whole herb is used being accounted cephalic and good against diseases from cold and phlegmatic causes; it opens obstructions of the Liver and Spleen, helps the Jaundice and Gout, and applied outwardly is reckon'd vulnerary and good for sore watery inflamed eyes."

Preparation: Fluid extract: Dose, $\frac{1}{2}$–1 dr.

VIOLET

Viola odorata, Linn.
Fam. Violaceae

Synonyms: Blue Violet, Sweet Violet.

Habitat: Widely found in Europe, Asia, and the British Isles.

Description: The leaves are cordate-ovate, obtuse, with long stalks bearing deflexed hairs. Flowers blue, with a hooked stigma, and a short spur inflated at the end and channelled above. In a blue variety of *Viola tricolor*, sometimes preferred for colouring purposes, the stigma is inflated, not hooked. The flowers of *V. calcarata*, with oblong sepals and a corolla spur twice as long as the sepals, are also sold under this name.

Parts Used: Leaves, flowers.

Medicinal Use: Antiseptic, expectorant. Violet leaves contain certain glucosidal principles, not yet fully investigated, but of distinct antiseptic properties.

The flowers possess expectorant properties, and have long been used in syrup form for coughs, colds, etc.

It has been recommended and used with benefit to allay pain in cancerous growths—some even say to cure cancer. In 1902 Lady Margaret Marsham, of Maidstone, cured from cancer of the throat by infusion of Violet Leaves, published the recipe. The relief was almost immediate. In a week the external hard swelling had gone, and in a fortnight the cancer on the tonsil had disappeared. Pour a pint of boiling water on to a handful of fresh Violet Leaves and stand for twelve hours. Strain when required. Apply to the affected part and cover with a piece of oilskin. Change the lint when dry or cold. Another report states that a gentleman aged 45 was cured of cancer by drinking 1 pt of infusion of Violet Leaves prepared from the dry leaves, and also by fomentation with the hot liquor. Or a poultice may be made and used in similar manner.

W

WAFER ASH *Ptelea trifoliata*, Linn.
Fam. Rutaceae

Synonyms: Wingseed, Hop Tree, Shrubby Trefoil, Ptelea, Swamp Dogwood.
Habitat: U.S.A. and Canada.
Description: The root-bark occurs in quilled or curved pieces, about $1\frac{1}{2}$–3 in. long, $\frac{1}{2}$–$\frac{3}{4}$ in. in diameter and $\frac{1}{8}$–$\frac{3}{4}$ in. thick, transversely wrinkled, with a whitish-brown, or pale-buff, exfoliating surface of thin, papery layers, the inner surface nearly smooth, with faintly projecting medullary rays. Transverse fracture short, yellowish white, the papery layer pale buff. Taste, bitter; inodorous.
Part Used: Root-bark.
Medicinal Use: Tonic, antiperiodic, stomachic. In all cases of debility and during intermittent and remittent febrile diseases, where a tonic is indicated, this drug can be employed with benefit. It has a soothing influence upon the mucous membrane and promotes appetite, being tolerated when other tonics cannot be retained. The powdered bark is given in doses of 10–30 gr. The infusion is taken in tablespoonful doses three to four times a day.

WAHOO *Euonymus atropurpureus*, Jacq.
Fam. Celastraceae

Synonyms: Indian Arrowroot, Burning Bush, Spindle Tree, Euonymus.
Habitat: U.S.A.
Description: The root-bark occurs in quilled or curved pieces about $\frac{1}{12}$ in. thick, ash grey, with blackish ridges or patches, outer surface whitish or slightly tawny. Fracture friable, smooth, whitish, the inner layer appearing tangentially striated. Taste, sweetish, bitter, and acrid; nearly inodorous. The stembark is in longer quills, with a smooth outer surface with lichens usually present on it, and a greenish layer under the epidermis.
Parts Used: Root-bark, bark.
Medicinal Use: Tonic, alterative, cholagogue, laxative. Valuable in liver disorders, especially those following or accompanied by fever. For constipation due to inactivity of liver it may be given with every confidence, especially as its action is mild and non-irritant. The concentration "Euonymin" is generally used in pill form and in combination with other tonics, laxatives, etc.

Preparations: Elix. Euonym. et Pulsat: Dose, 1–4 dr; Ext. Euonym. B.P.C. 1949 (Syn., Euonymin): Dose, 1–2 gr; Liq. Euonym. et Iridin: Dose, ½–1 dr; Liq. Euonym. et Pepsin: Dose, ½–1 dr; Tinct. Euonym. B.P.C. 1949: Dose, 10–40 min.

WAKE ROBIN, AMERICAN

Arum triphyllum, Linn.
Fam. Araceae

Synonyms: Wild Turnip, Indian Turnip, Dragon Root, Jack-in-the-pulpit, *Arisaema triphyllum*, Schott.

Habitat: U.S.A.

Description: Root about 1–2 in. broad, depressed globular, with a ring of simple rootlets above, the surface wrinkled below, brown-grey, internally white and mealy, with scattered wood bundles. In slices 1–2 in. in diameter and ¼ in. thick, brownish white at the margins, the transverse surfaces white, starchy, with numerous pale-brown dots indicating the scattered wood-bundles. Taste, burning and acrid; odour, none.

Part Used: Root.

Medicinal Use: Expectorant, diaphoretic. Recommended in croup, whooping cough, cough, bronchitis, laryngitis, pains in chest, etc. Also useful in flatulence, asthma, and colic.

Preparation: Powdered root: Dose, 10–30 gr.

WALNUT

Juglans regia, Linn.
Fam. Juglandaceae

Habitat: Probably a native of Persia but now cultivated in many countries including Great Britain.

Flowering Time: April and May. The nut ripens towards the end of September.

Description: The leaflets vary in size on the same leaf, which is composed of seven to nine leaflets. They average 2¼–4 in. in length and 1–1½ in. wide, rather paler below, parchment-like when dry, leafstalks brown. Taste, bitter and astringent; odour, aromatic and characteristic. By long keeping the leaves become brown and lose their aroma.

The bark occurs in quilled or curved pieces 3–6 in. long or more, and ¾–1½ in. broad, dull blackish brown, with traces of a thin, whitish epidermal layer, tough and fibrous, and somewhat mealy; the inner fibres tough and flattened, those in the outer, mealy portion white and silky. Taste, bitter and astringent; odour, none.

Parts Used: Bark, leaves.

Medicinal Use: Alterative, laxative, detergent. Used in herpes, eczema, scrofula. The infusion of 1 oz of bark or leaves in 1 pt of boiling water is taken in wineglassful doses. Externally this is also used as an application to skin eruptions, ulcers, etc. Many uses have been ascribed to many different parts of the Walnut tree. Because the nut resembled in appearance the brain it was thought, according to the Doctrine of Signatures to be good for the headache, etc.

Waller states: "The roots of the Walnut Tree laid bare and perforated, in the month of February yield a copious juice; it relieves chronic pains of the teeth, and even cures the pain of gout, and affords almost miraculous relief to those arising from stone and gravel both externally applied and internally drank. . . ."

Preparation: Liquid extract, leaves: Dose, 1–2 dr.

Domestic Use: The timber is used for furniture. A dye made from the shells has been used to darken the hair.

WATER BETONY

Scrophularia aquatica, Linn.
Fam. Scrophulariaceae

Synonyms: Brownwort, Bishop's Leaves, *Betonica aquatica.*

Habitat: A wild plant in Europe and Great Britain growing as Culpeper says "by the ditch side, brooks and other water courses."

Flowering Time: July.

Description: Stem and leafstalks winged, leaves cordate-oblong, obtuse, crenate-serrate, bracts linear, blunt. Flowers greenish purple, small, with two long and two short stamens, and a roundish, kidney-shaped staminode; ovary two-celled, with numerous seeds. Taste, bitterish; odour, none.

Part Used: Leaves.

Medicinal Use: Vulnerary, detergent. Used externally as poultice for ulcers, sores, and wounds, or boiled in lard as an ointment.

WATER DOCK

Rumex aquaticus, Linn.
Fam. Polygonaceae

Synonyms: Red Dock, Bloodwort.

Habitat: Europe and Great Britain, mainly in the North, usually on the banks of rivers and by pools and ditches.

Flowering Time: July and August.

Description: The root appears in vertical slices, taken through the top-shaped root-stock, the outer surface blackish or dark brown, with the remains of a few branches, and transverse rings of scars of rootlets. The transverse section shows a porous bark, and a large pith, with honeycomb-like cells, and a short zone of woody bundles, with porous medullary rays between them. Taste, astringent and somewhat sweet; odour, none.

Part Used: Root.

Medicinal Use: Alterative, deobstruent, detergent. Used for cleansing ulcers in affections of the mouth, etc. As a powder it has cleansing and detergent effects upon the teeth. Internally the dose of the infusion is a wineglassful.

The root finely powdered has been recommended as an excellent dentifrice to strengthen the gums.

Preparation: Liquid extract: Dose, $\frac{1}{2}$–1 dr.

WATER DROPWORT

Oenanthe crocata, Linn.
Fam. Umbelliferae

Synonyms: Hemlock Water Dropwort, Water Lovage, Hemlock Dropwort, Dead Tongue.

Habitat: Europe and Great Britain. Barton and Castle say they frequent watery places and are particularly abundant on the banks of the Thames between Greenwich and Woolwich.

Flowering Time: July.

Description: The root is white, or yellowish when dried, spindle-shaped, containing a milky juice which, in the fresh root, exudes in scattered drops that quickly turn orange when the root is broken. Exceedingly poisonous, and should not be used except under a doctor's order.

Part Used: Root.

Medicinal Use: Narcotic, poisonous. This is an exceedingly poisonous plant, producing severe gastro-intestinal disturbances and convulsions. A tincture made with 2 oz in 1 pt of diluted alcohol has been used with benefit in epilepsy resulting from injury, the dose being 1–5 drops, administered with great caution.

WATER FENNEL

Oenanthe Phellandrium, Lamk.
Fam. Umbelliferae

Synonyms: *Phellandrium aquaticum*, Linn., Fine-leaved Oenanthe.

Habitat: Europe and Great Britain by water courses.

Flowering Time: July.

Description: The fruit is oblong, about $\frac{1}{5}$ in. long and $\frac{1}{12}$ in. in diameter, tapering a little towards the apex, and crowned with four minute, subulate teeth. There are four vittae (oil cells) on the convex surface, and two on the flat surface of each half fruit. Taste, acrid; odour, strong, aromatic, and characteristic.

Part Used: Fruit.

Medicinal Use: Expectorant, alterative, diuretic. In chronic affections of the air passages, such as asthma, laryngitis, catarrh, etc., this is considered to have a beneficial effect. The powder may be given in doses of 4–5 gr, cautiously administered, as large doses produce dizziness, pains in the head, and other undesirable symptoms. Dr. Turnbull, of Liverpool, recommended it highly in bronchitis to relieve cough, ease expectoration, and produce sleep.

WATER GERMANDER

Teucrium scordium, Linn.
Fam. Labiatae

Habitat: Europe. It also grows in Great Britain but is rather rare. According to Barton and Castle it was found in Cambridgeshire, Oxfordshire, and a few other counties.

Flowering Time: July and August.

Description: Stem velvety. Leaves opposite, sessile, oval-oblong, $\frac{3}{4}$ in. long and $\frac{1}{5}$ in. broad, narrowed at the base, coarsely serrate at the margin, and softly hairy on both sides. Taste, bitter. The fresh leaves, when rubbed, have a penetrating, alliaceous odour.

Part Used: Herb.

Medicinal Use: Antiseptic, diaphoretic, stimulant. Will be found an excellent remedy in all inflammatory diseases. The infusion of 1 oz of herb in 1 pt of boiling water is taken in wineglassful doses. It was recommended by the ancients as an alexipharmic, sudorific, and antiseptic. Galen even goes so far as to declare that after battle the bodies found lying on these plants were much slower in decaying that those not so found.

Preparation: Liquid extract: Dose, $\frac{1}{2}$–1 dr.

WATER PLANTAIN

Alisma plantago, Linn.
Fam. Alismaceae

Synonyms: Mad-dog Weed, Greater Thrumwort.

Habitat: Europe and Great Britain along water-courses.

Flowering Time: July to September.

Description: The leaves are greyish green, on long stalks, cordate-ovate, or lanceolate, with prominent veins. Taste, acid; odour, none.

Part Used: Leaves.

Medicinal Use: Diuretic, diaphoretic. An excellent remedy in gravel and other urinary and kidney diseases, where there is irritation and uneasiness in passing water, pains in the loins, etc. The powdered leaves are given in doses of 1–2 dr, or taken in an infusion of 1 oz to 1 pt of boiling water in teacupful doses three or four times a day.

The plant was greatly praised in Russia some years ago as a remedy for hydrophobia, hence its synonym Mad-dog Weed.

WHITE POND LILY, AMERICAN

Nymphaea odorata, Soland.
Fam. Nymphoeaceae

Synonyms: Water Nymph, Water Cabbage.

Habitat: U.S.A.

Description: The root in pieces about 2 in. in diameter, with circular leaf scars on the upper, and remains of rootlets on the lower, side; externally brown, internally greyish white, spongy, with scattered wood bundles. Taste, mucilaginous, astringent; inodorous. The English White Water Lily is *N. alba*, Linn.

Part Used: Root.

Medicinal Use: Antiseptic, astringent, demulcent. Will be found of service in bowel complaints, where an astringent is needed. A decoction of 1 oz of root boiled in 1 pt of water for twenty minutes is taken internally in wineglassful doses. For external application the decoction can be used as an excellent lotion for bad legs and sores generally. As an injection in leucorrhoea, fluor albus, and gleet it is very useful. In putrid sore throat it may be used as a gargle, and it is a good wash for sore eyes, ophthalmia, etc. The powder is often used as a poultice, when it should be combined with equal parts of crushed Linseed or powdered Slippery Elm.

Preparation: Liquid extract: Dose, $\frac{1}{2}$–1 dr.

WILD CARROT

Daucus carota, Linn.
Fam. Umbelliferae

Synonyms: Bird's Nest, Queen Anne's Lace.

Habitat: Europe and Great Britain, growing wild in fields and pastures.

Flowering Time: July.

Description: Leaves oblong, or obovate-oblong, bipinnate, with acute segments, the whole plant hairy. In taste and odour it resembles the garden carrot, but the root is small and white, not large. The umbel of white flowers has generally one central, crimson flower, and the fruit is margined with prickles, which are tipped with one to three minute, recurved bristles.

Part Used: Herb.

Medicinal Use: Diuretic, deobstruent, stimulant. An active and valuable remedy in the treatment of dropsy, retention of urine, gravel, and affections of the bladder. The infusion of 1 oz in 1 pt of boiling water is taken in wineglassful doses.

Preparation: Liquid extract: Dose, $\frac{1}{2}$–1 dr.

WILD CHERRY

Prunus serotina, Ehrh.
Fam. Rosaceae

Synonyms: Virginian Prune, *Cerasus serotina*, Loisel.

Habitat: North America.

Description: The bark occurs in curved or flat pieces $\frac{1}{12}$ in. or more thick, externally smooth, greenish-brown or yellowish-brown and glossy; or if from older trees, rust-brown, uneven, and deprived of most of the corky layer. Fracture short, granular, radiately striate, under surface often porous, with a network of fibres. When soaked in water it gives off a bitter almond odour; taste, bitter, astringent, and aromatic.

Part Used: Bark.

Medicinal Use: Astringent, tonic, pectoral, sedative. Used as a tonic in convalescence from fevers, etc. Also as a valuable remedy in catarrhal affections; given in consumption, nervous cough, whooping cough, and dyspepsia.

Preparations: Linct. Tolu. Co. pro infant. B.P.C.: Dose, 30–60 min; Syr. Prun. Serot. B.P.C.: Dose, 30–120 min; Syr. Prun. Virg. U.S.P.; Tinct. Prun. Serot. B.P.C. 1949: Dose, 30–60 min.

WILD INDIGO

Baptisia tinctoria, R. Br.
Fam. Leguminosae

Synonyms: Baptisia, Indigoweed, *Sophora tinctoria*, Linn., *Podalyria tinctoria*, Michx.

Habitat: Eastern United States of America.

Description: Crown of the root with knotty branches and a few little-branched roots about 20 in. long and $\frac{1}{4}$–$\frac{1}{2}$ in. thick, furrowed longitudinally, becoming warty and scaly externally. Fracture tough and fibrous. Bark brown, rather thick, with tough bast fibres in radial lines. Wood whitish, with concentric lines, finely porous, medullary rays indistinct. Taste, bitterish, acrid, and disagreeable; the wood tasteless.

Parts Used: Root, leaves.

Medicinal Use: Antiseptic, stimulant, purgative, emmenagogue. In small doses it is a mild laxative; in large a powerful cathartic. Used in rheumatism, scarlatina, etc., and as an antiseptic injection in foul discharges.

A decoction of 1 oz in 1 qt of water boiled down to 1 pt is taken in tablespoonful doses. An ointment made from 1 part of fluid extract to 8 parts of simple ointment is applied to inflamed tumours and ulcers.

WILD MINT

Mentha sativa, Linn.
Fam. Labiatae

Synonyms: Marsh Mint, *Mentha aquatica*, Linn., Hairy Mint.
Habitat: Europe and the British Isles.
Flowering Time: August.
Description: Leaves opposite, shortly stalked or nearly sessile, ovate, acute, serrate, hairy, the upper ones smaller. Flowers forming axillary clusters. Taste, aromatic; odour, characteristic.
Part Used: Herb.
Medicinal Use: Emetic, stimulant, astringent. Used in diarrhoea and in difficult menstruation. The infusion of 1 oz to 1 pt of boiling water is taken in wineglassful doses.

Parkinson writes: "Applyed to the forehead or the temples of the head it easeth the paines therof. It is also good to wash the heads of young children therewith against all manner of breaking out therin, whether sores or scabs."

"Aristotle and others in the ancient times forbade Mints to be used of souldiers in the time of warre, because they thought it did so much to incite to Venery, that it tooke away, or at least abated their animosity or courage to fight."—Parkinson.

WILD YAM

Dioscorea villosa, Linn.
Fam. Dioscoreaceae

Synonyms: Dioscorea, Colic Root, Rheumatism Root.
Habitat: Most tropical countries.
Description: Tuber cylindrical, compressed, branched at intervals of about 2 in., and curved, about 4–6 in. long, and $\frac{1}{2}$–$\frac{3}{4}$ in. thick, pale brown externally, with sunk stem scars on the upper and remains of rootlets below. Fracture short, internally hard, white, with yellowish wood bundles. Taste, insipid, afterwards acrid; inodorous.

Part Used: Root.

Medicinal Use: Antibilious, antispasmodic, diaphoretic. Is valuable in all forms of colic, abdominal and intestinal irritation, etc., in spasms, spasmodic asthma, vomiting, and hepatic congestion. A decoction of 1 oz of root in 1 pt of water may be taken in tablespoonful doses until relieved. Large doses may produce emesis.

Preparations: Liquid extract: Dose, ½–1 dr; Dioscorein: Dose, ½–4 gr.

WILLOW, BLACK, AMERICAN

Salix discolor, Muhl.
Fam. Salicaceae

Synonyms: Pussy Willow, *Salix nigra*, Marsh.

Habitat: U.S.A.

Description: In quilled pieces, 2–6 or more in. long and about ¾ in. broad, blackish grey externally, with numerous dark-brown, round lenticels, inner surface pale buff. Transverse section pale buff, rough, with flat, pointed fibres. Taste, bitter, astringent; odour, none. There are many varieties of the English Willow, and probably the one nearest approaching the American Black Willow is the *Salix phylicifolia*, the Tea-leaved Willow, which we illustrate.

Parts Used: Bark, berries.

Medicinal Use: Anaphrodisiac, sexual sedative, tonic. Is highly recommended and largely used in the treatment of spermatorrhoea, nocturnal emissions, etc. Also relieves ovarian pain. The infusion of 1 oz of bark to 1 pt of boiling water is used in wineglassful doses. A poultice made by simmering the powdered bark in cream is unrivalled in gangrene and indolent ulcers, etc.

Preparation: Ext. Salic. Nig. Liq.: Dose, ½–1 dr.

WILLOW, WHITE

Salix alba, Linn.
(and other species)
Fam. Salicaceae

Synonym: European Willow.

Habitat: A tree growing in moist places and specially by running streams.

Description: The tree is well known and needs no description. The bark, which is chiefly employed in medicine, appears in quills or fragments of varying lengths, $\frac{1}{24}$–$\frac{1}{12}$ in. thick, somewhat glossy, brownish, striated longitudinally, with ellipsoid leaf scars. Inner surface cinnamon brown, finely striated. Fracture short, slightly laminated. Taste, bitter; inodorous.

Parts Used: Bark, leaves.

Medicinal Use: Tonic, antiperiodic, astringent. Has been used with benefit in febrile diseases of rheumatic or gouty origin, also in diarrhoea and dysentery. The usual form of administration is the decoction, given in wineglassful doses four to five times a day.

Gerard writes: "The green boughs with the leaves may very well be brought into chambers and set about the beds of those that be sicke of fevers, for they do mightily coole the heate of the aire which thing is wonderful refreshing to the sicke patients."

Dioscorides states that "the bark being burnt to ashes and steeped in vinegar takes away cornes and other risings in the feet and toes."

Parkinson writes: "The water that is gathered from the willow while it flowereth, the barke being slit and a vessell apt to receive it, being fitted to it, is very good for rednesse and dimme eyesight and films that begin to grow over them. . . ."; also: "The decoction of the leaves and barke in wine is good to bathe . . . the places pained with the gout . . . and to cleanse the head or other parts of scurfe. . . . The juyce of the leaves and green barke mingled with some Rosewater and heated in the rinde of a pomegarnet is singular good to helps deafnesse to be dropped into the eares."

Preparation: Salicin B.P.C. is prepared from various species of Salix. Dose 5–15 gr.

Commercial Use: The twigs and branches are used in basket making and the wood in furniture and for the making of cricket bats. In days gone by the charcoal from the willow made the finest gunpowder.

Biblical References: Leviticus XXIII, 40; Psalm CXXXVII, 2; Job XL, 22; Isaiah XV, 7 and XLIV, 4; Ezekiel XVII, 5.

WINTER'S BARK

Drimys Winteri, Forst.
Fam. Magnoliaceae

Synonyms: Wintera, Winter's Cinnamon, True Winter's Bark, *Wintera aromatica*, Murr.

Habitat: South America. Said to have been discovered by Capt. Winter on Drake's expedition to the South Seas.

Description: Now very rare in commerce, but sometimes imported under the name of pepper bark. In short pieces $\frac{1}{4}$–$\frac{1}{3}$ in. in thickness, and 2–3 in. long, dark brown throughout. Fracture short and granular, showing pale medullary rays in the bark, which project on the inner surface, giving it a striated appearance. Taste, very pungent; odour, feeble. False Winter's Bark, *Cinnamodendron corticosum*, grown in the West Indies, has similar properties. As the true Winter's Bark is now unobtainable, this has taken its place and is invariably supplied. The bark closely resembles Canella, but is more astringent, owing to the presence of tannin.

Part Used: Bark.

Medicinal Use: Stimulant, aromatic, stomachic. This bark has been highly recommended in indigestion, flatulence, colic, etc., and also as an anti-scorbutic. The powdered bark is given in doses of 30 gr. An infusion made from 1 oz of bark in 1 pt of boiling water is given in wineglassful doses.

Although very little used in Europe today, it is still used in South America as a remedy for diarrhoea.

WINTER CHERRY

Physalis alkekengi, Linn.
Fam. Solanaceae

Synonyms: Alkekengi, Strawberry Tomato, Ground Cherry.

Habitat: Grows wild in some parts of Europe and Asia and is cultivated in gardens in Great Britain and America.

Flowering Time: July and August. The berries ripen in September.

Description: The dried berries are dull red, about $\frac{1}{3}$–$\frac{1}{2}$ in. in diameter, globular, two-celled, containing numerous whitish, ovoid, flattened seeds. The red inflated calyx, about 1 in. in diameter, is sometimes left attached to the berries. Taste, sweet and bitterish; odour, none. The plant sold in pots as Winter Cherry is *Solanum pseudocapsicum.*

Part Used: Berries.

Medicinal Use: Diuretic, febrifuge. Has been employed with success in intermittent fevers; also in urinary disorders caused by rheumatism and gout.

Joseph Miller recommends the berries boiled in milk and sweetened with sugar for the Kidneys and Bladder. They are also recommended for Jaundice.

WINTERGREEN

Gaultheria procumbens, Linn.
Fam. Ericaceae

Synonyms: Teaberry, Boxberry, Chickerberry.

Habitat: United States and Canada.

Description: The leaves are obovate or broadly elliptical, short-stalked, faintly serrate at the margin, leathery, glossy green above, paler beneath. Taste, astringent, and aromatic; odour, that of methyl salicylate.

Part Used: Leaves.

Medicinal Use: Aromatic, astringent, stimulant. A very valuable remedy in the treatment of rheumatism, for which it is often used, especially in combination with other herbal agents. May be employed in diarrhoea, and as an infants' carminative. The infusion of 1 oz in 1 pt of boiling water is taken in wineglassful doses.

Preparations: Ol. Betul. B.P.C. 1949 was originally distilled from the plant but is now made from *Betula lenta.* It can also be made synthetically, when it is known as Methyl Salicylate B.P. From this is made Lin. Methyl. Salicyl. B.P.C.; Lin. Methyl Salicyl. et Eucalyp. B.P.C.; Ung. Iod. Denig. c. Methyl. Salicyl. B.P.C.; Ung. Methyl. Salicyl. B.P.C.; Ung. Methyl Salicyl. Co. B.P.C.; Ung. Methyl. Salicyl. Co. dil. B.P.C.; Ung. Methyl. Salicyl. dil. B.P.C. 1949.

WITCH HAZEL

Hamamelis virginiana, Linn.
Fam. Hamamelidaceae

Synonyms: Spotted Alder, Winter Bloom.

Habitat: United States of America.

Description: Bark in quilled pieces about $\frac{1}{16}$ in. thick, from 2–4 or more in. long, the outer surface greyish, scaly, with transverse lenticels, pinkish brown, the inner surface striated longitudinally. Fracture fibrous and laminated. Taste, astringent; odour, feeble. The leaves are broadly obovate, usually 3 or 5 in. long, and about 2–2½ in. broad, the margins serrate-dentate, feather-veined, the erect veins prominent below, each ending in a tooth. The hairs, when remaining on the dried, rather brittle, leaves, are stellate.

Parts Used: Bark, leaves.

Medicinal Use: Astringent, tonic, sedative. Most valuable in checking internal and external haemorrhages; also in the treatment of piles. A decoction made from the bark or leaves makes an excellent injection for bleeding piles. An ointment made by adding 1 part fluid extract bark to 9 parts simple ointment is also used as a local application. The distilled extract from the fresh leaves and young twigs forms an excellent household remedy for internal or external use. For varicose veins it should be applied on a lint bandage, kept constantly moist. The concentration "Hamamelin" is used for piles, mostly in the form of suppositories.

Preparations: From bark: Tinct. Hamam. B.P.C. 1949: Dose, 30–60 min.

From leaves: Ext. Hamam. Liq. B.P., from which is made Ung. Hamam. B.P.; Ext. Hamam. Sicc. B.P., from which is made Supp. Hamam. B.P.; Supp. Hamam. et Zinc. Ox.; Past. Hamam. B.P.C. 1949; Ung. Benzocain. Co. B.P.C.

Aqua Hamamelidis or Distilled Witch Hazel B.P.C. 1949 is prepared from the twigs of the tree by distillation.

WOOD BETONY

Stachys betonica, Benth.
Fam. Labiatae

Synonyms: Bishopswort, *Betonica officinalis.*

Habitat: This plant grows wild, chiefly in woods, as it prefers shady places.

Flowering Time: It flowers in July and the seed ripens quickly after.

Description: The plant has many broad leaves rising from the root, roundly dented at the edges. The stems are upright and hairy, producing leaves at the joints smaller than the lower leaves. The flowers are reddish or purple in colour, spotted with white, labiate, and arranged in a terminal oval spike interrupted below. The calyx is smooth. The roots are white and thread-like.

Part Used: Herb.

Medicinal Use: Culpeper says the herb is appropriated to the planet Jupiter and the sign Aries.

Parkinson states: ". . . it is said also to hinder drunkenness being taken beforehand and quickly to expell it afterwards. . . ."

The root is not used in medicine. It has an obnoxious flavour and produces vomiting. Today, Wood Betony is regarded as an aromatic, astringent, and an alterative. It is usually combined with other herbs and used as a tonic in dyspepsia and an alterative in rheumatism.

Preparation: Liquid extract: Dose, ½–1 dr.

BOTH Parkinson and Culpeper quote Antonius Musa, physician to the Emperor Augustus Caesar, who wrote on the virtues of Wood Betony saying amongst other things that ". . . it preserves the liver and bodies of men from the danger of epidemic diseases and from witchcraft also; it helps those who loath and cannot digest their meat, those that have weak stomachs and sour belchings. . . ."

WOODRUFF

Asperula odorata, Linn.
Fam. Rubiaceae

Synonyms: Woodroof, Waldmeister Tea.

Habitat: A wild English plant growing in the woods.

Flowering Time: May and June.

Description: Herb about 6–8 in. high, with a slender, quadrangular, brittle stem, and whorls of usually eight narrowly elliptic, rather rigid leaves about 1 in. long and 1¼ in. broad, entire at the margins, and tipped with a sharp point. Taste, like coumarine; odour, when dried, like new-mown hay.

Part Used: Herb.

Medicinal Use: Diuretic, tonic. Useful for removing biliary obstructions of liver, etc., and strengthening to the stomach.

Gerard states: "It is reported to be put into wine to make man merry and to be good for the heart and liver: it prevaileth in wounds as Cruciata and other vulnerary herbes do."

WOOD SAGE

Teucrium scorodonia, Linn.
Fam. Labiatae

Synonym: Garlic Sage.
Habitat: A British wild plant.
Flowering Time: July.
Description: Stems obtusely quadrangular. Leaves opposite, stalked, ovate, with a cordate base, obtuse, crenate-serrate, the upper surface reticulated with prominent veinlets beneath; about $1\frac{1}{2}$ in. long, $\frac{3}{8}$ in. broad. The yellow flowers grow in long spikes at the tops of the branches. Taste, bitter, resembling that of hops; odour, slightly aromatic.
Part Used: Herb.
Medicinal Use: Diaphoretic, astringent, emmenagogue, tonic. Used in fevers, colds, inflammations, and in obstructed menstruation. The infusion of 1 oz in 1 pt of boiling water is taken warm in wineglassful doses.

Joseph Miller recommends this herb for gout and rheumatism and also as a vulnerary plant, stating that it prevents mortification and gangrene.
Preparation: Liquid extract: Dose, $\frac{1}{2}$–1 dr.

WOOD SORREL

Oxalis acetosella, Linn.
Fam. Geraniaceae

Synonym: Common Wood Sorrel.
Habitat: It grows in Great Britain chiefly in woods and shady places.
Flowering Time: April.
Description: Leaves trifoliate, stalked, the leaflets broadly obcordate and emarginate, reflexed when dry, the leafstalk slender, often reddish toward the base. Flowers white, bell-shaped, with delicate purplish veins. Taste, pleasantly acid; odour, none.
Part Used: Herb.
Medicinal Use: Diuretic, refrigerant. Reputed of value in febrile diseases, urinary affections, catarrh, and haemorrhages. The herb may be infused with water or boiled in milk and administered freely, although excess should be guarded against.

Joseph Miller says: "The juice, when clarified is a fine red colour and makes a very agreeable syrup."

WORMSEED

Chenopodium ambrosioides, Linn.
Var. *anthelminticum*, A. Gray
Fam. Chenopodiaceae

Synonym: American Wormseed.

Habitat: America.

Description: Fruit depressed globular, about $\frac{1}{12}$ in. in diameter, greenish or brown, glandular. The single seed is glossy, black, lenticular, with an obtuse edge, the albumen containing a curved embryo. Taste, acrid, astringent, and turpentiney; odour, camphoraceous and turpentiney. It is known in New Zealand as Californian Spearmint. Contains about 3 per cent volatile oil, to which the anthelmintic properties are due.

Part Used: Seeds.

Medicinal Use: Anthelmintic, antispasmodic. Chiefly used to expel intestinal worms. It should be given at bedtime and in the morning before food, for two or three days, followed by some cathartic.

Preparations: Powdered seeds: Dose, 15–60 gr; Liquid extract: Dose, $\frac{1}{2}$–1 dr; Ol. Chenopod. B.P.: Dose, 3–15 min.

WORMSEED, LEVANT

Artemisia cina, Berg.
Fam. Compositae

Synonyms: Santonica, Semen sanctum, Semen contra Vermes, Semen Santonici, *Artemisia lercheana*, Kar. & Kir., *Artemisia maritima*, var. *pauciflora*, Web., *Artemisia maritima*, var. *Stechmenniana*, Bess., *A. chamaemelifolia*, Vill.

Habitat: Russia.

Description: This drug consists of minute flowerheads containing three to five minute, tubular flowers without pappus. The flowerheads are about $\frac{1}{8}$ in. long and $\frac{1}{16}$ in. in diameter, greenish yellow when fresh, brown when kept for some time; each has 18 oblong-obtuse scales closely overlapping each other and bearing minute, yellow glands on their surface. Taste, bitter and aromatic; odour, when rubbed, that of cineol.

Part Used: Unexpanded flower buds.

Medicinal Use: Vermifuge. The seeds are used in domestic practice combined with honey or treacle. Their vermifuge action is due to the presence of Santonin, the flowerheads containing from 2 to 3·5 per cent. The chief use of Levant Wormseed is for the extraction of Santonin, which is official in the B.P. The flowerheads (commonly called seeds) may be administered in doses of from 10–30 gr night and morning to expel round worms. It has less effect upon thread worms and little action on tape worms. When the flowerheads expand, the Santonin content rapidly decreases.

Parkinson mentions Wormseed and its use as a vermifuge specially for children.

Preparations: Santonin B.P.: Dose, 1–3 gr, from which are made Tab. Santonin B.P.C.: Dose, 1–3 gr; Tab. Santonin et Hydrarg. Subchlor. B.P.C.: Dose, 1–2 tablets; Tab. Santonin et Scammon Co.: Dose, 1 tablet; Troch. Santonin (each lozenge contains 1 gr. Santonin).

WORMWOOD

Artemisia absinthium, Linn.
Fam. Compositae

Synonyms: Old Woman, Ajenjo.

Habitat: It is a plant that grows freely in many parts of the world and of it there are many varieties. Culpeper describes three varieties—the Sea Wormwood, Common Wormwood, and lastly the Roman Wormwood of which he writes: "and why Roman seeing it grows familiarly in England? It may be so called because it is good for a stinking breath which the Romans cannot be very free from, maintaining so many bad houses by authority of his Holiness."

Flowering Time: July and August.

Description: Stem 2–2½ ft high, whitish-like leaves, with fine silky, appressed hairs. Leaves about 3 in. long by 1½ in. broad, about three times pinnatifid, the leafstalks slightly winged at the margin, and the lobes linear and obtuse. The small, nearly globular flowerheads are arranged in an erect, leafy panicle, the leaves being reduced to three or even one linear segment. The flowers have a greenish-yellow tint, and have no pappus. Taste, very bitter; odour, characteristic, resembling that of thujone.

Part Used: Herb.

Medicinal Use: Tonic, stomachic, febrifuge, anthelmintic. A good remedy for enfeebled digestion and debility. It may also be used to expel worms. The infusion of 1 oz to 1 pt of boiling water is taken in wineglassful doses.

Joseph Miller states: ". . . a Cataplasm of the green leaves beat up with Hog's Lard was commended to Mr. Ray by Dr. Hulse as a good external remedy against the swellings of the Tonsils and Quinzy."

Culpeper writes: "Take the flowers of Wormwood, Rosemary and Black Thorn of each a like quantity, half that quantity of Saffron; boil this in Rhenish wine but put it not in Saffron till it is almost boiled; this is the way to keep a man's body in health, appointed by Camerarius in his book entitled *Hortus Medicus* and it is a good one."

Gerard states: "Being taken in wine it is good against the poison of IXIA (being a viscous matter proceeding from the thistle Chamoelion) and of Hemlock and against the biting of the shrew mouse and of the sea dragon."

Domestic Use: It is said that Wormwood stored where clothes are kept, keeps away the moth. It also forms an ingredient of the drink known as Vermouth.

Preparations: Liquid extract: Dose, ½–1 dr; Tinct. Absinth: Dose, 1–4 dr.

Biblical References: It is said that where the Bible refers to Wormwood it refers to the variety *Artemesia Judaica*, a native of Palestine. The writers frequently refer to Wormwood to compare its bitterness with sin and its consequences. There are references in Deuteronomy XXIX, 18; Proverbs V, 3 and 4; Jeremiah IX, 15 and XXIII, 15; Lamentations III, 15 and 19; Amos V, 7; Revelation VIII, 10 and 11.

CULPEPER states that Wormwood is good for preventing drunkenness. He quotes that when Saturn met with Venus and found her "drunk as a hog" Saturn said "What, thou a fortune and be drunk? I'll give thee antipathetical cure; Take my herb Wormwood and thou shalt never get a sufiet by drinking."

WOUNDWORT

Stachys palustris, Linn.
Fam. Labiatae

Synonyms: Allheal, Panay, Opopanewort, Downy Woundwort, Clown's Woundwort, Rusticum Vulna Herba, Stinking Marsh Stachys.

Habitat: Ditches and watery places in England.

Flowering Time: June and July.

Description: Distinctive character: Leaves narrowly lanceolate, nearly sessile, hairy. Flowers, dull purple. Taste, astringent; odour, unpleasant. There is another variety, *Stachys sylvatica*, Linn., known as Hedge Woundwort (synonym, Clownswort), with leaves cordate-ovate, serrate, long-stalked, hairy. Flowers reddish purple. Stems square. Taste, astringent; odour unpleasant.

Part Used: Herb.

Medicinal Use: Antiseptic, antispasmodic. It relieves gout, cramp, and pains in the joints, falling sickness, and vertigo. The bruised leaves, applied to a wound, will stop bleeding and heal the wound. The fresh juice is made into a syrup and taken internally to stop haemorrhages, dysentery, etc. Gerard praises its virtues in healing grievous and mortal wounds, and writes: "I took foure handfuls of the herbe stamped and put them into a pan whereunto I added foure ounces of Burrowes grease, half a pint of Oyle Olive, wax three ounces which I boyled into the consumption of the juyce (which is known when the stuffe doth not bubble at all) then did I straine it, putting it to the fire againe, adding thereto two ounces of Turpentine the which I suffered to boil a little, reserving the same for my use. The which I warmed in a saucer dipping therein small soft tents which

I put into the wound, defending the parts adjoining with a plaister of calcithcos relented with oyle of roses; which manner of dressing and preserving I used even until the wound was perfectly whole. . . ."

GERARD writes of a case of a shoemaker's servant in Holborn "who intended to destroy himselfe. His attempt was thus; First he gave himselfe a most mortall wound in the throat in such sort that when I gave him drinke it came forth at the wounde which likewise did blow out the candle: another deepe and grievous wound in the breast with the said dagger, and also two others 'in abdomine' or the nether belly . . . which mortall wounds by God's permission and the virtues of this herbe [woundwort] I perfectly cured within twenty daies: for which the name of God be praised."

Y

YARROW *Achillea millefolium*, Linn.
Fam. Compositae

Synonyms: Milfoil, Thousand-leaf, Nosebleed.

Habitat: A common herb growing in pastures.

Flowering Time: August.

Description: Stem angular, rough. Leaves alternate, about 3–4 in. long and 1 in. broad, bipinnatifid, clasping the stem at the base: the segments very narrow, short, and linear acute. The whole plant more or less hairy with white, silky, appressed hairs. The flowerheads small, white, minutely daisy-like, in flattened-terminal corymbose cymes. Taste, insipid; odour, feeble.

Part Used: Herb.

Medicinal Use: Diaphoretic, stimulant, tonic. Most useful in colds, obstructed perspiration, and the commencement of fevers. It opens the pores freely and purifies the blood. The infusion of 1 oz to 1 pt of boiling water is taken in wineglassful doses, drunk warm, with a teaspoonful of Composition Essence added to each dose. Combined with Elder Flowers and Peppermint it forms a speedy cure for influenza, colds, etc.

Culpeper places this herb under the influence of Venus and states: "An ointment of them cures wounds and is most fit for such as have inflamations. . . ."

Parkinson writes: "The powder of the dryed herbe taken with Comfrey and Plantaine water doth also stay inward bleedings, and put into the nose as I said before will doe the same. . . ."

Preparation: Liquid extract: Dose, ½–1 dr.

YELLOW DOCK *Rumex crispus*, Linn.
Fam. Polygonaceae

Synonym: Curled Dock.

Habitat: A common weed growing freely in the British Isles.

Description: The root occurs in short, shrivelled pieces, about ¾–1 in. long or more, brown, and more or less rough and wrinkled externally, showing on transverse section a yellowish-brown, rather thick bark, surrounding a woody centre with concentric rings and a radiate structure. Leaves narrow, oblong, lanceolate, crisped at the margins. Taste, mucilaginous, bitterish; odour, none.

Part Used: Root.

Medicinal Use: Laxative, alterative, tonic. Can be freely used in rheumatism, skin diseases, bilious complaints, piles, bleeding of the lungs, etc. A syrup may be made by boiling ½ lb of crushed root in 1 pt of syrup, and is taken in teaspoonful doses. The dose of the infusion of 1 oz of powdered root in 1 pt of boiling water is a wineglassful.

Preparations: Liquid extract: Dose, ½–1 dr; Solid extract: Dose, 5–15 gr; Rumin: Dose, 3 gr.

YELLOW FLAG

Iris pseudacorus, Linn.
Fam. Iridaceae

Synonyms: Yellow Iris, Flower-de-luce, *Iris lutea, Iris aquatica*, Fleur-de-Lys.

Habitat: Widely spread in Europe and Africa and a well-known garden plant in the British Isles.

Description: Rhizome brownish externally, cylindrical, compressed, with transverse scars of fallen leaves, and scars of roots beneath, dark red internally. Flowers yellow. Taste, very acrid; odour, none.

Part Used: Rhizome.

Medicinal Use: Astringent, cooling. It is reputed of value in dysmenorrhoea and leucorrhoea as an astringent lotion.

YELLOW PARILLA

Menispermum canadense, Linn.
Fam. Menispermaceae

Synonyms: Moonseed, Canadian Moonseed, Moonseed Sarsaparilla, Texas Sarsaparilla, Yellow Sarsaparilla, Vine Maple.

Habitat: Canada and U.S.A.

Description: Root cylindrical, about ¼ in. thick, varying in length, finely wrinkled longitudinally, yellowish brown, with slender, branching, brittle rootlets, internally yellowish. Fracture, tough, woody. Taste, bitter; nearly inodorous.

Part Used: Root.

Medicinal Use: Alterative, laxative, diaphoretic, tonic. A valuable alterative, considered to excel Sarsaparilla in treatment of scrofula, blood disorders and cutaneous diseases generally. It also acts as a tonic and nervine, and may be given in all cases of debility and dyspepsia.

Preparations: Powdered root: Dose, ½–1 dr; Liquid extract: Dose, ½–1 dr; Menispermin: Dose, 1–4 gr.

YERBA REUMA

Frankenia grandifolia, Cham. & Schlecht.
Fam. Frankeniaceae

Synonyms: Flux Herb, Frankenia.

Habitat: California, N. Mexico.

Description: Stem slender, about $\frac{1}{16}$ in. in diameter, forked. Leaves opposite, $\frac{1}{4}$ in. long and $\frac{1}{16}$ in. in diameter, linear, with strongly-revolute margins, short hairy, as is also the stem. Taste, saline; odour, none.

Part Used: Herb.

Medicinal Use: Mild astringent. Is of service in diarrhoea, dysentery, leucorrhoea, gleet, and catarrh. It may be applied locally as an injection.

Preparation: Liquid extract: Dose, $\frac{1}{2}$–1 dr.

YERBA SANTA

Eriodictyon glutinosum, Benth.
Fam. Hydrophyllaceae

Synonyms: Eriodictyon, Mountain Balm, Bearsweed, Gum Bush.

Habitat: California.

Description: A low, evergreen shrub, leaves elliptic-lanceolate, about 2–4 in. long and $\frac{3}{4}$ in. broad, irregularly dentate at the margins. The upper surface is green and more or less varnished with resin, the lower surface reticulated and white with hairs. Taste, balsamic; odour, aromatic and agreeable.

Part Used: Leaves.

Medicinal Use: Aromatic, tonic, expectorant. Is highly recommended for bronchitis, asthma, and all similar catarrhal affections. To increase its effects in asthmatic complaints it is generally combined with Grindelia. An aromatic syrup of Yerba Santa is used to mask the taste of quinine.

Preparations: Liquid extract: Dose, $\frac{1}{2}$–1 dr; Powdered leaves: Dose, $\frac{1}{4}$–1 dr.

YEW

Taxus baccata, Linn.
Fam. Taxaceae

Habitat: It grows in England and America and other parts of the world.

Flowering Time: April or May. The berries are ripe in September or October.

Description: A large, evergreen tree. Male and female flowers are born on separate plants. The fruit is a single oval seed nearly covered with a thick red coat resembling an abortive acorn. The leaves are about $\frac{1}{2}$ in. long, alternate, and curve outwardly and upwardly. Excepting the pulp of the fruit all parts are poisonous, both to man and animals.

Part Used: Leaves.

Medicinal Use: Owing to its poisonous nature and uncertain action it is seldom employed in medicine. At one time it was thought to be good for epilepsy.

Preparation: Powdered leaves: Dose, 1–5 gr.

Domestic Use: In ancient days the best longbows were made from Yew.

YOHIMBE BARK

Pausinystalia yohimbe, Pierre
Fam. Rubiaceae

Habitat: Cameroons and French Congo.

Description: Bark usually in channelled pieces, outer and inner surface reddish brown. Gives a red coloration when shaken with solution of ammonia.

Part Used: Bark.

Preparations: Liquid extract: Dose, 5–15 min; Yohimbine hydrochloride B.P.C.: Dose, $\frac{1}{20}$–$\frac{1}{8}$ gr, usually administered in the form of pills or tablets.

HAS a reputation on the Continent as an aphrodisiac owing to the presence of the poisonous alkaloid Yohimbine.

Z

ZEDOARY *Curcuma zedoaria*, Rosc.
Fam. Zingiberaceae

Habitat: India.

Description: The rhizome is usually sold in transverse slices about $\frac{3}{4}$–$1\frac{1}{4}$ in. broad and $\frac{1}{4}$ in. thick. The outer surface is greyish, with a few circular striae and small spiny points of root bases. The transverse section is greyish white, hard, and horny. Taste, bitterish and camphoraceous; odour, recalling cardamoms and ginger.

Part Used: Rhizome.

Medicinal Use: Aromatic, stimulant. It is chiefly employed as a carminative and stomachic, and acts in a manner very similar to ginger, only milder. The infusion of $\frac{1}{2}$ oz to 1 pt of boiling water is given in tablespoonful doses as required.

Preparation: Liquid extract: Dose, 10–30 drops.

It formed an ingredient in the original Warburg's Tincture.

APPENDIXES

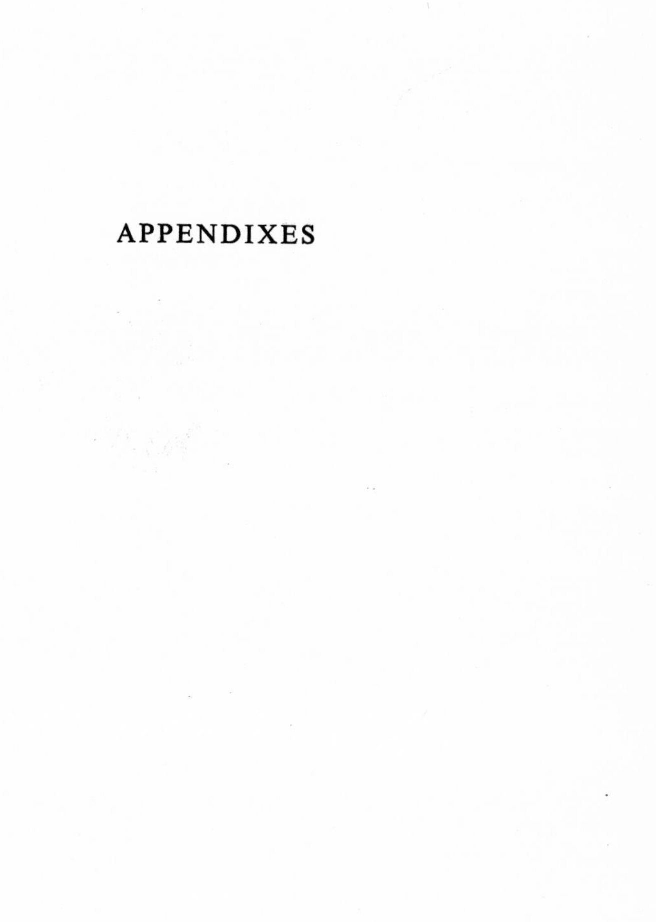

GUIDE TO THERAPEUTIC ACTION

Alterative. Blue Flag, Burdock, Echinacea, Figwort, Mezereon, Poke Root, Queen's Delight, Red Clover, Sarsaparilla, Turkey Corn, Yellow Dock.

Anodyne. Aconite, Coca, Henbane, Hops, Indian Hemp, Jamaica Dogwood, Poppy.

Anthelmintic. Aloes, Butternut, Kousso, Male Fern, Pinkroot, Tansy, Wormseed, Wormwood.

Antibilious. Balmony, Mandrake American, Wild Yam.

Antiperiodic. Alstonia, Ash, Cinchona, Feverbush, Quebracho, Wafer Ash, Willow White.

Antiscorbutic. Lemon, Lime Fruit, Scurvy-Grass, Shepherd's Purse.

Antiscrofulous. Adder's Tongue American.

Antiseptic: Barberry, Echinacea, Eucalyptus, Golden Seal, Southernwood, Thyme, White Pond Lily, Wild Indigo.

Antispasmodic. Asafoetida, Black Haw, Chamomile, Cohosh Black, Cramp-bark, Gelsemium, Lady's Slipper, Lobelia, Mistletoe, Pulsatilla, Scullcap, Stramonium, Sundew, Valerian.

Aperient. Rhubarb, Rose Pale.

Aphrodisiac. Damiana, Muirapuama, Saw Palmetto, Yohimbe.

Aromatic. Allspice, Angelica European, Angostura, Basil, Bugle, Burnet Saxifrage, Calamus, Canella, Cinnamon, Condurango, Cubebs, Golden Rod, Magnolia, Meadowsweet, Melilot, Musk Seed, Orange, Savory Summer, Tonka Beans, Winter's Bark.

Astringent. Avens, Bayberry, Bistort, Blackberry, Catechu, Cranesbill, Nettle, Oak, Pinus Bark, Rhatany, Tormentilla, Witch Hazel.

Balsamic. Clary, Larch.

Bitter. Angostura, Bugle, Canchalagua, Cascara Amarga, Cedron, Chiretta, Feverfew, Gentian, Gold Thread, Horehound, Osier Red American, Quassia.

Cardiac. Asparagus, Birch European, Butterbur, Foxglove, Hawthorn, Hellebore American, Hellebore False, Kola, Lily-of-the-Valley, Mescal Buttons, Mountain Laurel, Night-Blooming Cereus, Strophanthus, Tonka Beans, Tree of Heaven.

Carminative. Allspice, Angelica, Aniseed, Balm, Calamus, Cinnamon, Cloves, Fennel, Ginger, Peppermint.

Cathartic. Alder Bark American, Bitter Apple, Black Root, Broom, Bryony White, Buckthorn Alder, Butternut, Cabbage Tree, Castor Oil, Colchicum, Copaiba, Croton, Dyer's Greenweed, Gladwin, Hedge-Hyssop,

Hellebore Black, Hemp Agrimony, Holly, Hydrangea, Indian Physic, Ivy, Jalap, Mandrake American, Mountain Flax, Poke Root, Rhubarb, Senna, Squill, Swamp Milkweed, Turpeth.

Corrective. Oliver Bark.

Demulcent. Arrowroot, Comfrey, Couchgrass, Iceland Moss, Irish Moss, Linseed, Liquorice Root, Marshmallow, Slippery Elm.

Deobstruent. Bladderwrack, Buckbean, Butcher's Broom, Eternal Flower, Liverwort English, Water Dock, Wild Carrot.

Depurative. Figwort.

Dermatic. Chaulmoogra.

Detergent. Adder's Tongue English, Balmony, Black Currant, Goa, Golden Seal, Ragwort, Soap Tree, Soapwort, Southernwood, Walnut, Water Betony, Water Dock.

Diaphoretic and Sudorific. Angelica, Balm, Boneset, Crawley Root, Ipecacuanha, Jaborandi, Pennyroyal, Prickly Ash, Yarrow.

Digestive. Paw-Paw, Paw-Paw Seed.

Diuretic. Broom, Buchu, Clivers, Couchgrass, Hydrangea, Juniper Berries, Pareira, Parsley, Parsley Piert, Pellitory, Pipsissiwa, Shepherd's Purse, Stone Root, Uva-Ursi, Wild Carrot.

Emetic. Bitter root, Ipecacuanha, Lobelia, Mustard, Tag Alder, Vervain.

Emmenagogue. Aloes, Arrach, Black Cohosh, Blue Cohosh, Corn Ergot, Ergot, Ground Pine, Hellebore Black, Life Root, Motherwort, Mugwort, Pennyroyal, Rue, Southernwood, Tansy, Wood Sage.

Emollient. Linseed, Liquorice Root, Marshmallow, Slippery Elm.

Expectorant. Benzoin, Elecampane, Horehound, Ipecacuanha, Lobelia, Lungwort, Mouse-ear, Mullein, Pleurisy Root, Polypody Root, Senega, Squill, Wild Cherry, Yerba Santa.

Febrifuge and Refrigerant. Aconite, Angostura, Alstonia, Avens, Balm, Boneset, Catnep, Crawley Root, Devil's Bit, Five-leaf-grass, Gelsemium, Hellebore American, Peruvian Bark, Wormwood.

Hemostatic. Bistort, Cranesbill, Corn Ergot, Ergot.

Hepatic. Dodder, Pichi, Toadflax Yellow.

Hydrogogue. Bryony White, Mandrake American.

Hypnotic and Narcotic. Belladonna, Bittersweet, Bugleweed, Hemlock, Henbane, Indian Hemp, Mistletoe, Passion Flower, Poppy, Stramonium.

Insecticide. Musk Seed, Pyrethrum.

Irritant: Bitter Apple, Bryony, Cayenne, Mustard, Poison Oak, Thuja.

Laxative. Buckthorn, Cascara Sagrada, Dandelion, Golden Seal, Mandrake, Manna, Mountain Flax.

Mydriatic. Belladonna, Henbane, Stramonium.

Myotic. Calabar Bean.

Nervine. Arrach, Black Haw, Cramp Bark, Guarana, Kola, Lady's Slipper, Lime Flowers, Mistletoe, Motherwort, Muira-Puama, Oats, Pulsatilla, Scullcap, Snake Root, Sumbul, Valerian, Vervain.

Nutritive. Arrowroot, Iceland Moss, Irish Moss, Salep, Saw Palmetto, Slippery Elm.

Oxytocic. Cotton Root.

Parasiticide. Cocculus indicus.

Parturient. Corn Ergot, Cotton Root, Squaw Vine.

Pectoral. Aniseed, Beth Root, Blue Mallow, Euphorbia, Hartstongue, Hyssop, Irish Moss, Jujube Berries, Labrador Tea, Life Root, Linseed, Liquorice Root, Liverwort American, Lungwort, Maiden Hair, Mullein, Polypody Root, Sarsaparilla American, Slippery Elm, Sundew, Wild Cherry.

Purgative. Aloes, Bitter Apple, Jalap, Mandrake, Scammony.

Resolvent. Bittersweet, Galbanum.

Rubefacient. Bryony Black, Cayenne, Cowhage, Croton, Pellitory, Pine Oil, Turpentine.

Sternutatory. Asarabacca, Soapwort Root Egyptian.

Stimulant. Ammoniac, Blood Root, Cascarilla, Cayenne, Cinnamon, Cloves, Ginger, Horseradish, Jaborandi, Kola, Mustard, Nux Vomica, Paraguay Tea, Pennyroyal, Peppermint, Peruvian Balsam. Poplar, Prickly Ash, Snake Root, Wintergreen.

Stomachic. Allspice, Avens, Calamus, Centaury, Chamomile, Condurango, Cubebs, Peppermint, Quassia, Rhubarb, True Unicorn Root.

Styptic. Avens, Cranesbill Root American, Lady's Mantle.

Sudorific. Sarsaparilla American, Vervain.

Taenifuge. Kamala, Kousso, Male Fern.

Tonic. Alstonia, Barberry, Bitter Root, Buckbean, Calumba, Chamomile, Chiretta, Centaury, Damiana, Gentian, Gold Thread, Hops, Kola, Nux Vomica, Peruvian Bark, Pipsissiwa, Popular, Prickly Ash, Quassia, Strophanthus, Turkey Corn, Unicorn Root, Wild Cherry, Wormwood.

Vermifuge. Butternut, Cabbage Tree, Cohosh Blue, Corsican Moss, Goat's Rue, Horehound Black, Male Fern, Pink Root, Primrose, Stavesacre, Wormseed.

Vulnerary. Arnica, Crosswort, Myrrh, Water Betony.

FORMS OF MEDICINAL PREPARATIONS

INFUSIONS

These preparations are generally made of ground or bruised roots, barks, herbs, or seeds, by pouring boiling water over the drug, letting it stand for half an hour, occasionally stirring, and finally straining the clear liquid carefully off. Sometimes cold water may be used, as in the case of a few bitters, such as Calumba, Quassia, etc., when the ground drug will be found to yield its properties to water without heat. The usual quantity of drug to 1 pt of water is 1 oz, but in a few cases where the drugs contain very active principles, less is sufficient. The dose of most infusions varies from a tablespoonful to a wineglassful or a teacupful.

DECOCTIONS

As a rule decoctions are made by pouring cold water upon the cut, bruised, or ground drug, the mixture being boiled for twenty minutes to half an hour, cooled, and strained. Roots and barks are generally treated in this manner, as they need longer subjection to heat to extract their virtues. Decoctions are generally made in a strength of 1 oz to 1 pt, but, as the water boils away, it is best to use 1½ pt, and the decoction should then when finished measure 1 pt. The length of time depends upon the readiness with which the drug gives up its active principles to the liquid. The dose varies from two teaspoonfuls to a wineglassful or two.

LIQUID EXTRACTS

These are most popular and convenient preparations, inasmuch as, if properly made, they are the most concentrated fluid forms in which vegetable drugs may be obtained. Liquid extracts are made in a variety of ways—evaporation by heat, *in vacuo*; cold percolation; high pressure, etc.—each drug being treated in that manner by which its properties may best be extracted and held in concentrated solution. The strength of a Liquid extract is 1 in 1, or 1 oz fluid represents 1 oz of crude drug—for instance, 1 oz of Liquid Ext. Golden Seal would represent the medicinal value of 1 oz of Golden Seal Root. Liquid extracts are daily becoming more popular, and, as they may be easily obtained, bid fair to rival the Tinctures and Preparations which have made Homoeopathy so popular with those who seek an easy way of keeping a household stock of domestic remedies.

SOLID EXTRACTS

Are prepared by evaporating to the consistence of honey the fresh juices or strong infusions of vegetable drugs. They may also be manufactured by a spirituous process, in which case the alcohol is recovered by means of distillation from a strong tincture of the drug. Solid extracts are employed chiefly in the manufacture of pills, plasters, ointments, and compressed tablets.

TINCTURES

Are spirituous preparations made with pure or diluted spirits of wine of drugs containing gummy, resinous, or volatile principles, or of any drugs rendered useless by the application of heat in any form, or of the great number of drugs which will not yield their properties to water alone, as their active principles are more readily extracted by spirit, better held in solution and preserved from deterioration.

Tinctures are generally made in a strength of 1 or 2 oz of drug to 1 pt. The dose varies according to the active principles contained in the drug.

PILLS

Are perhaps the best known and most largely used form of medicines, chiefly because of their handy form and general convenience, and also because of their comparative tastelessness. Pills are for the most part composed of concentrated extracts and alkaloids in combination with active crude drugs. They may be obtained coated or uncoated, but the pearl-coated pill is the general favourite, as it is quite tasteless, and the coating, if properly made, is readily soluble in the stomach.

TABLETS

Are made by compressing drugs into a very small compass. It is claimed for them that they are superior to pills, because they are more easily administered and by reason of their rapid dissolution in the stomach are quicker in their action.

CAPSULES

Are gelatine containers of convenient sizes for swallowing and holding oils, balsams, etc., which, because of their nauseous taste or smell, would be difficult to administer. Such drugs as Cod Liver Oil, Castor Oil, Copaiba, Sandalwood Oil, etc., are largely given in this form, because objection is made to the remedies in their natural state.

SUPPOSITORIES

Are small cones made of some convenient and easily soluble base, and used where it is desired to apply medicines *per rectum*. They are invaluable in the treatment of internal piles, cancers, fistula, etc. They are also made of nutrient ingredients, and passed into the bowels where patients are unable to take nourishment in the usual manner.

PESSARIES

Are similar to Suppositories, but are made in a suitable shape to be used in female complaints, where it is desirable to apply remedies to the walls of the internal passages.

CONCENTRATIONS

Are a class of medicinal resins or resinoids obtained from medicinal drugs by precipitation from their alcoholic preparations, either by water, distillation, or other suitable means.

Those at present in use contain one or more, but not always all the therapeutic virtues of the drugs from which they are made, and in many cases are only powdered extracts.

WEIGHTS AND MEASURES

1 grain	equals	0·0648	grammes
1 scruple (20 grains	,,	1·2959	,,
1 drachm (60 grains)	,,	3·8879	,,
1 ounce avoirdupois (437·5 grains)	,,	28·3495	,,
1 ounce Apothecaries' or Troy (480 grains)	,,	31·1035	,,
1 pound (7,000 grains)	,,	453·59	,, , or
		0·4356	kilogrammes

1 minim	equals	0·0592	millilitres
1 fluid drachm (60 minims) ..	,,	3·5515	,,
1 fluid ounce (8 drachms)	,,	28·4123	,,
1 pint (20 ounces)	,,	0·5682	litres
1 gallon (8 pints)	,,	4·5459	,,

1 metre	equals	39·3701	inches
1 decimetre, 0·1 of metre ..	,,	3·9370	,,
1 centimetre, 0·01 of metre ..	,,	0·3970	,,
1 millimetre, 0·001 of metre ..	,,	0·0397	,,

DOMESTIC DOSES AND THEIR EQUIVALENTS

1 teaspoonful	.. equals approximately		1 drachm
1 dessertspoonful ..	,,	,,	2 drachms
1 tablespoonful ..	,,	,,	½ fluid ounce
1 wineglassful ..	,,	,,	1½–2 fluid ounces or 3–4 tablespoonfuls.
1 teacupful	,,	,,	4–5 fluid ounces or 8–10 tablespoonfuls

HERBAL COMPOUNDS

(CONTINENTAL)

These are compounds used largely in France and Germany as household remedies. They are called "Species," and the liquid made, a "Tisane" or "Tee" (tea). They are prepared as ordinary infusions or decoctions (1 in 20), and the dose is a wineglassful frequently.

ANTICATARRH

Goosefoot, Rupturewort } of each equal parts (Infusion)

ANTILACTEOUS

(Restraining the secretion of milk)

Elder Flowers	1 part
Lady's Bedstraw	1 ,,
St. John's Wort	2 parts
Senna Pods	3 ,,

(Infusion)

ANTISPASMODIC

Yarrow Herb	1 part
Orange Flowers	2 parts
Valerian Root	3 ,,

(Infusion)

AROMATIC

Sage, Rosemary, Thyme, Wild Thyme, Hyssop, Marjoram, Wormwood, Peppermint } of each equal parts (Infusion)

ASTRINGENT

Bistort Tormentilla Pomegranate	of each equal parts	(Decoction)

BITTER NO. 1

Germander Centaury Holy Thistle	of each equal parts	(Infusion)

BITTER NO. 2

Holy Thistle Germander Centaury Buckbean	of each equal parts	(Infusion)

CARMINATIVE

Aniseed Fennel Caraway Coriander	of each equal parts	(Infusion)

CEPHALIC

(Nervine, for headache)

Rosemary Thyme Wild Thyme Wild Marjoram Peppermint Lavender Flowers Rose Flowers Marjoram	of each equal parts	(Infusion)

COOLING

Melon Seed Cucumber Seed Water Melon Seed	of each equal parts	(Infusion)

COUGH

Maidenhair Hart's Tongue Poppy Capsules Vervain Hyssop Ground Ivy	of each equal parts	(Infusion)

DIAPHORETIC

Marshmallow Root	8 parts
Liquorice Root	4 „
Orris Root	4 „
Ground Ivy	4 „
Aniseed	1 part
Coltsfoot Leaves	4 parts
Red Poppy Flowers	2 „
Mullein	2 „
	(Infusion)

DIAPHORETIC AND ALTERATIVE

(Espèces ou bois)

Sassafras Wood Guaiacum Wood China Root Sarsaparilla Root	of each equal parts	(Decoction)

DIAPHORETIC AND ALTERATIVE

Sassafras Wood Elder Flowers Red Poppy Flowers Borage Leaves	of each equal parts	(Infusion)

DIAPHORETIC AND ALTERATIVE

Guaiacum Wood	1 part
Burdock Root	2 parts
Elm Bark	1 part
Bittersweet	1 „
	(Decoction)

DIAPHORETIC, SMITH'S

Sarsaparilla Root	4 parts
China Root	2 „
Liquorice Root	2 „
Guaiacum Wood	2 „
Sassafras Wood	2 „

(Decoction)

DIURETIC, NO. 1

Asparagus Root
Parsley Root
Celery Root
Fennel
Butcher's Broom

} of each equal parts

(Decoction)

DIURETIC, NO. 2

Marshmallow Root
Asparagus Root
Liquorice Root
Strawberry Root
Couchgrass Root

} of each equal parts

(Decoction)

EMMENAGOGUE

Black Hellebore Root
Valerian Root
Mugwort Herb
Wormwood Herb
Wormseed

} of each equal parts

(Decoction)

EMOLLIENT

Marshmallow Flowers
Mallow Flowers
Mullein Flowers
Pellitory-of-the-Wall

} of each equal parts

(Infusion)

INFANTS' CORRECTIVE

Fennel	2 parts
Aniseed	2 ,,
Couchgrass	5 ,,
Polypody	5 ,,
Liquorice Root	10 ,,
Figs	10 ,,
John's Bread	10 ,,
Lime Flowers	10 ,,
Hartshorn	10 ,,

(Infusion)

PECTORAL, FRUIT

Dates (stoned)
Jujubes (fruit)
Figs
Currants

} of each equal parts

(Infusion)

PECTORAL, NO. 1 (FLOWERS)

Marshmallow Flowers
Mallow Flowers
Coltsfoot Flowers
Violet Flowers
Mullein Flowers
Red Poppy Flowers
Catsfoot Flowers

} of each equal parts

(Infusion)

PECTORAL, NO. 2

Mallow Flowers	1 part
Red Poppy Flowers	2 parts
Ground Ivy	2 ,,
Maidenhair	2 ,,
Hyssop	2 ,,
Liverwort	2 ,,
Balm	2 ,,
Mullein Flowers	4 ,,
Jujubes (fruit)	6 ,,
Currants	6 ,,
Raisins	6 ,,
Marshmallow Root	10 ,,
Liquorice Root	12 ,,
Figs	20 ,,
John's Bread	20 ,,
Barley	24 ,,

(Infusion)

PECTORAL, NO. 3
(*Brusttee*)

Aniseed	2 parts
Mullein Flowers	2 ,,
Coltsfoot Leaves	4 ,,
Orris Root	1 part
Liquorice Root	3 parts
Marshmallow Root	8 ,,

(Infusion)

PURGATIVE (ST. GERMAIN)
(*Thé de santé*)

Fennel	1 part
Cream of Tartar	1 ,,
Elder Flowers	2 parts
Aniseed	2 ,,
Senna Leaves	4 ,,

(Infusion)

PURGATIVE (SWISS)

Wormwood
Wood Betony
Bugle
Mountain Mint
Water Germander
Hyssop
Ground Ivy
Yarrow
Marjoram
Periwinkle
Rosemary
Sanicle
Sage
Thyme
Wild Thyme
Germander
Vervain
Arnica Flowers
Catsfoot Flowers
Coltsfoot Flowers

} of each equal parts

(Infusion)

VERMIFUGE

Tansy
Wormwood
Wormseed (Levant)
Chamomile

} of each equal parts

(Infusion)

GLOSSARY OF BOTANICAL TERMS

Achene. A one-seeded fruit, or part of a compound fruit, as in the Buttercup and Clematis, that does not open when ripe, and distinguishable from a seed by the remains of a style or stigma at the apex.

Acrid. Leaving a more-or-less burning sensation in the mouth and throat when chewed.

Acuminate. Tapering gradually to a fine point.

Albumen. The substance in the seed surrounding the germ or embryo when it is small. It is present in the Castor Oil seed (oily), in the Nux Vomica (horny), and in others fleshy or starchy, but it is not present in all seeds, those like the Bean and Almond, having the nourishment stored up in their large seed-lobes.

Alliaceous. Having an odour like garlic or onion.

Amplexicaul. The base of the leaf developed so as to clasp or surround the stem.

Annular or Annulated. Applied to the root when constricted at intervals so as to form rings, as in Ipecacuanha.

Anthers. The part of the stamens containing the (usually powdery) pollen.

Apetalous. Having no petals. When only one row of floral leaves is present, even if coloured, it is considered to be the calyx, as in the Clematis, which is consequently apetalous.

Apocarpous. Carpels free, each forming a single ovary, style, and stigma.

Appressed or Adpressed. A term applied to hairs when they lie close against the stem.

Arillus. A fleshy growth from the point where the seed is attached to the ovary, as in the Nutmeg, of which mace is the arillus.

Aromatic. Having a more or less agreeable odour.

Ascending. Applied to the stem when half-way between erect and prostrate.

Awn. A tapering thread-like body, terminating the flower scales in grasses or the seed in some of the Apocynezceae, as in Strophanthus seed.

Axillary. Proceeding from the axil or angle where the leaf or bract is attached to the stem.

Balsamic. Having a sweet odour like benzoin, usually due to the presence of compounds of benzoic or cinnamic acids.

Barbed. Furnished with sharp points bent backwards as in a fish-hook.

Berry. A soft fruit containing, when ripe, seeds loose in pulp, and usually crowned with calyx at the top, as in the Gooseberry; when the calyx is not present at the apex of a berry-like fruit it is called baccate.

Bifid. Having two lobes or divisions about half-way through.

Bipinnatifid. A leaf twice divided in a pinnate or feather-like manner about half-way to the stalk or midrib.

Biserrate. Applied to the margin of a leaf where the margin is serrate, i.e. cut with oblique teeth like a large saw, each tooth being again cut with lesser saw-like teeth.

Bracts. Any leaf under a flower is a bract, whether scaly, coloured, or only a green leaf diminished in size. See Involucre and Phyllaries.

Bristles: A term applied to stiff or rigid hairs.

Bulbs. The bulb is usually more or less globular, composed of fleshy scales (modified leaves crowded on a short stem, as in the Madonna Lily). In some bulbs the outer scales become thin and membranous and enclose the fleshy scales, as in the Onion. In the Garlic all the modified leaves are membranous and only the leaf-buds developed in their axils are fleshy, these fleshy buds being called cloves.

Calyx. The cup or outer row of floral leaves enclosing the rest of the flower, usually consisting of five pieces either free from each other as in the Buttercup, or united into a tube as in the Rose, only the upper portion being free.

Capsule. A fruit dry when ripe and opening at maturity, either by pores as in the Poppy, or by valves as in Stramonium, or transversely as in Henbane. It consists of two or many carpels.

Carpels. Fruits are composed of one or more modified leaves which bear on the margin one or more seeds. Each of these leaves is known as a carpel. In the Buttercup they are distinct; in the Pea and Bean only one is developed. In the Orange many are united, but their internal sides are absorbed.

Catkins. A spike of male or female flowers usually without petals or calyx, as in the Willow and Alder. In the Alder the bracts under the female flowers become hard and woody.

Channelled. Applied to leaves having the upper surface concave.

Ciliate. Furnished with a row of hairs along the margin, like eyelashes.

Cluster Crystals. Minute globes of crystals contained in leaf cells; sometimes called sphaeraphides, and usually consisting of calcium oxalate.

Concentric. Having several circles inside one another.

Conchoidal. Having a fracture somewhat concave, with curved lines, as in Aloes.

Conical. Broad and round at the base and tapering towards the top.

Cordate. Shaped like the heart on playing cards.

Coriaceous. Having a leathery texture.

Corm. A more or less globular shortened stem, having membranous scales, but no fleshy ones, as in Colchicum and Crocus.

Corolla. Applied collectively to the inner row of coloured floral leaves, whether distinct or united into one piece. When the calyx and corolla are similar in colour and size, the term perianth is applied, as in the Lily and Hyacinth, in which there are two similar rows of three pieces; the outer row alternate and overlapping the inner row at the base.

Cortex. Applied to the outer separable portion of a stem or fruit.

Corymb. An arrangement of flowers in which the flowerstalks are of different lengths, but all rise to a level at the top, the outside flowers opening first. When the central flower opens first it is called a corymbose cyme.

Cotyledons. The seed lobes as seen when splitting open a nut or almond. They contain the nourishment to support the young plant while the root is being developed, when albumen is not present.

Crenate. Leaves having rounded, not saw-like, teeth.

Cruciform. Arranged like a Maltese cross, as in the flowers of Wallflower, and other cruciferous plants.

Cuneate. Wedge-shaped.

Cuticle. The thin outer skin coating the epidermis, but not usually separable.

Cyme. This term is added to any inflorescence in which the central flower of the whole, or of a branch, opens first; thus the Elder has an umbellate cyme.

Deciduous. Falling off; applied to trees which are bare of leaves in winter, or to the flowers which fall when the fruit forms. If the calyx falls off as the flower opens, as in the Poppy, it is said to be caducous.

Decurved. Curved downwards.

Dehiscence. A term applied to the opening of fruits.

Dentate. Having sharp, nearly straight incisions in the margin of the leaf.

Didynamous. Having two stamens longer than the other two, as in plants of the Labiatae and Scrophulariaceae.

Digitate. Having five or more narrow segments, as in the leaf of the Lupin.

Disc. The name given to a growth between the stamens and the pistil, as in the *Ruta graveolens* and to the centre of flowers in Compositae.

Disciform. Shaped like a disc. Applied to the circular depressions on a rhizome where a deciduous stem has arisen, as in Solomon's Seal.

Efflorescence. A covering of fine powder, which is not permanent.

Elliptic. Shaped like an ellipse.

Emarginate. Having an indentation at the apex of the leaf.

Embryo. The young plant in the seed, consisting of one or two cotyledons, with a minute leaf-bud above and a minute root below.

Endocarp. The inner layer of the fruit, corresponding to the inner surface of the carpel (which, like the leaf, has three layers). In the Plum, the endocarp forms the stone, the inner layer or mesocarp forms the flesh, and the outer or epicarp forms the skin.

Entire. Not toothed at the margin.

Epidermis. The skin of the leaf. In the Windsor Bean leaf it can easily be peeled off.

Epigynous. Inserted upon or into the pistil, e.g. stamens of the Orchis.

Epipetalous. Stamens attached to the petals.

Exfoliating. Splitting off in layers like the bark of the Plane Tree and Sycamore.

Falcate. Curved like a scythe blade.

Feather-veined. Having the lateral veins proceeding straight to the margin, as in the leaf of *Rhamnus fragula*.

Female Plant. When the male and female flowers are on distinct plants. This arrangement is called dioecious, and when on separate flowers on the same plant, monoecious.

Filiform. Thread-shaped.

Florets or Flowerlets. Applied to the central flowers in the flowerheads of the Compositae. The central tubular florets are distinguished as florets of the disc, and the outer strap-shaped ones as florets of the ray.

Flowerheads. An arrangement of flowers in a compact group surrounded usually with several rows of bracts. *See* Involucre and Phyllaries.

Fluorescence. Applied to liquids which present two different colours when viewed at different angles.

Fluted: Cylindrical but channelled vertically like a column.

Foliaceous. Leafy. Applied to the Thallus, or stemless growths of Lichens, Hepaticae, and Algae, when the segments are broad; also to bracts when they resemble the leaves except in being smaller.

Fracture. The transverse surface of a bark or root when broken; if not fibrous or in layers it is described as short.

Galbulus. A fleshy fruit consisting of three fleshy bracts united together, with naked seeds under each, i.e. having no proper ovary, as in the Juniper fruit. The three lines at the top indicate the lines of juncture of the bracts. The term is also applied to the rounded woody cone of some species of Cupressus.

Gamopetalous. Petals joined at the base.

Gamosepalous. Sepals joined at the base.

Glands. Cells containing oily or mucilaginous secretions, sometimes forming a distinct receptacle as in the Eucalyptus leaves, and sometimes forming the terminal head of a hair as in the Geranium, or they may be stalkless as in the Hop.

Halberd-shaped or Hastate. Shaped like a halberd, as in the leaf of *Rumex acetoselia*.

Heartwood. The central portion of a tree trunk, often filled with a deposit of colouring matter or resin, as in Lignum vitae.

Hermaphrodite. Having male and female organs, i.e. stamens and pistil, in the same blossom.

Hilum. The scar on a seed indicating where it has been attached by a stalk to the wall of the ovary; this name is also applied to the central spot in starch grains.

Hypogynous. Calyx or corolla situated below the ovary.

Imbricated. Overlapping like the tiles of a roof.

Imparipinnate. A pinnate leaf having an odd leaf at the apex.

Inciso-serrate. The term incised is applied when the teeth are deeper at intervals.

Indusium. The membranous covering over the sori, or groups of spore cases, of ferns.

Inflorescence. The arrangement of flowers in plants.

Internodes. The intervals between the leaves on the stem.

Interruptedly pinnate. Having smaller leaflets between the ordinary leaflets, as in Agrimony.

Involucre. A ring of bracts outside a flowerhead in the Compositae. In the Umbelliferae the basal ring is called the general involucre, and the ring under the secondary umbels, the partial involucre.

Keeled. Having a projecting line underneath, or formed like the keel of a boat.

Laminate. Formed in thin layers. The name of lamina is also given to the blade or flat part of a leaf.

Lanceolate. Oval, but pointed at both ends, like a lance-head.

Leaflet. The parts of a compound leaf when they are divided down to the midrib or rachis.

Legume. A fruit consisting of a single carpel, which opens on one side only, corresponding to the margin of the carpellary leaf.

Lenticels. Corky developments of the stomata or breathing pores of the bark.

Lenticular. Shaped like a lens, as in the Lentil.

Lichen. A group of cryptogamic plants growing on rocks and trees, usually greyish or yellowish, without distinction of stem and leaf, but variously branched; the fructification forms a small disc, usually brown or blackish on the surface, or black points, dots, or lines.

Ligulate. Strap-shaped.

Linear. Leaves narrow and short with parallel margins as in the Juniper.

Lyrate. Applied to pinnatifid leaves in which the terminal lobe is larger than the others and rounded.

Medullary Rays. Slender lines of soft tissue that connect the pith with the bark; usually paler than the wood, as seen in a transverse section of the wood.

Micropyle. The minute opening of the seed through which the radical of the embryo pushes out. In the Bean it can be seen near the hilum.

Moss. Minute plants with green leaves with or without a single vein, or a forked vein, and bearing stalked or stalkless capsules, usually opening transversely, containing spores, and often furnished with teeth.

Mucronate. Furnished with a short, sharp point at the apex.

Muller-shaped. Shortly cylindrical with one flat end and the opposite one rounded, like a muller.

Multicellular. Hairs, or fruits, composed of many cells.

Mycelium. The loose thread-like mass forming the plant of fungi. In the Mushroom it is loose and cottony, and known as mushroom spawn; in Ergot it is compacted into a hard mass known as a sclerotium.

Node. The point of the stem whence the leaves arise.

Nucleus Sheath. The line in endogenous roots which separates the outer ring from the central portion.

Nut. A fruit originally composed of three carpels, which ultimately becomes one-celled and contains one seed, as in the Cocoa Nut and Hazel Nut. In the young state the three carpels are indicated by the presence of three stigmas.

Obconical. Pointed at the base, broadening towards the top.

Oblanceolate. Lanceolate, but wider at the upper end. As a rule the prefix "ob" means the reverse shape.

Obovate. Ovate reversed.

Opposite. Applied to leaves when two arise from opposite sides of the same node.

Ovary. The young fruit-containing seeds, surmounted by a stigma, or a stigma borne on a stalk, called the style. The stigma represents the apex of the carpellary leaf, and therefore indicates the number of carpels present in the fruit, as in the Poppy fruit. The presence of the stigma distinguishes a small fruit from a seed.

Ovate. Egg-shaped.

Ovoid. Nearly, but not quite, egg-shaped.

Paleae. The two scale-like bracts enclosing the stamens and pistil in the flower of a grass, the outer usually larger and often furnished with an awn; also the membranous scales forming the bract of each floret of the disc in the flowerhead of the Compositae.

Palisade. Closely-packed, narrow, cylindrical cells forming the upper half of the leaf under the epidermis in most plants.

Palmate. Shaped like the palm of the hand, with five or more lobes as in the Sycamore leaf.

Panicle. An infloresence in which the first branches are branched again, the outside flowers of each branch opening first.

Papilionaceous. Shaped like a Pea blossom.

Papillae. Small raised points, or very short threads.

Pappus. The limb of the calyx in a composite flower, the veins being developed in the form of hairs; if the hairs are simple the pappus is said to be pilose; if feathery, i.e. laterally branched, it is called plumose.

Perianth. The floral envelope surrounding the internal organs of the flower.

Pericarp. The whole of the husk of the fruit, consisting of three layers—epicarp, mesocarp, and endocarp.

Perigynous. Growing upon a body surrounding the ovary.

Petals. The inner, usually coloured, row of the leaves of the flower.

Petiole. The stalk of the leaf.

Phyllaries. The bracts forming one or more rings outside the flowerhead of a composite flower.

Pilose. See Pappus.

Pinnate. Divided in a feather-like manner to the rachis. When there are smaller leaflets between the larger ones, the leaf is said to be interruptedly pinnate; if the leaflets are in pairs with a terminal odd one, it is imparipinnate.

Pinnatifid. Divided in a feather-like fashion about half-way to the midrib or rachis.

Pinnatisect. A pinnate leaf divided about three-quarters of the distance to the midrib.

Pistillate. The flower bearing the female organ or pistil, which consists of ovary, style, and stigma.

Pitted. Having very small depressions.

Placenta. The portion of the ovary to which the seeds are attached. It usually consists of the thickened edges of the carpellary leaf turned inside the ovary, but sometimes is a growth formed from their edges, as in the Poppy capsule.

Polypetalous. Having many petals.

Polysepalous. Having many sepals.

Procumbent. Prostrate branches with the end slightly raised.

Protosalt. Salts consisting of the lower oxide of metals combined with an acid; they contain less oxygen than the persalts, and usually differ in colour, e.g. the protosalts of iron are green, and the persalts, red.

Pubescent. Having short, downy hairs.

Pyrenes. The fruit of the Labiatae and Boraginaceae, resembling seeds, but each consisting of a half carpel containing one seed.

Pyriform. Shaped like a pear.

Quilled. Applied to bark which becomes inrolled when dry, as in Cinnamon and Cinchona.

Raceme. An inflorescence in which flowers having stalks of equal length are arranged along a central stem, the lowest flower opening first.

Rachis. The backbone or central rib of a large, much divided leaf, like a Fern.

Radical. Leaves arising from the top of the root or rootstock.

Raphe. A thread in the inner seed coat consisting of vessels connecting the interior of the ovule with the placenta, as in the Orange seed.

Raphides. Needle-like crystals of oxalate of calcium, found in the cells of plants, as in the Squill root.

Receptacle. The name given to the disc-like top of the stem to which the florets of a composite flower are attached. The same name is also given to the cavities in plant tissues containing oil or mucilage.

Reniform. Shaped like a kidney.

Reticulated. Covered with a network of veins or lines.

Revolute. Rolled back at the edges.

Rhizome. A prostrate stem more or less embedded in the soil, giving off leaves from the upper, and roots from its lower, surface. The name is also sometimes given to the short, upright stem covered with the remains of fallen leaves, and ringed, as in Gentian root. This is preferably distinguished as the root-stock, as it is stem continuous with the root.

Rhombic. Shaped like a rhomb.

Rhomboidal. Irregularly rhombic.

Root-stock. See Rhizome.

Rosettes. Leaves closely and spirally arranged, as in the House-leek and in double flower of the Rose.

Rotate. Wheel-shaped.

Ruminated. Albumen is said to be ruminated when the inner seed coat is folded into its substance, as in the Nutmeg and Areca Nut.

Schizocarp. A dry, many-seeded fruit which splits when ripe into one-seeded parts.

Scyphi. The wineglass-like organ bearing the fructification at the apex in the genus of lichens called Cladonia.

Secondary Umbels. Called also partial umbels; when each stalk of an umbel bears a smaller or secondary umbel at its apex.

Sepals. The leaves of the calyx.

Serrate. Having oblique teeth like a saw.

Sessile. Having no leafstalk, and therefore, so to speak, sitting on the stem.

Sinuate. Having incisions rounded at the base, as in the Oak leaf.

Spatulate. Shaped like a spatulate or flattened spoon.

Spike. An inflorescence in which flowers without stalks are arranged along a central stem, either loosely or densely, as in Agrimony and Plantain.

Spine. The hardened, projecting vein of a leaf, as in the Holly and Thistle.

Spore Cases. Receptacles containing spores.

Spur. A more-or-less tubular projection at the base of the corolla, as in the Toadflax and Columbine.

Stamens. The male organ of the flower, consisting of two anthers, usually oblong or reniform in shape, containing pollen, and often borne on a stiff thread or filament.

Staminode. A barren stamen, containing no pollen, as in Scrophularia.

Stellate. With rays like a star.

Stigma. The sticky apex of the style of the female organ of the flower, to which pollen is carried by insects or the wind.

Stipules. Small, leaf-like organs, at the base of the leafstalks, or attached to the stem between the leaves. In the Polygonaceae membranous stipules form a sheath, called an ochrea, round the stem.

Stipulets or Stipels. Small leaflets at the base of the leaflets in compound leaves, as in the Dwarf Elder.

Stomata. Microscopic openings in the surface of the leaf, mostly on the under surface, whereby air enters the tissues.

Stone Cells. Cells hardened by internal deposits, appearing to the naked eye or under a lens as hard points, in bark, etc.

Striated. Marked with more-or-less parallel lines.

Style. The filament connecting the stigma and ovary.

Subulate. Shaped like an awl.

Suckers. Underground branches from the stem or root that arise at a distance from the stem, as in the Raspberry.

Syconus. A name given to the fruit of the Fig, derived from the Greek name of the Fig.

Syncarpous. Carpels all joined to form a single ovary.

Tangential. A vertical section at right angles to the centre of the stem.

Terminal. At the end of a shoot or branch.

Ternate. A leaf divided into three distinct segments.

Tetrahedral. Having four sides.

Thallus. The flat, branching growth, of uniform texture, of cryptograms.

Toothed. More-or-less pointed, equal-sided incisions in the margin of the leaf.

Tortuous. Twisted and undulated.

Trifid. Nearly divided into three segments.

Trifoliate. Having three distinct leaflets, as in Clover and Bogbean.

Tripinnate. Three times divided in a pinnate manner.

Truncate. Appearing as if cut off at the end, as in the leaf of the Tulip Tree.

Tuber. An underground, more or less globular stem, bearing leaf-buds, as in the Potato and Artichoke.

Umbel. An arrangement of flowers having stalks proceeding from one point, and of equal length, so as to form a level surface, the outer flowers opening first.

Unisexual. Flowers having either stamens or pistils, but not both together.

Vascular. Consisting of vessels or minute tubes.

Vittae. The oil receptacles in the fruits of the Umbelliferae; they usually appear as dark, vertical lines between the ridges of the fruit.

Whorl. A circle of leaves around a node, as in Galium.

PLANT FAMILIES

Plants are divided into groups known as "Families," and each family displays certain characteristics which distinguish it from others. These characteristics are dealt with here in broad outline for the principal families. Any good text-book on Botany will allow the reader to go into considerably greater detail.

ALISMATACEAE. Plants that grow in marshy, wet soil, and Water plants.

Leaves Radical. Leafless flower stems.
Flowers Terminal umbels, panicles or racemes.
Perianth 6 segments sometimes all similar and sometimes 3 sepal-like and 3 petal-like.
Stamens Indefinite.
Carpels Indefinite.
Example Water Plantain.

AMARANTHACEAE. An exotic family similar to Chenopodiaceae but characterized by 2 or 3 bracts under each flower.

APOCYNACEAE. Principally tropical plants. Possesses similar characteristics to Gentianaceae but with ovary divided into two cells.

Examples Periwinkle, Alstonia.

AQUIFOLIACEAE. A small order including Holly and various species of Ilex.

ARALIACEAE. Trees and shrubs similar in many respects to Umbelliferae, but bearing simple umbels and frequently a succulent fruit in the form of a berry.

Example Common Ivy.

ARISTOLOCHIACEAE. Herbs and tall climbers. A small family widely distributed but found principally in the tropics.

Leaves Alternate, often with stipules.
Perianth Combined with the base of the ovary.
Stamens 6 or 12 attached to ovary.
Fruit 3- or 6-celled each containing several seeds.
Examples Asarabacca, Snake Root, Birthwort.

ASCLEPIADACEAE. An exotic family closely allied to Apocynaceae.
Example Calotropis.

BERBERIDACEAE. Shrubs.
Leaves Alternate.
Petals 2 to 8 but never 5.
Sepals 2 to 8 but never 5.
Stamens Same number as petals.
Carpel Single.
Examples This is a small family and the best-known examples are the Barberry and Berberis.

BETULACEAE. A subdivision of Cupuliferae including Birch, Alder, and Hazel.

BIGNOLIACEAE. A branch of Scrophulariaceae including Caroba.

BORAGINACEAE. Usually coarse, hairy herbs.
Leaves Alternate.
Flowers One-sided spikes or racemes.
Stamens 5 developed on the petals.
Examples Borage, Bugloss, Comfrey.

BUXACEAE. A subdivision of Euphorbiaceae.

CANNABINACEAE. A branch of Urticaceae including Indian Hemp.

CAPRIFOLIACEAE. Shrubs, trees, and herbs.
Leaves Opposite.
Flowers Gamopetalous and epigynous. In corymbs or panicles. Usually 5 lobes.
Stamens Usually 5 developed on petals.
Pistil 2 to 5 united carpels.
Ovary Inferior. 3- to 5-celled.
Fruit Succulent, usually 1- to 5-celled.
Seeds 1 or a few in each cell.
Examples Black Haw, Dwarf Elder, Elder.

CARYOPHYLLACEAE. Mostly herbs.
Leaves Opposite, growing from swollen nodes.
Flowers Polypetalous, hypogynous, usually in cymose inflorescence.
Stamens Usually twice as many as petals.
Pistil 2 to 5 united carpels joined to 1 ovary.
Fruit 1-celled capsule.
Examples Plants of the Pink type. Chickweed, Soapwort, *Arenaria rubra*.

CHENOPODIACEAE. Herbs, usually growing near the sea-shore, some of which have succulent stems and leaves for the storage of water.

Leaves Usually alternate.
Flowers Small and inconspicuous in sessile clusters.
Stamens 5.
Pistil 2 united carpels.
Fruit Contains one seed frequently flattened in shape.
Examples Wormseed (Chenopodium), Arrach.

COMPOSITAE. Herbs.

Leaves Radical or alternate, rarely opposite.
Flower What is usually recognized as the flower is composed of numerous florets collected together into one head with a common calyx.
Examples Dandelion, Chamomile, Coltsfoot.

CONVULVULACEAE. The Bindweed family, which twines round other plants and by means of suckers feeds on its host. In some cases the roots attach themselves to the roots of other plants. It is a well-known family and the gardener's constant worry.

Examples Dodder and the exotic plant Scammony.

CORNACEAE. Mainly composed of tropical plants.

Examples Fever Bush, American Boxwood, Red Osier.

CRASSULACEAE. Herbs and shrubs.

Leaves Succulent.
Flowers Terminal racemes or cymes. Polypetalous, perigynous. Number of sepals and petals varies from 5 to 20.
Stamens Usually twice as many as petals.
Pistil Apocarpous and as many as stamens. Each forms a distinct capsule.
Examples Houseleek, Stonecrop.

CRUCIFERAE. Herbs.

Leaves Alternate.
Flowers Terminal racemes. Polypetalous, hypogynous. Petals and sepals usually 4, cruciform.
Stamens 6, of which 2 are frequently shorter.
Ovary Solitary. 2-celled.
Fruit A pod divided into 2 cells; the seeds are attached to the edges of the partition.
Examples Hedge Mustard, Mustard, Horseradish.

CUCURBITACEAE. The Gourd family. It includes such plants as Melons, Cucumbers, Pumpkins, Marrows, etc.

CUPULIFERAE.

Flowers In catkins, usually unisexual, the male and female catkins being borne on the same plant.

Pistil 2 or 3 carpels.

Fruit A nut.

Examples Oak, Chestnut.

CYPERACEAE. Herbs, resembling to a large extent Graminaceae, but with solid, three-angled stems with sheaths of leaves closed round them.

Flowers Small green or brown spikes either solitary and terminal or compound clusters, each with an outer bract.

DIOSCORIDACEAE. Climbing plants.

Leaves Alternate.

Flowers Small. Unisexual. 6 petals, 6 sepals.

Stamens Male flowers 6.

Pistil 3 carpels (female flower).

Ovary 3-celled inferior.

Example Black Bryony.

DROSERACEAE. A family of carnivorous plants, which produce sticky tentacles on the leaves which exude a fluid to digest insects that settle on them.

Example Sundew.

EQUISETACEAE. The horsetail family. A family of leafless herbs with articulate and whorled stems, represented only by the genus Equisetum.

ERICACEAE. Shrubby plants and heaths usually found on moorlands.

Flowers Usually drooping, solitary or in clusters and globe-shaped with 4 or 5 lobes. Calyx of 4 or 5 divisions.

Stamens Usually twice as many as lobes.

Fruit A capsule or berry each containing one or more seeds.

Examples Trailing Arbutus, Uva Ursi.

EUPHORBIACEAE. Herbs, shrubs, or trees.

Flowers Unisexual, hypogynous.

Ovary 3 united carpels each with 1 or 2 pendulous ovales.

Fruit A schizocarp, often explosive.

Examples Euphorbia, Cascarilla.

FUCACEAE. Seaweeds, exemplified by Bladderwrack.

FUMARIACEAE. Allied to Papaveraceae, but distinct because of its irregular flowers and 6 definite stamens.

GERANIACEAE. The Geranium family. Annual or perennial herbs and shrubs.

Leaves Opposite. Rarely alternative, palmately veined.
Flowers Polypetalous, hypogynous. 5 sepals, 5 petals.
Stamens 5 to 10.
Pistil 5 carpels.
Fruit A 5-lobed schizocarp.
Examples Cranesbill.

GENTIANACEAE. Bitter-tasting herbs.

Leaves Opposite.
Flowers Terminal cymes or panicles. One flower to each fork.
Ovary A single cell or partially divided into two.
Fruit A capsule, many seeded.
Examples Buckbean, Gentian, Centaury.

GRAMINACEAE. Most cereals and grasses.

HYPERICACEAE. Limited in this country to the genus Hypericum, the best known being St. John's Wort.

IRIDACEAE. Perennial herbs with creeping rhizomes.

Leaves Radical or vertical either side of the stem, embracing it in a sheath.
Flower Superior with 6 petal-like segments.
Stamens 3.
Pistil 3 carpels.
Ovary 3-celled, inferior.
Examples Blue Flag, Yellow Flag, Gladwin.

JUGLANDACEAE. The Walnut family. A subdivision of Amentaceae which includes Butternut and Walnut.

LABIATAE. Herbs, with quadrangular stems.

Leaves Opposite.
Flowers Usually in cymes in the axils of the upper leaves. Calyx 5-toothed. Corolla is tubular and usually forms two lips.
Stamens 2 or 4 in two pairs.
Ovary 4-lobed, each containing 1 seed.
Pistil Rises from centre of ovary and has a cleft top.
Examples Catnep, Red Sage, Scullcap.

LAURACEAE. A family of evergreen laurels.

LEGUMINOSAE. Commonly recognized as plants with flowers similar to the pea and producing a fruit or legume, such as Broom, Bean, and the various vetches.

LILIACEAE. Perennial herbs with bulbous root-stocks.
Leaves Radical.
Perianth Petal-like with 6 divisions.
Stamens 6.
Ovary 3-celled. Usually more than one seed in each cell.
Examples Lily of the Valley, Asparagus, Colchicum.

LINACEAE. The Phlox family.
Leaves Entire.
Flowers Regular. Sepals 5. Petals 5.
Stamens As many as petals.
Pistil 5 carpels slightly connected at base.
Ovary 5 cells.
Fruit A capsule. Each cell contains two seeds.
Example Linseed.

LYCOPODIACEAE. The Moss family.
Examples Clubmoss, American Ground Pine.

MALVACEAE. The Mallow family. Herbs and soft-wooded shrubs.
Leaves Alternate.
Flowers Polypetalous, hypogynous. Calyx 5 divisions. Petals 5.
Fruit Dry and many seeded.
Examples Blue Mallow, Marshmallow.

MORACEAE. Trees and shrubs producing a latex.
Flowers Petals and sepals usually of 4 segments.
Stamens Usually 4.
Pistil 2 united carpels.
Fruit Usually composite.
Examples Mulberry, Contrayerva, Hops.

MYRICACEAE. A subdivision of Amentaceae confined to the genus Myrica such as Bayberry and Sweet Gale.

MYRSINACEAE. A tropical branch of the Primulaceae family.
Example Embelia.

MYRTACEAE. A very large tropical family, similar to Rosaceae but leaves opposite, inferior ovary and united carpels. It includes Bayberry and Allspice.

OLEACEAE. Shrubs, trees, and tall climbers.
Leaves Opposite, entire or pinnate.
Flowers Regular, hypogynous, and in terminal clusters.
Stamens 2.
Pistil 2 carpels.
Fruit 2-celled, each cell with 1 or 2 seeds.
Examples Ash, Olive.

ONAGRACEAE. Herbs.
Leaves Usually opposite and undivided.
Flowers Terminal spikes or racemes. Lower flowers solitary in leaf axils. Polypetalous, epigynous. Calyx tube adhering to ovary and sometimes prolonged beyond it.
Stamens 8, 4, or 2.
Fruit Capsule or berry.
Example Evening Primrose.

ORCHIDACEAE. The Orchid family. Rhizome thickened into tubers.
Leaves Entire. Parallel-veined.
Flowers Irregular. Solitary or in spikes, racemes or panicles each in the axle of a bract. Superior perianth, petaloid. Sepals 3, petals 2, the third petal forming the labellum or lip.
Stamens 1 (rarely 2) combined with pistil.
Ovary 1-celled with numerous tiny seeds.
Examples Crawley, Salep.

PALMACEAE. The Palm family.

PAPAVERACEAE. The Poppy family.
Leaves Radical or alternate. Usually divided.
Flowers Usually 4 petals.
Stamens Numerous.
Ovary 1-celled and subdivided. Many-seeded. Capsule. The stems exude a milky juice when broken.
Examples Poppy, Blood Root, Celandine.

PINACEAE. The Conifer family, including many trees and shrubs yielding a resinous juice.
Examples Colophony, Larch, White Pine, Pinus.

PIPERACEAE. A tropical family, including peppers such as Cubebs, Black Pepper, Kava Kava.

PLANTAGINACEAE. The Plantain family.
Leaves Radical, ribbed, spreading. Leafless flower stalks.
Flowers Inconspicuous, gamopetalous, hypogynous and formed into a simple spike. Sepals 4. Corolla of 4 spreading lobes.
Stamens 4 and usually long.
Ovary 1-, 2-, or 4-celled with 1 seed in each.
Examples Plantain, Psyllium.

PLUMBAGINACEAE. Hard, stiff herbs.

Leaves Radical.
Flowers Terminal heads. Tubular calyx. Corolla of 5 petals.
Stamens 5.
Ovary 1-celled, bearing 5 styles.
Fruit A capsule with 1 seed.
Examples American Sea Lavender, English Sea Lavender, Thrift.

POLEMONIACEAE. A small group of herbs.

Flowers Terminal cymes or panicles. Calyx 5-cleft, corolla 5-lobed.
Stamens 5.
Pistil 3-lobed.
Fruit Capsule, 3-celled, each containing several seeds.
Examples Jacob's Ladder, Abscess Root.

POLYGONACEAE. Herbs.

Leaves Alternate. Stipules form a tubular sheath round the stem.
Flowers Small. Polypetalous. Formed in leaf axils or in terminal panicles. 3 sepals. 3 petals.
Ovary Free, with 2, 3, or more styles.
Fruit Seed-like nut.
Examples Bistort, Yellow Dock, Knotgrass.

POLYPODIACEAE. A branch of the Fern family.

PRIMULACEAE. The Primrose family.

Leaves Undivided, opposite, alternate, or radical.
Flowers Gamopetalous, hypogynous. Calyx 3 petals usually divided into 5 but occasionally into 4, 6, or 7 divisions.
Stamens Epipetalous, antipetalous.
Pistil Syncarpous.
Fruit 1-celled capsule containing several seeds.
Examples Cowslip, Primrose.

RANUNCULACEAE. Herbs.

Leaves Alternate or radical (except in the Clematis which is a climber with opposite leaves).
Flowers Hypogynous, solitary, or in terminal racemes or panicles. Petals, 5 polypetalous.
Stamens Numerous.
Pistil Several carpels, apocarpous.
Examples Anemone, Pilewort, Buttercup.

RHAMNACEAE. The Buckthorn family.
Leaves Alternate.
Flowers Small and green, clustered in axils of leaves.
Fruit Berry.
Examples Buckthorn, Alder Buckthorn, Cascara.

ROSACEAE. Herbs, shrubs, and trees.
Leaves Alternate and usually toothed.
Flowers Polypetalous, perigynous in clusters or solitary.
Stamens Numerous in whorls.
Pistil Apocarpous.
Examples Rose, Agrimony, Almond.

RUBIACEAE. A subdivision of Euphorbiaceae forming a large family of exotic plants.
Example Ipecacuanha.

RUTACEAE. Principally tropical plants such as Buchu and other plants common to South Africa and Australia. One growing in this country is the Common Rue.

SALICACEAE. A subdivision of Amentaceae embracing Poplar, Willow, Balm of Gilead.

SARACENIACEAE. The Pitcher Plant family. Part of the family of carnivorous plants that feed on insects decomposed by bacteria formed in the flower.

SAXIFRAGACEAE. Herbs and shrubs.
Leaves Opposite, or alternate.
Flowers Calyx 4- or 5-lobed and sometimes joined to ovary. Petals 4 or 5, perigynous or epigynous.
Stamens 8 or 10.
Pistil 2 to 5 carpels.
Ovary One- or many-celled.
Fruit Capsule or berry. Each cell contains several seeds.
Example Black Currant.

SCROPHULARIACEAE. Herbs.
Leaves Opposite, or alternate.
Flowers Calyx 5 segments. Corolla gamopetalous usually 2-lipped.
Stamens Usually 4. Sometimes 2. Rarely 5.
Fruit 2-celled. Several seeds in each.
Examples Speedwell, Mullein, Foxglove.

SOLANACEAE. Herbs and shrubs.

Leaves Alternate.
Flowers Gamopetalous. 5 lobes. Calyx 5 teeth.
Stamens 5.
Pistil 2 carpels.
Fruit A capsule or berry with several seeds.
Examples Belladonna, Henbane, Bittersweet.

UMBELLIFERAE. Herbs and shrubs with hollow stems.

Leaves Alternate. Much divided.
Flowers Small in terminal or lateral umbels. Petals 5.
Stamens 5 alternating with petals.
Ovary 2-celled. 1 seed in each.
Examples Celery, Aniseed, Angelica.

VACCINIACEAE. Similar to Ericaceae, but with inferior ovary.

Example Bilberry.

VALERIANACEAE. Herbs.

Leaves Opposite.
Flowers Terminal corymbs or panicles, small and numerous. Calyx adheres to ovary. Gamopetalous, tubular at base, 5 lobes.
Stamens Fewer than lobes of corolla.
Fruit Small, dry, and seed-like with single seed suspended from top of cell.
Example Valerian.

VERBENACEAE. The Vervain family. Herbs, shrubs, and trees.

Leaves Usually opposite.
Flowers As Labiatae except for ovary which is entire with style proceeding from top.
Fruit 2- to 4-celled, 1 seed in each.
Examples Vervain, Lemon-Scented Verbena.

ZINGIBERACEAE. An exotic family of aromatic plants including Ginger and Cardamoms.

GLOSSARY OF MEDICAL TERMS

Alterative. A vague term to indicate a substance which hastens the renewal of the tissues so that they can to better advantage carry on their functions.

Anodyne. Pain-easing.

Anthelmintic. Causing death or removal of worms in the body.

Antibilious. Against biliousness.

Antiperiodic. Preventing the return of those diseases which recur, such as Malaria.

Antiscorbutic. Preventing Scurvy.

Antiscrofulous. Preventing or curing scrofulous diseases.

Antiseptic. Preventing putrefaction.

Antispasmodic. Preventing or curing spasms.

Aperient. Producing a natural movement of the bowels.

Aphrodisiac. Exciting the sexual organs.

Aromatic. Having an aroma.

Astringent. Binding. Causing contraction of the tissues.

Balsamic. Of the nature of a balsam. Usually applied to substances containing resins and benzoic acid.

Bitter. Applied to bitter-tasting drugs which are used to stimulate the appetite.

Cardiac. Products which have an effect upon the heart.

Carminative. Easing griping pains and expelling flatulence.

Cathartic. Producing evacuation of the bowels.

Cholagogue. Producing a flow of bile.

Corrective. Restoring to a healthy state.

Demulcent. Applied to drugs which sooth and protect the alimentary canal.

Deobstruent. Clearing away obstructions by opening the natural passages of the body.

Depurative. A purifying agent.

Dermatic. Applied to drugs with an action on the skin.

Detergent. Cleansing.

Diaphoretic. Drugs which promote perspiration.

Digestive. Aiding digestion.

Emetic. Applied to drugs which cause vomiting.

Emmenagogue. Applied to drugs which have the power of exciting the menstrual discharge.

Emollient. Used in relation to substances which have a softening and soothing effect.

Expectorant. Promoting expectoration and removing secretions from the bronchial tubes.

Febrifuge. Reducing fever.

Haemostatic. Drugs used to control bleeding.

Hepatic. Used in connexion with substances having an effect upon the liver.

Hydrogue. Having the property of removing accumulations of water or serum. Causing watery evacuations.

Hypnotic. Producing sleep.

Insecticide. Having the property of killing insects.

Irritant. Causing irritation.

Laxative. A gentle bowel stimulant.

Mydriatic. Causing dilation of the pupil.

Myotic. Contracting the pupil.

Narcotic. Applied to drugs producing stupor and insensibility.

Nephritic. Drugs having an action upon the kidneys.

Nervine. Applied to drugs used to restore the nerves to their natural state.

Nutritive. Nourishing.

Oxytocic. Hastening birth by stimulating the contraction of the uterus.

Parasiticide. Destroying parasites.

Parturient. Applied to substances used during childbirth.

Pectoral. Used in connexion with drugs used internally for affections of the chest and lungs.

Purgative. Drugs which evacuate the bowels. More drastic than a laxative or aperient.

Refrigerant. Relieving thirst and giving a feeling of coolness.

Resolvent. A term used to denote substances applied to swellings in order to reduce them.

Rubefacient. Applied to counter-irritants. Substances which produce blisters or inflammation.

Sedative. Drugs which calm nervous excitement.

Sternutatory. Producing sneezing by irritation of the mucous membrane.

Stimulant. Energy producing.

Stomachic. Applied to drugs given for disorders of the stomach.

Styptic. Substances which clot the blood and thus stop bleeding.

Sudorific. Producing copious perspiration.

Taenicide. Applied to drugs used to expel tape-worm.

Tonic. Substances which give tone to the body producing a feeling of well-being.

Vermifuge. Substances which expel worms from the body.

Vulnerary. Used in healing wounds.

ABBREVIATIONS FOR THE AUTHORS OF BOTANICAL NAMES

Ach.	Acharius, Erick
Adam	Adam, Johan Friedrich
Adans.	Adanson, Michel
Ait.	Aiton, William Townsend
Allem.	Allemao, Francisco Freire
Aguiar	Aguiar, J. M. de
Arcang.	Arcangeli, Alceste
Arg.	d'Argenville, Antoine Joseph
Arn.	Arnott, George Arnold Walker
Aubl.	Aublet, Jean Baptiste Christophore Fusée
Baill.	Baillon, Henri Ernest
Baker	Baker, John Gilbert
Balf.	Balfour, Francis Maitland
Bart. & Wendl.	Bartling, Friedrich Gottlieb Wendland, Heinrich Ludwig
Batsch	Batsch, August Johann Georg Karl
Beauv.	Beauvois, A. M. T. J. Palisot
Becc.	Beccari, Odoardo
Benn.	Bennett, John Joseph
Benth.	Bentham, George
Bercht.	Berchtold, Friedrich, Graf von
Berg & Schmidt	Berg, Otto Carl Schmidt, C. F.
Bernh.	Bernhardi, Johann Jakob
Bess.	Bessey, Charles Edwin
Bieb.	Bieberstein, L. B. Fr. Marschal von
Blume	Blume, Carl Ludwig
Boiss. & Buhse	Boissier, Edmond Buhse, F.
Bonducella, G.	Bonducella, G.
Borkh.	Borkhausen, Moritz Balthasar
Brandis	Brandis, Joachim Dieterich
Buch.-Ham.	Buchanan-Hamilton, Francis
Bunge	Bunge, Alexander von
Burkhill	Burkhill, J. H.

Burm.	Burmann, Johannes
Br., R.	Brown, Robert
Carr.	Carrière, Elie Abel
Cass.	Cassini, Alexandre Henri Gabriel
Cav.	Cavanilles, Antonio José
Chaix	Chaix, Dominique, Abbé
Cham.	Chamisso, Adalbert von
Choisy	Choisy, Jacques Denys
Colebr.	Colebrooke, Henry Thomas
Correa	Correa da Serra, José Francisco
Craib	Craib, William G.
Crantz	Crantz, Heinrich Johann Neptomuk, von
Cyrill.	Cyrillus, Patriarch of Alexandria
D.C.	De Candolle, Augustin Pyramus
Decne. & Pl. ..	Decaisne, Joseph Planchon, Gustav
Del.	Delile, Alire Raffeneau
Deppe	Deppe, Ferdinand
Desf.	Desfontaines, René Loniche
Desr.	Desrousseaux, Louis Augustin Joseph
Don, G.	Don, George
Dry.	Dryander, Jonas
Duchesne	Duchesne, Antoine Nicholas
Dum.	Dumortier, Barthélemy Charles
Dunal	Dunal, Michel Felix
Dur.	Du Roi, Johann Philipp
Ehrh.	Ehrhart, Friedrich
Ell.	Ellis, John
Eng.	Engler, Adolf
Fisch.	Fischer, Friedrich Ernst Ludwig von
Focke	Focke, William Olbers
Forsk.	Forskal, Pehr
Forst.	Forster, John Heinhold
Fries	Fries, Elias Magnus
Gaertn.	Gaertner, Joseph
Gay, C.	Gay, Claudio
Goldb.	Goldbach, Karl Ludwig
Grah.	Graham, John
Grah., R.	Graham, Robert
Gray, A.	Gray, Asa
Greene	Greene, Edward Lee
Griff.	Griffin, William
Griseb.	Grisebach, August Heinrich Rudolf
Haenke	Haenke, Thaddaeus

Han.	Hanbury, Daniel
Hance	Hance, Henry Fletcher
Harms	Harms, Hermann
Haw.	Haworth, Adrian Hardy
Hayne	Hayne, Friedrich Gottlob
Henn.	Henning, Paul
Heyne	Heyne, Benjamin
H., B., & K. ..	Humbolt, Friedrich Alexander von Bonpland, Aimé Kunth, Karl Sigismund
Hill	Hill, Sir Arthur W.
Hoffm.	Hoffmann, George Franz
Holmes	Holmes, Edward Morell
Hook.	Hooker, William Jackson
Hook., f.	Hooker (*filius*), James Dalton
Host	Host, Nicolaus Thomas
Houtt.	Houttyn, Martin
Huds.	Hudson, William
Huss	Huss, Olavus E.
Jacq...	Jacquin, Joseph von
Kar. & Kir. ..	Karelin, Georg Kilirow, Johann
Ker-Gawl.	Ker, John Bellenden, *alias* Gawler
King	King, George
Koch	Koch, Wilhelm Daniel Joseph
Klotsch	Klotsch, Johann Friedrich
Kunth	Kunth, Karl Sigismund
Kuntze	Kuntze, Otto
Kütz.	Kutzing, Friedrich, Traugott
Labill.	Labillardière, Jacques Julien Houten de
Lam. or Lamk. ..	La Marck, Jean Baptiste Antoine Pierre Mounet, Chevalier de
Lamb.	Lambert, Aylmer Bourke
Ledanois	Ledanois, E.
Lemaire	Lemaire, Charles
Léveillé	Léveillé, Joseph Henri
L'Hérit.	L'Héritier de Brutelle, Charles Louis
Lindl.	Lindley, John
Linn.	Linnaeus, Carl
Linn., f.	Linnaeus (*filius*), Carl von
Loisel.	Loiseleur-Destongchamps, Jean Louis Auguste
Marsh.	Marshall, Humphry
Mart.	Martius, Karl Friedrich Philipp von
Maton	Maton, William George

Medik.	Medikus, Friedrich Casimir
Mich., or Michx. ..	Michaux, André
Miers	Miers, John
Mill.	Miller, Philip
Miq.	Miquel, Friedrich Anton Wilhelm
Moench	Moench, Konrad
Mol.	Molina, Juan Ignazio
Muell., F.	Mueller, Ferdinand von
Muhl.	Muhlenberg, Henry
Murr.	Murray, Johann Andreas
Neck.	Necker, Noel Joseph de
Nees	Nees von Esenbeck, Christian Gottfried
Nees, T. & Eberm.	Nees von Esenbeck, Theodor Friedrich Ludwig Ebermaier, Karl Heinrich
Nichols.	Nicholson, George
Nutt.	Nuttall, Thomas
Oliver	Oliver, Daniel
Olivier	Olivier, Guillaume Antoine
Ort.	Ortega, Casimir Gomez
Osbeck	Osbeck, Pehr
Pav.	Pavon, José
Pell. or Pellet. ..	Pelletier-Sautelet
Pers.	Persoon, Christian Hendrik
Pierre	Pierre, Jean Baptiste Louis
Planch.	Planchon, Gustav
Pohl	Pohl, Johann Emmanuel
Presl	Presl, Karel Boriwog
Pursh	Pursh, Friedrich Traugott
Rafin.	Rafinsque, Schmaltez Constantino
Retz.	Retzius, Anders Johan
Reg.	Regel, Edward
Rich., A.	Richard, Achille
Risso	Risso, J. A.
Rosc.	Rosco, William
Ross	Ross, John
Roth..	Roth, Albrecht Wilhelm
Roxb.	Roxburgh, William
R. & P.	Ruiz, Lopez Hipolito Pavon, Joseph
R. & S.	Roemer, Johann Jakob Schultes, Joseph Auguste
Salisb.	Salisbury, Richard Antony
Schlecht.	Schlechtendal, Diedrich Friedrich Leonhard von
Schneid.	Schneider, Camillo K.

Schott	Schott, Heinrich Wilhelm
Schrad.	Schrader, Heinrich Adolphus
Schreb.	Schreber, Johann Daniel Christian von
Schum.	Schumann, Karl
Scop.	Scopoli, Johann Anton
Sieb. & Zucc. ..	Siebold, Philip Franz von Zuccarini, Joseph Gerhard
Sims	Sims, John
Sm.	Smith, Sir James Edward
Soland.	Solander, Daniel
Sprague	Sprague, T. A.
Spreng.	Sprengel, Kurt
Stackh.	Stackhouse, John
Stapf	Stapf, Otto
Steinh.	Steinheil, Adolf
Steud.	Steudel, Ernest Gotlieb
St. Hil.	St.Hilaire, Augustin François César
Stokes	Stokes, Jonathan
Sw.	Swartz, Olaft
Sym.	Symons, Jelinger
Tausch	Tausch, Ignaz Friedrich
Thunb.	Thunberg, Carl Pehr
Torr.	Torrey, John
Trev.	Trevisan, Victore Conte
Triana	Triana, José
Tul.	Tulasne, Louis René
Urb. or Urban ..	Urban, Ignatz
Vahl	Vahl, Martin
Vell.	Vellago, Josepho Mariano a Conceptione
Vent.	Ventenat, Etienne Pierre
Vis.	Visiani, Roberto de
Waldst. & Kit. ..	*See* W. & K.
Wall.	Wallich, Nathan Wolff styled Nathaniel
Walpers	Walpers, Wilhelm Gerard
Walt.	Walter, Thomas
Warb.	Warburg, Otto
Wats., S.	Watson, Sereno
Web.	Weber, Friedrich
Weddell	Weddell, Hugh Algernon
Wend.	Wenderoth, Georg Wilhelm Franz
Wiggers	Wiggers, Fredericus Henricus
W. & K.	Waldstein, Franz Adam, Graf von Kitaibel, Paul
Willd.	Willdenow, Karl Ludwig

INDEX OF BOTANICAL NAMES APPEARING IN HEADINGS

INDEX OF COMMON NAMES AND SYNONYMS

Common Names are in Capitals, as in ACACIA.
Botanical Names are in Italics, as in *Actaea racemosa.*
Synonyms are in Roman type, as in Adderwort.